Andrés González

Governance for the 21st Century

Fragen politischer Ordnung in einer globalisierten Welt

herausgegeben von

Prof. Dr. Friedrich Kratochwil

(Universität München)

Band 6

LIT

Andrés González

Governance for the 21st Century

The Fight Against Corruption in Latin America

LIT

Cover Picture: OSWALDO GUAYASAMIN "MANOS DEL MENDIGO",
OIL ON CANVAS

Bibliographic information published by the Deutsche Nationalbibliothek
The Deutsche Nationalbibliothek lists this publication in the Deutsche Nationalbibliografie; detailed bibliographic data are available in the Internet at http://dnb.d-nb.de.

ISBN 978-3-03735-014-0 (Schweiz)
ISBN 978-3-8258-9916-5 (Deutschland)
Zugl.: München, LMU, Diss., 2004

A catalogue record for this book is available from the British Library

Dufourstr. 31
CH-8008 Zürich
Tel. +41 (0) 44-251 75 05
Fax +41 (0) 44-251 75 06
e-Mail: zuerich@lit-verlag.ch
http://www.lit-verlag.ch

LIT VERLAG Dr. W. Hopf
Berlin 2007
Auslieferung/Verlagskontakt:
Fresnostr. 2
D-48159 Münster
Tel. +49 (0)251–62 03 20
Fax +49 (0)251–23 19 72
e-Mail: lit@lit-verlag.de
http://www.lit-verlag.de

Distributed in the UK by: Global Book Marketing, 99B Wallis Rd, London, E9 5LN
Phone: +44 (0) 20 8533 5800 – Fax: +44 (0) 1600 775 663
http://www.centralbooks.co.uk/acatalog/search.html

Distributed in North America by:

Transaction Publishers
New Brunswick (U.S.A.) and London (U.K.)

Transaction Publishers
Rutgers University
35 Berrue Circle
Piscataway, NJ 08854

Phone: +1 (732) 445 - 2280
Fax: + 1 (732) 445 - 3138
for orders (U. S. only):
toll free (888) 999 - 6778
e-mail:
orders@transactionspub.com

To my parents Alfredo and Olga,
for being the real fighters throughout the years…

To my brother Alfredo,
for never giving up…

To Ana,
for all the things you are…

To my parents Alfredo and Olga,
for being the real fighters throughout the years…

To my brother Alfredo,
for never giving up…

To Ana,
for all the things you are…

ACKNOWLEDGEMENTS

This dissertation project started some time ago, after I thought I was actually leaving Munich in search of other academic endeavours in another country. However, I did stay here and pursued the most ambitious project of my academic career. I call it "ambitious", because I had nothing but ideas and proposals, yet there were many times where the means to undertake this research and complete the written version were not always given. There are so many people who helped me in so many different ways that 'thank you' does not even begin to say enough.

First of all, I thank my parents Alfredo and Olga, to whom this thesis is dedicated, for being always there, always supportive and understanding, I thank immensely for not ever giving up on my ideas and projects. It is due to their efforts that I have made it so far here in Germany. My brother Alfredo I thank for being a great friend and a constant source of inspiration. I whish I could be always as strong as you are.

Also, gigantic thanks to Ana Dujic, for being there from the very beginning to the very end and for believing in me the whole time, even when I was convinced that I would never finish the dissertation on time. Without your love and support, none of this would have been possible.

I also thank my teachers, Prof. Friedrich Kratochwil, for accepting the tutorship of the dissertation and for all the valuable comments and positive critiques during all phases of the elaboration of this dissertation. And I also thank him for being a constant support during my many "entanglements" as a teaching assistant at the GSI in Munich. Prof. Dietmar Herz I thank for jumping in at the very last minute and assuming the role of second thesis advisor. His positive attitude towards my work was pivotal in the last months.

At the GSI, I found many friends who always showed me the good side of things and who never doubted neither on my work nor on my persona. In this regards, an immense amount of gratitude go to Astrid Gernig, who has become an unconditional friend during good times and bad times, and who showed me the great value of loyalty throughout my years at the Chair of International Politics. All the other colleagues at the *Lehrstuhl* I thank for putting up with me for so many years. Also, thanks to Dr. Manuela Glaab, for the office space I was granted at the GSI. This was such an important resource for the entire workload of the dissertation.

From the students who attended my classes, I received valuable input that opened my eyes to new aspects of the topic. Thank you all for being so engaged in the discussion and for constantly posing questions I would have never thought of. Special thanks to Robert Johnson, who became my editor

over night and had to put up with my handicap of using too many sentences for just saying one word.
The friends I have found in Munich were more than a family and I would have certainly never ever found myself at home without them. Anja Jakob, Evi Zingraf, Tinka Enard, Eva Zieschank, Sebastian Brökelmann, Danie Samaniego, Markus Niedermeier, you all deserve nothing less than all my gratitude.
I spent most of my "dissertation free" time working for Siemens Business Services. This gave me the opportunity to finance my dissertation project for nearly two years. More important than the pay however, was the incredible human capital I was blessed to find at the Press Department and at Analyst Relations. In this regard, I thank Axel Grüter, since without him, I would have found myself back in Ecuador ahead of time with no complete thesis at all. Moreover, Jörn Roggenbuck, who constantly kept me in a good mood, even though I was going through tough times balancing three or four projects at the same time. Bettina Rother-Neumann, Andreas vom Bruch, Martin Schubert, Monika Friedrichs, Anne Hunecke, Bettina Meierhofer and all the others I thank so much for opening the doors of your lives to me and make me realize how incredible you all are.
It has been a while since I have left high school. However, there are certain people who have been involved in my life supporting me, as if graduation day had been just yesterday. Karin Abarca, Susanne Baumgartner, Tanja Andrade, Santiago Páez, Claudia Oemer, Kai Köster and all the others, I thank you for constantly reminding me where I come from and that suits do not always make people.
Lastly, and certainly not least, my "second family" at the NMUN Conference in New York, especially Vivian Nilson, Jennifer Kim, Christine Richmond, Jennifer Franco, Dave Koller, Brian Halma, Peter Gussone, Veevek Thankey, as well as the Conference Staffs of 2000-2004 for believing in me all the way. You have changed my life in so many ways, that I have nothing but the greatest respect for each and every one of you. And as always, and somehow, thanks to Hamid Rezai.

A TODOS GRACIAS MONUMENTALES!

TABLE OF FIGURES

INTRODUCTION

THE GLOBALIZATION OF CORRUPTION

The changing nature of contemporary world politics, especially since the end of the Cold War, has reached virtually all fields of human activity. The main feature of current globalization processes is that national borders seem to disappear and create space for greater and faster interaction between states, organizations, and individuals.[1] The most visible manifestations of this phenomenon can be found in the fields of communication, economics and finance, international organizations, and the environment.[2]

In the field of communication, it can be easily observed that with the appearance and spread of the World Wide Web and other modern information technologies, individuals all over the planet are able to establish contact and share information within seconds, regardless of their geographical location. More than ever before, communication has taken so many different formats, that it has become almost impossible to remain 'disconnected' from world affairs. The media has benefited from these improvements and is able to reach a wider range of audiences, locate global problems and project them onto international agendas.[3] Through the use of systems such as satellite television and live streams via Internet, individuals can witness global events as they take place anywhere at any time. And with the improvement of information and communication technologies, a telephone line and a small hardware device are sufficient components for retrieving massive amounts of information.

---

[1] "Global politics" are understood as "[…] the stretching of political relations across space and time; the extension of political power and political activity across the boundaries of the modern nation-state. […] Associated with this 'stretching' is a frequent 'deepening' impact of global political processes such that, unlike in ancient and modern empires, 'action at distance' permeates with greater intensity the social conditions and cognitive words of specific places or political communities." In: Held, David, Anthony McGrew, David Goldblatt and Jonathan Perraton. Global Transformations. Politics, Economics and Culture. (Cambridge, UK: Polity Press, 1999), p. 49.

[2] *Ibid.* In their book, Held and his co-authors distinguished between pre-modern globalization (7000-9000 BC), early modern globalization (1500-1850 AD), modern globalization (1850-1945), and contemporary globalization (after the end of World War II). In this section, as well as for the rest of the book, the latter term will be used to locate 'globalization' within a time line. Further uses of the term are based on the authors' categorization, however focusing on the years after the end of the Cold War.

[3] This notion has been observed in recent cases of humanitarian intervention. As mentioned by Robinson, Piers. "The CNN effect: can the news media drive foreign policy?" Review of International Studies (1999), Vol. 25, pp. 301-309.

Contemporary globalization has also strengthened the role of economics and finance in current international relations. In current world politics money markets have transcended national borders to become the most global of all markets.[4] Hardly a day passes without analysts and policy-makers paying utmost attention to the emergence of a 'global economy'. For the nation-state of the 21st Century, capital flows and financial markets seem to have become equally – if not more important – issues beyond military and security affairs.

In terms of organizations, the processes of globalization have brought an increase in the variety and number of companies, associations, and regulatory agencies that postulate global problems as their *raison d'être.*[5] Besides traditional world fora such as the United Nations (UN), the North Atlantic Treaty Organization (NATO), or the International Monetary Fund (IMF), new bodies of non-governmental nature take the stage to debate international issues. These so called 'transnational' actors include multinational corporations such as Sony or BMW and non-governmental associations such as Greenpeace or Amnesty International who are, nowadays, considered equal existing forces in the international arena.[6] Transnational actors create networks through which several groups of non-specific association, representing many sectors of national societies, have been able to articulate their interests outside their national boundaries. This development has led to the debate on the emergence of a 'global society', a theoretical construct that derives from the existence of a global economic system and worldwide communication networks.[7]

Lastly, contemporary globalization has brought the inclusion of environmental issues as a fundamental part of world governance.[8] Problems such as climate change, the exhaustion of natural resources and waste management have led to the establishment of international environment

---

4 Pauly, Louis. Who Elected the Bankers? Surveillance and Control in the World Economy. (Ithaca and London: Cornell University Press), p. ix.

5 Sholte, Jan Aart. "The Globalization of World Politics." In: Baylis, John and Steve Smith. The Globalization of World Politics. An Introduction to International Relations. (Oxford: Oxford University Press, 1997), p. 15 ff.

6 On transnational actors see also Risse-Kappen, Thomas (ed.) Bringing Transnational Relations Back In. Non-State Actors and International Institutions. (Cambridge, UK: Cambridge University Press, 1995).

7 Shaw, Martin. Global Society and International Relations. Sociological Concepts and Political Perspectives. (Cambridge, UK: Polity Press, 1995). See also Clark, Anne Marie, et. al. "The Global Limits of Civil Society." World Politics (October 1998), Vol. 51, pp. 1-35.

8 Lipshutz, Ronnie. "From Place to Planet: Local Knowledge and Global Environmental Governance." Global Governance. (1997), Vol. 3, pp. 83-102.

regimes as a sign of willingness by the international community to approach these issues with joint efforts.[9] Although the effectiveness of these initiatives has not always been as promising as their initial goals, the importance of such regimes has not only added repeatedly neglected topics to the world political agenda, but has also changed the simplistic tone of power politics posed by the realist tradition of international relations theories.[10] As no state in today's world is completely immune to environmental problems, these topics have become top priorities for national governments and international organizations.

GLOBALIZATION AND THE DEVELOPMENT OF INTERNATIONAL RELATIONS

Since this book is primarily a contribution to the field of International Relations, the effects of contemporary globalization processes on this area of study must be, at least briefly, mentioned. With respect to the scholarship of International Relations theory (IR), contemporary globalization since the end of the Cold War brought along new issues for the debate on how international politics should be studied. The rapidly increasing transnational circulation of goods, services, people, information and capital altered the ways in which international relations were both created and approached.[11] The classic antagonisms between idealism and realism and the methodological disjuncture between traditionalism and scientism seem to have become "relics" of a scholarship that was mainly influenced by the confrontation between East and West.[12] The end of the Soviet Empire raised new questions for the long tradition of IR theory, as the events in world politics did not remain consistent with the provisions of many IR approaches.[13] The

[9] See Young, Oran. International Cooperation: Building Regimes for Natural Resources and the Environment (Cornell Studies in Political Economy). (Ithaca: Cornell University Press, 1989.)

[10] Krasner, Stephen. "Structural Causes and Regime Consequences: Regimes as Intervening Variables." International Organization (1982), Vol. 36, pp. 185-205. And *ibid.*, "Regimes and the Limits of Realism: Regimes as Autonomous Variables." International Organization (1982), Vol. 36, pp. 497-510.

[11] A comprehensive review of the impact of globalization in IR theory can be found in: Clark, Ian. Globalization and International Relations Theory. (Oxford: Oxford University Press, 1999.)

[12] The development of the academic field of IR can be found in: Dunne, Tim, Michael Cox and Ken Booth. The Eighty Year's Crisis. International Relations 1919-1999. (Cambridge: Cambridge University Press, 1998.) See slso Knutsen, Torbjørn L. A History of International Relations Theory. 2nd Edition, (Manchester, University of Manchester Press, 1997)

[13] One of the most remarkable examples in this regard is the critique to Kenneth Waltz' structural realism, as it said to have been inadequate to predict and explain the collapse of the Soviet Union and the Eastern Block. On this point see Ashley, Richard. "The Poverty of Neorealism." International

established theoretical approaches proved to contain analytical weaknesses and the focus of the debate drifted from classic issues of international institutionalization to a discussion on greater issues such as democracy, democratization, and the concepts of sovereignty and legitimacy in the context of modernization and globalization.[14]

As some IR scholars rightly postulated in the late 1990s, after the demise of the Communist bloc, the shape of international politics – traditionally characterized by empires as the principal form of political rule and world political organization – changed into a worldwide system of nation-states with multilateral, regional, and global systems of regulation and governance.[15] Two key developments can be observed at this point. First, states are increasingly becoming more of a functional part in a larger conglomerate of transnational relations shaped by other non-state forces, rather than remaining the key actors of the international stage.[16] And second, this particular structure of increasingly global relationships has started a wave of other "types" of globalization in various areas of international life, as stated earlier on.[17] These sub-categories of globalization – economic, trade, culture, industrial production, migration, communication – have established certain patterns in current world politics that deserve the attention of policy makers and scholars.

On the one hand, the neoliberal world economic order has developed strict mechanisms of multilateral economic surveillance and regional supervision in order to set the rules under which international finance and trade regimes should be regulated.[18] At the same time, improvements in the field of communication make it possible to share a great amount of information on a worldwide scale. On the other hand, the immense number of institutions and regimes of regional and global governance make it impossible to track every single interaction across boundaries. In this sense, regardless of the implemented control mechanisms established by

---

Organization (1984), Vol. 38, pp. 225-286. And Lebow, Richard Ned. "The Long Peace, the End of the Cold War and the Failure of Realism." International Organization (Spring 1994), Vol. 48, pp. 249-277.

14 Sørensen, Georg. "IR theory after the Cold War." In: Dunne, Cox and Booth. The Eighty Year's Crisis. International Relations 1919-1999, p. 83 ff.

15 Held, et. al., Global Transformations. Politics, Economics and Culture, p. 425 ff.

16 For the role of the state in the age of globalization see also contributions by: Moravscsik, Andrew "Taking Preferences Seriously: A Liberal Theory of International Politics." International Organization, (Autumn 1997), Vol. 51, pp. 513-554; Wolf, Martin. "Will the Nation State Survive Globalization?" Foreign Affairs, (January/February 2001) Vol. 80 No. 1, pp. 178-191.

17 Held, et. al., Global Transformations. Politics, Economics and Culture, p. 426 ff.

18 Ibid.

international financial institutions, the globalization of politics has, unfortunately, also turned into the globalization of organized violence and organized crime.[19] Military conflicts used to be the *locus clasicus* in which politics became international and transnational. However, since the fall of the Berlin Wall and the disappearance of bloc politics, conflicts erected from organized violence, organized crime and terrorism have expanded to become global threats as the events in New York and Washington in 2001, and most recently in Madrid in 2004 have shown. [20]

Among problems of this nature, there is one particular form of organized crime, which deserves the attention of social scientists as well as policy-makers, namely the issue of corruption. This phenomenon traditionally refers to "one of the world's oldest part-time professions: proffering and accepting bribes."[21] It also denotes a problem that was widely known, but hardly approached during the years of the Cold War. However, over the past ten years, corruption has changed from an isolated national problem into an international concern with unprecedented effects for world politics. The last decade of the 20th century witnessed the emergence of corruption as an international political issue demanding a comprehensive political response on a global scale.[22]

THE INTERNATIONALITY OF CORRUPTION

Numerous reasons can be outlined for the current perception of corruption as an increasingly important international problem. This study identifies six key factors that emerge from the prior discussion on globalization and its consequences for international affairs.

First, the end of the Cold War concluded an era where cases of political corruption in some countries were "covered" by powerful nations in recognition of political support for either East or West.[23] Donor countries and institutions no longer tolerate statesmen who traditionally used the public

---

[19] *Ibid.*, p. 87 ff.

[20] This argument is presented at length by: Mittelman, James H. and Robert Johnston. "The Globalization of Organized Crime, the Courtesan State, and the Corruption of Civil Society." Global Governance (1999), vol. 5, pp. 103-126.

[21] Glynn, Patrick, Stephen J. Kobrin and Moises Naim. "The Globalization of Corruption." In: Elliott, Kimberly Ann (ed.) Corruption and the Global Economy. (Washington D.C.: Institute for International Economics, 1997), pp. 7-27.

[22] Ibid.

[23] Tanzi, Vito. "Corruption Around the World. Causes, Consequences, Scope and Cures." IMF Staff Papers. (December 1998) Vol. 45, No. 4, pp. 559-594.

treasury as their personal bank in the interest of political expediency.[24] Nowadays, the prevention of corruption is regarded as an essential condition for "good governance" and sustainable economic development.[25] Without the traditional division of world affairs into two camps, there has been a growing awareness of corruption as being a problem, which concerns every country, regardless of its political affiliation.[26]

Second, the lack of information about this phenomenon, especially in centrally planned economies, made the topic of corruption either a less discussed or completely ignored issue.[27] There is now evidence, that in many countries with this type of economic model, high-level corruption was a widely occurring phenomenon. However, governments did not bring the topic out in the open as they only benefited from being silent and careless about these practices.[28]

Third, as liberalism ran its course after the defeat of communism, the world-wide implementation of democratic models of government provided the media with enough space for the discussion of corruption without any kind of restrictions.[29] Investigative journalism on the subject of corruption has increased and has helped to bring traditionally hidden corrupt practices into the public light with unprecedented consequences for those involved.[30] Therefore, independent media have been identified as an essential institutional mechanism in the fight against corruption, especially in emerging democracies.[31] Moreover, recent studies have shown that a high degree of freedom of the press is associated with low levels of corruption.[32]

---

[24] Doig, Alan and Robin Theobald (eds). Corruption and Democratization. (London: Frank Class and Co. Ltd, 2000), p. 7 ff.

[25] Ibid.

[26] Glynn, Kobrin and Naim. "The Globalization of Corruption", p. 10.

[27] Ibid.

[28] Tanzi, "Corruption Around the World. Causes, Consequences, Scope and Cures", p. 5.

[29] Ibid.

[30] The corruption scandals around the presidents Abdala Bucaram of Ecuador, Carlos Andres Perez of Venezuela and Fernando Collor de Melho of Brazil in the 1990s serve as good examples. In all these cases, investigative journalists dared for the first time to challenge high-level authorities endangering their positions within their respective governments. As seen in Stapenhurst, Rick. "The Media's Role in Curbing Corruption." The World Bank Institute (2000).

[31] Lewis, Charles. "The Role of the Media and NGOs in Fighting Corruption." In: Trang Duc V. (ed.) Corruption and Democracy. Political Institutions, Processes and Corruption in Transition States in East-Central Europe and in the former Soviet Union. (Budapest: Institute for Constitutional & Legislative Policy, 1994), pp. 179-183

[32] This is the conclusion of a study at the University of Basel by Aymo Brunetti and Beatrice Weder. "A Free Press is Bad News for Corruption." WWZ Discussion Paper Nr. 9809. (Basel: Center of

Fourth, as it was observed earlier, the transnational nature of current international relations has made contact between countries increasingly varied. Therefore, individuals in less corrupt countries and those in endemically corrupt ones have been able to exchange their views of and experiences with corruption on a broader basis.[33] This intellectual and empirical exchange has led to increased awareness in the international community of the expansion of this problem.[34]

Fifth, if political and intellectual interdependence can be attributed to the globalization of corruption, then economic interdependence is an even greater factor for the internationalization of this phenomenon. The broadening and deepening of global financial and economic integration enables corruption to "spill over" throughout the world economy.[35] As national boundaries seem to disappear with globalization, it becomes increasingly difficult to separate domestic economic structures from international ones.[36] In addition, the emergence of an electronically networked global financial system creates more fluid mechanisms for the movement of capital.[37] Currency markets have now become the most global of all markets and the transfer of money at the international level is vital for making international business work.[38] Thus the establishment of a more technologically advanced, free and open regime of international trade and finance has made money transfers easier, quicker to occur, and almost impossible to track.[39] It is especially in this realm where international corruption seems to expand at its best, since both the scope of the problem and the difficulties of controlling it remain somehow endless.

Lastly, the appearance and increasing importance of non-governmental organizations (NGOs) specifically concerned with combating corruption has created a new kind of international public awareness for this problem.[40] The leading institution in this regard is the Berlin-based organization Transparency International (TI). As a typical NGO, the work of

Economics and Business Administration, University of Basel, 1998.) Reprinted in: Journal of Public Economics. (2003) Vol. 87, pp. 1801-1824.

[33] Tanzi, "Corruption Around the World. Causes, Consequences, Scope and Cures", p. 5.

[34] Ibid.

[35] Glynn, Kobrin and Naim. "The Globalization of Corruption", p. 12.

[36] Ibid.

[37] Ibid.

[38] Pauly, Who Elected the Bankers? Surveillance and Control in the World Economy, p. ix.

[39] Morris-Cotterill, Nigel. "Money Laundering." Foreign Policy (May/June, 2001) Issue 124, p. 19.

[40] Tanzi, "Corruption Around the World. Causes, Consequences, Scope and Cures", p. 5.

TI is aimed at creating international networks, in this particular case, networks against corruption.[41] Thus, the focus of TI's strategy is to build coalitions around the world, which would help combat this phenomenon.[42] With over 85 national chapters, TI has been able to develop and foster anti-corruption movements in all regions of the world. These non-governmental movements have launched corruption onto the agendas of governments worldwide.

SCHOLARLY PERSPECTIVES ON CORRUPTION

Just as the issue of corruption has been "re-discovered" by international politics, this phenomenon has also become a more intensively studied topic by analysts and policy-makers. In past years, the vast majority of available research on corruption came from economics.[43] Studies from this area were the most commonly cited and provided the most valuable recommendations on how to cope with this problem.[44]

Nevertheless, the scope of corruption studies has broadened into the social sciences to include political scientists, sociologists, and most recently anthropologists to undertake extensive research on this topic, who concentrate on the meaning of illegal practices in different societies and on people's assessment of courses of action in diverse cultural backgrounds.[45] Sociological and anthropological approaches to corruption entail explorations of how individuals evaluate social practices in their respective country.[46]

---

[41] Galtung, Fredrik und Jeremy Pope. "The Global Coalition Against Corruption: Evaluation Transparency International." In: Schedler, Andreas, Larry Diamond und Marc Plattner (Hrsg.) The Self-Retaining State – Power and Accountability in New Democracies. (Boulder, London: Lynne Rienner Publishers, 1999), pp. 257-282.

[42] Ibid.

[43] Poelchau, Daniel. Normativer Wandel im Internationalen System. Ein Erklärungsansatz für das zunehmende Engagement im Kampf gegen die Korruption. (Munich: Geschiwster-Scholl-Institut für Politische Wissenschaft, 2002), p. 117. This recent study at the Ludwig-Maximilians-University of Munich showed that between 1990-2000, the number of online publications at the World Bank on the area of corruption grew as much as 30 percent over all other topics researched at the Bank.

[44] Andvig, Jens, Odd-Helge Fjeldstad, et. al. Research on Corruption. A Policy Oriented Survey. Stockholm: Chr. Michelsen Institute (CMI) & Norwegian Institute for International Affairs (NUPI), December 2000, p. 51 ff.

[45] *Ibid,* p. 63. An introduction to anthropological views on corruption can be found in: Sissener, Tone Kristin. "Anthropological perspectives on corruption." Chr. Michelsen Institute. CMI Working Paper, 2001.

[46] Andvig, Fjeldstadt, et. al. Research on Corruption. A Policy Oriented Survey, p. 63.

Approaching the issue from a different perspective, most political scientists have studied the phenomenon of corruption as part of the debate on the role of the state as an indispensable instrument for economic development, welfare and the distribution of goods, especially in developing countries.[47] The traditional proposals of "state-dominated" or "state-less" governance models have not achieved the desired results in the quest for socio-political and economic development.[48] Therefore, many conclude that the best solution to plausible patterns for development must refer to a medium-sized government structure with adequate economic policies and strong political commitment.[49] Political scientists have acknowledged that development is not solely a problem of economics; it entails strong political factors that cannot be left out of the discussion. In this context, political scientists analyze corruption by taking a country's political dimensions into consideration.[50] Within this analytical posture, political science has delivered an analysis of corruption that covers various regime types such as authoritarianism, democracy, development-oriented models and neo-patrimonial rule.[51] The political science study of corruption focuses further on the struggle between different state institutions and on their struggle for influence within the government apparatus.[52] In this regard, the independence of the judiciary, the strength of the parliament as a counterpart to the executive, the hierarchical relationship among bureaucracies, the reform of the public sector and modernization efforts such as privatization, deregulation and decentralization are the political factors that need to be included in the assessment of corruption.[53] Lastly, political scientists also explore the different internal control mechanisms within the government's structure as possible effective tools for the fight against corruption.[54]

In the area of International Relations, scholars have mainly concentrated their analysis of corruption within the discussion on the role of norms in international politics.[55] The key questions of this debate are: a) where do norms come from; b) how do norms develop and situate themselves

---

47 *Ibid.*, p. 51.
48 Ibid.
49 Ibid.
50 Ibid.
51 Ibid.
52 Ibid.
53 *Ibid.*, p. 52.
54 Ibid.
55 Poelchau. Normativer Wandel im Internationalen System, p. 6.

as an explaining factor for the behavior of different actors in international relations; and c) through which mechanisms do norms gain constitutive effects for the actions, not only of states, but also of individuals and social networks.[56] In this context, the initial concern of IR Theory might not be corruption *per se*. However, as it was mentioned earlier on, corruption has become an international problem and thus requires international solutions. Therefore, the contribution of IR Theory in the approach of global corruption appears when the community of states develops international mechanisms and sets up international norms to curb corruption.[57] IR scholars then analyze how these anti-corruption "norms" work, how they should be implemented and how they contribute to the perception of the problem on a global scale.[58]

Most recently, there has been a further analytical area in which IR Theory and the study of corruption are linked: the traditional concept of state sovereignty. The example of tax havens should clarify this point.[59] Since the late 1960s, the number of states that serve as tax havens has increased dramatically and it has been estimated that as much as half of the world's stock of money is either permanently placed in or has passed through tax havens.[60] As tax haven regulations foster money laundering – a common form of international corruption – governments in these countries have the discretion to make the rules to which their benefactors have to comply.[61] Due to this discretion of tax havens of making decisions on the funds deposited therein, an international jurisdictional vacuum develops and national sovereignty becomes somehow "commercialized" by tax havens, as these states directly establish the costs of legal protection and economic

[56] Selected works on the current debate of norms in the scholarship of International Relations Theory are: Finnemore, Martha and Kathryn Sikkink. "International Norm Dynamics and Political Change." International Organization (Fall 1998), Vol. 52, pp. 887-917; Florini, Ann. "The Evoution of International Norms." International Studies Quarterly (September 1996), Vol. 40, pp. 363-390; Kratochwil, Friedrich. "How do Norms Matter?" In Byers, Michael (ed.) The Role of Law in International Politics. (Oxford: Oxford University Press, 2000), chapt. 3; Kratochwil, Friedrich. Rules, Norms and Decisions. (Cambridge: Cambridge University Press, 1989); and Legro, Jeffrey. "Which Norms Matter?" International Organization (Winter 1997), Vol. 51, pp. 31-64.

[57] Poelchau. Normativer Wandel im Internationalen System, p. 6.

[58] *Ibid.* At this point, I thank Daniel Poelchau for bringing this issue to my attention and for the comprehensive discussions on the topic.

[59] As seen in Palan, Ronen. "Tax Havens and the Commercialization of State Sovereignty." International Organization (Winter 2002), Vol. 56, no. 1, pp. 151-176.

[60] *Ibid*, p. 151.

[61] *Ibid*, pp. 152. The author makes an analogy comparing tax havens with parking lot proprietors stating that, "they could not care less about the business of their customers, only that they pay for parking the vehicles there."

benefit for those who use them.[62] IR theorists analyze this problem by re-assessing the traditional notions on sovereignty and the problems that corrupt practices such as money laundering can bring upon these concepts.[63]

This short introductory review has shown that the phenomenon of corruption is a vast area that still demands thorough analysis. Summarizing, these remarks serve as the initial *motives* for this book. As it was observed at the beginning, current globalization has brought changes not only to international politics, but also to almost every area of human activity. Further, it was noted that the events that lead to the end of the Cold War gave rise to new questions for the analysis of International Relations both from an empirical as well as theoretical tenure. Within these new issues, it became clear that not only international politics, but also organized crime have become transnational. In this realm, the problem of corruption was identified as an increasingly important and equally endangering phenomenon both for states and for international institutions. Moreover, in the last decade of the 20th century, numerous reasons have accounted for the growing international concern of corruption, all of them demanding comprehensive solutions from analysts and policy makers. And lastly, but certainly no less important, it was noted that corruption studies seemed to have experienced a shift in their analytical diversity. As economics used to be the classical field from which most studies of corruption emerged, now the social sciences, especially sociology, anthropology, political science and IR theory have become equally involved in the scholarly assessment of corruption. The purpose of this book is thus to make a social scientific contribution on one of the greatest problems of current international life.

DEMOCRACY AND CORRUPTION IN LATIN AMERICA

The political landscape of Latin America has experienced profound changes over the last 50 years. After having shared a nearly 500-year long common history of colonialism and thereafter liberation and republican independence, the region's political landscape in the first decade following the end of World War II was characterized by new governments willing to engage in multilateral efforts to promote human rights and democracy

---

[62] *Ibid.* This point based on Palan's article was taken out of a paper I presented to the National Collegiate Conference Association under the name "Preventing and Combating the International Flow of Illicit Funds within the International Business and Trade Regime. A Background Guide." The National Model United Nations Conference. (October, 2002)

[63] Palan. "Tax Havens and the Commercialization of State Sovereignty", p. 153 ff.

throughout the region.[64] The democratic endeavors of the post-war Latin America did not last long enough and in the following decades nearly every country in the region experienced the rise of authoritarian military rule and the installment of economic protectionism.[65] Since the beginning of the 1980s, however, there has been an important shift in politics and economics similar to the changes implemented during the 19th century's *independencia.*[66] The last 20 years are a particular point in the history of Latin America, as this time brought a revival of the democratic idea of governance, as totalitarian regimes failed to guarantee economic prosperity and political freedom for most Latin Americans.[67] The general consensus of many Latin American nations in the 1980s was based on the assumption that the transition (or in this case, the return) to democratic governance combined with free-market economic policies would set the patterns for adequate economic, social, and political development in the region.[68] With the end of the Pinochet-regime in Chile, it was clear that the choice of democracy in the Americas had turned into a norm accepted in almost every country.[69] As a consequence, the implementation of liberal economic reforms for more open markets, state deregulation, and regional integration raised the expectations

---

64 The Declaration of Principles on Inter-American Solidarity and Cooperation entailed the acknowledgement on the "existence of democracy as a common cause in America." This document was adopted at the Inter-American Conference on the Consolidation of Peace in Buenos Aires in 1936. Cited in: Muñoz, Heraldo and Joseph Tulchin (eds.) Latin American Nations in World Politics. (Boulder: Westview Press, 1996), p. 19.

65 Between 1945 and 1980, only Costa Rica and Mexico did not experience coups and, thereafter, military regimes of any kind. As seen in: Calvert, Peter and Susan Calvert. Latin America in the Twentieth Century. (London: Macmillan Press, 1990.)

66 The strive for independence from Spain and Portugal in Latin America changed the political shape of the continent as former colonies claimed their territories back from the *conquistadores*. European thinkers and practitioners involved in the French and American Revolutions inspired the initial independence movements. The first important outbreak of the rebellion against the European rulers took place in the former Real Audiencia de Quito in Ecuador on 10th August 1809, when the Spanish governor Conde Ruiz de Castilla was suddenly supplanted by a group of local citizens, who installed a provisional "government of the people". Although royal forces crushed this sublevation only ten months later, it became the first symbol of independence on the continent. This episode known as the "first shout of independence" (sp. *"primer grito de independencia"*) gave birth to other resistance movements across Spanish and Portuguese colonies in the Americas. For further reference see also: Lynch, John. Latin America Between Colony and Nation: Selected Essays (London: Palgrave Macmillan, 2001.)

67 Lopez, George A. and Michael Stohl. "Liberalization and Redemocratization in Latin America: The Search for Models and Meanings." In: Lopez, George A. and Michael Stohl (eds.) Liberalization and Redemocratization in Latin America. (New York: Greenwood Press, 1987), p. 1-13.

68 Tulchin, Joseph S. and Ralph H. Espach. Combating Corruption in Latin America. (Washington, D.C.: The Woodrow Wilson Center Press, 2002), p. 1.

69 *Ibid.* The authors note Cuba as the only exeption.

of both leaders and the electorate in a new economic doctrine which would supplant the obsolete barriers of protectionism.[70]

At the dawn of the authoritarian regimes era in Latin America, the lack of basic national consensus and the emergence of politically motivated violence constituted the main breaking elements of the still young democracies in the region.[71] Nowadays, corruption is perhaps a comparable threat for the new democratic institutions because of its corrosive and destabilizing effects.[72] Moreover, this phenomenon has disillusioned all those who predicted a more efficient and transparent kind of governance, after democracy and liberalism had been installed as political an economic *modi operandi* on the continent.

Corruption is currently a highly debated topic in the political, economic, social, and cultural agenda of Latin American affairs. But the concern about this problem goes beyond an intellectual and theoretical debate. During the last ten years, most governments in the region have directly suffered the effects of systematic corruption. The population, moreover, has suddenly been directly confronted with the negative results of corrupt practices, which for many Latin Americans is traditionally seen as a 'way of life'.[73] From Mexico to Argentina, the catastrophic reactions to corruption have exposed the idea of democracy and economic liberalism to severe criticism, undermining the intentions of policy makers and weakening the citizen's confidence in the political and economic discourses of the last two decades.[74] This lack of trust in government institutions has served as the seed for internal crises with high political and economic costs attached.[75] Recent Latin American history has witnessed the dismantling of entire governments after corruption scandals have been brought to the public eye.[76]

---

[70] Ibid.

[71] Ferreiro, Alejandro. "Dinero, Política y Transparencia: el imperativo democrático de combatir la corrupción." Working Paper for the 9th International Anti-Corruption Conference. (Durban: Transparency International, 1999.)

[72] Ibid.

[73] This observation was made by the Argentine journalist Mario Diament. Quoted in: Little, Walter and Eduardo Posada-Carbó. Political Corruption in Europe and Latin America. (London: Macmillan Press Ltd., 1996), p. 10.

[74] Tulchin and Espach. Combating Corruption in Latin America, p. 2. Moreover, the authors note that "[a]lthough unsupported by the historical record, a troublesome perception persists throughout the region that authoritarian leaders of the past were more honest and more committed to serving the nation's interest than today's democratic politicians."

[75] Ibid.

[76] The recent events in Argentina and Ecuador can serve as examples. As a result of economic mismanagement and endemic corruption within the administration in 2001, President Fernando de la

The regional and international effects were soon visible to the Latin American community of states. Foreign investors and multilateral donor agencies were deterred in offering their traditional contribution to the development of the region, as high levels of corruption became a "trade mark" in many Latin American countries.[77] Thus it can be easily observed that international efforts for economic reform and sustainable growth in the region cannot be adequately undertaken if the perception of Latin American countries of being endemically corrupt still prevails.[78]

METHODOLOGY: PUZZLE, HYPOTHESES, VARIABLES

Out of the recent development of corruption in Latin America, a key question arises: *why is corruption still so present in this region?* This is the puzzle this book seeks to solve. Moreover, the nature of the problem as a regional phenomenon catches the attention of any observer. Are Latin American politics culturally or normatively bound to corrupt practices, or does corruption work as the "grease" in the Latin American political and economic machinery? The research will seek to provide a comprehensive answer to this question by analyzing corruption from a theoretical point of view and by documenting its nature, causes and effects in the political and economic systems of three selected cases within Latin America.

The attempt to provide a solid and unbiased answer to the question of why corruption is still present in Latin America is not an easy task. At first, a comparative systematic analysis of corruption in different countries in and outside Latin America may seem appropriate. However, inter-regional comparisons have not been effective in explaining why this problem persists in this region.[79] As many nations outside the continent – such as the United States of America and some European countries – have acknowledged that corruption does exist within their political systems, for Latin America, instead, the acknowledgement is that "corruption *is* the system."[80] An inter-

Rúa was forced to step down from power. In a similar situation just one year before, Ecuadorian President Jamil Mahuad faced a civil "coup" as different civil movements marched into the government's facilities protesting against corruption and demanding a change in the administration.

[77] Tulchin and Espach. Combating Corruption in Latin America, p. 2. The authors note, that in 2000, for the first time, the standby agreement between the International Monetary Fund (IMF) and the Argentine government explicitly contained measures for reducing corruption as a requirement to qualify for currency support.

[78] Ibid.

[79] Little and Posada-Carbó. Political Corruption in Europe and Latin America, p. 10.

[80] Ibid.

regional comparative analysis of corruption thus faces considerable obstacles due to political, social and historic differences among countries, even if they are on the same continent. The structure of the political system and the social public perception of the term "corruption" vary from region to region thus making such analytical efforts highly questionable.[81]

Nevertheless, if an inter-regional approach seems loaded with analytical pitfalls, an effective understanding and explaining of corruption in Latin America is perhaps best gained if we focus on the region *per se*. As corrupt practices have become a common danger for most governments in Latin America, the research should then try to first analyze national and local characteristics of different countries in the region, compare them, and then make general assumptions for the entire scope of the problem on the continent.

Such a procedure will be effective if the core elements to any scientific approach – variables and hypotheses – are established first. Due to the scope of the topic at hand, there are endless mechanisms through which the puzzle can be solved. Therefore, this book will postulate selected hypotheses from different scholarly traditions, particularly from the social sciences. The main dependent variable will be the incidence of corruption, measured by the levels of perceived corruption indicated in Transparency International's Corruption Perceptions Index. Although this tool does not permit more than the interpretations of perceptions, it has become the only useful index containing a cross-country ranking.

As for the independent variable, it was noted earlier that corruption has become a multidisciplinary topic studied by economists, political scientists, sociologists and anthropologists, and theorists of International Relations. This variety of approaches enables a wide range of analytical views of this phenomenon. Since the objective of this book is to provide a comprehensive explanation for the levels of corruption and their effects in Latin American nations, it seems adequate to use elements from each of these academic disciplines and set them as independent variables in to deliver proper answers to the initial questions.

Under this premise, there will be four main working hypotheses in this analysis. The first will focus on the economic perspective of corruption and the costs implied for countries affected by this problem. Corruption is seen as a major threat towards economic growth in developing regions and emerging markets. This study builds on the causal relation between corrupt practices and the different stages of economic development and will test that

[81] Ibid.

in the case of Latin America the state of the economy might be the reason for the incidence of corruption, therefore *if economic development is low, then corruption levels remain high.*[82]

Second, taking the sociological and anthropological view into consideration, this book seeks to understand the incidence of corruption in Latin America from a normative and cultural perspective. Some simplistic explanation for the existence of corruption in this region is to believe – as most policy makers and analysts have done in the past – that corruption is inevitable in Latin American politics. Political scientists Joseph Tulchin and Ralph Espach are right to note that this posture entails a "fatalism [which] is both unjustified and untrue."[83] Moreover, the authors point out that, despite differences in history and political culture, Europe, Asia and the United States deserve similar criticisms when it comes to the presence of corruption in these regions since

> "[c]lientelist political systems, tight familial and communal bonds, and rigid social hierarchies are a legacy of the region's history of conquest, colonialism, and racial division. The region's social and economic development, the prominence of government and church hierarchies, the patrimonialist style of the Spanish and Portuguese monarchies, and other factors created an environment favorable to clientelism and the use of public office for private enrichment or protection. Also the influence of Enlightenment philosophy, which had such dramatic effect in England and much of Europe, spread more slowly through Spain, Portugal, and their colonies and was obstructed there by entrenched political and economic interests. As a result of these legacies, political systems in Latin America have tended to exhibit an exorbitant mixing of the public and private spheres and a tradition of clientelist governance. The same can be said, however, for Spain, Portugal, and Italy, the region's cultural progenitors in southern Europe. Japanese and other Asian societies receive similar criticism, and Africans reputed to be worse

---

82 An introduction to the debate of corruption as a constraint for development can be found in: Gray, Cheryl and Daniel Kaufmann. "Corruption and Development." Finance & Development (1998), pp. 7-10.

83 Tulchin and Espach. Combating Corruption in Latin America, p. 9.

> than Latin America. This determinist argument ignores the fact, however, that all systems have suffered from extensive corruption at one time or another, including that of Britain and – rather often, it seems –from the United Stares."[84]

Accordingly, cultural attitudes do play an important role in either accepting or rejecting corrupt practices, however these attitudes are "far from fixed."[85] Precisely because there is a lack of understanding of the normative element of the phenomenon of corruption in Latin America, this book explores the relationship between history and political culture and the acceptance and/or rejection of corrupt behavior. Therefore, this study intends to find out if, within a country, *national history and political culture influence the levels of corruption.*

The third working hypothesis emerges from the political study of corruption. As political scientists have concentrated the research of corrupt practices on the role of the state, the efforts have led to an analytical debate on "how much state" is necessary to effectively combat corruption.[86] As the political systems in most Latin American countries have made the jump from authoritarian regimes into modern liberal democracies, this research will give credit to the relationship between levels of corruption and the political systems of the different countries in the region. In the early 1980s, the hope was to use democracy as an effective tool to diminish corruption. However, the recent scandals in almost all Latin American countries have dramatically proven the contrary.[87] Is there more corruption in a democratic system, or is corruption the political *herencia* of authoritarian regimes? The task will be to either confirm or falsify the claim that corruption and the government systems in Latin America are directly linked, thus *if the modern liberal democratic model of governance is followed, corruption levels will be low.*

Lastly, as current IR theory has contributed to the study of corruption by bringing the issue of norms into the discussion on how to cope with this problem, this book seeks to establish the role of international norms against corrupt practices by observing how the emergence, development, and implementation of these norms (in form of regional agreements and treaties) can be used as an effective mechanism to lower the levels of corruption in

---

84 *Ibid.*, p. 10.

85 Ibid.

86 Andvig, Fjeldstadt, et. al. Research on Corruption. A Policy Oriented Survey, p. 51.

87 For a review of recent cases see Transparency International. Global Corruption Report 2001. (Berlin: Transparency International, 2001), pp. 168-179.

Latin America. Therefore, the fourth working hypothesis for the case of Latin American countries is that *if international norms against corruption are established and effectively implemented, levels of corruption will diminish.*

Confirming and/or falsifying four hypotheses can become a hard enterprise. Therefore, there is a need to choose a method and develop a concrete plan for achieving the desired results. As such, the following observations will present both the chosen methodological approach and the plan of the book through which I will proceed in order to solve the puzzle and address each one of the proposed hypotheses.

THE COMPARATIVE METHOD AND CASE STUDY SELECTION

It is the task of every social scientist to make a choice for the method to be used in the analysis. This is a highly difficult – and at times even polemic – issue as there are several ways in which social scientific analysis can be undertaken.[88] Therefore, the following observations shall introduce the reader to several arguments and reasons for the chosen method used in the forthcoming chapters and sections.

First, the main purpose of analyzing the topic of corruption in the following book is to understand the different relationships that arise from this phenomenon on the political, economic, socio-cultural levels of national life. In this context, corruption will be also treated as an international problem that has transcended borders thus creating a danger to which no country is entirely immune. In order to provide the reader with empirical findings, case studies will illustrate, and either confirm or falsify these hypotheses, fulfilling the analytic-scientific nature of this book.

Second, as it will be observed in the initial chapters, reliable data on corruption is extremely difficult to obtain. Even the studies which have been able to work with statistical methods warn us about the absolute validity of their findings. This shall be a very important point for the proceedings of this book. Due to this fact, it seems plausible to focus the analysis on the problem of understanding and explaining the difference *facettes* of corruption and not on numerically measuring corruption for an evidentialistic statistical analysis.

These two observations are the main reasons for choosing the path of comparative politics and use the widely discussed, though notably valid method of cross-country comparison for the analysis of corruption undertaken in this book. As it was observed above, the comparative method

[88] A modern comprehensive overview of the methodological debate in the social sciences can be found in: Chalmers, Alan F. What Is This Thing Called Science? (Indianapolis: Hackett Pub. Co., 1999.)

seem have proven to be useful for the analysis of corruption in Latin America.[89] Nevertheless, in order to justify this choice and without going too far into the never ending methodological debate in the social sciences, I shall include in the following a few arguments from the scholarship on the positive use of the comparative method, as well as its possible problems and fallacies.

In one of the classic scholarly contributions on the comparative method, political scientist Arend Lijphart explores this sub-discipline by arguing about its efficacy and applicability for the analysis of politics.[90] Some of his findings have been considered for the methodological construction of this book. First of all, Lijphart notes that the main goal of the comparative method is to discover empirical relationships among variables rather than numerically measuring them.[91] Moreover, he defends the position that although statistical/experimental methods could bring more palpable results to the observer, the comparative method proves its validity as it concentrates on a smaller amount of cases and variables, rather than on large and at times endless sets of data and numeric values. This reduction will allow a more controlled and focused analysis.[92]

Lastly, Lijphart advocates in favor of the method of comparison when it comes to a cross- national analysis, which is precisely what this book intends to do. According to the scholarship, the comparative method would allow to establish both differences and similarities of the chosen cases in order to explain the general propositions and thus solve the main puzzle of a social scientific treaty.[93]

On the discussion of working with case studies, political scientist Harry Eckstein provides an extensive overview of how to use case studies for theory building and explaining in the social sciences as well as the implications therein.[94] He differentiates between several types of cases and their purposes for the scientific method coming to one conclusion (among several others), namely that using case studies to test theories is useful, because

[89] Little and Posada-Carbó. Political Corruption in Europe and Latin America, see page 12 and note 79.

[90] Lijphart, Arend. "Comparative Politics and the Comparative Method." American Political Science Review. (September 1971) Vol. 65, No. 3, pp. 682-693.

[91] *Ibid.*, p. 682.

[92] *Ibid.*, p. 684.

[93] *Ibid.*, p. 685 ff.

[94] Eckstein, Harry. "Case Study and Theory in Political Science." In: Greenstein, Fred and Nelson W. Polsby. Handbook of Political Science. Volume 7: Strategies of Inquiry. (Reading, MA. Addison Wesley Publishing Company, 1975), pp. 79-137.

> "[o]ne can use a well-constructed experiment, conducted to simulate as closely as possible the specified conditions under which a law must hold, and compare its result with that predicted by the law. In the history of science the decisive experiments have been mostly of that kind a fact that makes on wonder how the comparative observation of unmanipulated cases could ever have come to be regarded as any sort of equivalent of experimental method in the physical sciences."[95]

Using this assumption, it can be clearly justified what the intention of this book is: to elaborate an analytical framework based on the theories of a particular area of study, namely corruption, and provide with case studies and their comparison for explaining this phenomenon's implications in the chosen countries. These observations might enable a yet more general assessment of the problem for the field of International Relations.
Lijphart's and Eckstein's contributions denote the preliminary validity of the comparative method and the use of case studies as a procedure for the social scientific analysis proposed in this book. Both authors do acknowledge the limitations of comparison and highlight the analytical weaknesses it might have, especially when related with the results of the statistical/experimental approach, which may seem more "real".[96] However, the arguments explained above are plausible enough for the purposes of this book and will be therefore defended and implemented in the course of the following chapters.
The next question would be how to choose the cases (in terms of "how many and why") as well as to determine the basis on which the comparison should be undertaken. For these two points, Lijphart again provides the necessary answers. He argues that cases can be chosen for multiple reasons. There can be choices based on the scope of the proposed hypotheses or selections can be intentionally chosen to either falsify or confirm them.[97] This creates a preliminary bias, in terms of choosing the cases that would fit better with the

[95] *Ibid.*, p. 116-117.

[96] For a detailed analysis of the contrasts between the experimental/statistical and the comparative method see also George, Alexander L. and Timothy L. McKeown. "Case Studies and Theories of Organizational Decision Making." In: Coulam, Robert F. and Richard A. Smith. Advances in Information Processing in Organizations, Vol. 2. (Greenwich, CN.: JAI Press, 1985), pp. 21-58.

[97] Lijphart, "Comparative Politics and the Comparative Method", p. 686. The author makes reference to Johan Galtung who regards this procedure as the "quotation/illustration methodology."

theories before putting them to a test.[98] Therefore, Lijphart suggests that cases should be chosen systematically and the scientific approach should lead to probabilistic and not universal generalizations. This means that just because one case falsifies a hypothesis, it does not mean that the result can be universally postulated and applied to all other cases. A scientific case-related rejection can be easily turn relative when one presents a contrary case.[99]
For this book, it must be noted that the choice for the countries does not follow any exclusive intended pattern of selection for a higher possibility of confirming the working hypotheses. It can be said that there is a personal interest of the author, vested on his cultural background, which serves as the main motivation for choosing both the region and the countries. However, as it will be observed in Section III, all cases provide good opportunities for an adequate comparison as they may seem similar at first, but present substantive differences, especially when it comes to the incidence of corruption. Precisely these similarities and differences will permit an adequate answer of the puzzle and a solid testing of the hypotheses.[100]
Furthermore, this book recognizes three main points made by Lijphart for a comprehensive implementation of the comparative method. *First*, a successful comparative approach should "reduce the property space of the analysis" meaning that the number of variables should be kept low by combining variables and avoiding an overflow in order to not lose the general objectives of the entire book.[101] *Second*, when choosing cases for the comparison, onc should lean towards selecting "comparable" cases, entailing both similarities and differences which will be used to recognize constants or variables for the analytical treatment of the hypotheses. Through the use of "comparable" cases, the number of variables will be reduced and the study of the relationships among them can be undertaken under controlled conditions.[102] And *third*, cases selected within the same regional area (the

[98] On this point see also: Geddes, Barbara. "How the Cases You Choose Affect the Answers You Get: Selection Bias in Comparative Politics." In: Stimson, James A. (ed.) Political Analysis. An Annual Publication of the Methodology Section of the American Political Science Association. Vol. 2 (Ann Arbor: The University of Michigan Press, 1990), pp. 131-150.

[99] Lijphart, "Comparative Politics and the Comparative Method", p. 686.

[100] Political scientists Mattei Dogan and Dominique Pelassy note moreover, that "[v]iewed from apart, South American countries present a series of analogies that become much less evident when one looks at them more closely, allowing the contrasts to appear." In: Dogan, Mattei and Dominique Pelassy. How to Compare Nations. Strategies in Comparative Politics. (Chatham, NJ: Chatham House Publishers, Inc., 1990), p. 132.

[101] Lijphart, "Comparative Politics and the Comparative Method", p. 686.

[102] *Ibid.* The author explains that "[i]f such comparable cases can be found, they offer particularly good opportunities for the application of the comparative method, because they allow the establishment

"area approach") shall provide a cluster of political, economic and socio-cultural similarities that would make the testing of the hypotheses easier and more solid as if the cases were chosen randomly across different regions.[103]
Using these premises as valid methodological directives and bearing in mind the initial considerations on the topic of corruption, this book presents two main constitutive elements. On the methodological side, the analytical framework uses the levels of corruption (as indicated mostly by TI's Corruption's Perception Index) as the main independent variable to be tested in all four main hypotheses. The dependent variables may differ in each one of the case studies, however, the main interest is to test the hypotheses and make an assessment of how the independent variable reacts to the exposure of the above mentioned factors (level of economic development, political culture/history, political system, and applied international mechanisms.)
It must be noted that Lijphart recommends having at least two cases in the analysis, as the study of just one case will miss any ground for having an *ex post facto* valid generalization and applicability.[104] In this regard, the plan of the book foresees the analysis of three comparable case studies within the same geographical region, namely Argentina, Chile and Ecuador. This number should allow making comprehensive, solid and controlled attempt towards an explanatory generalization of the topic at hand for the entire region.

PLAN OF THE BOOK

This study hopes to combine the analytical advantages of International Relations Theory and comparative politics in order to provide answers to the most recent concerns raised by the problem of corruption in Latin America. The structure of the book is divided into three main sections.

---

of relationships among a few variables while many other variables are controlled." The author quotes John Stuart Mill, who referred to this approach to as the "method of difference" and the "method of concomitant variations." See: Mill, John Stuart. A System of Logic. (London: Spottiswoode, Ballantyne & Co. Ltd. Reprinted Version, 1967.)

103 On this aspect of intra-regional case study selection and comparison, Lijphart makes reference to the contribution of authors such as political scientist Bruce Russet, who noted that "[t]he rigorous delineation of regions or groups of countries which have, compared with the rest of the world, a high degree of social and cultural homogeneity should help the analyst of comparative politics to decide in which comparisons he must be especially sensitive to the 'many roads' problem and where he can fairly secure in ignoring it." In: Russet, Bruce M. International Regions and the International System. A Study in Political Ecology. (Chicago: Rand McNally & Company, 1969), p. 9. See also Dogan and Pelassy. How to Compare Nations. Strategies in Comparative Politics, p. 132 ff.

104 Lijphart, "Comparative Politics and the Comparative Method", p. 688.

Section I includes a review of the definition and the different typologies of corruption. Also included are its main normative causes and general effects on both states and international relations. Special attention will be given to the perception of corruption as a constraint for regional and national development.[105] This initial step will set the analytical framework within which the entire "plot" of the book will develop.

After a thorough theoretical treatment of corruption, the Section II provides the reader with an overview of the major approaches that have been discussed in the scholarship on the topic as well as on anti-corruption practices. Four major areas will be analyzed, public sector reform, the role of non-governmental organizations, the position of the media and the latest international mechanisms against corruption implemented by the community of states. This section will allow locating the different strategies and initiatives against corruption and will portray both the successes and failures of each approach.

In Section III, a comprehensive analysis of the major problems of corruption in three Latin American countries, namely Argentina, Chile and Ecuador, will be provided. At first, a short summary of each country's history and political system will be provided in order to sketch out the major characteristics, similarities, and differences among them. Thereafter, the countries will be analyzed in terms of corruption. This means, that major incidents related to this phenomenon in the last years will be documented and taken into consideration. The findings of this section are pivotal for either confirming or falsifying the four working hypotheses and for testing the theories presented in the first section.

By combining theoretical and empirical findings, the conclusion intends to elaborate appropriate answers to the main puzzle and test the four hypotheses. The main argumentative concern will be to compare the cases and, out of the comparison, to draw common patterns for determining how corruption "operates" and possibly establish some general postulations on why this phenomenon is still so prevalent in these countries. In this context, it will be evaluated if corruption can be seen as a general phenomenon for Latin America, or if it varies from country to country.

At this point, it is important to note, that it is not the goal of this analysis to prove "how corrupt" some countries may or may not be. This should be the focus of other research treatises on the topic. Besides, any attempt to answer such a question will face the problem of data reliability, which is one of the most discussed problems in the scholarship of corruption. More specifically,

105 See Gray and Kaufmann. "Corruption and Development."

this book seeks to explain why corruption persists in these countries and if there is a possible link between the different independent variables related to the problem and its persistence in the selected countries and, beyond this, in the region.

MECHANISMS: CORRUPTION RESEARCH, EMPIRICAL FOUNDATION AND PITFALLS

> "Ideally the data applied in research on corruption should be based on direct and first-hand observations of corrupt transactions made by unbiased observers who are familiar with the rules and routines in the sector under scrutiny."[106]

This observation made by researchers at the Norwegian Agency for Cooperation and Development (NORAD) clearly denotes the primary problem of obtaining the data needed for the analysis proposed in this book. If the puzzle and the four working hypotheses are to be tested and solved, adequate material constitutes the key to making the findings of this book a solid contribution towards the scholarship of corruption. Therefore, the following lines will present the research tools used in this book, including their empirical foundation and explanatory power. Nonetheless, weaknesses and theoretical pitfalls of the chosen mechanisms will be addressed as well, since they are of considerable importance for the overall evaluation of corruption presented in this contribution.

For Section I, the current scholarly debate on the topic of corruption should be used for locating the definition of corruption, its causes and effects on international relations. Authors such as Samuel Huntington, Gunnar Myrdal, Magnus Blomström, and Michael Bratton will portray the different positions and the so-called "debates" of the scholarship towards the issue of corruption. No current analysis of corruption can spare the use of "classics" on the topic from authors such as Susan Rose-Ackerman and Kimberly Ann Elliot.[107] The former focuses on understanding the relationship between the government and corrupt practices. Rose-Ackerman's books have comprehensively shaped the debate on how to adequately explain the persistence of this phenomenon within the public administration. Elliot is also especially important, as she has conducted research on corruption from

[106] Andvig, Fjeldstadt, et. al. Research on Corruption. A Policy Oriented Survey, p. 35.

[107] Rose-Ackermann, Susan. Corruption and Government. (Cambridge: Cambridge University Press, 1999); and Elliott (ed.) Corruption and the Global Economy.

an international angle, which is the main perspective of this book. Other economic analysts have influenced the discussion and the research on corrupt practices throughout the world. Vito Tanzi, Paulo Mauro and Jens Andvig are the most prominent of this group.[108] Arnold Heidenheimer and Michael Johnston published what many refer to as the foremost book on political corruption, Political Corruption – Concepts and Contexts.[109] Their work is a great asset to the discussion on the politics of corruption. Lastly, the recent survey on corruption research presented by NORAD is worth mentioning as it provides one of the most complete overviews of this entire field of studies.

As Section II explores the most recent approaches for combating national and international corruption, new material will be introduced and discussed. The last working hypothesis will be tested by first highlighting the role of international institutions in the fight against corruption. This will be undertaken by reviewing recent reports and case studies from the World Bank, the IMF, and other international institutions. The reports of these organizations will enable one to create a comprehensive overview of solutions such as public sector reform and the implementation of more transparent economic and political structures for "cleaner" governance. These contributions are also important, since they document the latest efforts undertaken by countries to effectively combat corruption within their administration.

Moreover, the latest reports and articles on the role of NGOs and the media will enable us to illustrate how effective these institutions can be at creating a global public awareness on the negative effects of corruption worldwide. Aimo Brunnetti and Beatrice Weder at the University of Basel and the University of Mainz are among the few who analyze the relationship between press freedom and levels of corruption. Therefore, their findings will be included and discussed in the last section of the book. Recent articles by Johan Galtung and Jeremy Pope at TI will be used to examine the general role of NGOs as effective international civil coalitions against corruption.

---

[108] Relevant works include: Tanzi, "Corruption Around the World. Causes, Consequences, Scope and Cures"; Tanzi, Vito and Hamid R. Davoodi. "Corruption, Growth and Public Finances." IMF Working Paper 00/182 (2000); Andvig, Fjeldstadt, et. al. Research on Corruption. A Policy Oriented Survey; Mauro, Paolo. "Corruption: Causes, Consequences, and Agenda for further Research." Finance & Development (1998), pp. 11-14.

[109] Heidenheimer, Arnold and Michael Johnston (eds.) Political Corruption. Concepts and Contexts. Third Edition. (New Brunswick, New Jersey: 2002.) See also the previous edition: Heidenheimer, Arnold, Michael Johnston, and Victor LeVine (eds.) Political Corruption – A Handbook. (New Brunswick and Oxford: Transaction, 1989.)

The material chosen for Section III is twofold. On the one hand, the current literature on Latin American affairs, especially those relating to the chosen case studies will be used in order to describe the different aspects of the political landscape of the continent. Special attention will be given to how corruption has been a damaging factor for the democracies in the region. In this particular focus, the work of Joseph Tulchin at the Woodrow Wilson International Center for Scholars is of particular importance. Tulchin, among other authors such as Heraldo Muñoz, Laurence Whitehead and Ralph Espach, undertake valuable analyses of the different shapes corruption has taken in Latin America.

On the other hand, the empirical data on corruption will primarily rely on the most widely used tool for describing corruption to date: the Corruption Perception Index of Transparency International (CPI). Since this study is neither an article of investigative journalism nor a police report, the indicators for the existence of corruption in Latin America – recognizable for each country – should be taken from a reliable source a social scientific analysis. At the moment, the CPI presents the most prominent and widest-used tool for research and public debate on corruption.[110] In this context, the work of Johann Graf Lambsdorf at the University of Göttingen should be highlighted. Together with TI, he has been able to produce valuable data on the perception of corruption within public administrations in over 80 countries worldwide. Therefore, his findings as well as the latest CPI report will be useful for assessing the current status of corruption in the chosen countries. Nevertheless, it is important to note from the very beginning of this book, that the CPI does contain certain weaknesses that need to be briefly mentioned. As the name reveals, the CPI deals mainly with the *perception* of corruption obtained from different polls. The methodology of interviewing or directly asking business people, policy analysts, scholars and even practitioners could lead to inconsistencies of the objectivity of such polls. The CPI combines various surveys in order to explain the range in which countries are ordered. However the definition of corruption varies from questionnaire to questionnaire and so do the opinions of those interviewed.[111] Therefore, the CPI – as the primary tool to illustrate the status of corruption in Latin America – should be used under careful observance of these possible pitfalls. These problems will be thoroughly analyzed in Chapter Six.

---

[110] *Ibid.*, p. 39.

[111] *Ibid.*, p. 42. It is noted that "[...] the responses may depend on the respondents' cultural backgrounds, and if they are residents or non-residents in the country in question. Furthermore, the responses may vary between income groups, among experts and the general public."

Since the conclusion addresses the main questions of this analysis in order to solve the puzzle and the test the hypotheses, no new material will be added to this part of the book. Due to the intended comparison among the cases and the establishment of a general pattern highlighting the damage from corruption in the region, the conclusion will build upon the mechanisms and sources used in the theoretical and empirical sections.

CHAPTER ONE

THE BATTLE OF DEFINITIONS

> "The first thing that needs to be said is that corruption [...] tends to evoke a particular pattern of reactions. First, there is evasion. Then excuses. And finally, with luck, useful analysis."[112]

One of the starting challenges of any study in the social sciences is the quest for proper definitions. This initial step is of utmost importance, since provides the basis of the analytical framework as well as its boundaries. In the area of corruption studies, the search for an adequate definition has been the subject of an extended academic discussion. The lack of a single widely accepted definition of corruption has been the initial obstacle for most papers in this area of study.[113]

The purpose of this Chapter is to offer an overview of the different analytical postures on corruption research as well as to discuss the main theoretical traditions within the scholarship. This revision will lead to the choice of an operational definition for the specific purposes of this book, which will then be used throughout the rest of the analysis.

As it was observed in the introduction, the study of corruption has become rich in its multidisciplinarity. Therefore, current attempts to define corruption come from different fields of the social science disciplines, creating extensive academic debates and fostering a considerable amount of analytical discourses.[114] An important common feature of the academic work on corruption until today has been the classification of its distinctive forms, striving for an adequate operationalization of the concept for analytical and practical purposes.[115]

Since there are simply too many elements to consider within one single phenomenon, scholars have tried not to over-define the term "corruption", but to rather elaborate several categories within which corrupt

---

112 Klitgaard, Robert. Controlling Corruption. (Berkeley: University of California Press, 1988), p. ix.

113 Nas, Tevfik F., Albert C. Price and Charles T. Weber. "A Policy-Oriented Theory of Corruption." The American Political Science Review (March 1986), Vol. 80, No. 1, pp. 107-119.

114 Andvig, Fjeldstadt, et. al. Research on Corruption. A Policy Oriented Survey, p. 10.

115 Ibid.

practices can be located and recognized as such.[116] These categories are not final, however, they enable a first look at the many dimensions corruption might take. Moreover, they present the initial criteria under which this phenomenon has been classified in the social sciences.

SETTING UP THE INITIAL CRITERIA

Political scientists Arnold Heidenheimer and Michael Johnston were among the first scholars to propose a set of definitions of corruption based on different behavioral categories.[117] Reviewing the findings of economists and social scientists in the 1970s, the authors made an initial classification of social science definitions of corruption.[118] They identified three main areas from which most of these definitions derive: *public-office-centered* definitions, *market-centered* definitions and *public-interest-centered* definitions.[119]

The first category refers to the basic misuse of public authority for personal gain.[120] The *public-centered* definition is mainly political, as its origins can be found within the public administration. It also denotes that corruption occurs as a violation of the trust an official has been given by the public.[121]

The second category drifts away from politics and considers corruption from the economic perspective. *Market-centered* definitions see corruption as a form of making business with a public office by maximizing the income of the public servant in charge of it.[122] Moreover, corruption

116 Johnston, Michael. "The Political Consequences of Corruption: A Reassessment." Comparative Politics (July 1986), Vol. 18, Issue 4, pp 459-477.

117 Heidenheimer and Johnston (eds.) Political Corruption, p. 7 ff.

118 Ibid.

119 *Ibid.*, p. 8.

120 *Ibid.*, p. 8. A classic definition in this category was posed by Joseph Nye as he considered corruption to be "...behavior which deviates from the normal duties of a public role because of private-regarding (family, close private clique), pecuniary or status gains; or violates rules against the exercise of certain types of private-regarding influence. This includes such behavior as bribery (use of reward to pervert the judgement of a person in a position of trust; nepotism (bestowal of patronage by reason of ascriptive relationship rather than merit); and misappropriation (illegal appropriation of public resources for private-regarding uses)." Original citation in: Nye Joseph. "Corruption and Political Development: A Cost-Benefit Analysis." American Political Science Review (June 1967), Vol. LXI, No.2, pp. 417-427.

121 Nas, Price and Weber. "A Policy-Oriented Theory of Corruption", p. 108.

122 Heidenheimer and Johnston quote, among others, the German author Jacob van Klaveren who states that corruption occurs when "a civil servant regards his public office as a business, the income of which he will...seek to maximize. The office then becomes a – maximizing unit. The size of his

becomes an effective tool to gain influence over actions within certain sectors of a bureaucracy.[123]

Lastly, the *public-interest-centered* definitions recognize corruption as a damaging factor to what many authors understand as "the public interest."[124] In this category, a public official takes advantage of his position by acting in favor of whoever offers the reward and thereby provokes a detrimental damage within the government and thus to the public interest.[125]

Although these categories are a helpful start for realizing the many dimensions corruption can take, even the same authors as well many of their colleagues do acknowledge that these categories are directly bound to a great analytical pitfall. In their review of the scholarship of corruption, economists Tevfik Nas and Charles Weber, and political scientist Albert Price asserts that these classifications contain descriptive merits, however "they lack the generality essential for an analytically useful definition of corruption."[126]

Within their own framework of analysis, Heidenheimer and Johnston raise a key question to consider for the further search of a proper definition of corruption: which norms should be used to determine whether a specific action is corrupt or non-corrupt?[127] Thus he problem of properly defining corruption has normative component, which makes any attempt easily relative, as norms vary among countries, governments and citizens. And since most of the authors come from Western-Christian societies, the search for a definition becomes even more difficult. As political scientists John Peters and Susan Welch put it,

> "[…] the systematic study of corruption is hampered by the lack of an adequate definition. What may be "corrupt" to

income depends … upon the market situation and his talents for finding the point of maximal gain on the public's demand curve." Original citation in: van Kleveren, Jacob. "Die historische Erscheinung der Korruption, in ihrem Zusammenhang mit der Staats- und Gesellschaftsstruktur betrachtet." In: Vierteljahreszeitschrift für Sozial- und Wirtschaftsgeschichte. (December 1957), Vol. 44, No. 4, pp. 294-302, 312-318. Translated by Peggy Hoffmann and Karl Kurtz. Re-printed in: Heidenheimer and Johnston (eds.) Political Corruption, pp. 83-94.

123 *Ibid.*, p. 8. As originally stated by Leff, Nathaniel. "Economic Development Through Bureaucratic Corruption." American Behavioral Scientist. (November 1964), Vol. 8, No. 3, pp. 8-14.

124 *Ibid.*, p. 9. Carl Friedrich represents this position.

125 Friedrich, Carl. "Corruption Concepts in Historical Perspective." In: The Pathology of Politics: Violence, Betrayal Corruption, Secrecy and Propaganda. (New York: Harper & Row, 1972), pp. 127-141. Re-printed in: Heidenheimer and Johnston (eds.) Political Corruption, pp. 15-25.

126 Nas, Price and Weber. "A Policy-Oriented Theory of Corruption", p. 108.

127 Heidenheimer and Johnston (eds.) Political Corruption, p. 10.

one citizen, scholar or public official is "just politics" to another, or "indiscretion" to a third."[128]

Therefore, the first attempt to categorize the numerous definitions of corruption encounters several normative disagreements within the scholarship of this area of study. However, these fallacies challenged social scientists of this early generation of corruption research to try and locate these norms and criteria somewhere beyond norms, namely in law.

One of the widely accepted proposals for setting the analytical cardinal points within which corrupt activities can be found from a more legal perspective was made by political scientist and anthropologist James Scott.[129] His position entails a legal-positivist tone and proposes to delineate corruption within a specific legal framework and make the distinction between what is corrupt and what is not. Scott postulates three possible sources to establish the criteria to locate corruption, namely *legal definitions, public interest* and *public opinion.*[130] As for the first category, corruption is to be found in such acts that do not compel with laws established by the government.[131] Second, similar to Heidenheimer and Johnston, corruption is located within activities that harm he public interest, even if these actions are legal.[132] Consequently, if an act turns out to be beneficial to the public interest, it is not viewed as "corrupt" even if it is against the law.[133] Lastly, a further source for determining the criteria of corruption can be found within public opinion, which is defined as the perception of the people of one nation towards this phenomenon.[134] In this context, political scientist John Gardiner adds to Scott's postulates that the consideration of public opinion as a factor for defining corruption is of great importance, for

[128] Peters, John G. and Susan Welch. "Political Corruption in America: A Search for Definitions and Theory, or If Political Corruption Is in the Mainstream of American Politics Why Is it Not in he Mainstream of American Politics Research?" The American Political Science Review (September 1978), Vol. 72, Issue 3, pp. 974-984.

[129] Scott, James C. Comparative Political Corruption. (Englewood Cliffs, NJ: Prentice Hall, 1972.)

[130] The summary of Scott's position is made by John Gardiner in "Defining Corruption." In: Punch Maurice, et. al (eds.) Coping with Corruption in a Borderless World: Proceedings of the Fifth International Anti-Corruption Conference. (Deventer and Boston: Kluver Law and Taxation Publishers, 1993), pp. 21-38. Reprinted in: Heidenheimer and Johnston (eds.) Political Corruption, pp. 25-40.

[131] *Ibid.*, p. 29. Gardiner states on this point that "[t]hese criteria are very straight forward: if an official's act is prohibited by laws established by the government, it is corrupt; if it is nor prohibited, it is not corrupt even I it is abusive or unethical."

[132] *Ibid.*, p. 32.

[133] Ibid.

[134] Ibid.

> "[i]f there are significant differences between what a nation's laws say and how most citizens define corruption, it is likely that officials and government employees will be guided more by local culture than by the word of law, and thus will be more likely to violate the law." [135]

Public opinion is regarded as an important factor in the fight against corruption, since it enables authorities to take notice of corrupt activities and puts pressure for their prosecution.[136] Moreover, the citizen's opinion about what is corruption and what it is not also tends to lead to their political favoritism, thus meaning that candidates and officials sharing the same values will be more likely election winners.[137]

NORMS AS DEFINITIONAL STANDARDS

Although Scott and Gardiner were able to expand the definitional framework within which corruption could be found, they have also faced several criticisms, which underlie the explanatory power and analytical usage of their proposals. Similar to the criticisms made to Heidenheimer and Johnston, there are certain disadvantages to Scott's criteria for defining corruption. Most of these fallacies are again related to the normative element entailed in corruption after relating it to laws, the public interest and public opinion.

The first problem is that defining corruption primarily breach of law faces a simultaneous dilemma, as stated by Peters and Welch: "[…] all legal acts are not necessarily corrupt and all corrupt acts are not necessarily illegal."[138] Second, the relationship between corruption and the public interest, as in the case of Heidenheimer, demands from any researcher a clear picture of what he/she understands under "the public interest" before categorizing any actions as being corrupt.[139] And third, determining the existence of corruption through the acceptance or rejection from the public

---

135 Ibid.

136 Ibid.

137 Ibid.

138 Peters and Welch. "Political Corruption in America: A Search for Definitions and Theory", pp. 975.

139 *Ibid.* The authors note that "[t]he possibility exists that a behavior may be proscribed by law as corrupt but be beneficial to the common good, such as 'fixing' the papers of an illegal alien who contributed his labor and skills to a rapidly expanding economy. Furthermore, this definition enables a politician to justify any act by claiming that it is in the public interest."

contains similar problems as with the public interest. In this category, the "public" becomes a matter of definition. Numerous studies have used polls in order to measure the public opinion on corruption and reveal problems such as determining who the public is and what it really stands for.[140] Moreover, studies in this area have revealed either complete public ambiguity (e.g. no response) or polarized opinions on the matter, thus making the explanatory power of such methods seem somehow low.[141] Peters and Welch point out a final problem of public opinion criteria when differences exist between the public and the political elites in terms of considering what differentiates corrupt acts from legal ones.[142]

After reviewing the different aspects of the definitional efforts of the scholarship towards corruption, some primary observations can be made. It is quite obvious that the quest for a universal definition of corruption that suits all possible analytical elements entailed in this word is mostly impossible. The issue of whose norms to follow when defining corruption is the major impediment of most approaches. Three basic reasons can be observed for this argument. First, there are conceptual differences among the various scholars, despite the fact that most of them agree on the basic analytical pitfalls and fallacies.[143] Second, the elements around the classifications of a corrupt act need adequate definitions as well (public interest, public opinion, etc.) And third, even if we were able to locate whose norms to follow, who the public is and what interests do they represent, the universal definition of corruption will not be equal across the different regions of the world. Gardiner – as well as other major scholars – adverts that definitions of corruption and thus criteria such as legal standards, public interest and public opinion do vary considerably between countries.[144]

THE FAILURE OF REDUCTIONISM

The review of the theoretical traditions in the study of corruption has shown that this term is loaded with different elements that make a universal

---

140 Gardiner. "Defining Corruption." The author makes reference to Michael Johnston's book Political Corruption and Public Policy in America. (Monterey: Brooks/Cole, 1982.)

141 Peters and Welch. "Political Corruption in America: A Search for Definitions and Theory", pp. 975.

142 Ibid.

143 Gardiner. "Defining Corruption", p. 35 ff.

144 *Ibid.*, p. 36. The author explains that "[i]n some nations, laws deal only with blatant bribery; other nations however have added laws to regulate nepotism, conflicts of interest, election campaign contributions, etc. Some nations feel that 'gift-giving' or 'dash' payments are acceptable while other nations have very detailed codes of conduct regulating both legislators and bureaucrats."

definition impossible, if not to say inadequate. However, the purpose of this Chapter is not only to reassess the problems and findings of the scholarship on corruption. Moreover, the task is to choose an appropriate operational definition, which will allow to further explain the causes and consequences of this phenomenon as well as its impact on international relations and especially on the case studies. This choice is not easy, since corruption seems to vary from country to country, from legislation to legislation, and even from person to person.

There are, however, two basic similarities that can be drawn out of findings from scholars discussed above. These similarities have been recognized in one of the latest research reviews on the topic, a policy oriented survey made by scholars at the Norwegian Institute of International Affairs.[145] First, according to the authors, most of the attempts to define corruption reflect the role of the state in society.[146] It is true, that state-society relations can be found in almost every category of the definitions described above. In this context, corruption is mostly referred to as a breach or treason between officials representing the state and the public representing society. And second, most market-oriented definitions of corruption observe the intersecting point between the public and the private sector.[147] Therefore, corruption is seen as a private transaction to obtain wealth in an illegal manner abusing from a public charge.

These two factors become the pillars of one of the most widely used operational definition of corruption in the current academic discussion, as well as within the most relevant international institutions related with the topic: *the abuse of public office for private gain.*[148] This simple formulation seems to summarize all the important elements in one sentence. Although this might be at first glance an adequate working definition – as it has been for

---

145 Andvig, Fjeldstadt, et. al. Research on Corruption. A Policy Oriented Survey, p. 11.

146 Ibid.

147 *Ibid.* The authors make reference to Susane Rose-Ackerman's contributions. Her focus is mainly on the economics of corruption and how this can affect the government. See: Rose-Ackerman, Susan. Corruption and Government. Causes, Consequences, and Reform. (Cambridge: Cambridge University Press, 1999.)

148 *Ibid.* The World Bank and Transparency International base their entire framework against corruption on this operational definition. However, this does not mean that these institutions alone created the definition. For example, Tevfik Nas, Albert Price and Charles Weber already stated their definition of corrupt acts as [...] any illegitimate use of public power or authority for private benefit." In: Nas, Price and Weber. "A Policy-Oriented Theory of Corruption", p. 108. Similar to these authors, Michael Johnston observed that "[a]t its most basic level, corruption is the abuse of public roles and resources for private benefit." In: Johnston. "The Political Consequences of Corruption: A Reassessment", p. 460.

most papers on corruption – there are at least two aspects that must be discussed.

First, the fact that corruption seems to be a decay of the state apparatus in order to damage the citizens does not necessarily mean that corruption finds it beginning and its end only within the public sector. Corruption also emerges from private businesses and most organized sectors of civil society.[149] Although most cases of corruption present the public breach of law as the *locus classicus*, there are also non-state actors that take part in such practices. In this regard, the relationship between the private and the public sector should not be neglected when considering the definition posed above. Many cases of corruption, as Rose-Ackermann has pointed out, occur precisely when these two sectors, private and public, meet, then

> "[c]orruption describes a relationship between the state and the private sector. Sometimes, state officials are the dominant actors; in other cases private actors are the most powerful forces. The relative bargaining power of these groups determines both the overall impact of corruption on society and the distribution of the gains between bribers and bribees."[150]

And second, there are certain conceptual aspects that should be considered when using such a compact definition for the term "corruption." Political scientist Mark Phillip warns about two key problems when reducing the definitional scope of corruption solely to the public sector. On the one hand, the area corresponding to the "public office" is far too extensive to be strictly delineated.[151] On the other hand, the intrinsically added political dimension of corruption – mostly asserted to its direct linkage with the official government – has jeopardized the validity of any definition from the simpleness of its original encyclopedic meaning.[152] For corruption, according

---

[149] *Ibid.*, p. 14. The authors note that "[t]here is corruption in terms of bribing, swindling and mafia-methods in businesses, and there are disloyal employees in private firms, non-governmental organizations and associations."

[150] Rose-Ackerman. Corruption and Government, p. 113.

[151] Phillip notes that [s]ome civil servants may have tightly defined and constrained activities permitting little substantive discretion, but many do not. Similarly, politicians do not act simply as functionaries to fulfill promises made to an electorate which is fully cognizant of its interest." In: Phillip, Mark. "Conceptualizing Political Corruption." In: Heidenheimer and Johnston (eds.) Political Corruption, pp. 41-57.

[152] *Ibid.*

to the Oxford English Dictionary is referred to as "a thing being changed from its naturally sound condition, into something unsound, impure, debased [...] etc."[153] According to the author, there is a general lack on consensus on what the "nature" of politics is, thus concluding,

> "[o]ne line definitions of political corruption are inherently misleading because they generally obscure the extent to which the concept and its components are rooted in ways of thinking about the distinctive ends to which political activity is directed."[154]

This point reaffirms a pivotal factor for the establishment of the operational definition, namely the decisive role of politics in the conceptualization of corruption. As we shall see in further chapters, corruption takes many forms and appears in different levels. However, the notable role it plays for the decay of the "body politic" makes politics – or furthermore the political arena – the defining element for the operationalization of corruption.[155] Therefore, a basic aspect of the working definition shall be the perception of corruption as deviant political behavior, which takes place not only within the public sector, but also within all sectors of society. Nevertheless, we shall be reluctant of the fact that corruption should clearly differ from bad political performance and "political incompetence", since we are seeking to gain a general understanding of this phenomenon based on the initial criteria explained above and not on a mere comparison to a particular political feature.[156]

CORRUPTION AND THE ABUSE OF POLITICS

Before choosing a working definition for the study of corruption, we should first briefly recapitulate some of the major findings and observations made earlier. First, corruption is primarily related to the public sector and its relation to the citizens.[157] Second, corruption denotes a form of deviant

[153] Ibid.

[154] Ibid.

[155] The theoretical analysis of corruption as the decaying instance in politics – from a political theory perspective – can be found in: Dobel, J. Patrick. "The Corruption of the State." The American Political Science Review (September 1978), Vol. 72, No. 3, pp. 958-973.

[156] Phillip. "Conceptualizing Political Corruption", p. 52.

[157] Heidenheimer and Johnston (eds.) Political Corruption, p. 8 ff.

behavior to an established norm.[158] This behavior is understood as person committing an act of corruption defying the norm, abusing it in his/her own terms and benefiting from this action. Third, this behavior creates distrust from the environment (e.g. public opinion) towards the perpetrator thus damaging the standing of the established norm. Lastly, the appearance of corruption within the public sector makes this term primarily a political one, although several other manifestations of this phenomenon can be recognized, also within the private sector and other non-political organizational forms in the society.

These points make it clear that corruption is a special form of abuse, particularly in the sphere of public politics. The reciprocal relationship between the state apparatus and society make this kind of abuse a highly problematic issue, as citizens see a form of betrayal by public officers. The betrayers are not solely politicians or public servants, but could also private entrepreneurs or corporate entities. The beneficiaries are not only individuals. They can also be groups and lobbies within society. In this regard, the definition proposed above to see corruption as the *abuse of public office for private gains*, can be adapted – for the purposes of this analysis – as to *the illegitimate or illegal use of public (and private) authority for personal or corporate benefit.*[159] This shall be, however, a working definition and not a definitive postulate, for it entails elements that are open for different interpretations.[160] Therefore, an explanation of the key elements in this operational definition shall justify this choice and illustrate the different elements contained therein.

Illegitimate or illegal. It was noted earlier that one criterion to differentiate between corrupt and legal activities is the legal-constitutional framework, which legitimates most actions within the political apparatus of a country.[161] Therefore, the illegitimate character of any action is an effective element for defining corruption, as it allows to directly classify any case within or without the legal perimeter. Although the legal framework varies from country to country, this does not affect the explanatory power laws can have on considering an action consistent or inconsistent with national law

158 See Nye, "Corruption and Political Development", pp. 417-427.

159 This definition is adapted from Nas, Price and Weber. "A Policy-Oriented Theory of Corruption", p. 108.

160 *Ibid.* The authors do acknowledge that there acre certain forms of legally influence political behavior.

161 As seen in Scott. Comparative Political Corruption.

regulations. This shall be the first step when considering if there is a case of corruption within activities of both the government and the private sector.

Public (and private) authority. Corruption does not only take place on a "one way street" between the government sector and the private sector.[162] Corruption may take the opposite path, especially when transnational corporations and other private organizations engage in contracts with national governments.[163] It was already mentions, that in present international politics, governments are not the only source of authority. Private citizens, groups or corporations can also dictate the rules on "how to run business" with very good chances of being heard.[164] Adding the factor of the private sector as an equally important actor in the process of corrupt activities shall make the working definition more useful for understanding this phenomenon from these two different perspectives.

Personal or corporate benefit. The gains from corruption cannot be attributed to a single person. Interest groups and associations at every level of society can benefit from bribes, fraud and other related acts of corruption.[165] Political clans, families, co-workers and perhaps even entire firms can be involved. Therefore, it becomes necessary that a working definition of corruption emphasizes the multiplicity of this phenomenon on the recipient's side.

THE 'PRIVATE' SIDE OF CORRUPTION

Many political scientists refer to Harold Lasswell's contribution Politics: Who Gets What, When, How as he provided a major guideline to approach corruption by arguing that the study of politics is the study of influence and the influential.[166] Scholars from various disciplines in the social sciences, who study the causes of corrupt activities, see this analogy as the starting point for their approaches. Although this question was primarily aimed at gaining an understanding of politics, it has also become a useful tool to understand corruption, since this phenomenon denotes a two-way

162 Andvig, Fjeldstadt, et. al. Research on Corruption. A Policy Oriented Survey, p. 14 ff.

163 Ibid.

164 On this point, see Pauly, Who Elected the Bankers? Surveillance and Control in the World Economy.

165 Andvig, Fjeldstadt, et. al. Research on Corruption. A Policy Oriented Survey, p. 14 ff.

166 Lasswel, Harold D. Politics: Who Gets What, When, How. (New York: Peter Smith, 1950. Reprinted version. Originally published by the McGraw-Hill Book Company, 1936.)

influence relationship between the originator and the receiver, between the principal and its agent.[167]

If we focus on Lasswell's *"who"*, corruption has been commonly subjected to the practices and structures of the public sector. However there is no doubt that an equal assessment of the other side of corruption, namely the private sector, is necessary to achieve a wide-range understanding of these practices: Therefore, the concluding part of this Chapter focuses on the role of the private sector as a scenario for the development of corrupt activities.

The analysis of corruption in the private sector is two-leveled. The first level focuses on transactions of private companies with the public offices. The second level deals with activities that take place within the private sector itself.[168] It is important to note, that the main incentive of private sector corruption is to maximize the company's profit. Thus a first differentiation to public sector corruption can be observed, as the interests in this case are mainly economic and not necessarily political although politicians can try – at times- to influence firms for political purposes and vice versa.[169] The emerging moment of private sector corruption on the first level however is when a private company breaks the established rule in order to maximize profit. As Rose-Ackermann observes,

> "[i]t is easy to see that corporations single-mindedly concerned with profit maximization will choose an 'optimal' amount of fraud or corruption [...] Some illegal behavior will be encouraged because it increases profits,

[167] Political scientist Harvey Kebschull points out, that "[...] if students of politics are to achieve an understanding of 'who gets what, when, how,' [...] they need to have an appreciation of the causes of scandal and corruption as well as of the formal institutions of government and politics." In: Kebschull, Harvey G. "Political Corruption: Making it the 'Significant Other' in Political Studies." PS: Political Science and Politics. (December 1992), Vol. 25, Issue 4, pp. 705-709.

[168] Pope, Jeremy. "The Private Corporate Sector." In: *Ibid.* and Transparency International. TI Source Book 2000 – Confronting Corruption: The Elements of a National Integrity System. (Berlin: Transparency International, 2000), pp. 137-151.

[169] In this case "[w]hen managers control firms, politicians use subsidies and bribes to convince them to pursue political objectives. When politicians control firms, managers use bribes to convince them not to push firms to pursue political objectives." In: Shleifer, Andrei and Robert W. Vishny. "Politicians and Firms." The Quarterly Journal of Economics. (November 1994), Vol. 109, No. 4, pp. 995-1025.

and other behavior will be tolerated because it is too costly to eliminate."[170]

The most common *malheur* in private sector corruption are bribes, which are usually offered to public officials in order to obtain licenses, permits, contracts and the like.[171] This is the particular case, in which bribes or *"facilitation payments"* can become beneficial for the company, since it allows business to flow instead of getting stuck behind a bureaucrat's desk. In fact, there is evidence for supporting the argument, that in a bureaucratic-overloaded environment, a private company may find bribes adequate to reduce the time and costs some processes can demand.[172] Pope recognizes three areas of vulnerability in which companies can feel "tempted" to offer bribes. First, in certain countries, there are few possibilities for any company to engage in a government contract without having to pay a bribe. Second, there is a tendency to think that offshore bribes are condoned because they have become customary in the international trade and business regime *("everybody does it.")* And third, companies may seek to create job opportunities and profit thereof by bribing decision-makers to approve unnecessary acquisitions and projects.[173]

However the difference to public sector corruption here is that the interaction between bribers and bribees is more layered, meaning that managers do not necessarily want to engage directly in corrupt activities but rather designate intermediary agents that do the "dirty work" on their behalf.[174] This so called *"buffers"* provide special information and valuable insights to possible business partners, be them governments or private firms. Therefore, they offer a more effective bargaining position than individual companies. Rose-Ackermann asserts to say, that these middlemen are often the best way for private enterprises to "save face and escape legal liability by

---

170 Rose-Ackermann, Susan. "Corruption and the Private Sector." In: *Ibid.* Corruption. A Study in Political Economy, p. 189.

171 Pope. "The Private Corporate Sector."

172 Kaufmann and Wie. "Does ‚Grease Money' Speed Up the Wheels of Commerce?"

173 All these three points seen in: Pope. "The Private Corporate Sector", p. 142. On international bribery see also: Vogl, Frank. "The Supply Side of Global Bribery." In: New Perspectives on Combating Corruption. (Kuala Lumpur: Transparency International and the World Bank, 1998), pp. 55-64.

174 Rose-Ackermann. "Corruption and the Private Sector", p. 192.

avoiding direct knowledge of corruption", organizing their business to allow such practices to take place.[175]

The second level of private sector corruption, which could be referred to as inter- and intra-firm corruption is not as clear-cut as public sector corruption. As Jeremy Pope points out, while some jurisdictions have explicit regulations against "kickbacks" or "commissions" taken by a company's employees, in many cases, these regulations are neither properly codified nor existent at all.[176] Fraud within large companies has become a common scenario to exemplify cases of corruption within the private sector. Particularly in the area of financial management, the incidence of corruption is said to be no less than in the public sector.[177] Pope best describes the example of such an event:

> "[An] accountant who warned her superiors that a book-keeper was fiddling the books by raking money from the payments system. The book-keeper was prosecuted and sacked, but the company did nothing to improve its management scrutiny. As a result the very same accountant started running identical scams, but for even larger amounts, writing cheques to suppliers who were, in fact, supplying herself."[178]

There are several more cases in which employees or even entire departments are the main causes of intra-firm corruption. Rose-Ackermann observes that, similar to the case of the public sector, there can be *petty* corruption on low-employee level as well as *grand* corruption at top managerial level.[179] However, Pope rightly concludes that still the most frequent form of private sector corruption occurs through bribes offered to public officials in return of bureaucratic facilitations.[180]

---

175 Ibid.

176 Pope. "The Private Corporate Sector", p. 139.

177 *Ibid.* In the United States, the case of the fall of its seventh biggest company Enron is a good example of how internal mismanagement, fraud and corruption take place in a private corporation leading to its collapse. A recent account of the events and technicalities that led to Enron's collapse can be found in: Swartz, Mimi and Sherron Watkins. Power Failure: The Inside Story of the Collapse of Enron. (New York: Double Day, 2003.)

178 Pope. "The Private Corporate Sector", p. 139.

179 Rose-Ackermann. "Corruption and the Private Sector", p. 191.

180 Pope. "The Private Corporate Sector", p. 141; and Rose-Ackermann. "Corruption and the Private Sector", p. 196.

Despite the fact that private companies seek mostly economic interests, there are further similarities between the incidence of corruption in the private and public sectors. Conflicts of interests can occur within and between firms. Just as politicians may sell out voters, managers at the top level may sell out stockholders.[181] In this scenario, corporate boards of directors assume the role of elected top government officials, and create the dependent relationship between voters and authorities. Although this relationship is not identical (stockholders can sell their shares if they disagree with corporate policies), both managers and politicians have the discretionary power to either combat of foster corruption within their organizations assuming similar responsibilities for political scandals and economic failure.[182] Moreover, in some companies, the board of directors may impose decisions and policies on illicit practices that reach every level of their organizational structure, similar to the case of the public sector. Control instruments such as internal codes of conduct and penalty systems for offenders are directly linked to the power of the board of directors to decide up to which level these mechanisms can curb or ignore corruption.

Among the critical differences between public sector and private sector corruption at the second level lies the fact, that boards may have less legal restraints since the jurisdiction of a company is mostly smaller than that of an entire country. Also, not every company has effective and extended internal sight mechanisms to monitor the policies and directives of all the employees, including the members of the board.[183] Moreover, the relationship between the board of directors, shareholders and employees is – in some cases – not as "public" as in the government sphere. In many corporations, shareholders and employees do not have any kind of contact with the top-level management and thus are poorly informed on the activities of the board of directors. Therefore, the information they have about the company's practices and performance (balance, profit, dividends, etc.) may be deviant from their own personal experience. In the public sector, voters know candidates in a better way and are aware of why he was elected in the first place. Citizens have more channels than employees to obtain information and the control mechanisms are more extended for a politician than for a manager. In this context, corruption in the private sector can be "hidden" in a better way by the top management, since the patterns of information are relatively narrow than in the public sphere.

181 Ibid.

182 Ibid.

183 Ibid.

Lastly, within the many forms of private corporations, those of non-profit nature are commonly said to be less prone to corruption.[184] However, charity institutions, educational organizations, research facilities and cultural communities are not entirely free from corruption.[185] This has basically two reasons. First, the somehow noble and "altruistic" missions of such organizations lead to a considerable misinformation on their books. And just because some organizations tend to "fight for a good cause", this does not make them unable to engage in illicit activities. As Rose-Ackermann notes,

> "[b]y tacking advantage of a popular presumption that the nonprofit label implies benevolent trustees, an organization may instead permit kickbacks or self-dealing schemes that enrich individuals in charge of allotting the organization's funds. The advantage of the nonprofit form seems to rest on the rather slim reed of trust and on the notion that entrepreneurs select profit-making firms if they are narrowly self-seeking and choose nonprofits organizations if they have altruistic temperaments."[186]

This last point leads us to conclude, that the private sector is as prone to corruption as its public counterpart for a variety of reasons as it was explained above. The variety of causes and scenarios attached to corruption should therefore not only be related to political practices of government. As seen above, managers and private entrepreneurs can also engage in illicit practices due to the fact that corruption seems to be a present temptation to every institution, since the benefits are on the prevailing side of decision-makers and corporate managers.

As Robert Klitgaard pointed out at the beginning, the main difficulty around the concept of corruption is the lack of useful analysis. The key to any effective analysis is to have the right analytical tools. In this regard, the working definition proposed in this chapter can be a first useful tool for the rest of the analysis proposed in this book. Although the single characteristics

---

[184] Rose-Ackermann. "Corruption and the Private Sector", p. 202.

[185] *Ibid.* The author makes also reference to two cases in which charity organizations became involved in several corruption scandals in: Mendelson. Mary Adelaide. Tender Loving Greed. (New York: Alfred A. Knopf, 1974.)

[186] *Ibid.* See as example the case of NGOs in post-Suharto Indonesia as found in: Holloway, Richard. "Corruption and Civil Society Institutions in Indonesia." Working Paper for the 10th International Anti-Corruption Conference. (Berlin: Transparency International, 2000.)

contained in the definition are not definitive and could be relativated, they provide all the basic elements needed for the steps to be followed in the next chapters. Lastly, it is important to remark that the four working hypotheses presented in the introduction should have several advantages from the chosen definition, since all the elements included in the chosen definition are present in each of the hypotheses this book intends to test. However, the analytical framework is not yet complete. In order to effectively use the working definition, a deeper look into the different characteristics of the phenomenon of corruption should be taken. Therefore, task of the following chapters is to analyze the different causes and the various forms corruption takes within the political, economic and social structures of a country.

CHAPTER TWO

FORMS, CAUSES, AND TYPOLOGIES OF CORRUPTION

> "If the study of corruption teaches us anything at all, it teaches us not to take a political system or a particular regime at its face value [...] How for example could we have adequately explained the rule of Boss Tweed in New York of the 1890s, the structure of Chiang Kai-shek's Koumitang Party, the methods of 'Papa Doc' Duvalier in Haiti or the failure of the parliamentary system in Indonesia without examining corruption?"[187]

Most cases of corruption are usually engendered when a person or an organization obtains monopoly power over a good or a service requiring a rent on it and thus having the discretion to its allocation. Consequently, the availability of this good or service depends directly upon this individual or corporate entity. Klitgaard notes that whoever has the discretion also has the power and tendency to: 1) decide who receives the particular good or service; 2) settle how much someone has to pay for it, and 3) become less accountable.[188] According to the author, corruption is the result of *"monopoly plus discretion minus accountability"* – a formula known as C = M + D - A.[189]

This explanation seems easy and suitable at first. Nevertheless, the analysis of corruption as a mainly political phenomenon shows in the last chapter, that the problem at hand is far more complex than the monopolization of a rent, good, or service. As it was seen earlier, the extension of the term "corruption" turns its definition into an uneasy task for the scholarship. However, the literature on the topic has not only focused on a definitional location for this phenomenon. Moreover, the multiple causes and forms corruption might take have been given equal importance as well. It was observed earlier, that corruption is mostly related to a certain deviation of norms in the role of a public servant. This might denote at first that the

---

[187] Scott. Comparative Political Corruption.

[188] Klitgaard, Robert. "International Cooperation Against Corruption." In: Finance and Development. (March 1998), pp. 3-6.

[189] Ibid.

primary causes of corruption lie within the public sector. Such a simplistic postulate is too narrow since corruption can also originate in the private sector, as we shall see in the following chapter.

The working definition also postulates, that corruption is primarily a form of illegitimate or illegal abuse. This behavior can be certainly attributed to a case of norm deviance. Consequently, a key question arises: where does this deviance originate? Furthermore, it also becomes legitimate to ask how corrupt activities emanate both in the government and in the private sector, and what different forms of these phenomena can be recognized.

BASIC FORMS OF CORRUPTION

In order to make an appropriate analysis of the causes, forms and typologies of corruption, two points must be reconsidered. First, corruption includes social, political, economic and cultural elements that make an exact classification of its forms very hard to achieve. In most scholarly attempts, several categories and varieties of corruption partly overlap and even become interchangeable with other concepts.[190] And second, the causes of corruption are always contextual and rooted within a country's policies, bureaucratic traditions, political development and social history.[191] Similar to the definition, the causes and forms of corruption may also vary from nation to nation, as the term has become a matter of personal interpretation.

Therefore, an exact listing of all activities that fall into the category of "corrupt acts" is neither exclusive nor definitive. However, there have been some useful differentiations elaborated by scholars and observers on the topic. In the early 1990s, John Gardiner's contribution towards defining corruption proposed a preliminary distinction of the term by relating it to common public problems. The first of these problems is associated with corruption by public officials, followed by the *abuse* of office by public officials *(nepotism, patronage, conflicts of interest), business corruption, fraud theft, abuse, error and waste*, and finally *organized crime and racketeering*.[192] Although these categories might be useful at first, but in a broader sense, they cover almost every illicit act in human life. Therefore, we

---

[190] Andvig, Fjeldstadt, et. al. Research on Corruption. A Policy Oriented Survey, p. 15.

[191] Bannon, Ian. "The Fight Against Corruption, A World Bank Perspective." Workshop on Transparency and Governance. Consultative Group Meeting for the Reconstruction and Transformation of Central America.
<http://www.iadb.org/regions/re2/consultative_group/groups/transparency_workshop6.htm> (04.06.2000.)

[192] Gardiner. "Defining Corrupion", p. 27 ff.

need to focus on the activities that fall within the working definition of Chapter One, which dealt mostly with the illegal use of authority, be that public or private, for personal or corporate gain.

Another classification, by IMF economist Vito Tanzi, focuses more specifically on the initial momentum of corruption. The author classifies corruption in *bureaucratic* or *political*, *cost-reducing* or *benefit enhancing* (for the briber), *briber-initiated* or *bribee-initiated*, *centralized* or *decentralized*, and *predictable* or *arbitrary*.[193] Most of these forms are related to the role of the public sector in politics and the economy, despite the fact, that Tanzi does not neglect the existence of corruption in private corporations. This classification relates however more to the characteristics corruption might take once it has happened, thus saying less about the concrete acts that start corruption.

Political scientist Inge Amudsen recognizes mainly five manifestations of corruption, namely *bribery*, *embezzlement*, *fraud, extortion*, and *favoritism* and makes one of the most current differentiations.[194] Her classification is useful for specifically locating the forms of corruption, as she clearly documents what is behind each category. *Bribery* is primarily referred to as "the payment (in money or kind) that is given or taken in a corrupt relationship." *Embezzlement* denotes "theft of resources by people who are put to administer it; it is when disloyal employees steal from their employers." *Fraud* means "an economic crime that involves some kind o trickery, swindle or deceit [It] includes a manipulation or distortion of information, facts and expertise, by public officials positioned between politicians and citizens, who seek to draw a private profit." *Extortion* is related to "money and other resources extracted by the use of coercion, violence or the threats to use force. Lastly, *favoritism* denotes "a mechanism of power abuse implying 'privatization' and a highly biased distribution of state resources, no matter how these resources have been accumulated in the first place."[195]

Despite the distinctive the classifications, most of the authors agree, that an understanding of the emerging moment of corruption both within modern society and the body politic should be achieved if we are to

193 Tanzi, Vito. "Corruption Around the World. Causes, Consequences, Scope and Cures" IMF Staff Papers (1998), Vol. 45, No. 4, pp. 561-594.

194 Amudsen, Inge. "Political Corruption: an introduction to the issues." Chr. Michelsen Institute Working Paper (1999.)

195 *Ibid.* All citations from Amudsen as seen in: Andvig, Fjeldstadt, et. al. Research on Corruption. A Policy Oriented Survey, p. 15 ff.

understand the various forms describes above. Therefore, we shall focus the following parts of this Chapter to the causes of corruption from the different perspectives the scholarship has to offer.

CORRUPTION AS A PROBLEM OF MODERNIZATION

Political philosopher Jean Jacques Rousseau adverted both in *Social Contract* and in the *Discourse on the Origins of Inequality* about the pureness of men, which was tainted by the advances of society.[196] According to him, the more complex society and thus the state became, the more individuals drifted away from their original natural status. In this context, Rousseau saw corruption as a product of societal evolution and of the turbulent relations between individuals and the political apparatus.[197] The progress in society, according to Rousseau made man more eager and ambitious to gain power and thus to be corrupted thereby.

History has witnessed many periods of change, which have established new norms, new ideals, new forms of political, social and economic organization as well as new patterns of behavior. Similar to Rousseau's arguments, political scientist Samuel Huntington uses these periods in human history – referred to as "modernization" – and attributes the causes of corrupt activities to such processes.[198] In his opinion, corruption is a phenomenon that can be related to rapid social and economic modernization for three main reasons.[199] First, processes of modernization always involve a change in the basic value of a society. This means that appeals to universal values such as equal rights among citizens and equal obligations towards the state are proclaimed from different groups in society. These norms are

[196] Rousseu, Jean-Jacques and Donald A. Cress (Translator.) Discourse on the Origin of Inequality. (Indianapolis: Hackett Pub. Co, 1992); and *Ibid.* and Maurice Cranston (Translator.) The Social Contract (New York: Penguin , June 1968.)

[197] *Ibid.* Book IV of The Social Contract focused on the precarious disproportion between government and the sovereign. In this relationship, Rousseau saw a possibility for corruption to emerge. For a deeper analysis see also: Dobel. "The Corruption of the State."

[198] Huntington, Samuel. "Modernization and Corruption." In: Political Order in Changing Societies. (New Haven and London: Yale University Press, 1970), pp. 59-71. Re-printed in: Heidenheimer and Johnston (eds.) Political Corruption, pp. 253-264.

[199] *Ibid.*, p. 59. As explanation, the author states that "[p]olitical life in eighteenth-century America and in twentieth-century America, it would appear, was less corrupt than in nineteenth century America. So also political life in seventeenth-century Britain was, it would appear, less corrupt than it was in eighteenth-century Britain. Is it merely coincidence that this high point of corruption in English and American public life coincided with the impact of the industrial revolution, the development of new sources of wealth and power and the appearance of new classes making demands on government?"

assimilated by society contending the old values and patterns of behavior. Thus Huntington concludes, that corruption in modernizing societies denotes the deviance of norms of the newly established patterns of behavior, rather than the deviance of behavior from already accepted norms. As new standards develop, both the public and the government recognize corrupt activities in different ways. In these terms, corruption is as a product of this distinction, which comes along with modernization.[200]

Second, modernization processes create new sources for wealth and power. The appearance of these new sources means that new groups will strive for access to them in legal and illegal manners. Huntington observes as a consequence, that most societies fail to integrate these new groups into the political system thus creating the necessity to adapt them into the system by irregular means.[201]

And third, modernization imposes changes on the "output side of the political system." This means that during these periods of time, government authority tends to expand and the amount of areas subjected to legal regulations multiplies. Consequently, new laws not only create more space for "legal perpetrations". Moreover, some groups of society may be put in a disadvantaged position by the new legal frameworks, making them prone to break the law and thus becoming a further source of corruption.[202]

The effects of corruption on modernizing societies and their politics are most observable at the end of Huntington's argument. For he concludes by stating that the implementation of modern values makes a society extremely critical about its own practices. This only promotes the identification of certain political activities directly with corruption. As societal standards constantly rise and become stricter through modernization, politics cannot meet these demands and is mostly rejected and looses its original value. Huntington names this the "victory of the values of modernity over the needs of society."[203]

If we follow Huntington's argumentation, it becomes plausible that modernization processes have provided the adequate scenario for corruption

---

[200] Ibid.

[201] *Ibid.*, p. 61. As an example, the author observes that "[t]he new millionaires buy themselves seats in the Senate or in the House of Lords and thereby become participants in the political system rather than alienated opponents of it, which might have been the case if this opportunity to corrupt the system were denied them. So also recently enfranchised masses or recently arrived immigrants use their new power of the ballot to buy themselves jobs and favors from the local political machine."

[202] *Ibid.* Huntington notes that this posture depends highly on the level of acceptance, which laws obtain from the population, and also on the case with which laws can be broken without detection.

[203] *Ibid.*, p. 63.

to breed within society and politics. Changes in the original patterns of behavior give rise to resistance and sub-ordinance, thus deviance of established norms, from those who do not agree with or do not benefit from the new established order. Considering the processes of modernization as a key variable for the specific appearance and deployment of corruption in politics and society, Huntington's postulate underlines that the causes of corruption can be attributed to the failures of both society and the government to consequently maintain a political order and to adapt new norms and patterns of behavior to it. Moreover, corruption is caused due to the lack of political cohesion and of political authority for keeping the established order functioning maintaining both the general agreement compliance with legal regulations. Thus modernization and the intrinsic set of changes it contains can be considered a first major cause for spread of corruption in contemporary societies. This position will be contended in the Part II of this study, as the working hypotheses are tested on the case studies. Giving the fact that most countries in Latin America have experienced drastic periods of modernization, it will be useful to apply Huntington's postulate for assessing the causes of corruption in the selected countries.

Before doing so however, there are still many forms in which corruption manifests itself in politics, society and the economy. These typologies deserve equal attention as they describe the different patterns in which corrupt activities develop. In order to gain a clearer understanding of the causes of corruption, a categorization of its multiple forms is needed. Therefore, the various types of corruption will be presented considering political, economic, social and cultural characteristics.

A MATTER OF LEVEL: POLITICAL AND BUREAUCRATIC CORRUPTION

The *locus classicus* for corruption is politics, and, more specifically, the public sector. The first part of the working definition focuses on the abuse of public authority. In this context, the role of the public servant takes considerable importance for a first differentiation of corruption forms. Within the sphere of politics and the government sector, there are two kinds of corrupt activities based on the level in which they appear. First, there is *"grand"* corruption, which is the denomination for classic *political* corruption and involves mostly high-level authorities misusing their public positions for private benefit.[204] In this category, representatives are usually

[204] The exact formulation for "grand corruption" is [...] the misuse of public power by heads of state, ministers and senior officials for private pecuniary gain." In: Moody-Stuart, George. "Grand

involved in great national and transnational deals, accepting or giving bribes to either further authorities at the same level or to private entrepreneurs, mostly from transnational corporations.[205] In developed countries, *political "grand"* corruption is said to be less spread than in developing and underdeveloped nations.[206] This difference is caused mostly by two elements of modern developed economies: a large-sized private sector offering great opportunities for illicit self-enrichment and lesser intervening role of the public sector in national affairs.[207] By no means does this denote, that the public sector in developed countries is not prone to corruption, since "[...] everywhere the state is active in economy and society presents an opportunity for rent seeking."[208]

The second type of corruption, which takes place in lower spheres of the public sector, is referred to as *"petty"* or *bureaucratic* corruption.[209] In this scenario, corruption occurs in the every-day business of public entities such as hospitals, schools, police stations, customs offices, taxing authorities, etc.[210] This scenario differs from the first category in the amount of money which is at stake. *"Petty"* corruption describes the "extortion of small payments by low level officials in order to expedite business by cutting through red tape [...]"[211] Although at first glance, bureaucratic corruption seems to be less damaging than political corruption due to the lower amount of financial benefits involved, it does have serious consequences as well. For example, this type of corruption is especially harmful to the poorer sectors of the population who might lack access to certain public goods that require bribes.[212] In some instances, the poor may even be required to pay more for

---

Corruption in Third World Development" Transparency International (1994.) Original citation found in: Doig and Theobald. Corruption and Democratization, p. 3. For further reference see Moody-Stuart, George. Grand Corruption. How Business Bribes Damages Developing Countries. (Oxford: WorldView Publications, 1997.)

205 Doig and Theobald. Corruption and Democratization, p. 4. According to the authors, the cases of Mobutu Sese Seko in former Zaire, Benazir Bhutto in Pakistan and Indonesia's Suharto correspond to this category of corrupt activities.

206 Ibid.

207 *Ibid.* It is further explained that "[...] fraud in the form of illegally using, diverting or simply stealing funds from private firms and other non-governmental organizations is much more evident in developed countries than in theor less developed counterparts."

208 Ibid.

209 Andvig, Fjeldstadt, et. al. Research on Corruption. A Policy Oriented Survey, p. 18.

210 Ibid.

211 Doig and Theobald. Corruption and Democratization, p. 5. This is also referred to as "speed" or "grease" money.

212 Ibid.

bribes than people with higher incomes.[213] Surveys show that wealthier households pay more bribes than poor ones, but the latter are more affected by the burden of *"petty"* corruption.[214] This type of corruption is highly dangerous for public institutions, as it creates general apathy and a lack of trust towards the government.[215]

Although this differentiation is important for realizing the scope of corruption, its validity will depend on the separation of politics from the administration, which is at times difficult to observe in many countries.[216] Moreover, it can be said that in some instances political and bureaucratic corruption tend to condition each other and take place at the same time.[217]

This classification is of considerable analytical importance, as it helps to delineate the particular forms of corruption in the public sector.[218] It is important to note again, that although these first categories of corruption directly involve the public sector, this does not deny the presence of the private sector as an actor equally involved in these processes. As we shall see later on the analysis of economic corruption, the private sector is involved in most of both political and bureaucratic corruption.[219]

A Matter of Profit: Economic Sources of Corruption

From a political perspective, the common initial scenario for the emergence of corruption is when government institutions are weak and public officials misuse their position to obtain private or corporate gain, mostly in form of economic benefits. Similarly, the vast majority of economic studies on corruption conclude that this phenomenon originates primarily in the public sector. More specifically, malfeasant activities occur when rents exist,

---

213 Bannon. "The Fight Against Corruption, A World Bank Perspective."

214 Ibid.

215 Doig and Theobald. Corruption and Democratization, p. 6.

216 Andvig, Fjeldstadt, et. al. Research on Corruption. A Policy Oriented Survey, p. 19.

217 Ibid. According to the authors, this occurs when "[p]olitical corruption is usually supported by widespread bureaucratic or *petty* corruption, in a pyramid of upward extraction. And corruption in high places is contagious to lower level officials, as these will follow the predatory examples of, or even take instructions from, their principals."

218 In a similar attempt, Heidenheimer suggested to classify the degree of corruptness of public activities between "black", "gray", and "white" corruption. The first will correspond to the category of "grand" corruption, the latter refers to "petty" corruption. See: Heidenheimer Arnold. Political Corruption: Readings in Comparative Analysis. (New York: Holt, 1970.) Cited in: Peters and Welch. "Political Corruption in America: A Search for Definitions and Theory", pp. 975.

219 Klitgaard, Robert. "International Cooperation Against Corruption."

mostly as a result of government regulation.[220] The intervention of the government in the economy and the vast number of rules and regulations in most everyday-activities (from opening a bank account to obtaining a passport or a driver's license to the closing of a financial deal) creates the necessary monopoly power for the officials who authorize or control these activities.[221] Therefore, the first major economic cause of corruption is mostly attributed to rent seeking. Economists define this term as "situations where people use resources both for productive purposes and to gain an advantage in dividing up the benefits of economic activity."[222] IMF economist Paulo Mauro notes that the most commonly recognized sources of rent seeking behavior can be found in basic forms of governmental economic intervention such as trade restrictions (e.g. tariffs and import quotas), subsidies, price controls, multiple exchange rate practices and foreign exchange allocation schemes, as well the provision of monitored credits.[223] Also, natural resource endowments (e.g. oil, precious minerals) are a further proper scenario for rent seeking practices.[224] Although bribes are not entirely a synonymous for rent seeking, they are the most recognizable form for these kinds of activities.

In order to understand the economic causes of corruption, a brief assessment of rent seeking can be helpful. From an economic perspective, such practices have to do mostly with adequate levels of market competition, as it is the economist's natural approach to believe that bribes are uncommon where perfect competition prevails.[225] Therefore, rent seeking in form of bribes can – but not necessarily must – occur when market failures in the

220 Mauro. "Corruption: Causes, Consequences, and Agenda for further Research", p. 11. "The classic example of a government restriction resulting in rents and rent-seeking behavior is that of an import quota and the associated licenses that civil servants give to those entrepreneurs willing to pay bribes."

221 Tanzi, "Corruption Around the World. Causes, Consequences, Scope and Cures", p. 566.

222 Rose-Ackermann. Corruption and Government, p. 2. For a more comprehensive approach see also: Hartle, D.G. "The Theory of 'Rent Seeking': Some Reflections." The Canadian Journal of Economics. (1983) Vol. 16, No. 4, pp. 539-554.

223 Mauro. "Corruption: Causes, Consequences, and Agenda for further Research", p. 11; and *Ibid.* "Why Worry About Corruption?" Economic Issues. No. 6 (Washington D.C.: International Monetary Fund, 1997.)

224 *Ibid.* The author explains that in this case, natural resources "can typically be sold at a price that far exceeds their cost of extraction and their sale is usually subject to stringent government regulation, to which corrupt officials can turn a blind eye."

225 Ades, Alberto and Rafael Di Tella. "Rents, Competition, and Corruption." The American Economic Review (September 1999), Vol. 89, No. 4 , pp. 982-993. On this point, reference is also made to Rose-Ackerman, Susan. Corruption: A study of political economy. (New York: Academic Press, 1978.)

provision of public goods exist.[226] Based on government intervention, market competition and market failures, most of the research on rent seeking focuses on two scenarios, depending on the level at which rent seeking takes place.[227] At the top level, a regulation that has effects on a particular sector of the industry is set up by the government, and a lower-rank official misuses his position to obtain bribes.[228] At the bottom level, the bureaucrat himself affects the level of competition by directly setting up a limit or a tariff to a particular good or service. Then, he charges a bribe to those companies or persons who benefit from this limited access.[229]

An adequate explanation of the relationship between these two levels can be found in the principal-agent model of bureaucratic control.[230] In this approach, regulatory actors are hierarchically ordered. At the top, there are various political principals who seek to control the behavior of their agents at the lower levels of the bureaucratic pyramid. The latter have the direct discretion and an information advantage to avoid a total control from the top. Therefore, the relationship between principals and their agents is characterized by a divergence of interests at each level and by the degree in which both parts have – or are willing to use – control mechanisms to influence each other.[231] In this context, most economists conclude that the failure of the government to create perfect market conditions for the delivery of public goods creates a proper scenario for rent seeking. This phenomenon involves top-level politicians, lower-rank bureaucrats and other sub-ordinates who create a market for themselves by accepting and, in some cases, legally competing for bribes.[232]

---

226 Gradstein, Mark. "Rent Seeking and the Provision of Public Goods." The Economic Journal (September 1993) Vol. 103, No. 420, pp. 1236-1243.

227 Bliss, Christopher and Rafael Di Tella. "Does Competition Kill Corruption?" The Journal of Political Economy (October 1997), Vol. 105, No. 5, pp. 1001-1023.

228 Ibid.

229 Ibid.

230 This classic model was introduced to the study of corruption as a tool for explaining the deviant behavior of American public officials during the mid-1970s. Relevant works include: Rose-Ackerman, Corruption: A study of political economy; and Banfield, Edward C. "Corruption as a Feature of Governmental Organization." The Journal of Law and Economics (1975) Vol. 18, pp. 587-605.

231 The entire explanation adapted of the model adapted from: Hedge, David M., Michael J. Sticchitano and Patricia Metz. "The Principal-Agent Model and Regulatory Federalism." The Western Political Quarterly (December 1991) Vol. 44, No. 4, pp. 1055-1080.

232 See also: Appelbaum, Elie and Eliakim Katz. "Seeking Rents by Setting Rents: The Political Economy of Rent-Seeking." The Economic Journal (September 1987) Vol. 97, No. 387, pp. 685-699; and Krueger, Anne O. "The Political Economy of the Rent-Seeking Society." The American Economic Review (June, 1974) Vol. 64, No. 3, pp. 291-303.

A second major economic cause of corruption according to the economic literature is the problem of low wages in the public sector.[233] This is an intrinsic problem of any administration and is highly related to rent seeking. It deems, nevertheless, a separate analysis. Undoubtedly, honesty in the civil service is an integral part of effective national governance. However, in any bureaucracy, most members pursue a maximization of their budgets.[234] The causes for this kind of behavior lie mostly in the wages public officers obtain for their services. When salaries are low, civil servants may misuse their positions "as a way of making ends meet."[235] Control mechanisms and thus the probability of "getting caught" become a closely related factor of corruption propensity.

IMF economists Caroline Van Rijckeghem and Beatrice Weder note that in the past, research on this area concludes that high-earning officials tend to be less corrupt, since they have more to loose.[236] In an equal fashion, some classic studies reveal that when the level of bribes is high and the detection level is low, the wage at which corruption is eliminated is high.[237] This means, that rising up penalties could easily eradicate corruption, however, such a measure could end up costing more than just increasing salaries.[238]

In this scenario, the behavior of the public official becomes the key explanatory variable. As Mauro pointed out, public officials might *de facto* engage in illicit activities in order to compensate a bad salary. In other cases, the perception of the civil servant is that he/she is being paid to less for his/her services and this might lead to corruption as well. Tanzi refers to these two behavioral types by stating that there may be *"corruption due to*

---

233 Tanzi, "Corruption Around the World. Causes, Consequences, Scope and Cures", p. 572.

234 Niskanen, William A. "Bureaucrats and Politicians." The Journal of Law and Economics (1975) Vol. 18, pp. 617-643.

235 Mauro, "Why Worry About Corruption?", p. 5.

236 Van Rijckeghem, Caroline and Beatrice Weder. "Corruption and the Rate of Temptation: Do Low Wages in the Civil Service Cause Corruption?" Working Paper of the International Monetary Fund WP/97/73 (1997.)

237 *Ibid.* The authors refer to the classic "shirking-model" established by Carlo Shapiro and Joseph Stiglitz and note, that in this model "[...] it may be cost-effective for governments to pay 'capitulation wages' (wages below reservation wages, which attract only the dishonest) rather than raise wages to the high levels required to deter corruption [...]" For a closer look on the economic efficiency of wages see: Shapiro, Carlo and Joseph Stiglitz. "Equilibrium unemployment as a worker-discipline device." American Economic Review (1984), Vol 74 ,pp. 433-444.

238 Ibid.

need and corruption due to greed."[239] The following graphic illustrates the relationship between these two distinctions:

FIGURE 1: WAGE LEVEL CORRUPTION TRADE-OFF

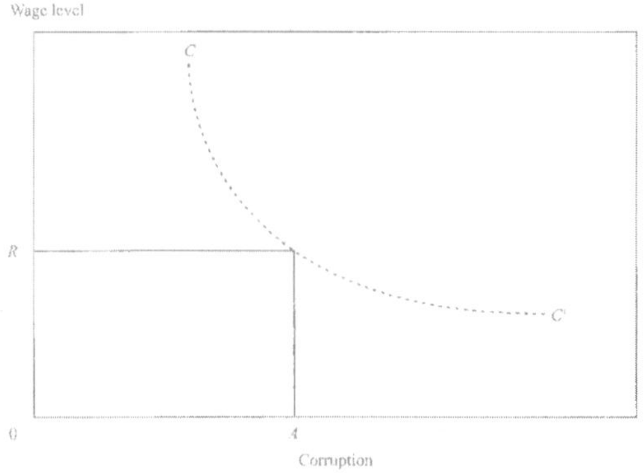

Source: Tanzi, "Corruption Around the World. Causes, Consequences, Scope and Cures", p. 573.

> The X-axis shows the level of corruption and the Y-axis shows the level of wages. CC' is the trade-off between these two levels. The curve denotes, that when wages are high, corruption is low. OR represents the minimum level of civil servant's wage needed for an adequate living standard. Therefore, OA is attributed to "*corruption due to greed*", while the area beyond OA is "*corruption due to need.*"[240]

Van Rijckeghem and Weder base their analysis on two premises. The first one is similar to Mauro's and Tanzi's postulates that civil servants may engage in corrupt activities in order to achieve a "fair" income.[241] However the second premise becomes interesting for this book, since it states that in some countries, civil servant wages lead society to condone corruption thus

[239] Tanzi, "Corruption Around the World. Causes, Consequences, Scope and Cures", p. 572.

[240] Ibid.

[241] Van Rijckeghem and Weder. "Corruption and the Rate of Temptation", p. 6.

resulting in a low probability of crime detection and high corruption levels.[242] This point should be kept in mind when the analysis turns on the case studies.

Using data on civil service and manufacturing wages in developing countries and correlating them to a corruption index (Political Risk services), Van Rijckeghem and Weder come to the conclusion that there is in deed a negative association between public wages and corruption noting, that the quality of the bureaucracy and the rule of law are closely related to a civil servant's payment.[243] The relationship between wages and corruption depends on several factors beyond the payment itself. Internal and external controls, the legal penalty system and economic distortions can also have an influence in this particular case.[244]

Most recently, Transparency International and its Global Corruption Report have added some considerable explanatory power to this argument. Based on household surveys in Madagascar, the report examined the relationship between civil wages and the incidence of corruption. The results led to same conclusion that there is in deed a strong negative correlation between these two variables.[245] Although this relationship is not entirely free from the influence of other factors – as pointed out by Van Rijckeghem and Weder – the study revealed, that despite these factors, the performance of civil servants mostly depends on their salaries.[246]

Looking ahead, most economists note that increasing the wages alone could not solve the problem in its entirety, as there will always be officials who pursue more enrichment than necessary *("corruption due to greed.")* However, the link they established between low salaries in the public sector and the propensity of corruption can be certainly attributed to a major economic cause for the spread of illicit activities.

---

[242] *Ibid.*, p. 7.

[243] Ibid.

[244] *Ibid.*, p. 19 ff.

[245] Razafindrakoto, Mireille and François Roubaud. "Wages and Corruption: the case of Madagsacar." In: Transparency International. Global Corruption Report 2003. (Berlin: Transparency International, 2003), pp. 292-294. The authors observe, that the incidence of *petty* corruption in Madagascar dropped continuously from 42 percent in 1995 to 10 percent in 2001. During the same period, wages were raised by 50 percent in real terms.

[246] Ibid.

A MATTER OF ATTITUDE: SOCIO-CULTURAL AND ANTHROPOLOGICAL PERSPECTIVES

In the previous debate on the efforts of the scholarship towards an adequate and perhaps "universal" definition of corruption, cultural elements attached to this term became of particular importance. It was said, that no matter how precision any definition could become, its applicability would always depend on the individual's degree of acceptance thereof. Gardiner was right by pointing out that, when it comes to corruption, public officials (and private citizens as well) are more likely guided by local culture than by established legal frameworks.[247]

Therefore, a review of how socio-cultural and even anthropological factors can explain the causes of corruption might be useful, in order to understand this phenomenon from different perspectives. As it was noted in the Introduction, this field is particularly new to the scholarship on corruption. Some of the results of this field are yet to be tested at length. Nevertheless, the input they have added to the understanding of corruption is notable.

In a contending position to political scientists and economists, social anthropologist Tone Sissener makes a review of the issues that this field has to offer for understanding the roots of corruption.[248] According to the author, the actions of individuals cannot be explained from a universal set of invariable norms that distinguishes corrupt practices from legal ones. Furthermore, she observes that the political and economic scholarly debate on the definition of corruption and thus on its causes is flawed due to three main reasons. First, the concept of the "public office" is an analytical enterprise established by western social thinkers.[249] Second, the logic of legal frameworks is not always given, thus meaning, that at some stages, corruption might be the better path to choose from its legal opposite.[250] And

---

[247] Gardiner. "Defining Corruption", p. 32.

[248] Sissener, Tone Kristin. "Anthropological perspectives on corruption." Chr. Michelsen Institute Working Paper (2001.)

[249] *Ibid.* The author relies her assumptions on the Weberian conceptualization of bureaucracy. For further reference on this point see: Weber, Max, Mills C.Wright (ed.) Gerth Hand (Translator.) Essays in Sociology. (Oxford: Oxford University Press, 1958); and – as cited by the author – Handelman, John. "Introduction: The Idea of Bureaucratic Organization." Social Analysis (December 1981), Vol. 9.

[250] For similar considerations see also Kaufmann, Daniel and Shang-Jin Wie. "Does 'Grease Money' Speed Up the Wheels of Commerce?" IMF Working Paper 00/64. (Washington DC: International Monetary Fund, 2000.); and Wei, Shang-Jin. "Corruption in Economic Development: Beneficial Grease, Minor Annoyance, or Major Obstacle?" Discussion Paper for the Workshop on Integrity in Governance in Asia. (Bangkok, June 19-July 1, 1998.)

third, most legal approaches are based on the presumption, that legal frameworks are unbiased and apolitical, however corruption is not an objective practice. Therefore, Sissener considers corruption a "social" act thus demanding that its origins should be found within the social relationships between citizens and throughout history.[251] As anthropologist Akhil Gupta observes,

> "[a]nalyzing the discourse of corruption draws attention to the powerful cultural practices by which the state is symbolically represented to its employees and to citizens of the nation [...] Representations of the state are constituted, contested, and transformed in public culture. Public culture is a zone of cultural debate conducted through the mass media, other mechanical modes of reproduction, and the visible practices of institutions such as the state."[252]

Therefore, anthropological, ethnological and socio-cultural studies on corruption focus on the normative and *social* dimensions of this phenomenon. In this context, both the private relationships of citizens and their attitude towards the government are the crucial elements for the appearance of corrupt practices in society and in politics. Accordingly, corruption depends strictly on the personal point of view of the actors involved.

In order to strengthen this position, Sissener evaluated the findings of ethnological studies in different countries, especially in the developing world. She concentrated her analysis on two main areas: practices referred to as *"gift-giving"* and the establishment of social informal networks. On the former, she was able to observe, that in some cultures, *"gift-giving"* is not only an obligation, but also can also become a legitimate mechanism to obtain material and non-material goods.[253] As for the latter, Sissener notes that in many countries, people are sometimes traditionally "obliged" to recur

---

[251] Sissener. "Anthropological perspectives on corruption."

[252] Gupta, Akhil. "Blurred Boundaries: The Discourse of Corruption, the Culture of Politics and the Imagined State." American Ethnologist (May 1995), Vol. 22, No. 2, pp. 375-402.

[253] Sissener. "Anthropological perspectives on corruption", p. 13. In the Chinese case, reference is made to the works of Yunxiang Yan and Mayfair Mei-Hui Yang, who studied the normative meaning of gift-giving in Chinese society and are cited by the author in her paper.

to one another to gain access to public or private goods.[254] Moreover, there is a strong commitment between social groupings to help each other out at all times, at all levels. This is, however, not only bound to normative or cultural circumstances. When the policies of a government become economically adverse or turn politically oppressive, there can be a general access restriction to certain areas of public life, be that consumer goods or job vacancies. In some societies, individuals tend to create their own networks within which they can meet their needs.[255]

This clearly shows, that there is a great importance amounted to the sociological and anthropological causes of corruption. It is the personal point of view, or even the manifestation of particular interests of family members and those of other social units that determines what is corruption and what is not. The examples provided above prove, for instance, that the concept of bribery – as understood in most western societies – could be easily relativated in other societies. Therefore, the causes of corruption shall be determined not only from universal political and economic perspectives. As Sissener concludes, "discourses on corruption can only be understood when seen as part of wider social and cultural contexts."[256] This is a key variable that we shall consider for the empirical analysis of the case studies, especially when testing the second hypothesis that questions if the degree of acceptance of corruption can depend on factors such as the above mentioned..

However, it is important at this stage, to consider the fallacies of the socio-cultural approaches as well. Sociologist Anthony P. Maingot has pointed out two major problems of viewing corruption from a socio-cultural point of view.[257] First, the tendency towards personalization has a limited explanatory power. This means that attributing corruption to a single

254 *Ibid.*, p. 15. The author explains, that some developing countries, this scenario is see more often. For example, in Bangladesh, "[b]etween family, friends, neighbours, etc. [...] there exists an almost general obligation of mutual assistance. One cannot refuse a service, a favour, and a bit of string pulling or compliance without sever consequences."

255 In socialist Cuba, observers agree that two generations have grown under an over-regulated system in which stealing from the state is regarded as a necessary means for daily survival. As seen in: Casals, Beatriz C. and Sergio Díaz-Briquets. "Policy Framework to Address Corruption in the Cuban Transition." Cuba in Transition. (ASCE), (August 1999), Vol. 9, pp. 443-452. Moreover, the Russian *blat* , referred to as "the use of personal networks and informal contact to obtain goods and services in short supply and to find a way around formal procedures", is a legitimate mode to solve business in which all parties are equally served. See Sissener. "Anthropological perspectives on corruption." On *blat* see also the works of Alena Ledeneva cited by the author in her paper.

256 *Ibid.*, p. 18.

257 Maingot, Anthony P. "Confronting Corruption in the Hemisphere: A Sociological Perspective." Journal of Interamerican Studies and World Affairs. Special Issue: Summit of the Americas – Issues to Consider. (Autumn, 1994), Vol. 36, No. 3, pp. 49-74.

individual and expecting that the more he/she advances within the system, the more corruption and damage he/she can cause, does not reflect a clear difference to what others have been doing before or after he/she got into office.[258] And second, there is an imminent analytical failure by comparing corruption between cultures and expecting a certain degree of *cultural surrender* especially towards western standards. Maingot observes, that for instance, North Americans have long seen Latin Americans as "inherently corrupt" and in the same fashion, Latin Americans perceive US-American practices as "profoundly corrupt."[259] Therefore, the author warns on two specific problems related with cross-cultural comparison. On the one hand, there are authors who believe that one particular culture can teach another "how to become less corrupt." And on the other hand, there is a belief that such transfer is ultimately impossible between cultures. These two antagonistic positions lead Maingot to the conclusion that while it is difficult to "impose" moral standards on different cultures, these cultures are particularly capable of making the necessary arrangements ("translation of codes") to build an own view on corrupt practices, based on more generalized standards.[260] He therefore concludes by stating that

> "[…] there are certainly cultural differences in definition and adjudication, there is, nevertheless, a specific area or social problem called corruption with which every society must cope. It is this shared understanding that justifies attempts to formulate theories of corrupt behaviour and the mechanisms for combating it."[261]

Since all case studies belong to the same cultural sphere (Latin America), we shall take these points into consideration in order to avoid turning this analysis neither into a simplistic explanation, nor into a narrow observation of corruption practices in the chosen countries.

---

[258] *Ibid.*, p. 52. The author uses the case of Panama's former President Manuel Noriega to exemplify his point and asks "[…] how different was Noriega's modus operandi from what officers of the Panama National Gurad had been doing for three decades? How different was the behavior of that Guard from the practices of other sectors: business, banking, civilian politicians? Were they not all in some fashion part of an enterprise?"

[259] Ibid.

[260] Ibid.

[261] Ibid.

THE 'PRIVATE' SIDE OF CORRUPTION

Social scientist Harold Lasswell titled one of his major political books with the questions *"who gets, what, when"* arguing, that the study of politics is the study of influence and the influential.[262] Many political scientists and economists who study the causes of corrupt activities see this analogy as the starting point for their approaches. Although this question was primarily aimed at gaining an understanding of politics, it has also become a useful tool to understand corruption, since this phenomenon denotes a two-way influence relationship between the originator and the receiver, between the principal and its agent.[263]

If we focus on Lasswell's *"who"*, corruption has been commonly subjected to the practices and structures of the public sector. However there is no doubt that an equal assessment of the other side of corruption, namely the private sector, is necessary to achieve a wide-range understanding of these practices: Therefore, the concluding part of this Chapter focuses on the role of the private sector as a scenario for the development of corrupt activities.

When it comes to the analysis of the causes of corruption, there are basically three reasons for addressing the private sector. First, as it was noted before, corruption can and does occur within and between private organizations, NGOs and other private groupings within society, sometimes even at larger scales than public administrations.[264] Second, the danger of corruption emerges mostly when the interaction between the public and the private sector does not suit the interests either one of the involved parties.[265] Lastly, the propensity of corruption in the public sector can, in some cases, depend on the "willingness" of the private sector to either stick to the rules or break them and on the pressure it can apply to national governments, if circumstances so require.

The analysis of corruption in the private sector is two-leveled. The first level focuses on transactions of private companies with the public

---

[262] Lasswel, Harold D. Politics: Who Gets What, When, How. (New York: Peter Smith, 1950. Reprinted version. Originally published by the McGraw-Hill Book Company, 1936.)

[263] Political scientist Harvey Kebschull points out, that "[…] if students of politics are to achieve an understanding of 'who gets what, when, how,' […] they need to have an appreciation of the causes of scandal and corruption as well as of the formal institutions of government and politics." In: Kebschull, Harvey G. "Political Corruption: Making it the 'Significant Other' in Political Studies." PS: Political Science and Politics. (December 1992), Vol. 25, Issue 4, pp. 705-709.

[264] Andvig, Fjeldstadt, et. al. Research on Corruption. A Policy Oriented Survey, p. 14.

[265] See Rose-Ackermann. Corruption and Government.

offices. The second level deals with activities that take place within the private sector itself.[266] It is important to note, that the main incentive of private sector corruption is to maximize the company's profit. Thus a first differentiation to public sector corruption can be observed, as the interests in this case are mainly economic and not necessarily political although politicians can try – at times- to influence firms for political purposes and vice versa.[267] The emerging moment of private sector corruption on the first level however is when a private company breaks the established rule in order to maximize profit. As Rose-Ackermann observes,

> "[i]t is easy to see that corporations single-mindedly concerned with profit maximization will choose an 'optimal' amount of fraud or corruption [...] Some illegal behavior will be encouraged because it increases profits, and other behavior will be tolerated because it is too costly to eliminate."[268]

The most common *malheur* in private sector corruption are bribes, which are usually offered to public officials in order to obtain licenses, permits, contracts and the like.[269] This is the particular case, in which bribes or *"facilitation payments"* can become beneficial for the company, since it allows business to flow instead of getting stuck behind a bureaucrat's desk. In fact, there is evidence for supporting the argument, that in a bureaucratic-overloaded environment, a private company may find bribes adequate to reduce the time and costs some processes can demand.[270] Pope recognizes three areas of vulnerability in which companies can feel "tempted" to offer bribes. First, in certain countries, there are few possibilities for any company to engage in a government contract without having to pay a bribe. Second, there is a tendency to think that offshore bribes are condoned because they

---

[266] Pope, Jeremy. "The Private Corporate Sector." In: *Ibid.* and Transparency International. TI Source Book 2000 – Confronting Corruption: The Elements of a National Integrity System. (Berlin: Transparency International, 2000), pp. 137-151.

[267] In this case "[w]hen managers control firms, politicians use subsidies and bribes to convince them to pursue political objectives. When politicians control firms, managers use bribes to convince them not to push firms to pursue political objectives." In: Shleifer, Andrei and Robert W. Vishny. "Politicians and Firms." The Quarterly Journal of Economics. (November 1994), Vol. 109, No. 4, pp. 995-1025.

[268] Rose-Ackermann, Susan. "Corruption and the Private Sector." In: *Ibid.* Corruption. A Study in Political Economy, p. 189.

[269] Pope. "The Private Corporate Sector."

[270] Kaufmann and Wie. "Does ,Grease Money' Speed Up the Wheels of Commerce?"

have become customary in the international trade and business regime *("everybody does it.")* And third, companies may seek to create job opportunities and profit therefrom by bribing decision-makers to approve unnecessary acquisitions and projects.[271]

However the difference to public sector corruption here is that the interaction between bribers and bribees is more layered, meaning that managers do not necessarily want to engage directly in corrupt activities but rather designate intermediary agents that do the "dirty work" on their behalf.[272] This so called *"buffers"* provide special information and valuable insights to possible business partners, be them governments or private firms. Therefore, they offer a more effective bargaining position than individual companies. Rose-Ackermann asserts to say, that these middlemen are often the best way for private enterprises to "save face and escape legal liability by avoiding direct knowledge of corruption", organizing their business to allow such practices to take place.[273]

The second level of private sector corruption, which could be referred to as inter- and intra-firm corruption is not as clear-cut as public sector corruption. As Jeremy Pope points out, while some jurisdictions have explicit regulations against "kickbacks" or "commissions" taken by a company's employees, in many cases, these regulations are neither properly codified nor existent at all.[274] Fraud within large companies has become a common scenario to exemplify cases of corruption within the private sector. Particularly in the area of financial management, the incidence of corruption is said to be no less than in the public sector.[275] Pope best describes the example of such an event:

> "[An] accountant who warned her superiors that a book-keeper was fiddling the books by raking money from the

---

[271] All these three points seen in: Pope. "The Private Corporate Sector", p. 142. On international bribery see also: Vogl, Frank. "The Supply Side of Global Bribery." In: New Perspectives on Combating Corruption. (Kuala Lumpur: Transparency International and the World Bank, 1998), pp. 55-64.

[272] Rose-Ackermann. "Corruption and the Private Sector", p. 192.

[273] Ibid.

[274] Pope. "The Private Corporate Sector", p. 139.

[275] *Ibid.* In the United States, the case of the fall of its seventh biggest company Enron is a good example of how internal mismanagement, fraud and corruption take place in a private corporation leading to its collapse. A recent account of the events and technicalities that led to Enron's collapse can be found in: Swartz, Mimi and Sherron Watkins. Power Failure: The Inside Story of the Collapse of Enron. (New York: Double Day, 2003.)

> payments system. The book-keeper was prosecuted and sacked, but the company did nothing to improve its management scrutiny. As a result the very same accountant started running identical scams, but for even larger amounts, writing cheques to suppliers who were, in fact, supplying herself."[276]

There are several more cases in which employees or even entire departments are the main causes of intra-firm corruption. Rose-Ackermann observes that, similar to the case of the public sector, there can be *petty* corruption on low-employee level as well as *grand* corruption at top managerial level.[277] However, Pope rightly concludes that still the most frequent form of private sector corruption occurs through bribes offered to public officials in return of bureaucratic facilitations.[278]

Despite the fact that private companies seek mostly economic interests, there are further similarities between the incidence of corruption in the private and public sectors. Conflicts of interests can occur within and between firms. Just as politicians may sell out voters, managers at the top level may sell out stockholders.[279] In this scenario, corporate boards of directors assume the role of elected top government officials, and create the dependent relationship between voters and authorities. Although this relationship is not identical (stockholders can sell their shares if they disagree with corporate policies), both managers and politicians have the discretionary power to either combat of foster corruption within their organizations assuming similar responsibilities for political scandals and economic failure.[280] Moreover, in some companies, the board of directors may impose decisions and policies on illicit practices that reach every level of their organizational structure, similar to the case of the public sector. Control instruments such as internal codes of conduct and penalty systems for offenders are directly linked to the power of the board of directors to decide up to which level these mechanisms can curb or ignore corruption.

Among the critical differences between public sector and private sector corruption at the second level lies the fact, that boards may have less

---

[276] Pope. "The Private Corporate Sector", p. 139.

[277] Rose-Ackermann. "Corruption and the Private Sector", p. 191.

[278] Pope. "The Private Corporate Sector", p. 141; and Rose-Ackermann. "Corruption and the Private Sector", p. 196.

[279] Ibid.

[280] Ibid.

legal restraints since the jurisdiction of a company is mostly smaller than that of an entire country. Also, not every company has effective and extended internal sight mechanisms to monitor the policies and directives of all the employees, including the members of the board.[281] Moreover, the relationship between the board of directors, shareholders and employees is – in some cases – not as "public" as in the government sphere. In many corporations, shareholders and employees do not have any kind of contact with the top-level management and thus are poorly informed on the activities of the board of directors. Therefore, the information they have about the company's practices and performance (balance, profit, dividends, etc.) may be deviant from their own personal experience. In the public sector, voters know the elected officer in a better way and are reluctant of why he was chosen. Citizens have more channels than employees to obtain information and the control mechanisms are more extended for a politician than for a manager. In this context, corruption in the private sector can be "hidden" in a better way by the top management, since the patterns of information are relatively narrow than in the public sphere.

Lastly, within the many forms of private corporations, those of non-profit nature are commonly said to be less prone to corruption.[282] However, charity institutions, educational organizations, research facilities and cultural communities are not entirely free from corruption.[283] This has basically two reasons. First, the somehow noble and "altruistic" missions of such organizations lead to a considerable misinformation on their books. And just because some organizations tend to "fight for a good cause", this does not make them unable to engage in illicit activities. As Rose-Ackermann notes,

> "[b]y tacking advantage of a popular presumption that the nonprofit label implies benevolent trustees, an organization may instead permit kickbacks or self-dealing schemes that enrich individuals in charge of allotting the organization's funds. The advantage of the nonprofit form seems to rest on the rather slim reed of trust and on the notion that entrepreneurs select profit-making firms if they are

281 Ibid.

282 Rose-Ackermann. "Corruption and the Private Sector", p. 202.

283 *Ibid.* The author makes also reference to two cases in which charity organizations became involved in several corruption scandals in: Mendelson. Mary Adelaide. Tender Loving Greed. (New York: Alfred A. Knopf, 1974.)

> narrowly self-seeking and choose nonprofits organizations if they have altruistic temperaments."[284]

This last point leads us to conclude, that the private sector is as prone to corruption as its public counterpart for a variety of reasons as it was explained above. The variety of causes and scenarios attached to corruption should therefore not only be related to political practices of government. As seen above, managers and private entrepreneurs can also engage in illicit practices due to the fact that corruption seems to be a present temptation to every institution, since the benefits are on the prevailing side of decision-makers and corporate managers.

Summarizing the findings of this chapter, we have found the following elements, which should enhance the theoretical framework for the analysis of the case studies. First, following the working definition, corruption is a phenomenon that emerged within the processes of modernization in recent history. Technological and social advances created the opportunity to seek more power and money resources, therefore, corruption appeared in modern politics and society as a mechanism to gain access to these new resources.

Second, the causes of corruption are closely related to the different typologies of this phenomenon. From the political perspective, corruption was found in two main areas, namely, in the low-level bureaucracy ("petty corruption") and the political elites ("grand corruption.") The economic research on corruption denoted that there are two main causes for the engendrance of this problem, the high propensity towards rent seeking and low wages, especially in the public sector. In a contending explanation of this phenomenon, anthropological and socio-cultural studies based their findings on the normative components of corruption. These scholars see social relationships, cultural context and the anthropological composition of different societies as the emerging elements of corruption. The cases of China, Bangladesh and Russia supported this argument.

Lastly, it became quite clear that corruption cannot be solely attributed to the public sector. Rose-Ackermann and Pope made crucial observations for establishing similarities between the practices of companies and those of governments. At the end, managers face similar situations as

---

[284] *Ibid.* See as example the case of NGOs in post-Suharto Indonesia as found in: Holloway, Richard. "Corruption and Civil Society Institutions in Indonesia." Working Paper for the 10th International Anti-Corruption Conference. (Berlin: Transparency International, 2000.)

elected officials, and even face similar risks from engaging in corrupt practices. Moreover, the propensity of non-profit organizations towards corruption was also mentioned, leaving us with the certainty that, as Scott postulated in the beginning of the chapter, corruption teaches us not to take any government or institution for absolutely innocent, as this phenomenon can take place at many levels from different perspectives and with numerous possible explanations.

The analysis proceeds giving special attention in the next chapter to the multiple effects that corrupt practices can have on the government, the economy, society and culture. The intention is to analytically link the established causes and typologies of corruption to the different areas of impact this problem might have within and outside politics.

CHAPTER THREE

EFFECTS, COSTS AND CONSEQUENCES OF CORRUPTION

> "Neither definitions nor the study of corruption should lose sight of this wider perspective: dealing with corruption is not an end in itself but a means to resolving the [...] effects it has at all levels [...] It has distorted development priorities, led to massive human and financial capital flight, and undermined social and political stability."[285]

The discussion of corruption has shown until this point the multiple *facettes* of this phenomenon as well as its different manifestations. After having defined the main variable of this analysis, the last chapter provided a closer look at the forms, causes and typologies of corrupt practices. One of the major findings was, that corruption can occur at various levels and can be caused by several factors from political, economic and socio-cultural nature. Moreover, it became clear why corruption should not be solely attributed to the public sector, as private companies and even non-profit organizations seem to suffer from the same *malaise* as government institutions.

Turning the attention into the effects, consequences and costs of corruption, we can see a similar explanatory discourse. According to the literature, the effects of corruption appear at various levels and can be explained from different perspectives.[286] In this context there is, however, a danger to recognize the effects of corruption in almost every aspect of human life without giving a concrete account of what these effects in deed look like.[287]

Therefore, this chapter will focus on the main consequences implied in corrupt activities. Similar to the typologies established in Chapter Two, three categories will be analyzed. First, we shall have a closer look at the effects of corruption at the political level. These include the analysis of the quality of public services, the apparent lack of trust on public institutions as well as major political instability and leadership decay caused by corruption.

---

285 Doig, Alan and Stephanie Mclvor. "Corruption and its control in the developmental context: an analysis and selective review of the literature." Third World Quarterly (1999) Vol. 20, No. 3, pp. 657-676.

286 Tanzi, "Corruption Around the World. Causes, Consequences, Scope and Cures", p. 564 ff

287 Johnston. "The Political Consequences of Corruption: A Reassessment", p. 474.

Second, an overview of qualitative and quantitative damages of corruption on the economy will be addressed. Some of the economic literature attempted to state, that in some cases, corruption might bring out better business than practices within the legal framework.[288] However, this argument is currently far from being valid. For instance, even if a bribe does speed up business, the act itself is not entirely loose from economic negative side effects, not to mention the political, social and even moral problems it might involve.[289] And third, the social costs of corruption will be discussed. There is strong evidence that corruption can become a form of social repression and lead to crucial inequalities, for instance in terms of income and access to public goods.[290]

POLITICAL EFFECTS

The traditional approach to the political effects of corruption in the 1960s and 1970s was primarily influenced by Samuel Huntington's functionalist conception of this phenomenon. According to him, corruption was a necessary characteristic of politics without which, some government institutions would not be able to function.[291] Even some scholars prior to Huntington saw corruption as beneficial for political development and as a way to circumscribe the obtrusive bureaucratic state apparatus.[292] In this regard, the classification of corruption as the "grease" of the political machinery was broadly acknowledged.

However, more recent studies on corruption have challenged this position and have recognized the negative impact of this phenomenon in politics. According to political scientist Mitchell Seligson, the spread of democracy, especially in the Third World has opened the eyes of the

---

[288] See for example: Leff. "Economic Development Through Bureaucratic Corruption", p. 8 ff.

[289] *Ibid.*, p. 1323. The author notes, for instance, that bribes may even cause more delay in some transactions in order to attract more bribes.

[290] Klitgaard. "International Cooperation Against Corruption."

[291] Huntington notes, that [c]orruption may thus be functional to the maintenance of a political system in the same way reform is [and it] serves to reduce group pressure for policy changes, just as reform serves to reduce class pressures for structural changes." In: Huntington. "Modernization and Corruption", p. 64.

[292] Seligson, Mitchell A. "The Impact of Corruption on Regime Legitimacy: A comparative Study of Four Latin American Countries." The Journal of Politics. (May 2002), Vol. 64, No. 2, pp. 408-433. The author bases this assumption on the work of Key, V.O. Southern Politics in State and Nation. (New York: Vintage Books, 1949.)

scholarship towards the political consequences of corrupt activities.[293] These consequences, or often referred to as "political costs", deal mostly with the relationship between society and the state.

Political Participation and Political Development

Taking into consideration that the state and society are key elements for a functioning political apparatus, Johnston recognizes two main areas of political effects emerging from corruption.[294] The first area is referred to as "short-term effects" and includes the destruction and undermining of the political trust between voters and the elected officials. As he observes, every political process in society needs a minimal amount of trust from the citizens towards the leadership. In this regard, corruption has a direct negative effect on this basic relationship. The result is twofold. First, citizens develop a general anti-trust position towards the government, as they do not want to become the target of bureaucratic or political corruption. This point will be discussed separately below. And second, this lack of trust generates a climate of greed and competition within public official rows. Public servants know that they are either serving the interests of their principals or their own interests and therefore become cautious and selective about determining who gains access to their particular service. Johnston points out, that such a scenario can lead to a complete deprivation of political independence between administrative agencies, hindering them to perform their duties and serve the public.[295]

The second realm of effects pointed out by Johnston is "long-term based" and refers to the danger of corruption on what he calls "political development."[296] According to the author, diverse groups of society engage in multiple institutional forms and engage – at different levels – in the political building process of any nation. Corruption, in this context, inhibits the creation and the effective participation of such independent civil groups for political development. As it was observed in earlier chapters, the politics of corruption mostly include an individual or a limited group who has access to a certain good and has the discretion to provide the public therewith.

293 *Ibid.*, p. 412.

294 Johnston, Michael. "The Political Costs of Corruption." Paper presented at the First Latin American Conference on the Fight against Bureaucratic Corruption. (Santa Fe de Bogota: November, 1993)

295 Ibid.

296 *Ibid.* The author uses this concept as the "growth of a strong and active civil society as a balance to the state, and increasing peaceful interaction between the two."

Therefore, corruption creates a monopoly as it only serves particular interests. Independent groups, who might be still loyal to the system, mostly lack access to these monopolies, especially if they are not willing to pay the price. Consequently, as Johnston observes, that a long-term political effect of corruption is the "privatization of political life" resulting from the monopolization of public goods and services.[297]

Quality of Government Performance

Besides making restrictions, corruption also seriously damages to the quality of the performance of government institutions. This is widely recognized point by practitioners and scholars and can be best reviewed by considering two features of the public sector, namely government expenditure and the allocation of talent.

On the former, it has been recognized that corruption can have a negative effect on the way public spending decisions are made.[298] This means, that corrupt politicians and bureaucrats not only seek increasing benefits, but also carefully shape the composition of government expenditure, so that they can cash bribes in an easier and more effective way.[299] The result is that areas such as health and education often become neglected by government spending, as they do not offer the opportunities to obtain great revenues from illegal activities.[300] In this regard, tentative – yet not conclusive – data shows, that corrupt governments tend to raise expenditures on areas in which they can operate more efficiently in terms making benefits through illegal practices.[301] The performance of the government thus is severely affected, since the budgetary priorities are subjectively influenced by the proneness to corruption. This feature creates uncertainty on the affected sectors, as public servants cannot rely in the central apparatus for

---

[297] Ibid.

[298] Mauro, Paulo. "The Effects of Corruption on Growth, Investment, and Government Expenditure: A Cross-Country Analysis." In: Elliot. Corruption and the Global Economy, pp. 83-107. See also Tanzi, "Corruption Around the World. Causes, Consequences, Scope and Cures", p. 568.

[299] Mauro, "The Effects of Corruption on Growth, Investment, and Government Expenditure: A Cross-Country Analysis", p. 87.

[300] *Ibid.* Mauro concentrated on government spending on education. Using data produced by Political Risk Services, Business International and other research institutions, he came to the conclusion that the correlation between corruption levels and the expenditure on education showed to be indeed negative: when corruption increased by two points in a ten point scales, expenditures in this areas decreased by 0.5 percent.

[301] Ibid.

providing their services without being tempted to demand extra payments for them. Moreover, biased budgetary decisions originate a limitation for services, with rationing and queuing as a result.[302]

The allocation of talent is the second feature of the decay of public performance due to the danger of corruption. This term is referred to the amount of qualified personnel that is hired for government positions. According to Murphy, Shleifer and Vishny, a country's most talented individuals are the true engines of an adequate political and economic development.[303] However, the rewards that high-class employees become are different in every sector. From this perspective, talented individuals have two choices: either they become private entrepreneurs or they join the government bureaucracy. This latter option is bound to the option of becoming a rent seeker, because of the considerable differences in terms of wages and benefits in the public sector, as seen in the last chapter.[304] Murphy, Shleifer and Vishny note that when talented people become entrepreneurs, they mostly make technological advances and contribute to the growth of the economy. However, if they become rent seekers, most of their gains come from the redistribution of revenues from third parties.[305] In this scenario, talented rent-seekers absorb labor, reduce income and mislead the incentives to produce thus hindering growth and development.[306] Although these effects are mainly economic, there is certainly a political addendum to them. By making rent seeking the best option but with the most damaging effects, talented individuals with high qualifications and great ethical values might tend to stay away from becoming involved in public affairs. It is plausible to think that high profiles would show preference to provide their abilities to employers that reward them based on their qualifications and not choose to obtain these rewards in an illicit way. The result would be that less talented people become providers of public services thus diminishing the quality, availability and reliability of government institutions. This lack of qualified personnel leads then to a decay in the overall performance of the public sector.[307]

---

[302] Tanzi, "Corruption Around the World. Causes, Consequences, Scope and Cures", p. 569.

[303] Murphy, Kevin M., Andrei Shleifer and Robert W. Vishny. "The Allocation of Talent: Implications for Growth." The Quarterly Journal of Economics. (May, 1991) Vol. 106, No. 2, pp. 503-530.

[304] As described in: Van Rijckeghem and Weder. "Corruption and the Rate of Temptation."

[305] Murphy, Shleifer and Vishny. "The Allocation of Talent: Implications for Growth", pp. 505.

[306] Ibid.

[307] For a further elaboration of these arguments, see also Gradstein, "Rent Seeking and the Provision of Public Goods"; and Shleifer, Andrei and Robert W. Vishny. "Corruption." The Quarterly Journal of Economics. (August 1993), Vol. 108, No. 3, pp. 599-617.

Lack of Trust in Government Institutions

The existence of corruption benefits a few and damages many. In this regard, the relationship between state institutions and the citizens becomes distorted because general trust in the government decreases, since it is perceived to be serving the highest bidders only.[308] Seligson notes that the worldwide spread of the democratic model of governance in the last 20 years changed the idea of corruption from the classic functionalist notion (the "necessary" grease of the political machinery, as stated by Huntington) into a dangerous dysfunctional element for the confidence of the public in the government.[309]

Political scientist Susan Pharr analyzed the relationship between government performance and public trust therein by viewing corruption as a source of public mistrust.[310] Although the author recognizes that the traditional indicator for trust in national institutions has been the state of the economy, she also asserts to observe that performance of the leadership is yet the key to measure citizen's confidence.[311] In this context, Pharr categorizes the term "leadership" in two dimensions: the actual policy performance of politicians/bureaucrats, and their conduct or attitudes towards holding a public office.[312] The former is to be considered a main indicator for the *a priori* public response to policy measures from the government.[313] The latter dimension, referred by the author as 'character', addresses the problem of public officials getting involved in activities outside the scope of their mandate, many of them outside the legal jurisdiction. By conducting a time-series analysis, correlating levels of confidence with reports on public office misconduct, Pharr came to the conclusion that these two variables reflect the fact that the public does indeed lose confidence in the government, when corruption activities are present and revealed within the government's

308 Seligson. "The Impact of Corruption on Regime Legitimacy", p. 412.

309 Ibid.

310 Pharr, Susan J. "Public Trust and Corruption in Japan." In: Heidenheimer and Johnston (eds.) Political Corruption, pp. 835-859.

311 Ibid.

312 Ibid.

313 Pharr notes, that "[t]his approach is all the more compelling because of the close correlation in so many countries between low satisfaction with government and politics and negative evaluations of specific institutions of government, including the prime ministership, legislature and bureaucracy." In: *Ibid.*, p. 845.

rows.[314] Figure 2 shows moreover, how political mistrust and thus the belief in democracy can be severely affected by the existence of corruption in the government.

FIGURE 2: DISSATISFACTION WITH DEMOCRACY AND CASES OF CORRUPTION REPORTED IN THE ITALIAN PRESS BETWEEN 1976-1992

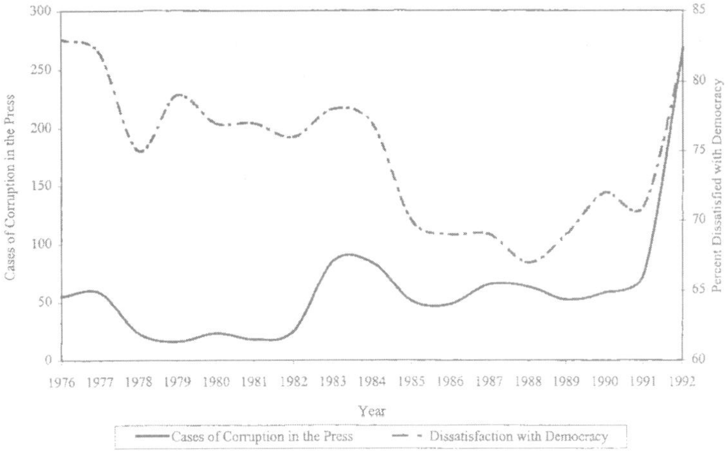

Source: Pharr and Putnam. Disaffected Countries: What's Troubling the Trilateral Countries? p. 214.

Pharr's conclusions foster the argument, that democratic institutions are the target of political corruption as their decay can be easily attributed to this problem. The lack of trust diminished the ability of such institutions to provide the services they are responsible for.

314 The research took place for the period between 1978 and 1996. It was based on corruption reports from one of Japan's major circulating newspapers, comprised by over 15,000 different documents. Furthermore, the author conducted a series of surveys on political dissatisfaction, which were correlated to the newspaper reports. Lastly, the study ran a Cochrane-Orcutt regression including indicators such as the number of seats of Japan's conservative Liberal Democratic Party (LDP), which ruled the country for nearly 40 years. An extended version of these findings can be found in: Pharr, Susan J. "Official's Misconduct and Public Distrust: Japan and the Trilateral Democracies." In: Pharr, Susan J. and Robert Putnam (eds.) Disaffected Countries: What's Troubling the Trilateral Countries? (Princeton: Princeton University Press, 2000.)

The relationship between corruption and the lack of trust towards the government is not entirely monocausal. Rose-Ackermann, reviewing the works of Diego Gambetta on the Sicilian Mafia, rightly points out, that when the citizen's faith in national institutions is low, the conditions for corruption can become even better.[315] When the level of trust towards the public sector is low, citizens will look for alternative channels for resolving their businesses and acquiring public goods and services.[316] Trust within a society can also be re-directed from trusting the government into trusting private entrepreneurs or personal business partners and/or family members. In this scenario, people might be better off if they do business with who they "trust" instead of relying on the official entities which at times can be more time and money consuming.[317] The author makes the following example:

> "[i]n one town a corrupt program administration became entrenched because of personal relationships between agents from different agencies who all lived close to each other and established friendships outside the work environment. In the second town the program was generally honestly administered because officials had few interpersonal links so that officials of one agency were willing to respond to citizen complaints about those in other agencies."[318]

This point clearly denotes that the level of citizen trust is an important element for avoiding the spread of corrupt activities. Therefore, this variable needs to be considered as one key political effect of corruption. Although the derivatives of the problem of confidence in the government and its relation to public misconduct entail social costs and social effects as well, this needs to be approached as primarily a political effect. Due to the basic relationship

---

315 Rose-Ackermann. Corruption and Government, p. 97. On Gambetta's work see: Gambetta, Diego. The Sicilian Mafia. (Cambridge, MA: Cambridge University Press, 1993.)

316 *Ibid.* A similar argument can be found for the case of Russia in: Ledeneva, Alena. Russia's Economy of Favours: Blat, Networking and Informal Exchange. (Cambridge, MA: Cambridge University Press, 1998.)

317 Rose-Ackermann makes the following example: "[i]n one town a corrupt program administration became entrenched because of personal relationships between agents from different agencies who all lived close to each other and established friendships outside the work environment. In the second town the program was generally honestly administered because officials had few interpersonal links so that officials of one agency were willing to respond to citizen complaints about those in other agencies."

318 Rose-Ackermann. Corruption and Government, p. 98.

between public trust and democracy, the lack of trust in national institutions as a consequence of corruption endangers the entire democratic apparatus of any country. As Pharr concludes in her contribution,

> "[i]n a post cold war world, democracy has emerged as the leading political system with no real rivals, but sustaining democracy requires, above all else, public trust. Taking steps to foster and maintain responsible leadership, political and bureaucratic, is thus a crucial issue for the millennium." [319]

Political Instability and the Decay of the Government Apparatus

One of the last but no less considerable political effects of corruption is increasing political instability. The factors explained above, lack of political development and participation, the poor delivery of public services and the loss of confidence on the political leadership act as catalyzers for an erosion of governability, especially in countries with weak institutions. Although it can interpreted both as a cause and as an effect, political instability will be used here as a pre-condition for a resulting scenario, namely the decay of the entire government.

Political instability is categorized in a twofold dimension covering both the legal changes of head of states and governments, as well as non-constitutional transitions, mostly in the form of violent "take-overs".[320] Within the context of the damaging effects of corruption, we shall give the latter category some consideration. As economists have showed, instability not only causes damages on growth and the levels of production.[321] It also creates a climate of uncertainly and political disorientation. In these scenarios, politicians tend to follow a "wait and see" policy for their course of action with the intention of avoiding confrontations with the population

---

[319] Pharr. "Public Trust and Corruption in Japan", p. 854.

[320] Berthélemy, Jean-Claude, Celine Kauffmann, Laurence Renard and Lucia Wegner. "Political Instability, political regimes and economic performance in African countries." OECD Development Center. March 2002.

[321] See also, as cited by Berthélemy et. al.: Fosu, Augustin Kwasi. "Political Instability and Economic Growth: Evidence from Sub-Saharan Africa." Economic Development and Cultural Change (1999) Vol.40, No. 4, pp. 87-107; and Alesina, Alberto, Sule Ozler, Nouriel Roubini and Phillip Swagel. "Political Instibility and Economic Growth." Journal of Economic Growth (1996) Vol. 1, pp. 189-211.

and the political opposition.[322] However, this strategy creates yet more dissatisfaction and thus more instability because the government becomes unable to meet any of its goals from a short-term perspective.[323]

The increase of social unrest resulting from all the factors explained above puts a considerable amount of pressure on the political leadership, as the state apparatus is no longer able to maintain law and order. Consequently governments that cannot put up with this pressure are literally "dismantled" as a consequence of political instability related to high levels of corruption in the administration.[324] Although some governments try to hold on to power by increasing corruption in exchange of loyalty from basic institutions such as the police and the military – as observed by Murphy, Shleifer and Vishny – the results have been all similar. The government fails and is overtaken either by a constitutional change (via new elections) or within a violent insurrection, rebellion, coup d' etat or revolution. This effect is considered one of newest areas to which the damage of corruption can be attributed.[325] As analysts Patrick Glynn, Stephen Kobrin and Moisés Naím remark,

> "[i]n less than a half-decade, the worldwide backslash against corruption has swept like a firestorm across the global political landscape. Governments have fallen. Longtime ruling parties have been hounded from office. Presidents, prime ministers, parliamentarians and once mighty chieftains have been grilled by prosecutors and herded onto the docket. Italy, France, Japan, South Korea, India, Mexico, Colombia, Brazil, South Africa: no region, and hardly any country, has been immune."[326]

ECONOMIC COSTS

As it was reviewed in Chapter One, most of the classic studies on corruption derive from economics. Therefore, the amount of sources on the economic impacts of this phenomenon is as big as the variety of elements

---

322 Berthélemy, et.al. "Political Instability, political regimes and economic performance in African countries", p. 6.

323 Ibid.

324 For examples see Klitgaard. Controlling Corruption, p. 1-12.

325 Rose-Ackermann, Susan. "The Political Economy of Corruption." In: Elliot. Corruption and the Global Economy, p. 45.

326 Glynn, Kobrin and Naim. "The Globalization of Corruption", p. 7.

analyzed therein. From the classic views of corruption as a factor for gaining economic advantage over an overloaded bureaucracy to corruption as the damaging factor for growth and economic development, the scope of effects is very wide.

In this section, selected effects relevant to the theoretical framework of the book as well as to the main questions and hypotheses will be considered. By no means is it intended to neglect the existence and importance of other factors that will be left out of this analysis. However, the focus on specific effects will enable the use of the economic variables on the case studies as a further explanatory mechanism to test the initial hypotheses. It is furthermore necessary to note, that the effects of corruption as a hindrance for economic development will be a separate area of analysis, which will be discussed in the next chapter, as there should be special attention given to this particular aspect of corruption. The economic effects taken into consideration in this chapter will focus growth and investment rates, the levels and consistency of public expenditure and public revenues as well as the quality of economic performance and the role of national institutions on the market economy.

The "Grease" Argument Revisited

Similar to the political effects, the academic debate on the economic consequences of corruption developed from traditional postures in which this phenomenon was seen as beneficial for the government economy. In this regard the works of Leff, Nye, and Huntington became mostly related with the argument that corruption was – in many cases – a better choice in economic terms. In the same fashion as with the political implications of corrupt activities, these authors perceived bribes as a necessary tax for cutting red tape and improving economic efficiency.[327] An overloaded bureaucracy would create more regulative burdens to impede rapid economic development. Therefore, according to these scholars, bribes reduce the speed of the numerous transactions of an over regulated economy. In terms of international economic competitiveness, this scenario would seem to make sense at some point of time, as countries engage in major deals with other

[327] Andvig, Fjeldstadt, et. al. Research on Corruption. A Policy Oriented Survey, p. 91. See also, Huntington. "Modernization and Corruption"; Nye. "Corruption and Political Development"; and Leff. "Economic Development Through Bureaucratic Corruption."

states and multinational corporations looking for "efficient" bureaucracies to implement contracts in the less possible period of time.[328]

Although there might be still some cases in which these arguments have not entirely lost their validity, there are many contradictions that can show a different perspective over time. For instance, Tanzi focuses on the incidence of bribes in the public sector to exemplify a much needed "revision" of past analytical postures on corruption.[329] First, he states, public officials may intentionally create regulations in order to extract bribes, therefore, this misusage creates more rules, because many bribers seek to maintain and expand their established monopolies.[330] Second, those who are engaged in bribes do not necessarily chose the most economical path. Bribes can be higher than real prices and bribees might require more than one payment to deliver the good or service.[331] Rent seeking becomes then a serious threat to economic growth as more money is directed towards illicit activities demanding more spending from the public sector. And third, bribes might not necessarily speed up transactions and bureaucratic processes, because bribees might intentionally reduce the pace of the processes in order to demand more bribes.

Tanzi's observations have received a great echo within the corruption scholarship and led to several studies neglecting the old perception of this problem as the " efficient grease" of politics and economics. In fact, the vast majority of current economic studies intend to empirically prove, that the economic impact of corruption is much greater than it was calculated in the past.[332] The arguments follow the same pattern: corruption is a *malaise* for the economy and threatens development and growth in unprecedented ways. Before going on to the analysis of the different effect of corruption on the economy, it becomes important to know that the results of these studies are by no means final. As we shall see, most economic studies have faced methodological problems and data collection and evaluation failures. Mauro explains that the empirical advances in this area have faced limitations, because a degree of efficiency of public institutions cannot be quantified

[328] This point is further explained in: Moody-Stuart. Grand Corruption, p. 11 ff.

[329] As seen in Tanzi, "Corruption Around the World. Causes, Consequences, Scope and Cures", p. 582.

[330] Ibid.

[331] Ibid.

[332] For example Daniel Kaufmann and Shang-Jin- Wei from the World Bank found out, that firms that pay more bribes actually spend more time dealing with bureaucrats leading to higher capital costs. In: Kaufmann and Wie. "Does "Grease Money' Speed Up the Wheels of Commerce?

making economic corruption a very hard to measure phenomenon.[333] For this reason, we shall consider the following arguments with caution.

Less Growth and Investment

The most prominent economic analysis on the complex relationship between corruption and growth and investment rates was undertaken by Mauro at the IMF.[334] The author bases his assumption on the fact that when doing business, corruption acts like a tax to speed up procedures and transactions as stated above. However, in such scenario, investors perceive this "tax" as an economic burden and therefore seek to invest in countries or areas in which this danger is minimal. Therefore, corruption is an intimidating factor for investment causing a direct impact on economic growth and development.[335]

In order to empirically test these assumptions, Mauro used two independent corruption indexes and three surveys on government expenditure. He then combined factors such as institutional efficiency, political stability, per capita income, investment rates, government spending, growth rates, incidence of corruption, among others into a statistical regression analysis obtaining some interesting results.[336] The results indicate that the levels of corruption negatively correlate with both the investment and the growth rate. This means, that if a country's corruption level is high, the increase of investment and growth will be negatively affected. In the same way, the statistical regressions showed that when a country improved its position within the corruption scale, the percentages of investment and growth tend to rise and improve as well, as he explains,

> "Regression analysis shows that a country that improves its standing on the corruption index from, say, 6 to 8 (0 being the most corrupt, 10 the least) will experience a 4

333 Mauro. "The Effects of Corruption on Growth, Investment, and Government Expenditure", p. 83.

334 Mauro, Paulo. "Corruption and Growth." The Quarterly Journal of Economics. (August 1995) Vol. 110, No. 3, pp. 681-712.

335 Mauro, "Why Worry About Corruption?" p. 6.

336 The surveys were obtained from Political Risk Services Inc. (International Country Risk Guide), and the Business International, see also note 16. Furthermore, three data sets were used for the regressions: 1) a data set from Robert J. Barro on government expenditure in different areas for over 100 countries; 2) a data set on expenditures from developing countries by Shantayanan Devarajan for nearly 60 countries; and 3) a data set comprising the overall expenditure rates of public enterprises for 96 countries. In: Mauro, "Why Worry About Corruption?", p. 7-8.

> percentage point increase in its investment rate and 0.5 percentage point increase in its annual per capita GDP growth rate."[337]

Although this seems like a solid statement at first, Mauro's findings should be only a preliminary indicator and should be therefore treated with "high" analytical caution.[338] This implicit reservation brings us back to the problems discussed in Chapter Two on the ability of the scholarship to explain corruption using empirical data. Among many of his colleagues, Mauro himself problematizes the results of his studies. He focuses on two key areas, in which analytical pitfalls could be easily found. First, he questions an overall validity of the arguments, as it is impossible to have absolute knowledge on how the surveys were conducted. And second, he warns about the causality of the chosen variables (expenditure, institutional inefficiency, incidence of corruption) noting that they could have been altered by subjective factors that do not appear in the data sets.[339]

Nonetheless, he is certain to observe that at least, a direct link between corruption and growth could be established, serving as a basic guideline for explaining the impact of this problem from an economic perspective. Following Mauro's work, some analysts have taken upon analyzing the long-term effects corruption on economic growth and obtained similar results on the negative correlation between these two variables.[340]

Less Revenue and More Expenditure

Besides its impact on growth, corruption can also cause negative effects on the quality of economic performance, especially in the area of public spending. In this context, Tanzi together with IMF economist Hamid Davoodi added strong arguments to the current discourse of the economic damages produced by corruption.[341] Focusing on the problems around *grand*

337 Mauro. "Corruption: Causes, Consequences, and Agenda for further Research", p. 12.

338 Ibid.

339 For instance, he questions whether it is plausible to consider that corrupt countries present slow growth rates is in deed a direct result from this phenomenon on the economy. Or does it appear like that because consultants in low growth countries give bad corruption grades in the surveys? In: *Ibid.*

340 See for instance: Ehrlich, Isaac and Francis T. Lui. "Bureaucratic Corruption and Endogenous Growth." The Journal of Political Economy (December 1999) Part 2: Symposium on the Economic Analysis of Social Behavior in Honor of Gary S. Becker. Vol. 107, No. 6, pp. 270-293.

341 Tanzi, Vito and Hamid Davoodi. "Corruption, Public Investment and Growth." Working Paper of the International Monetary Fund WP/97/139 (October, 1997.)

corruption within government projects, the authors note several key areas in which high levels of corruption act as a threatening factor to the national economy. Similar to Mauro, the authors based their assumptions on cross-country data analysis and statistical regressions obtained from surveys by Business International and Political Risk Services Inc.[342]

Tanzi and Davoodi expanded Mauro's argument in four major areas. First, the authors were able to prove again, that corrupt activities reduce public revenue and increase public spending.[343] The more illicit activities there are, the less money flows into the public treasury. Under these circumstances, the government has no other option than to rise public spending in order to compensate the losses created by corruption.[344] Economies in which corruption has the lead have low revenues, high spending, larger fiscal deficits and poor fiscal policies.[345]

Second, corruption increases public expenditure that is not accompanied by its recurrent current expenditure, for instance non-wage operations and maintenance expenditures.[346] In this regard, Tanzi and Davoodi show that a relatively high total expenditure on wages and salaries can be determined in economies with high corruption levels.[347]

A third area recognized by the authors is infrastructure. Corruption related operations reduce the quality of the existing infrastructure. This leads the government to spend more money on maintenance of basic facilities such as roads, power plants, telecommunication networks, etc. for doing business with other states and with the private sector. This raises transaction and operation costs for both government institutions and private entrepreneurs.[348]

Lastly, the revenues needed for financing so called "productive expenditures" are affected by public corruption. This means that projects that need financial assistance from the government can often suffer from cutbacks as a consequence of the economic damages of corruption as explained

342 *Ibid.*, p. 9.

343 *Ibid.*, p. 11. A further explanation of this point can be also found in: Tanzi, Vito. Policies, Institutions and the Dark Side of Economics. (Cheltenham, UK: Edward Elgar Publisching, 2000), p. 145 ff.

344 See also Mauro. "The Effects of Corruption on Growth, Investment, and Government Expenditure."

345 As seen in Tanzi, "Corruption Around the World. Causes, Consequences, Scope and Cures", p. 582.

346 Tanzi and Davoodi. "Corruption, Public Investment and Growth", p. 13.

347 *Ibid.*, p. 20.

348 *Ibid.*, p. 9. Additionally, some governments would allow a deterioration of infrastructure in order to hire companies to sustain the facilities. This would give high officials the opportunity to extract bribes from these companies as well.

above.[349] Tanzi and Davoodi observe that in cases of extreme corruption, "projects are chosen exclusively fore their bribe-generating capacity and not for their productivity."[350]

The Role of the Government in the Market Economy

A final area in which corruption has an increasingly negative influence from an economic perspective is the role of the government as the main regulating instance for the national economy. According to the literature, corruption undermines the position and the functioning of the public economic institutions in two ways.

First, in terms of internal control and the role of a sound economic and fiscal policy, Tanzi asserts to observe that corruption has a detrimental impact on public economic institutions, because it reduces their oversight ability thus making the government incapable of correcting market failures.[351] When institutions are weak and the proneness to corruption rises, public officials do not have the fear of being sanctioned. Such a scenario makes any kind of control practically irrelevant and both market weaknesses and failures are neither registered nor there are efforts to eradicate them. As Tanzi explains,

> "[w]hen civil servants appropriate, for their own use, the instruments that the government has at its disposal to influence the economy and to correct the shortcomings of the private market, they reduce the power of the state and its ability to play the intended and presumably corrective role."

Second, corruption also distorts the general incentives toward doing business with national economic institutions.[352] This observation can be made from a twofold perspective. From the international perspective, investors will surely dislike to engage in business with a country that denotes a high

349 *Ibid.*, p. 19 ff. The authors were able to show in their regressions, that, for example, the public expenditure for maintaining quality of roads depended on the incidence of corruption in the public sector.

350 *Ibid.*, p. 8.

351 Tanzi, "Corruption Around the World. Causes, Consequences, Scope and Cures", p. 583 ff; and *Ibid.*, Policies, Institutions and the Dark Side of Economics, p. 89 ff.

352 Ibid.

tendency towards corruption.[353] And from the internal perspective, many public officers do not feel enough motivation to "play by the rules" and perform their duties without misusing their positions for obtaining private rewards. This argument takes us back to the misallocation of talent, as stated by Murphy, Shleifer and Vishny, in which talented people do not get involved in the public sector for fear of becoming a further piece in the corruption puzzle.[354]

It is important to highlight, that there are many other economic effects of corruption that derive from the points made above or emerge from completely different angles. However, for the purposes of this study, this selection contains the most discussed issues in the academic community on this topic. These variables provide a comprehensive overview on the main economic fallacies engendered by corruption.

SOCIAL CONSEQUENCES

All contributions have concentrated thus far on the political effects and the economic costs of corrupt activities. There are certain areas in which the focus shifted from mainly political into mainly economic and vice versa, which reveals once again the diversity and flexibility of the phenomenon of corruption. However, after having analyzed political and economic fallacies, one aspect remains, namely the social consequences of corruption. The term "social consequences" entails those effects that could be easily added to the last two last categories, but which need a separate consideration as they tend to affect the relations of citizens in a society in a much more direct way.

The criteria presented in this category focus on factors that have an impact on different groups in the societal scale. These include are on the one side, distributional effects such as inequality and accessibility to public services, and on the other side, poverty and organized crime. These four main areas are known problems in most countries, which can be attributed to more general phenomena such as economic underdevelopment and lack of political cohesion. However, little attention has been paid to the fact that they can be in deed related to the existence of corruption both in the government and the public sector.

---

353 In 1999, the Control Risks Group (CRG), an international business risk consultant undertook a survey with nearly 200 international companies on general expectations when doing business with countries around the world. When asked what major deterrence could be named on first place while making foreign investment, nearly 40 percent of the companies gave corruption as an answer. In: Transparency International. Global Corruption Report 2001, p. 279.

354 Murphy, Schleifer and Vishny. "The Allocation of Talent: Implications for Growth."

Poverty and Unequal Access to Services

Out of the economic analysis by Mauro, Tanzi and Rose-Ackermann, we were able to see that corruption does diminish the quality of the economy by shrinking both growth and investment rates. A further aspect that accompanies these two problems is poverty. Following the IMF discourse on corruption, recent studies have included poverty as a key variable on the analysis of consequences of this phenomenon.[355]

From an economic perspective, poverty is seen as a problem that derives from the lack of adequate distribution of revenue and resources from the state to its citizens.[356] This scenario entails two major components. According to the World Bank, poverty is first attributed to the different levels of accessibility and quality of public services such as education, health, water and sanitation.[357] And second, poverty reduces the possibilities of many sectors of society to have strong representation in national political and economic processes as well as to enjoy fair access to information.[358] In these two areas, corruption acts as a catalyst for deepening the social gap between rich and poor.

As for the first relationship between corruption and poverty, it has been recognized that economic actors engaged in corrupt activities have a comparative advantage over those who are not, because they can afford to pay for the access to services and resources. The poor – meaning the bottom 20 percent of the population in terms of income growth – become an easy negative target of this unequal advantage.[359] As seen earlier, petty corruption delays the processes for the provision of public goods and increases the costs

---

355 See: Gupta, Sanjeev, Hamid Davvodi and Rosa Alonso-Terme. "Does Corruption Affect Income Inequality and Poverty?" Working Paper of the International Monetary Fund WP/98/76 (May, 1998.)

356 Ibid.

357 Teggemann, Stefanie. "Corruption, Poverty and Inequality." The World Bank. <www.worldbank.org> (26.03.2002)

358 Ibid.

359 Gupta, Davoodi and Alonso-Terme. "Does Corruption Affect Income Inequality and Poverty?", p. 10. The authors use this criterion based on previous economic works on the topic. They define the income growth of the 20 percent population "the average yearly growth rate in reral per capita GDP of the bottom quintile of the population measured in purchasing power parity-adjusted US dollars." See Birdsall, Nancy and Juan Luis Londoño. "Asset Inequality Matters: An Assessment if the World Bank's Approach to Poverty Reduction." American Economic Review, Papers and Proceedings. (1997) Vol. 87 No.2, pp. 32-37.

of their delivery, in which most cases, a bribe is entailed in the price.[360] Citizens, who cannot afford to pay this price, are mostly deprived from this particular service thus fostering poverty instead of reducing it. A UNDP report on this topic concludes, that

> "[a]nytime public benefits are distributed on the basis of ability to pay, the poor will suffer. Using an illegally price system to distribute pensions, public housing, education and health will disadvantage those unable to pay. This is true for legal user fees, and it is true for illegal bribes."[361]

The second direct effect of corruption on poverty appears within the power relations within society. The opportunities given to a few individuals to obtain the discretionary power over a good or a service by engaging in corrupt activities, create a social disequilibrium since an environment in which the access to people in political power and to financial resources is uneven supersedes the rule of law.[362] In this scenario, the poor sector of society lack equal opportunities to participate and shape policy and articulate their interest as a part of the whole. Corruption thus fosters the vulnerability of these groups to extortion, fraud and even social exploitation.[363] Although these factors affect the entire society, it is the poor, who suffer the most damage.[364]

Economists at the IMF have been able to prove that high levels of corruption can be related to high levels of poverty. Using statistical regressions on data such as natural resources, income, access to education and growth in corruption, the link between these two variables can become visible, as Figure 3 shows.

---

360 Teggemann, "Corruption, Poverty and Inequality." See also Gradstein, "Rent Seeking and the Provision of Public Goods."

361 United Nations Development Programme (UNDP). Corruption and Governance. Discussion Paper 3. New York, 1997.

362 Teggemann, "Corruption, Poverty and Inequality."

363 Ibid.

364 *Ibid.* A corruption survey conducted by the World Bank in Cambodia showed, that household with lower income spend nearly 2.3 percent of their income on bribes while rich households devoted only 0.9 percent of their income on such payments.

FIGURE 3: CORRUPTION AND INCOME GROWTH OF THE POOR

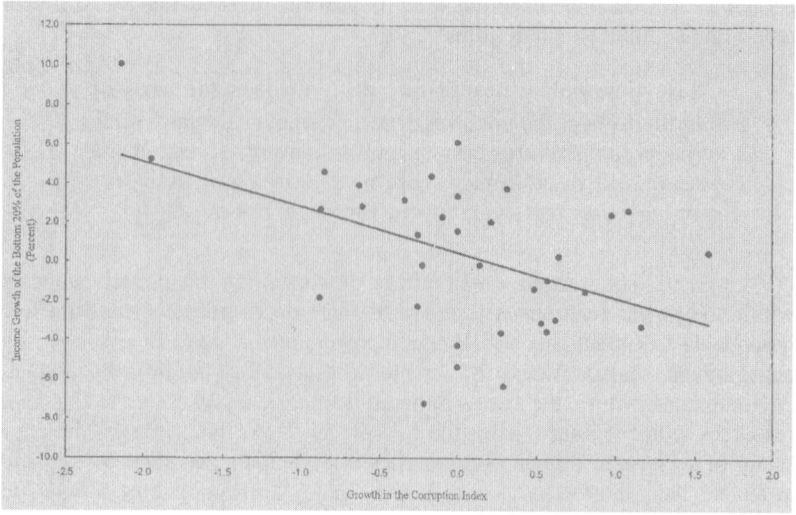

Source: Gupta, Davoodi and Alonso-Terme. "Does Corruption Affect Income Inequality and Poverty?"

> The relationship between corruption and poverty is obtained by several regressions associating higher growth in corruption with lower income growth of the poor. The results of one of the regressions show that one-standard deviation in the corruption growth scale (when this scale increases) directly relates to a decline in income growth of the poor.[365] Other regressions show similar scenarios, therefore, the authors come to the conclusion that countries with high levels of corruption have also high levels of poverty.[366]

As Figure 3 shows, if directly related to corruption, poverty can be interpreted as a further consequence of illicit activities. Moreover, it can be

[365] For instance, a deterioration of 0.78 percentage points on the corruption scale reduces the income growth scale by 7.8 percentage points per year. In: Gupta, Davoodi and Alonso-Terme. "Does Corruption Affect Income Inequality and Poverty?", p. 29 ff.

[366] Ibid.

seen that a failure of the government to distribute its resources and provide all sectors of society with equal access to public services, and a fair space within political and economic processes, creates an environment in which the consequences of corruption take a different shape, namely a dangerous factor for maintaining the social equilibrium and the societal cohesion.

Income Inequality

FIGURE 4: CORRUPTION AND INCOME INEQUALITY

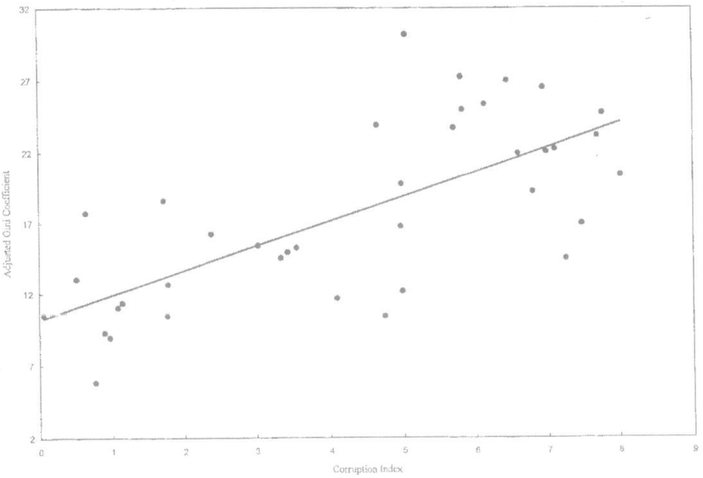

Source: Gupta, Davoodi and Alonso-Terme. "Does Corruption Affect Income Inequality and Poverty?"

The x-axis shows the levels of corruption based several corruption indexes. The y-axis is an adjusted Gini-Coefficient (this is composed of a number between 0 meaning everyone has the same income and 100 meaning one person has all the income and all the rest earn nothing). The curve shows, that an increase in the corruption scale corresponds to an increased Gini coefficient.[367]

A further social aspect of the dangers of corruption has to do with income inequality. Although this might be an economic factor, it does have a social component. The gap between the rich and the poor is a result of the failure of the state to adequately distribute revenues and resources. Consequently, there is a breach within society between those who earn more than the standard and those who manage to survive underneath the standard. This is not a new problem. However, the literature on corruption has been able to prove that a direct relationship between levels of corruption and the inequality of income can be established.[368]

Once again, statistical regressions are a helpful tool to establish and understand this link. The data used by Gupta, Davoodi and Alonso-Terme provide evidence for the argument that when high corruption is registered in one country, the degree of income inequality rises proportionately, as Figure 4 shows.

Furthermore, the results reviewed from the economic effects of corruption strengthen this particular point. It was noted that economic growth also suffers from corruption. A lack of adequate economic growth jeopardizes any attempt from the government to provide a clear structure in terms of distributing revenues and wealth and thus guaranteeing a minimum amount of income equality among its citizens.

Social Spending

Mauro already offered the first hint on how corruption affects the quality of public expenditure. He postulated that corrupt countries tend to direct funds and resources to areas from which corrupt government agents could demand bribes and seek rents in the most effective way. Big opportunities to obtain illegal payments can be found on military projects as well as on resources such as oil and its derivated goods. In these areas, corrupt bureaucrats and ambitious politicians spend most of their effort and time in order to maximize bribes and minimize the risk being discovered. A

[367] *Ibid.*, p. 17-18. The authors note however, that this is just an adjustment of the coefficient to selected variables. Other intervening factors could alter the relationship between corruption and income inequality and show different results.
[368] *Ibid.*, p. 12 ff.

lack of adequate decision-making from the political level arises, especially on issues related to social spending. As Moody-Stuart remarks,

> "[t]wo main areas of damage arise from the suspension of sound and critical decision-making. The first is that the wrong suppliers or contractors are liable to be chosen. The second, which has led to some of the worst development catastrophes, is that totally unnecessary or inappropriate purchases may be made or projects undertaken."[369]

In this regard, projects may be poorly targeted to sensitive areas such as education and health, as they do not bring the desires revenues as in the other cases. The sectors of society who need these services the most will directly suffer the consequences of such an environment.[370] Therefore, the lack of adequate public spending on areas and services within the frameset of "low politics" can be recognized as a further social consequence of corruption.

Evidence shows, that in some instances, corruption jeopardizes many aid projects for affected sectors of society (food programs, sanitation and fresh water facilities) and re-directs funds to those who are not in need, but want to take advantage in a corrupt environment.[371] In this context, we can assume with certainty, that

> "[t]he effects [of corruption] are not merely financial. They may also be profoundly economic, moral, and social. If rice in a government aid project disappears it erodes poor people's relationship with their community leaders and government officials. If a policeman or teacher takes advantage of his position to extract bribes it harms their reputation and relationship of trust, destroying social capital and decreasing moral standards."[372]

---

369 Moody-Stuart. Grand Corruption, p. 43.

370 UNDP. Corruption and Governance, p. 46 ff.

371 Teggemann, "Corruption, Poverty and Inequality." The author explains, that for example, it has been estimated, that over 10 percent of South Africa's social security budget is lost as a consequence of fraud, theft and bureaucratic inefficiencies.

372 Ibid.

Incidence of Crime

The last social consequence of corruption in many countries is the high level of criminality that becomes imminent in such environments. Since crime incidence has its own separate "analytical jurisdiction", it becomes difficult to specifically locate at the same time the link to corruption and the impact it has on society.

The relationship between corruption and organized crime is described by political scientists Donatella della Porta and Alberto Vannucci noting, that "[w]here organized crime is deep-rooted, corruption finds a fertile soil."[373] Turning the two key elements of this statement in the opposite way, it could be argued that, in the same way, a corrupt environment fosters the spread of organized crime. Corrupt activities can become general day-to-day business diminishing the sensibilization of citizens towards crime and guilt. If the standard between what is a felony and what is not disappears, other forms of criminal enterprises will spread.[374] In such an environment, citizens, and in particular public servants loose the fear of being sanctioned and the propensity towards corrupt practices and other criminal activities rises.[375]

A high incidence of crime can have several negative effects on society. At first sight, sociologists such as Emile Durkheim agree that crime can bring people together by building coalitions against crime perpetrators.[376] Nevertheless, there are many who observe that – to the contrary – the fear of crime can constrain social interaction and thus undermine the building of societal cohesion and social solidarity.[377] Using different examples of crime in urban cities, sociologists Liska and Warner were able to prove that in contemporary urban societies, high rates of criminality keep people apart, since their fear of becoming the next victim leads them to diminish routine activities from bigger groups such as municipalities and communities into smaller circles like close neighborhood and home.[378]

---

373 Della Porta, Donatella and Alberto Vannucci. Corrupt Exchanges. Actors, Resources, and Mechanisms of Political Corruption. (New York: Walter de Gruyter Inc., 1999), p. 221.

374 Pryce, William T. Congressional Testimony. Inter-American Convention Against Corruption. Council of the Americas. <www.americas-society.org> (02.05.2000)

375 As seen earlier in Mauro, "Why Worry About Corruption?", p. 5 ff.

376 In: Liska, Allen E. and Barbara D. Warner. "Functions of Crime: A Paradoxical Process." American Journal of Sociology. (May 1991) Vol. 96, No. 6, pp. 1441-1463.

377 *Ibid.*, p. 1441.

378 Ibid.

Although this seems like a plausible argument at first, the authors note, that a secondary effect of the fear of crime and the minimization of social activities can turn into a factor to control crime at the same time (as crimes seem to decrease when "everybody stays home".)[379] Nevertheless, the important element for the social consequences of the incidence crime and thus of corruption is that both do affect the relationships within the members of society. As Ambassador William T. Price concludes,

> "[s]ocially, corruption is destructive of morality and public decency. It undermines and weakens strong social values that are necessary for a true modern democratic system to function."[380]

It can be said with no doubt that the palette of effects and consequences of corruption can be extended *ad infinitum.* This Chapter has provided a selected overview of the main effects, causes and consequences of corruption activities. The selection was based on the consensus found within the different academic disciplines and on the analysis and interpretation of the major contributions on the topic. Summarizing, we can note the following points.

From the political perspective, the traditional conception of corruption as a beneficial element for the functioning of bureaucracy has been transformed into a more critical view of this term. Four key elements represent the main areas in which corruption damages politics, its system, and its actors. First, political participation and political development become severely affected as the relationship between citizens and representatives, especially in political building processes, becomes distorted by corruption causing political exclusion. Second, the quality of government performance is damaged by illicit activities, because in most cases, corrupt governments drift away from the role as the major provider of goods and services, focusing only on obtaining the most revenues out of corrupt deals. Third, corruption engenders a general civil mistrust in politicians undermining the authority of the government towards society. And fourth, the danger of political

---

379 *Ibid.* For similar views and extended analysis see also: Hollway, Wend and Tony Jefferson. "The Risk Society in Age of Anxiety: Situating fear of Crime." The British Journal of Sociology (June 1997) Vol. 48, No. 2, pp. 255-266; and Hartnagel, Timothy F. "The Perception and Fear of Crime: Implications for Neighborhood Cohesion, Social Activity, and Community Affect." Social Forces (September 1979) Vol. 58, No. 1, pp. 176-193.

380 Pryce. Congressional Testimony.

instability ending in the decay of the entire governmental structures has become, in recent years, a sensitive and damaging effect of corruption.

The economic literature provided a different perspective on the consequences of economic corruption for both national governments and the private sector. The key variables included in the analysis were, at first, growth and investment. The findings of economic experts on the area – though not definitive – provided insights on the intrinsic damage that corruption carries on to the economy. Mauro and Tanzi were able to prove that corruption negatively affects both growth and investment rates. Moreover, it became clear, that the national treasury receives fewer revenues and has a higher expenditure rates due to the existence of corrupt processes. These problems generate secondary effects such as a lack of presence of the government as the main regulating institution in the national market economy thus leading to more corruption.

Lastly, a social emphasis was given to the scope of corrupt related phenomena. Although this has not been a thoroughly researched area (most studies until present concentrate on politics or the economy), some social consequences could be obtained from the analysis above. Under the consideration that poverty is a social problem, the scholarship has been able to establish a causal relationship between the two variables, corruption and poverty. As Gupta, Davoodi and Alonso-Terme were able to explain, it seems like the more corruption there exists in a country, the higher poverty rates become. Furthermore, a basic determinant for social disrupture, namely inequality, was effectively related to the incidence of corruption practices. Once again, economists were able to observe that inequality tends to rise parallel to corruption scales. Government expenditure, an aspect that was mentioned earlier in the political effects of corruption, was picked up again – now from a social perspective – in order to locate a further element for the social consequences of corruption. It seems that the more corruption exists within the government, the less consequent decision making processes on social areas can be, as observed by Moody-Stuart. The last social consequence contained in this part was the great incidence of criminal activities, not necessarily related to corruption, which can lead to a lack of societal cohesion and a minimization of social solidarity.

This multifaceted analysis of the effects, costs and consequences of corruption builds the second cornerstone of the analytical framework of this book. As we closer to the case studies, all these elements will be re-introduced into the discussion in order to observe if they can be used as useful criteria to explain the incidence of corruption in the selected countries.

Chapter Four

International Perspectives: Towards a *Pax Corrupta*?

> "The scourge of corruption will, to some degree or another, always be with us. As we enter the new millennium, we are conscious that corruption, to a greater or lesser extent, poses a threat not only to the environment, human rights, democratic institutions and fundamental rights and freedoms, but it also undermines development and deepens poverty for millions over the world."[381]

It has been argued within the scholarly debate on corruption, that although this phenomenon has not entirely changed it its pathology over the years, its scope has extended beyond national borders, especially since the end of bipolarity and block politics. The so-called "internationality" of corruption was approached briefly during the introduction of this book. This aspect should not be left out without a proper discussion. Until this point, the theoretical framework has included a definition, the causes and the effects of corrupt activities. Taking the working definition as a starting point, it became clear, that corruption does not only relate to a problem of states. There is also a more "private" side to this phenomenon. On the one hand, the scope of corruption has extended beyond the borders of a single state thus turning into a regional and global issue. On the other hand, several non-state actors, such as international organizations, transnational corporations and private groupings or networks can and have become involved in corruption activities as well. These are two important features assessed in the newest debates on the "globalization" or extension of traditional national affairs onto the international arena.[382] These assumptions denote, that the relations and thus the problems of states transcend beyond borders, precisely because of the appearance of other agents of international relations, who are able to transfer political, economic, social and environmental issues beyond national borders and operate under different rules and frameworks than most states.

Based on this development and using the working definition presented in Chapter One, there seems to be a special kind of "privatization

[381] Eigen, Peter. "Preface." In: Pope and Transparency International. TI Source Book 2000, p. xv.

[382] Held, et. al. Global Transformations. Politics, Economics and Culture.

of corruption". This means, that there are certain areas, beyond the classic misuse of public authority within the modern nation-state, that require the attention of the scholarship on corruption.[383]

And the problem seems to grow even faster than in the past. Therefore, this chapter will focus on providing an overview on how big the threat of corruption has become for the community of states. As many observers conclude, the proportion of global corruption has gained the size and characteristics of a well-established – yet unofficial – international regime with its own rules, procedures and norms. Does this mean we are moving within some special kind of international order, a *pax corrupta*, when assessing the problem of corruption worldwide?[384] If this should be the case, then there need to be some areas in which the main manifestations of this order can be located.

Rather than recalling the earlier arguments for *why* corruption has become an international problem, this chapter seeks to explore *how* corruption related phenomena appear on a global scale. The analysis will concentrate on four main areas: first, corruption acting a promoting factor and platform for the spread of transnational organized crime; second, corrupt networks providing an effective mechanism for facilitating the flow of illegal funds within the international business and trade regime, a practice mostly referred to as money laundering; third, the effects of corruption seem – now more than ever – to have become one of the main constraints for regional development; and lastly, the chapter takes a closer look at the problems corruption engenders within the foreign development assistance regime.

TRANSNATIONAL ORGANIZED CRIME

One of the phenomena that changed the ways in which the international system works is the incidence of international crime. The activities referred to as "transnational organized crime" are not a feature of states, meaning that the main actors are mostly informal organizations

---

383 The working definition of corruption of this book referred to the illegitimate of illegal use of public (and private) authority for personal or corporate benefit.

384 This term is an adaptation based on the discussion about the global scope of transnational crime as particular international regime under the original name of "pax mafiosa." In: Sterling, Claire. Thieves World. (New York: Simon and Schuster, 1994.) As cited by: Shelley, Louise I. "Transnational Organized Crime: An Imminent Threat to the Nation-State?" Journal of International Affairs (Winter 1995) Vol. 48, No. 2, pp. 465-489. Although Shelley regards this idea as "premature", Sterling and other authors have explained that due to the great extent of international organized crime, a "pax mafiosa" is in deed rising as a regime of its own.

outside the governmental perimeter, which turns it into a highly complex issue for international affairs.

The relationship between corrupt practices and transnational organized crime is reciprocal. Della Porta and Vannucci rightly pointed out that within a criminal environment, corruption finds a fertile soil.[385] If we carry this relationship onto the international level, we find a similar causality. International criminals do seek adequate conditions for performing their business. Corruption thus acts as *ventile*, opening the doors and facilitating illegal businesses to develop across regions. This is a form of corruption that differs from the traditional definition of a public officer abusing his position for personal gain. In these scenarios, corruption takes place as well, however in a different, somehow "privatized" manner. Criminologist Michael Maltz asserted to say that "organized crime always involves corruption", while economist Peter Reuter states, that "corruption has a centrality for illegal markets that it does not have for legal markets generally."[386]

Transnational organized crime thus fosters corruption on an international scale as it spreads the range of such activities and transfers their obtained profit from one country to another, making it thus unreturnable to its country of origin. In this scenario, states are solely used as temporary stations in a continuous rotation of assets and personnel from international criminal networks. Although the international community has given special emphasis to tackle down this problem, it can be noted, that due to the technological advances in the world, transnational criminal networks and organizations continue to undermine the rules, norms and values of the international society, especially when it comes to international anti-corruption standards.[387] In this particular case, there sanctions imposed in case of non-compliance do not have a real destination, as the perpetrators are not even subjects of international law.

Moreover, if corruption is taken as an integral component of transnational organized crime, some possible threatening scenarios and dangers become visible.[388] International lawyer and criminologist Louise

---

[385] Della Porta and Vannucci. Corrupt Exchanges, p. 221 ff.

[386] Both citations found in: *Ibid.*, p. 227.

[387] On this point see also: Shelley, Louise I. "Crime and Corruption in the Digital Age." Journal of International Affairs (Spring 1998), Vol. 51, No. 2, pp. 605-620.

[388] Transnational organized crime is referred to the activities that are undertaken by groups that operate from a single state, but have hosts in several other states in which market conditions are favorable for their operations. Moreover, these groups work on the assumption that the risk of apprehension is low. As defined by: Williams, Phil. "Transnational Criminal Organizations and International Security."

Shelley notes that there are no prototypes for international criminal organizations, because these engage in several fields ranging from drug trafficking and drug smuggling onto arms trade, smuggling of stolen goods such as cars or works of art, and even to the illegal trade of human beings.[389] Therefore, she recognizes that the threats of transnational organized crime and thus of corruption are not only monetary but also affect political structures and the social order of the countries in which criminal organizations start and expand their operations.[390]

This connection can be observed on three different levels. First, the intimidation of political elites and the population, the repression against journalists and civil society groups and the domination of the political agendas in some countries, present the major political and social effects of transnational organized crime. As observed earlier, corruption plays a determinant role in all these areas, serving as the main platform and catalyzer for such practices.

Second, international criminal networks undermine the authority of the state by unofficially supplanting public officials with members of criminal organizations in order to represent and implement their objectives to the outside.[391] This is where private and public corruption clash. The illegitimate presence of individuals of organized-crime-affiliation within national political institutions fosters a special kind of political instability that can be transmitted on to the international levels. This would be the case if members who are involved in transnational criminal networks represented several countries.[392] Similarly, it was observed in Chapter Three that corruption does lead to an undermining of national institutions and to a general distrust of the population towards the leading elites. This leads to an inadequate representation of the country's policies, especially to the outside.

Survival (Spring 1994) Vol. 36, No. 1, pp. 96-113. Cited in: Shelley. "Transnational Organized Crime: An Imminent Threat to the Nation-State?", p. 472

389 *Ibid.*, p. 464.

390 *Ibid.* , p. 467.

391 As Shelley notes, "transnational organized crime groups in both developed and developing democracies seek to corrupt high-level government officials both on the groups' home turf and in the countries where they operate." In: *Ibid.*, p. 468.

392 Following this assumption Shelley's most recent contribution focuses on the example of post-Soviet Russia stating that "the globalization of Russian corruption has tarnished Russia's international image and undermined its state capacity." In: Shelley, Louise I. "Crime and Corruption: Enduring Problems of Post-Soviet Development." Demokratizatsiya (Winter 2003) Vol. 11, No. 1, pp. 110-114.

And third, transnational criminal organizations pose a security threat to the international community of states.[393] When it comes to drug trafficking and especially to illicit arms trade, transnational criminal actors turn into a potential danger, since their access to all kinds of military arsenal including nuclear and biological weapons cannot be controlled by any state or international organization. Due to the recent developments in the field of international business and trade regimes, not only money circulates faster, but also goods and services cross borders in an easier, faster way. In this scenario, the production and trade of weapons through transnational criminal cartels has become bigger and more attractive than ever before.[394] In this scenario, again, corruption facilitates, speeds up and covers the numerous business transactions of such groups.

MONEY LAUNDERING

The second area in which a more "privatized" side of corruption can be observed is the modern international economy, in which currency trade provides the most global of all markets.[395] This development makes the transfer of money at the international level become vital for undertaking international business transactions between states, transnational corporations and international finance institutions. Nevertheless, when doing international business and trade, countries and transnational corporations can often become engaged in the transfer of illicit funds in many different forms.[396] The money that is transferred from one country to another and then returned to the original country is illegal, thus making its transfer illegal as well. This form of international corruption referred to as money laundering, is one of the most critical problems of the emerging global economy. The existence and spread of international money laundering is based on two main factors. First, there is a lack of international regulation to comprehensively approach this problem. And second, similar to the case of transnational organized crime,

393 Shelley. "Transnational Organized Crime: An Imminent Threat to the Nation-State?", p. 468.

394 On the impact of transnational crime and arms trade see also: Robinson, Jeffrey. The Merger: The Conglomeration of International Organized Crime. (New York: Overlook Press, 2000.)

395 Pauly, Who Elected the Bankers? Surveillance and Control in the World Economy.

396 A major example taken from the previous chapters is the payment of bribes, especially between transnational corporations and governments. However, international bribery is not the only means through which funds are transferred illegally between states. Further problems of transnational kind such as narcotics trade and organized crime generate funds that circulate all over the world. In many cases, illicit drug sale revenues are directly used for money laundering and illicit investments. Also, funds required by terrorist groups and underground organizations depend greatly on international capital transfers.

the rapid advancements of the past decade in the field of information technologies and communications have made money transfers easier and quicker to make and thus almost impossible to track down.[397]

Hiding, moving, and investing the proceeds of criminal conduct compile the most used definition of money laundering today.[398] Disguising the illicit origin of funds has been an activity long performed by criminal individuals and enterprises around the world. Criminal entities use the financial system to cover the illegal origin of money and make it seem legitimately obtained.[399] Usually linked to other forms of organized crime, money laundering can be found in any crime that generates significant benefits such as extortion, drug trafficking, and illicit arms sales, among others.[400]

Money laundering is considered a special type of corruption.[401] Many observers also classify this phenomenon under international organized crime.[402] However, this phenomenon has certain individual features that need to be addressed, if we want to gain a proper understanding of corruption as an international problem.[403]

Since the transfer of illegal funds takes place on an international scale, there are several macroeconomic effects that can be attributed to

---

397 Morris-Cotterill. "Money Laundering" pp. 19.

398 Ibid.

399 Scott, David. "Money Laundering and International Efforts to Fight It." Public Policy for the Private Sector. Note 48 (May 1995.) Available online at: <http://rru.worldbank.org/viewpoint/HTMLNotes/48/48scott.pdf>

400 *Ibid.*

401 On this particular view see also Glynn, Kobrin and Naim. "The Globalization of Corruption", p. 24 ff.

402 Organization for Economic Cooperation and Development. "Basic facts about money laundering." Financial Action Task Force on Money Laundering. Paris, May 2002. <www1.oecd.org/fatf/Mlaundering_en.htm>

403 Money laundering usually takes place in three steps: placement, layering, and integration of cash or funds. In the initial phase, the launderer inserts illegally obtained money into the financial system. This is done by splitting up large cash amount in smaller sums, which are then deposited in multiple bank accounts or by purchasing monetary instruments such as cheques and money orders, which are then transferred to another location. After these funds are part of the financial system, the launderer enters the second phase of the process, layering, where funds are converted through the purchase and sales of investment instruments and deposited into different bank accounts around the world. In the third and final step, integration, the circulated funds re-enter the legal market in form of legitimate investments, such as real estate, luxury assets, or business ventures. As explained in: Scott. "Money Laundering and International Efforts to Fight It"; and OECD. "Basic facts about money laundering."

money laundering.[404] Misleading economic data and failed investments are two major effects. First, the amount of money involved in underground activities cannot be measured. Therefore it creates a distortion in economic data making it more difficult for governments to manage their own economic policies.[405] Due to the mobility of money between countries, monetary data also becomes erroneous and can have adverse effects on interest rates and exchange rate volatility, as the location of monetary aggregates is not known for certain.[406] Second, the ways in which income and revenues are distributed are also affected by money laundering. [407] During the stages of layering and integration of illicit funds, income is redirected from solid to low-quality investments in order to keep it unnoticed to central authorities. Investing in risky areas can therefore slow the pace of economic growth.[408]

Money laundering can also cause indirect macroeconomic effects. Legal transactions can be deterred because of the fear of getting involved in illegal activities, thus making foreign investment seem at times less attractive for economic actors.[409] Also, confidence in the markets and in the efficiency of profits becomes eroded through the existence of trading and fraud activities. Finally, money laundering can lead to a chain reaction in terms of undermining legal systems, since breaking one law makes it easier to break other laws subsequently.[410]

Although states are somehow involved in the international transit of illegal funds (some more than others), this problem is not an exclusive issue of governments. There are as much private actors involved as there are countries that make business through money laundering. The scholarship on corruption holds to the fact that in any act of corruption there are always two parties involved: those who pay, and those who receive. However, for the problem of money laundering, the role of governments, especially those who

[404] Quirk, Peter J. "Money Laundering: Muddying the Macroeconomy." In: Finance and Development (1997) Vol. 34 No. 1, pp. 7-9.

[405] Ibid.

[406] *Ibid.* The author notes that this is especially problematic for dollarized economies, since the dollar has been the traditional currency in money laundering. For this point see also: Morris-Cotterill. "Money Laundering".

[407] Ibid.

[408] *Ibid.* It is observed that "[...] there is evidence, that funds from tax evasion in the United States tend to be channeled into riskier but higher-yielding investments in the small business sector, and also that tax evasion is particularly prevalent in this sector. Fraud, embezzlement, and insider trading seem likely also to be more prevalent in rapid growing and profitable businesses and markets, because 'that's were the money is.'"

[409] Ibid.

[410] Ibid.

tolerate and even support the international flow of illicit funds is of considerable importance. Since the late 1960s, the number of states which serve as tax havens has increased dramatically.[411] Most, but not all, of these states are microstates and tourist resorts that are used as "booking centers" for the largest financial centers around the world.[412] It has been estimated that as much as half of the world's stock of money is either permanently placed in or has passed through tax havens.[413]

The main asset of these states is that their peculiar internal legal and political structures provide corporations with anonymity and protection from their home governments.[414] Tax haven regulations also favor international money launderers, because the governments in these countries have the discretion to make the rules as of to which of their benefactors they have to comply.[415] In this regard, a major issue for state and corporations who operate with tax havens is that, due to this discretion, the privilege of making decisions on funds deposited in tax havens can be neglected. In some cases, the holders of dirty money do not want to return the funds to the original depositor. Furthermore, there is no regulatory mechanism that could intervene and settle the dispute. Therefore, tax havens do create a problem for national governments, at least for those who frequently use alternative channels to transform illegal money into legal assets. There not only is a jurisdictional vacuum in terms of regulating the final destination of illegal money, but further, national sovereignty is said to be "commercialized" by tax havens, since these states directly establish the costs of legal protection and economic benefit for those who use them. This creates illicit advantages for individuals such as bank owners and financial officials.[416]

Since the scope of the problem of money laundering has taken transnational characteristics, a comprehensive solution against illicit flows of money must be found at the international level.[417] The main reason is the spread of international money laundering is caused by differences in controls and regulations across countries in which each jurisdiction has its own

411 Palan. "Tax Havens and the Commercialization of State Sovereignty."

412 *Ibid.* According to the author, there are around 70 identified tax havens worldwide.

413 *Ibid*, p. 151.

414 Ibid.

415 *Ibid.*, p. 152. The author makes an analogy comparing tax havens with parking lot proprietors stating that "they could not care less about the business of their customers, only that they pay for parking the vehicles there."

416 *Ibid.* The author discusses this issue at length in this article.

417 Tanzi. "Corruption Around the World. Causes, Consequences, Scope and Cures", pp. 586 ff.

provisions on the allocation and circulation of money.[418] This strengthens the assumption posed above on the special international corruption regime. In the context of money laundering, this regime has its own principles, norms, rules and procedures. Therefore, the more efficient control mechanisms are introduced in one country, the more likely international money launderers will try to take advantage of other less stringent systems to pursue their activities.[419] More than an international coordination of economic policy, the problem of international money laundering can best be approached by the development of international mechanisms, which diminish or even eliminate these differences.[420]

DEVELOPMENT CONSTRAINTS

During a symposium on the prevention and control of financial fraud, World Bank's Senior Advisor Pieter Bottelier pointed out that "like ignorance and environmental degradation, corruption is a great enemy of development."[421] This view has been spread throughout the entire academic debate on corruption as well as through the different practitioners' approaches on it.[422] It was said earlier, that before the end of the Cold War, the phenomenon of corruption was not as important as it has become nowadays.[423] Moreover, the effects of corruption were not considered an endangering factor, at least not for the underdevelopment of non-industrialized countries. Problems of different nature such as political instability, economic failure or social disruption were the main factor for the stagnation of the so-called "developing countries". Nevertheless, the consideration of the impact of illicit activities on political, social, and especially on economic development has become the focus of attention of many studies and approaches on the topic.

418 Ibid.

419 Ibid.

420 Ibid.

421 Bottelier, Pieter. "Corruption and Development – Remarks for the International Symposium on the Prevention and Control of Financial Fraud." The World Bank Group. <www.worldbank.org> (18.03.2002)

422 For an extended review of the literature on corruption within the topic of development see also: Doig and Mclvor. "Corruption and its control in the developmental context: an analysis and selective review of the literature."

423 *Ibid.* The author notes furthermore, that in the case of the World Bank, "[...] the subject of corruption was regarded as too difficult and controversial to deal with outside the context of Bank funded projects, or as not important enough to warrant the Bank's explicit attention."

In this context, the main inquiry is to find out how corruption affects the development of a nation. It is important to note at this point, however, that corruption should not be perceived as a stereotypical malaise of developing, less and least developed countries. Industrialized nations such as Japan, Germany and the United States have been recently shocked by corruption scandals denoting the presence of this problem within both their public and private sectors.[424] These cases differentiate to those cases of corruption in the developing world primarily in terms of the effects that they can have in a country's political, social and economic structures. Although the results of such cases have been of unprecedented magnitude and many who were involved did suffer direct consequences, we have not yet experienced a complete crash of the economy or the entire destruction of the political apparatus in industrialized countries as a result of corruption scandals. However, if we turn our attention to recent corruption cases in developing or less developed country, the picture will be completely different.[425] Due to the mostly desolate status of the economy in these countries, the damage of corruption becomes more visible. Political failure, poor economic performance and extended social discontent are the results that can lead to a complete breakdown of the governing apparatus implying a constant danger for the development of the affected country.[426]

The development literature does acknowledge that there is specific and differentiated damage of corruption on countries of the so-called "Third World" compared to industrialized nations. The former are mostly referred to in the scholarship as patrimonial or neo-patrimonial regimes.[427] In such states, the boundaries between the public and the private sphere are very thin, a central functioning administration does not really perform its duties (if it exists at all) and the private use or appropriation of public office is not regarded as illegitimate.[428] Social scientist Robin Theobald notes that,

---

[424] See for instance the recent prominent scandals around the Enron Corporation in the United States, the accusations against former German Chancellor Helmut Kohl on dubious party financing and, most recently, the disclosure of major irregularities in the Japanese national pension system including the bribing and illicit enrichment of several public officers at all levels.

[425] The chosen case studies will exemplify this point in Section Three.

[426] A good example of how corruption acts as a corrosive force against government institutions can be found in: Flanary, Rachel and David Watt. "The state of corruption: a case study of Uganda." Third World Quarterly (1999) Vol. 20, No. 3, pp. 525-536.

[427] Theobald, Robin. "So what is really the problem about corruption?" Third World Quarterly (1999) Vol. 20, No. 3, pp. 491-502.

[428] *Ibid.*, p. 492.

> "[j]ust as more perceptive analyses of city machines and other clientelist systems have highlighted their essentially manipulative and repressive character, so also with neo-patrimonialism [...] In the case of more backward economies, neo-patrimonial regimes often descend into pervasive and unabashed theft of public resources, large-scale institutional paralysis and, in some, situations, state collapse."[429]

If this difference is given, how does the damage for developing countries look like? In order to deliver an adequate answer to this question, the overall conditions for economic and political development should be briefly reviewed first. From the economic perspective, Johnston asserts to observe, that sustainable economic development is directly linked to functioning public institutions, along with private national and foreign investment as well as effective business management.[430] Adequate levels of growth and investment, as well as good public budgeting are key factors for such a scenario. On the other hand, political development can be only guaranteed if governments enjoy a great amount of credibility, legitimacy and civil participation combined with efficient mechanisms to provide public services to all citizens.[431]

The analysis on the effects of corrupt activities provided in Chapter Three described how corruption negatively affects the economy, the society and the political system in its entirety. If we take some of the results presented therein and expose them to the general criteria for development, as stated by Johnston, the following points can be determined on why corruption can be seen as a constraint for development:

- Corruption acts like a tax on business transactions. Therefore, private national and foreign investments are endangered by corruption since investors become deterred from engaging in business within a corrupt environment. The literature on this topic observes that investment is a pivotal element in any efforts towards achieving adequate economic development.

---

429 *Ibid.*, p. 493.

430 Johnston, Michael. "Unpredictable Rules, Dishonest Competition, and Corruption: Costs for Development and Good Governance." Paper submitted for the Conference on Combating Corruption in Asian and Pacific Economies. (29. September, 1999.)

431 Ibid.

- Corruption diminishes growth and thus slows development as pointed out earlier by Mauro. His findings proved – at least up to some point – that corruption scales relate negatively to growth rates. Therefore, in specific cases, corruption acts as the break for continuous growth.
- Furthermore, Mauro considered that the impact of corruption on growth also expands to the overall economic performance of one nation. This argument was related to the quality of public expenditure and the capacity of the government to effectively capture revenues. As these are also factors that promote economic development, their failure, especially in developing nations, can be linked to the existence of corruption within public and private spheres.[432]
- Pharr and Keohane provided us with valuable insights on the crisis of legitimacy and credibility that affects many countries of the world, regardless of their development status. A useful point of their contribution is that fact that corruption does affect a crucial factor for both legitimacy and credibility: public trust. If the confidence of society in their representatives is massively diminished, governments will lack the necessary stability to perform their duties. A climate of political uncertainty is not favorable for development, as it numbs the public sector thus keeping it from delivering services to the public and malfunctioning at all levels. We were able to observe in Chapter Three that this scenario could even lead to a complete collapse of national institutions, which would certainly mean a drawback for the development efforts of any country.

The list of factors could go on, however, this section specifically deals with how corruption affects selected criteria for development. Therefore, we should keep abreast of the fact, that the selection of these factors is not yet definitive and that there could be more points added to the entire argument. Nevertheless, the damage of corruption on development needs to be treated as a transnational issue, since this problem does transcend the scope of one single nation turning it into a regional and even global problem. It is interesting to observe, that this is yet another area in which corruption has become an international regime of its own, imposing constraints to most members of the international community, and, at the same time, being resistant to the efforts to eradicate it.

---

[432] Recalling Mauros' analysis, the author was able to determine that countries with higher rates of corruption have low levels of public expenditure in sensitive areas such as education and social affairs.

THE INTERNATIONAL FOREIGN AID REGIME

The last area of analysis for the recent "internationality" of corruption can be found in the international and bilateral development aid regime. Although this is a part of the entire discussion about the failure to develop in non-industrialized countries, the presence of corruption within development aid needs separate analysis. The main goal of official development assistance (ODA), as stated by the World Bank, is to reduce poverty and promote faster sustainable growth and achieve positive balances in social indicators.[433] Most of these funds are delivered via project related loans, as in the case of the World Bank, or, through direct cash flows, such as grants from the IMF. Some of the aid received in developing countries can also be obtained from bilateral agreements with donors.[434]

Traditionally, the issue of corruption was not a point of discussion in the international donors' agenda. However, in the last ten years, development institutions have started to seriously consider the implementation of anti-corruption measures as a condition of foreign assistance programs.[435] The rationale behind this posture derives from the general perception of developing assistance as being "a lot of waste" because of its presumable ineffectiveness.[436] In this context, leading international financial institutions have developed frameworks to ensure that the funds destined for development assistance are used in the right way and thus get to the right hands.[437] The assumption that corrupt activities affect all kinds of foreign assistance leads to the need to address this problem in a more comprehensive

---

[433] The World Bank. Assessing Aid. What Works, What Doesn't and Why. (New York: Oxford University Press, 1998), p. 2.

[434] For example, two-thirds of the total amount of Canada's official development assistance is bilateral and monitored by the Canadian International Development Agency (CIDA). In: Goldfarb, Danielle. "Who gets CIDA Grants? Recipient Corruption and the Effectiveness of Development Aid." Backgrounder. C.D. Howe Institute. (November, 2001.)

[435] Weder, Beatrice. "Institutions, Corruption and Development and their Ramifications for International Cooperation." In: van Ginkel, Hans et. al. (eds.) Human Development and the Environment – UNU Millennium Series. (Tokyo: United Nations University Press, 2002.)

[436] Goldfarb, "Who gets CIDA Grants? Recipient Corruption and the Effectiveness of Development Aid." The author observes, that most of Canada's aid recipients had negative annual per capita growth rates between 1994 and 1999. Although this is just one indicator among many, it is strong enough to maintain a certain caution about the effectiveness of ODA.

[437] For instance monitoring systems have been established for all funding projects within the institution itself. Moreover, special audit services are offered to recipient countries, which need extra assistance at the delivery of funds. See also: The World Bank. Helping Countries Combat Corruption. Progress at the World Bank Since 1997. (Washington D.C., August 2000.)

way than in the past. Moreover, going back to the findings of the last chapters, the typologies and causes of corruption denoted always malfunction within the public sector leading to engagement in illicit acts. The delivery of international assistance precisely tries to alleviate these problems first in order to create adequate conditions for development. However, the results have not yet been satisfactory. Therefore, two questions in this area are of particular interest. First, how does corruption affect the delivery and effectiveness of ODA? And second, can corruption levels be the criterion for deciding which countries should receive more aid?

Scholars and practitioners have been able to come up with some conclusions that could answer these questions. In terms of aid effectiveness, the problem of corruption is – at first – located within the quality of national institutions. This means, that in an environment in which the government apparatus is solid and policies are directed towards an effective and sound public management, the effects of ODA will more likely be positive.[438] However, in countries with poor management and fragile institutions, aid becomes ineffective, mostly because it does not reach its final destination. This is where corruption appears. The World Bank stated that the most direct effect of corruption on development aid is referred to as the "leakage of funds" within developing projects described as follows:

> "The distorting effects of corruption on projects take effect as early as the project design phase where project requirements are overstated or tailored to fit one specific company, they reach into the bidding process where collusion amongst firms or between public officials and bidders renders competition ineffective, leading to assigning of contracts to underperforming firms at inflated prices."[439]

---

[438] The World Bank. Assessing Aid. What Works, What Doesn't and Why, p. 20 ff. See also: Weder. ""Institutions, Corruption and Development and their Ramifications for International Cooperation." The author explains that in countries with a stable macroeconomic environment a 1 % point increase in foreign aid can be translated into a sustained increase in growth of 0.5 % point of GDP, 1.9 % of GDP higher private investment and a 1 % reduction in poverty. For further reference on the relationship between aid effectiveness and economic growth see also: Burnside Craig and David Dollar. "Aid Policies and Growth." World Bank Policy Research Paper No. 1777. (June 1997.)

[439] Teggemann, Stephanie. "Corruption and Development Assistance." The World Bank. <www.worldbank.org> (26.03.2002)

Moreover, there is a lot bribery and rent seeking between government officials and development agencies. In order to facilitate payments, bureaucrats may ask for an extra fee in order to speed up the processes. Or they may divert the funds into project from which they can easily obtain private benefits. This turns ODA into a game in which only those with the better connections, or with the greatest willingness to pay, have access to aid.[440] In such as scenario, weak governments suffer the consequences of falling behind in the development scale, even after aid has been provided.[441] Moreover, if the amount of development funds rises, in order to create a stable economic and political environment, the effects of corruption are by far not diminished. Quite to the contrary, in such cases, a quantitative increase of ODA usually creates further opportunities for corruption, as aid inflows provide new sources of wealth, which can be misused by public officials serving private purposes.[442] Hence the solution against corruption does not seem to be to increase ODA, but to make it more effective.

This particular feature of the relationship between corruption and international aid leads us to the second question posed earlier, if the delivery of development funds is granted proportionately to the corruption incidence in any given country. From the economic perspective, Alesina and Weder used several statistical regressions in order to prove whether this question could be answered based on the experience of several countries.[443] Similar to the methods used by Mauro, the authors chose data from five different surveys and tried to test if foreign aid could be linked to corruption.[444] One of the key findings of their contribution was that, based on the data, no sufficient empirical evidence could be found for verifying the assumption that less corrupt governments do receive more international aid.[445] The results show no negative correlation could be found between the two variables. This means, contrary to what many analysts think, the flows of foreign aid are independent from the incidence of corruption in any specific country. Moreover, countries with poor levels of governance and thus great

---

440 Ibid.

441 Goldfarb, "Who gets CIDA Grants? Recipient Corruption and the Effectiveness of Development Aid", p. 5.

442 Ibid.

443 Alesina, Alberto and Beatrice Weder. "Do Corrupt Governments Receive Less Foreign Aid?" Working Paper 7108. National Bureau of Economic Research. (May 1999.)

444 *Ibid.* The data was obtained from the International Country Risk Guide (ICRG), the 1997 World Development Report, Standard and Poors, Business International and TI's Corruption Perception Index.

445 Ibid.

propensity to corruption, have obtained equal amounts of aid from the international donor community to countries with positive governance indicators.[446]

Although these results might be disappointing at first, Alesina and Weder were able to make two interesting findings in their regressions. First, if foreign aid is scaled by the size of the public sector of the recipient country, corrupt governments seem to receive greater amounts of foreign aid.[447] This means that the bigger the country, the more extensive the amount of foreign aid, regardless of the level of corruption the country might present thus making the relation between these two variables seem even more questionable, as different measurements lead to opposite results. Second, the authors took a closer look at the different donors and recipients according to their geographical location. Accordingly, Scandinavian countries seem to give more to less corrupt governments while the United States neglects to support non-democratic regimes, but does not pay attention to the quality of government (in terms of corruption levels) of the supported democracies.[448] This tendency becomes plausible when historical factors are included in the analysis. It has been known, that countries with a colonial past are given special attention from their former administrators, as Teggemann explains "being a non-democratic colony attracted twice as much as aid as being a democratic non-colony."[449] In this context, development aid is based on a wide range of factors that go beyond the scope of corruption and its possible damaging effects.

Nevertheless, it is important to know that this traditional posture has changed. Due to the fact that the effects of corruption have been more visible than in the past – not only in individual countries, but also on the delivery and effectiveness of international development funds – the donor community is in need of quickly implementing mechanisms for the eradication of this problem. Development aid is not only a problem of economics. It is also a political issue. And, moreover, it is an issue of international relations. In this regard, it becomes clear why the community of states, especially the developing countries, is giving corruption a constantly growing importance in their agendas. As this phenomenon grows, it will probably have a greater impact on the decision-making processes about foreign development

---

446 Teggemann, "Corruption and Development Assistance." According to the author, this point can be explained by the different strategic interests donors have towards aid recipients.

447 Alesina and Weder. "Do Corrupt Governments Receive Less Foreign Aid?"

448 Ibid.

449 Teggemann, "Corruption and Development Assistance."

assistance than ever before thus compromising the position of developing, under developed and least developed nations on the international arena.

This chapter has summarized some of the most important aspects of the international corruption regime. The question at the beginning of the argumentation was if there could be such a regime, a so called *pax corrupta*, and if so, how it would look like. The subtopics discussed above show clearly how corruption has adopted the characteristics of an international regime of its own in four basic areas. Although there are many other forms for this phenomenon, it was pivotal for the following analytical steps of this book, to document the main manifestation corruption takes on a global scale. First, the links to transnational organized crime showed primarily how corruption has been "privatized" in terms of actors, and how it brings about damages, which go beyond borders and cross through entire regions. Second, the scourge of money laundering denoted the mechanisms through which corruption operates internationally, creating a legal *vacuum* and "commercializing" the sovereignty of those states, which become involved in such illicit activities. Third, the dangers corruption entails in terms of being a hindrance to development could be observed with the help of economic indicators and their interpretation. It became quite clear, how corruption acts as a corrosive on development and how, in recent years, it has engendered problems on all levels of society, economics and politics, even leading to complete government breakdowns, as in the case of many developing countries. And lastly, this chapter reviewed one of the latest findings about the internationality of corruption, namely the distorting effects it can have at the decision-making processes on delivery of development assistance. What many nations have considered as normal business in the past is now currently changing. Although there was not sufficient evidence to prove that less corrupt countries receive less foreign aid, the literature states that the international donor community is creating more mechanisms to monitor the destination of official development assistance.

These four areas denote a clear map of the international scope of corruption. At the same time, these features constitute the last piece in the theoretical framework proposed in this book. After a comprehensive evaluation and discussion on the definition, causes, effects and international perspectives of corruption, the analysis will move on to its second main part, namely the steps and measures that have been undertaken to directly address this problem.

CHAPTER FIVE

PUBLIC SECTOR REFORM

> "To its admirers in the late nineteenth and early twentieth centuries, bureaucracy offered the possibility of rationalized governance by apolitical specialists according to scientific principles, neutral rules, and fair procedures, the very antithesis of the abhorrent spoils system [...] Therefore, the occurrence of a corruption scandal meant that bureaucracy was not yet functioning properly and needed to be fine-tuned."[450]

After the theoretical framework of this book was developed in the first section, it is time to turn the focus on to the empirical aspects related to corruption. The plan of the book presented in the introduction foresaw the need for a combination of theoretical and empirical elements in order to solve the puzzle and either confirm or falsify the hypotheses. Therefore, this second section will explore four key areas in which the efforts and initiatives to eradicate corruption become the subject of analysis. Special emphasis will be given to the different areas that have developed tools and proposals for combating corruption. The leading questions are: what has been done to cope with corruption thus far? Which methods have proven to be successful? And what are the problems ahead?

There are four key areas in which the actions against corruption have concentrated in the last years. First, the traditional view of corruption as a problem of government agencies has led to a remarkable debate on how to reform the public sector.[451] Many agree to observe that tackling political corruption depends on successful structural changes within the government system. The new trend is referred to as "new public management" and seeks to transform the obsolete public apparatus into a more market-oriented model of government.[452]

---

[450] Anechiarico, Frank and James B. Jacobs. The Pursuit of Absolute Integrity. How Corruption Control Makes Government Ineffective. (Chicago and London: The University of Chicago Press, 1996.)

[451] Rose-Ackerman. Corruption and Government, p. 198 ff.

[452] Larbi, George A. "The New Public Management Approach and Crisis States" Occasional Paper No. 112. (Geneva: United Nations Research Institute for Social Development, September 1999.)

The second main area refers to the work of non-governmental organizations in the national and international fight against corruption. The most prominent example is the Berlin-based network from Transparency International. Not only has TI been able to project corruption and its detrimental effects onto the agendas of the international community in a very broad and comprehensive manner. Moreover, this organization has developed the most used tools for the analysis of corruption worldwide. TI's Corruption Perception Index (CPI) and Bribes Payers Index (BPI) has become a general benchmark for locating countries that are more affected by corruption than others. In addition, the work of the national chapters in terms of creating local and regional awareness of the dangers of corruption is a special feature in the work of TI.

Third, the role of the media should be addressed. It has been said lately, that the media is a powerful tool for preventing corruption.[453] The reason is that corruption scandals usually generate a considerable amount of media coverage. At the same time, the media has assumed the role of a 'watchdog' when it comes to the abuse of public or private authority for illicit purposes.[454] Assessing the recent effects of a functioning media on the political, economic and social landscape will portrait how non-governmental, independent actors influence the incidence of corruption. In this manner, we seek to provide an explanation to the causal relationship between a free press and the levels of corruption.

Lastly, this section will focus on the latest international efforts to combat corruption. Chapter Four portrayed the different areas in which corruption has become an international regime with its own rules and its own participants. However, it was also noted that, in the same fashion, the internationality of the problem demands international solutions. Therefore, this section ends with an introduction to the specific work of international organizations such as the UN and the World Bank on corruption. In this context, the effectiveness of international mechanisms against this phenomenon will be discussed focusing on the question on international law as an effective mechanism to fight, prevent and effectively eradicate the scourge of corrupt networks on a global level.

THE TRADITIONAL ROLE OF THE PUBLIC SECTOR

453 Brunetti and Weder. "A Free Press Is Bad News for Corruption", p. 1802 ff.

454 Utriainen, Terttu. "The Role of the Media in Preventing Corruption." Working Paper for the 8th International Anti-Corruption Conference. (Lima, 1997.)

The remark made by political scientists Frank Anechiarico and James B. Jacobs at the beginning of this chapter clearly shows that the bureaucratic model of governance is a key element of the modern nation-state.[455] Moreover, it denoted that the aims of the public administration were to establish a comprehensive system of "checks and balances" in which managerial power would be equally distributed and organized in a just and efficient manner. In order to achieve this goal, modern bureaucracies combined technical knowledge and specialized expertise with a unique set of "culturally determined and transmitted relations between superior and subordinate roles."[456]

The bureaucratic model of public administration was traditionally of great importance for the political functioning of states, especially in the Western Hemisphere.[457] After World War II, the public sector assumed the role of an enormous institution that dominated almost every aspect of the organizational life of each country.[458] This role expanded constantly and in a very similar way in many countries, despite the highly economic, social, political, and ideological diversities between the different public sectors of many states.[459] The more diverse societies became through their development, the more difficult became the tasks for the public administrations.[460]

As a consequence, the state became involved in almost all dimensions of national affairs through activities such as providing most public services and nationalizing private-owned or foreign companies. This involvement was first based on the general perception of governments that the private sector

---

455 Bureaucracy is defined as the "modern administrative organizations – organizations producing goods and services." In: Thompson, Victor A. Bureaucracy and Innovation. (Alabama: University of Alabama Press, 1969), pp. 3 ff.

456 Ibid.

457 One of the fundamental analytical elements for this notion is Max Weber's perception of bureaucracy as a necessary mechanism for the organization of state affairs. See: Weber. Essays in Sociology.

458 Between 1914 and the early 1950s, the amount of public revenue grew from 10 to 24 percent of GDP. At the end of the century, the total has stabilized at 44 percent. In: Boix Carles. "Democracy, Development and the Public Sector." American Journal of Political Science. (January 2001) Vol. 45, No. 1, pp. 1-17.

459 Bangura, Yusuf. "Public Sector Restructuring: The Institutional and Social Effects of Fiscal, Managerial and Capacity-Building Reforms." Occasional Paper No. 3. (Geneva: United Nations Research Institute for Social Development, February 2000.)

460 *Ibid.* The author notes that "[f]or instance, commitments to the welfare state and macro-economic stability in OECD countries encouraged acceptance of the state as central institution for redistributing wealth protecting the vulnerable and stimulating aggregate demand."

was too slow and inefficient to cope with the needs of the population with rapid economic expansion.[461] Since the 1950s, the need for achieving economic and social development was set at the very top of the political agendas in most regions of the planet. Most policy makers believed that the necessary element for achieving development was a strong state apparatus. This gave the public administration a leading role in the development efforts of both industrialized and developing countries. For these reasons, the state became a major institution that would "foster unity or solidarity, promote national development and micro-economic stability, regulate or check foreign domination, protect domestic markets and, in some cases, redistribute wealth."[462]

THE DECAY OF BUREAUCRACY

However these expectations were shattered as bureaucracies rapidly expanded and the scope of the public functions turned somehow blurry. A clear consequence of the overemphasis on the bureaucratic model was that the burden of the state grew inexorably and so did the failures of the government when it came to meeting the demands of the general public. Therefore, the 1970s witnessed a decay of the high expectations and ideals towards the bureaucratic model of administration.[463] Among other characteristics, the main manifestations of this decay were found within the so called "pathologies of bureaucracy" as explained by Anechiarico and Jacobs:[464]

- *decision-making delay,* referring to the classic accusations to the bureaucratic model of being obtrusively slow at making decisions and implementing them;

- *overcentralization*, meaning an excessive use of command and control;

- *inadequate authority,* in terms of government agencies losing the necessary authority to perform their duties;

---

461 Ibid.

462 Ibid.

463 See also: Wilson, James Q. Bureaucracy: What Government Agencies Do and Why They Do It. (New York: Basic Books, 1989); and Crozier, Michel. The Bureaucratic Phenomenon. (Chicago. University of Chicago Press, 1964.)

464 Anechiarico, and Jacobs. The Pursuit of Absolute Integrity, pp. 174 ff.

- *defensive management,* used to describe the rigid posture of bureaucrats on their orders and responsibilities;
- *goal displacement,* caused by the perception of following rules instead of achieving goals;
- *poor morale [of the bureaucrat],* created by the "mechanization" of the daily work load, combined with a low level of wages and remunerations;
- *barriers to interorganizational cooperation,* which takes place in form of a primary isolation of central agencies, leading to a total absence of internal communication, especially when it comes to finding solutions to similar problems; and
- *adaptive strategies,* recalling the efforts of public sector managers to circumvent bureaucracy by attributing tasks and duties to public authorities which would not be a part of the government apparatus.[465]

As observed in Chapter One, the public sector is the classic "first victim" of corruption. The pathologies explained above make even clearer why the state apparatus is more susceptible to the abuse of public office for private gain. Taking a closer look from an organizational and cultural theory point of view, political scientist Christopher Hood recognizes that one of the major weaknesses of the public sector occurs when "those managing or producing a service put their own interests and the interests of their clients or customers second."[466] In this scenario the logical consequences are embezzlement, fraud, and extortion, also known as the main typologies of corruption.

Therefore, the institutional weaknesses of the bureaucratic model and the decay of the public administration avert the need for a consequent reform of the public sector, in order to eliminate, or at least prevent illicit activities within government rows. Although authors such as Anechiarico and Jacobs assume that a comprehensive public sector reform seems to further complicate the diagnostic of a corrupt administration, this approach seems to

---

465 Some of these elements are analyzed in depth in: Crozier. The Bureaucratic Phenomenon, pp. 187 ff.

466 Hood, Christopher. The Art of the State. Culture, Rhetoric and Public Management. (Oxford: Oxford University Press, 1998), pp. 29 ff.

be the first classic solution that scholars look at, when searching for solutions for this problem.

SETTINGS AND PRESSURES FOR PUBLIC SECTOR REFORM

In order to understand why reform is an important element of any anti-corruption strategy, a proper evaluation of this approach is needed. From a simple standpoint, the steady aim of public reforms is to match the government's functions with the needs of its citizens. As stated by the OECD, "people want a government that does more and costs less."[467] In terms of corruption, public reforms should diminish both the propensity of corruption in the public administration as well as its damage on the population.

Public sector reforms are subject to many factors, both internal and external. At the very top, the political leadership can be the sole starting point of any reform endeavors. Strong leaders often identify themselves reform agendas in order to bring out their ideas to the public and strengthen the trust they have obtained from the population.[468] Nowadays, there is hardly any national government program that does not include efforts to change the structures of bureaucracy in order to make them easier and more transparent. However, any initiative of change within modern organizations requires certain preliminary considerations for its further development. The classic reason, as stated by political scientist Victor Thompson, is that

> "[i]n an organizational context dominated by the need to control [e.g. bureaucracies], innovation is dangerous because, by definition, it is not controlled behavior. It creates risks of errors and therefore of sanctions." [469]

In this context, Rose-Ackerman rightly points out that reform processes within any bureaucracy system are often attached to structural conditions within the political spheres. Reforms are seen as difficult and long lasting processes not just single isolated acts. Therefore, structural, mostly political

[467] OECD. "Government of the Future." OECD Public Management Policy Brief. (June 2001.)

[468] As Rose-Ackerman notes, 2[r]eforms sometimes occur simply because a charismatic and committed leader pushes them through. Strong leaders can inspire people to accept major reforms that lesser personalities could never achieve." In: Rose-Ackerman. Corruption and Government, p. 198.

[469] Thompson, Victor A. Modern Organization. A General Theory. (New York: Alfred A. Knopf, 1969), p. 163.

conditions can be decisive on the fate of any reform strategy in the public sector.

Rose-Ackerman considers five key elements that build the necessary conditions for domestic reform.[470] *First,* the willingness to reform needs to be widely accepted by the different political groupings in – and beyond – the government. Democracies must be able to gain wide support from the different sectors of politics and society and establish a broad consensus, which would even satisfy the opposition.[471] In authoritarian regimes, reforms could be brought up by leaders who seek to either gain absolute control over the bureaucracy (even if for private purposes) or pursue a specific form of legitimating their power.[472] Both patterns must include solid reform initiatives in order to be effective. If the political cohesion is not entirely given, reform approaches will be most likely vaguely implemented or, after some time, completely discarded.[473]

Second, pressures caused by political scandals and economic crises are often considered as "catalysts" for choosing the path of reform.[474] In many countries, the very fact of the disclosure of political misbehavior can move the leadership towards implementing reforms as a means to present an immediate reaction (yet not always a solution) to this problem.[475] Additionally, deep economic crises usually tend to raise the demand for rapid changes within the administration. As Rose-Ackerman notes, "during quiet, stable periods, when reform could be thoughtfully implemented, political support is lacking."[476] Although crises might end up in the total

---

[470] Rose-Ackerman. Corruption and Government, p. 198 ff.

[471] Rose-Ackerman argues that, for example, stable coalitions could bring in an acceptable degree of political stability within which reforms could be achieved. In: *Ibid.*, p. 199 ff.

[472] Ibid.

[473] Ibid.

[474] Ibid.

[475] *Ibid.* The case of Mexico presents a good example for this point. In the past decade, the increasing awareness on political corruption has led to major changes within the structure of government. Disclosures on corrupt activities during the administration of President Carlos Salinas de Gortari severely affected the image of Mexico's most influential party, the Party of the Institutionalized Revolution (PRI). For the first time, corruption related scandals fueled the electorate's disapproval with the government, leading to a first parliamentary defeat in 1997, in which the PRI lost its traditional majority in Congress, followed by the loss of the executive only three years later, when Vicente Fox was elected as the first non-PRI President since1929. These political changes have facilitated the implementation of initiatives for institutional checks on normal bureaucrats as well as high-level officials. In: Morris, Stephen. "Corruption and the Mexican political system: continuity and change." Third World Quarterly (1999) Vol. 20, No. 3, pp. 623-643.

[476] Rose-Ackermann. Corruption and Government, p. 209.

dismantlement of the government, in some instances, the pressures they create have been recognized by political leaders as opportunities for new measures and improvements.[477]

Third, natural resources and foreign aid influence the propensity of a government to pursue a reform of the public sector. On the former, Rose-Ackerman observes that in countries such as Venezuela, Nigeria or Indonesia, where natural resources are the main determinants of the national economy, public sector reform approaches do not have the desired impact. The reason is that basically, all businesses involved in the exploitation of these resources care much more about constantly making profit, rather than having an effective public sector.[478] Moreover, in such cases, the private sector does not offer profitable alternatives for bureaucrats other than engaging in the major national industry.[479]

Previously, in Section I, the role of foreign aid for reducing corruption was approached. The results of the latest empirical studies showed, that increasing the amount of foreign aid will not necessarily lead to less corruption in the public sector.[480] In a similar manner, Rose-Ackerman points out, that foreign aid, if not attached to a conditionality program, might postpone reform initiatives because governments might simply avoid such measures after receiving considerable amounts of development aid, due to the overflow of resources.[481] In such cases, all efforts are directed to secure as much ODA amounts as possible, instead of pursuing a re-structuring of the political institutions for a fair distribution of the obtained funds.[482]

The *fourth* aspect behind public sector reform according to Rose-Ackerman is the existing demand for new strategies for public office.

---

477 According to the World Bank, the vast majority of developing countries undertook reforms in the public sector as a response to adverse economic conditions. Institutional weaknesses, public deficits, high inflation rates and insufficient delivery of consumer goods fueled the impetus towards reform in most African, Latin American and Asian countries. In: Larbi. "The New Public Management Approach and Crisis States", pp. 6 ff.

478 Rose-Ackerman. Corruption and Government, p. 213. As the author explains, "[m]ineral-rich countries with few other sources of foreign exchange may be unlikely reformers both because the state can finance itself through its royalties [...]"

479 Ibid.

480 Goldfarb, "Who gets CIDA Grants? Recipient Corruption and the Effectiveness of Development Aid."

481 Rose-Ackerman. Corruption and Government, p. 214.

482 In most cases, the funds provided as official development assistance (ODA) are distributed and managed by public officers with low incomes, which can foster their inadequate use. In: Tavares, José. "Does Foreign Aid Corrupt?" Economic Letters (2003), No. (79), pp. 99-106. On the macroeconomic impact of foreign aid and the persistence of rent-seeking practices see also: Svensson, Jakob. "Foreign Aid and Rent-Seeking." Journal of International Economics (2000), Vol 51, pp. 437-461.

Whenever the organizational structure of a country becomes obsolete, the need for change automatically gains momentum. Although the issue of change – as observed by authors such as Thomson and Michel Crozier – is a highly difficult aspect within most bureaucratic organizations, when the performance of public duties and therein the delivery of public services begin to decay, innovative initiatives are mostly welcomed.[483] Additionally, the size and composition of the public sector might be a crucial factor for the demand of reform strategies:

> "[t]he best case for reform occurs when government employment is large in absolute numbers but a small share of the labor force. If most jobs are in the private sector, citizens, in general, will care more about whether the mail is delivered expeditiously, roads are built and maintained, and schools and hospitals function, rather than whether jobs within government are available."[484]

In this context, the inefficiencies of the public sector, combined with the solid position of the private sector (at least in terms of the working population) create the adequate conditions for implementing changes within the public administration. The main rationale behind this point is, as explained by Rose-Ackerman, that private businesses are eventually in favor of reforms which would endow more profit for them on the one side, while on the other side, public officers would tolerate cut backs if the opportunities for re-employment in the private sector remain high.[485]

The *fifth* and last condition for domestic reform deals with the long-term sustainability of innovative approaches. As explained above, political structures need cohesion, in order to accept reform packages. Within these structures, even opposing parties should be, if not entirely convinced by the reforms, at least "comfortable" with them. Here, Rose-Ackerman speaks about "compensating opponents for the losses they would otherwise

---

[483] Crozier notes that dysfunctions in a bureaucracy make it necessary to "resort to an innovator." In: Crozier. The Bureaucratic Phenomenon, pp. 202 ff.

[484] Rose-Ackerman. Corruption and Government, p. 216. The authors notes that in the case of the United States, the federal civil service reform in the 1970 was successful because of the relatively small size of the public sectors, as she observes, "[p]ublic employees were not a potent pressure groups, and the public generally supported reform.

[485] Ibid.

suffer."[486] In terms of corruption, this means, that reformers should not only encourage public officers to refrain from becoming involved in illicit activities. Public reforms include anti-corruption policies that target corrupt officers, who will most probably be dismissed, while others may just be deterred. The dismissal of the most corrupt elements is the logical first step. However, incentives given to honest bureaucrats become the basis for establishing effective public sector reform programs on the long run.[487] It is important for the long-term success of such policies, that the remaining public employees give reformers the necessary support for the entire initiative to succeed. This can only happen if changes within the public sector offer incentives and assistance to those who need to adapt to the new patterns of governability.[488]

Rose-Ackerman rightly points out that this form of "civil service protection" is an important pillar for maintaining the new system, since compensated and awarded public officers will most likely want to keep the new system working.[489] In this regard, the sustainability of public sector reforms depends directly on the ability of the government to keep civil servants "on track" and reassure them, that they will be the prime beneficiaries of the reform package.[490] The political leadership plays an important role as they are the key for "bridging the gap between the development and the implementations of reform.[491]

Rose-Ackerman's five conditions should enable to create an environment in which public sector reforms are thoughtfully planned, carefully developed and successfully implemented. Of course the list could be expanded and other elements might catch the attention of the scholarship in order to prove this

[486] *Ibid.*, p. 219.

[487] The OECD refers to this point as "changing organizational culture." This means, that governments should build incentives so that civil servants can be rewarded for complying with the objectives of reform strategies. Important elements include communicating expectations, accentuating the positive aspects of reform, building leadership for change, rewarding change and creating opportunities by offering employees the adequate training on the objectives of the reform package. In: OECD. "Government of the Future."

[488] Rose-Ackerman. Corruption and Government, p. 220.

[489] *Ibid.* Nevertheless, at the same time, the author stresses with caution, that employees can also undermine other projects of reform that might not suit their interests.

[490] For example, during the Clinton administration, US Vice President Al Gore established the "National Partnership for Reinventing Government" (NPR) in which teams of federal employees were awarded for creating innovative and effective processes or programs to make bureaucracy work better. The initiative was welcomed by civil servants and over 1,200 awards were presented. In: OECD. "Government of the Future."

[491] Ibid.

point.[492] Nevertheless, the author has provided us with valid starting considerations for evaluating the different efforts to reform the public sector for combating corruption. The case studies in Section III will illustrate Rose-Ackerman's views and will enable us to rather confirm the findings of the author or question their validity.

Reform from the Inside: Classic and New Approaches

After having established the initial patterns of public sector reform and their relation to the incidence of corruption, the question now turns from *how* to reform onto *what* to reform in the public sector in order to combat this problem. This turn will be approached on two levels. In general we should first ask: what kind of changes should be included in any comprehensive reform approach? Is it merely structural change, or does it include normative/cultural elements? Moreover, from a social scientific perspective, it becomes important to locate reforms in terms of visible and – up to some point – measurable results. How can we determine the success or failure of reforms programs? Secondly, we need to think about measures as mechanisms to cope with corruption within the public sector. Are reforms the only way to tackle down this problem? Do successfully undertaken reforms reduce corruption or can failures make it more likely to occur?

The "pathologies of bureaucracy", as explained above, showed that the evolving problem of the public sector during the 1960s and 1970s was based on the size and the functioning of its structures. In the past two decades, the main approaches towards public sector reform tried to specifically target these two aspects. Therefore, the main directives of the new models of state reform covered four policy goals namely fiscal stability, managerial efficiency, capacity building and public accountability.[493]

---

[492] Recent studies on public spending show further trends for the effectiveness of the public reform approach. For instance, the causality between the degree of decentralization, meaning the "total expenditure of subnational (state and local) governments over total spending by all levels (state, local and central) of government" and the incidence of corruption has proven to be negative. Such a conclusion favours the argument that public sector changes might be the effective tool to diminish public corruption. In: Fisman, Raymond and Roberta Gatti. "Decentralization and corruption: evidence across countries." Journal of Public Economics (2002), Vol. 83, pp. 325-345.

[493] Bangura. "Public Sector Restructuring", p. 7

Reactivating Fiscal Stability

As political scientist Carles Boix explained earlier, public sectors worldwide grew immensely during the first half of the 20th century as a consequence of economic modernization. However this growth did not necessarily mean that governments were able to meet the demands of the population in a better way. Therefore, when it came to the first policy goal of state reform, namely regaining fiscal stability, the goal was to directly address problems such as over-centralized decision-making, inappropriate incentives of public enterprises and economic failures.[494] The necessary measures included reforms on the size and structure of public expenditure, the privatization of many state sectors, and a comprehensive tax reform.[495]

One aspect of sinking public expenditure is downsizing personnel. This has had positive as well as negative effects. Cost reductions in this area can lead to better economic balances. However it might carry out political and social costs. As stated by UNDP,

> "[c]ost containment is an important aspect of civil service reform. But there are other equally important aspects. An efficient and motivated civil service is critical for governance, production and distribution of public goods. The broader aim of civil service reform is, therefore, the creation of a government workforce of the size and with the skills, incentives, ethos, and accountability needed to provide quality public services and carry out the functions assigned to the state." [496]

Through severance pays and early retirement schemes, downsizing could be undertaken with positive prospects, but general risks such as staff demoralizations, lower quality service and loss of credibility are always present.[497]

Moreover, public expenditure can also be diminished by implementing successful privatization programs. Privatization denotes a governmental measure to reallocate state assets from the public into the private sector. According to political scientist Yusuf Bangura, the effects of privatizations

494 United Nations Development Programme (UNDP). "Public Sector Downsizing. Early Retirement Schemes and Voluntary Severance Pay." (Beirut: 1999.)

495 Bangura. "Public Sector Restructuring", p. 8 ff.

496 UNDP. "Public Sector Downsizing."

497 *Ibid.* See also Bangura. "Public Sector Restructuring", p. 10 ff.

on the public sector are twofold.[498] First, fiscal expenditures can benefit from withdrawing subsidies to loss-making companies and from applying a rigid budgetary policy on national and local levels. And second, selling state companies will bring revenues to the public treasury in order to close fiscal gaps. Experience has shown however, that privatization is a risky enterprise and does not necessarily bring the desired results, if it is not undertaken under adequate terms and conditions.[499]

Privatization introduces market mechanisms between direct and indirect providers and users. Therefore, the framework of such steps is at the same time the main factor for both success and failure. Many experts conclude that although privatization might be a good way of reforming the public sector, it might become an obstacle towards economic and political problems.[500] One of the biggest impediments for adequate privatization efforts is, without a doubt, the incidence of corruption. In this regard, economists Nancy Birdsall and John Nellis assert to conclude, that

> "[p]rivatization has not been a popular reform. Economic assessments of the effects of privatization on economic welfare and growth in developing and transitional economies have generally been positive. But evidence of political chicanery and corruption, [...] fiscal mismanagement, [...] escalating prices [...] and lost jobs in a great many countries, has sullied its reputation even among proponents of the liberalizing reforms of the last two decades."[501]

Lastly, a comprehensive tax reform is the key to every attempt to achieve, or in some cases, reactivate fiscal stability. Taxes represent one of the biggest sources of revenue for some states. Usually, taxes are covered by laws that do not require the specific contact between tax payers and tax

---

498 Ibid.

499 In fact, the proneness to corruption in many countries has diminished the desired success of privatization measures. A recent example can be found in transition economies, which implements such measures after the decay of Soviet Communism See: Kaufmann, Daniel and Paul Siegelbaum. "Privatization and Corruption in Transition Economies" Journal of International Affairs (1996) Vol. 50, No. 2, pp. 419-58.

500 A good review of recent findings on the pros and cons of privatization can be found in:

501 Birdsall, Nancy and John Nellis. "Winners and Losers: Assessing the Distributional Impact of Privatization." Working Paper No 6. (Washington DC: Center for Global Development, May 2002.)

collectors.[502] However, Tanzi was right in pointing out previously, that taxation and custom administration systems build a perfect scenario for the spread of corruption. Endemic practices such as acts of corruption on the side of the tax administrators which remain unnotified and thus are neither discovered nor penalized make a tax reform much needed.[503] Tax payers are equally involved in this process, whenever they do not declare taxes and keep resources for themselves. Many cases even include joint-networks in which both tax administrator and tax payer benefit from dubious declarations and mutual fraud.[504] Approaches towards better taxation include transparency of taxation laws, as well a better mechanisms to monitor and control tax administrations.[505]

Managerial Efficiency: Old Public Administration vs. New Public Management

Any approach on reforming the public sector must and has included the term "efficiency" within its provisions. The goal is to make government work better for the citizens. Therefore, management reforms aim towards "deliberate changes to the structures and processes of public organizations with the objective of getting them to run better."[506]

The main debate in this area is between those who favor traditional forms of public administration and those who push for new managerial-like concepts of the state. The former is referred to as "Old Public Administration" where ministries, sections, and departments have an established hierarchical order and there is a system of top-bottom supervision.[507] The latter is an approach known as "New Public Management" (NPM) and it is a direct response to the failures of the traditional "command and control" concept of public administration with its

---

[502] Tanzi, "Corruption Around the World. Causes, Consequences, Scope and Cures", p. 567.

[503] *Ibid.* The author explains that in some cases, corruption within tax offices was so bad, governments started to replace entire departments by closing them down and hiring new personnel.

[504] This is particularly the case in local governments that allocate resources to smaller municipalities and sectional administrations. In such instances, taxes can be avoided due to informal reciprocally accepted agreements of non-compliance with official tax laws..

[505] For example, one of the latest trends in modernizing government is the concept of E-Government. The main idea is to enhance the communication between public offices and the citizens though the latest advancement of information technology. In this context, a possible scenario would be that citizens can make their tax declarations online by using a standard computerized system. In this way, the personal contact with any possible corrupt element would be drastically diminished.

[506] Pollit, Christopher and Geert Bouckaert. Public Management Reform. A Comparative Analysis. (Oxford: Oxford University Press, 2000), p. 8.

[507] Bangura. "Public Sector Restructuring", p. 22.

strong internal values of public interest and public accountability.[508] Both the failure of bureaucracy and the imminent spread of corruption led to the development of market oriented approaches for enhancing public governance.

NPM contains a set of doctrines which dominated the public agendas of most western countries in the 1970s. The central feature of NPM was the attempt to introduce market incentives and discipline models within the yet non-privatized sectors of the public administration.[509] Thus the main idea was to expose the public sector to market activities and to gain benefits in terms of efficiency and effectiveness. In the political practice, the approach is based on four key assumptions, postulated by public policy expert Martin Minogue: 1) the public interest state has failed and there is a strong need to replace it with private market mechanisms; 2) the efficiency of the public sector relies on a separation of "policy" from "execution"; 3) government performance will be better enhanced by an entrepreneurial culture based on managerial incentives than by a public service culture oriented towards the public interest; 4) the relationship between "managers" and "customers" is more accountable than the relationships in classic legal and political frames.[510]

The first countries that started to have success stories with NPM were Australia, New Zealand, United Kingdom, and the United States, among other developed economies.[511] Most recently, many countries in developing regions such as Africa, Asia, Latin America as well in transition economies in Eastern Europe have embraced NPM approaches, mostly to cope with the challenges of the globalized economy of the post Cold War era.

Although NPM has turned into a wide-spread model, it is still an approach with many ramifications and disputed opinions. While many traditionalists perceive the hierarchical model of bureaucracy as adequate for controlling all sectors of government, several pressures have emerged from political, economic and even social sides towards adopting more efficient and

---

508 Minogue, Martin. "Getting the Ideas Right: Public Management, Corruption and Development." Paper presented at the Workshop: "New Public Management: Challenges for Improved Accountability and Corruption Control. World Bank Annual European Conference on Development Economics (Oslo, June 2002.) Available online at <http://www.worldbank.org> (10.11.2003.)

509 Larbi. "The New Public Management Approach and Crisis States", pp. 2 ff.

510 Minogue. "Getting the Ideas Right: Public Management, Corruption and Development."

511 Some authors speak about a special kind of managerial revolution which started in these countries during the late 1970s and early 1980s. In: Minogue, Martin Charles Polidano and David Hulme (eds.) Beyond the New Public Management. Changing Ideas and Practices in Governance. (Cheltenham: Edward Elgar Publishing, 1998), p. xv. The case of New Zealand has been appointed as a classic example of this trend. An overview can be found in: Evans Lewis, Arthur Grimes, Bryce Wilkinson and David Teece. "Economic Reform in New Zealand 1984-95: The Pursuit of Efficiency." Journal of Economic Literature (December 1996) Vol. 34, No. 4, pp. 1856-1902.

flexible methods of public management.[512] The disparity between these two approaches is portrayed in ten basic points made in the early 1990s by political scientists David Osborne and Ted A. Gaebler:

1. Steer the ship, rather than row it.
2. Empower communities, rather than simply deliver services.
3. Encourage competition rather than monopoly.
4. Be mission driven rather than rule driven.
5. Fund outcomes rather than inputs.
6. Meet the needs of customers rather than the bureaucracy.
7. Concentrate on earning sources, not just spending.
8. Invest in prevention pf problems rather than cure.
9. Decentralize authority.
10. Solve problems by making use of the marketplace rather than by creating public programmes.[513]

The key elements of NPM include management decentralization, downsizing, performance contracting, contracting out, and the introduction of user fees.[514] These aspects are interrelated with each other and can be applied in several ways.

For example, decentralization refers to the efforts towards increasing managerial autonomy within public agencies by allowing them to operate more independently and drift away from traditional bureaucratic-hierarchical patterns.[515] Thereafter, re-structuring hierarchies and downsizing would reduce operational and personnel costs. Furthermore, NPM models include a separation between production costs for public services and their actual provision. This should help to have a clearer picture of which services have been purchased and what has been offered to the citizens.[516]

---

512 See for instance: Batley, Richard. "The Role of Government in Adjusting Economies 1994-1999 – An Overview of Findings." Research Programme at the International Development Department. University of Birmingham. Available online at <www.idd.bham.ac.uk/research> (04.11.2003.)

513 Osborne, David and Ted A. Gaebler. Reinventing Government: How the Entrepreneurial Spirit Is Transforming the Public Sector. (Reading, MA: Addison Wesley, 1992.) Quoted in: Minogue, Martin, "Changing the state: concepts and practices in the reform of the public sector." In: Minogue, Polidano and Hulme (eds). Beyond the New Public Management, p. 18.

514 Larbi. "The New Public Management Approach and Crisis States", pp. 17 ff.

515 *Ibid.* The approach also foresees "devolving" budgets to decentralized units and giving them control over their own finances.

516 *Ibid.*, p. 19.

Performance contracting, meaning to have legal agreements between the government and its service providers, is a further important feature of NPM.[517] According to the literature, such practices are aimed at improving both productivity and thus the delivery of public services. Performance contracts would create transparency within the bureaucracy as the relationship between governments and service providers would monitored from a closer angle. An additional feature in this approach is the use of contracts with private counterparts which will serve at the delivery of services. In the same fashion, contracting-out is based on a contract, however the involvement of non-state actors adds in the marketing feature. The goal is to create an environment in which there is a competitive supply side enabling the government to have a broader choice for the delivery of public services.[518] Bangura notes, that "contracting-out is often regarded as the most form of marketization in managerial reforms."[519]

The last point explained by Larbi and Bangura deals with the introduction of so called user fees or charges. It deals with the charges that are made to the user for his/her consumption of public utilities. According to the authors, such fees were traditionally minimal, and in some cases, governments guaranteed total subsidies for services such as public education and public health.[520] However, during the last ten years, governments have increasingly modified this policy and have implemented charging policies in order to re-vitalize some sectors of the economy.[521] The literature on NPM agrees that user charges aim at creating financial diversity and reshaping public spending. Lastly, fees should enable an improvement in the quality and services and make the user more cost-conscious by acquiring only those services which are really needed.[522]

---

517 Bangura. "Public Sector Restructuring", p. 29. The author defines this term as "a written agreement between government and public managers [...] in which quantifiable targets are specified and performance is measured against targets at the end of the period." Highlighted also on Larbi. "The New Public Management Approach and Crisis States."

518 Bangura. "Public Sector Restructuring", p. 30.

519 *Ibid.* The author further notes that contracting-out can take several forms and can be undertaken in most sectors of the government, be that health, education, construction and even security.

520 Larbi. "The New Public Management Approach and Crisis States", p. 31

521 The recent health sector reform in Germany provides a good example. Starting 2004 and for the first time in the history of the country, patients must pay a fee to attend any medical appointment. The main idea behind it is to use those funds to sustain the *marode* health system in the country by creating new revenues.

522 Larbi. "The New Public Management Approach and Crisis States", p. 31. For instance, the author describes, that "[w]here financial management and control are decentralized, the retention of user fees

Although NPM has proven to be the trendiest approach when reforming the public sector and it has been awarded in some cases as positive, there has been enough evidence that NPM has brought along institutional constraints, especially in developing countries.[523]

The critique has been made from different points of view and with different explanations for the fallacies found within this approach. Most of the problems in applying this model to developing countries are institutional weaknesses and incompatibilities.[524]

Minogue summarized the main critique to NPM by observing the following aspects. First, it seems to be that the market has become a severely flawed alternative to the state. Second, transaction costs have been greater than the revenues obtained from any cost savings. Third, the obtained autonomy in most public agencies has led to a blur – if not yet to the disappearance – of accountability thus creating more risks for policy errors and delivery failures. Fourth, public offices have been engaged in more conflicts (most of them of interest) than on collaboration after the introduction of competition mechanisms. Fifth, public servants have been rather demoralized in this scenario. And lastly, services, in some cases, have become worse than better after NPM.[525]

Furthermore Larbi observes that in many aspects, NPM provided short-term solutions such as cost and expenditure reduction, but ultimately undermined the capacity of the state in a long-term perspective.[526] In this regard, the author notes, that there are some concerns of a "destabilizing" effect of NPM programs on traditional bureaucratic processes, making some processes unmanageable after a sudden change in the chain of command.[527] Similar to Minogue, Larbi concludes, that there have been some complaints related to the loss of public and traditional channels of local

by hospitals will reduce dependence on the central ministry of health and this in turn will enhance managerial autonomy."

523 See for a comprehensive review of the critique Minogue, Martin. "Public Management and Regulatory Governance: Problems of Policy Transfer in Developing Countries." Working Paper No. 32 Centre on Regulation and Competition (Mancherster. December 2002.)

524 Latin America provides good example of the recent problems and failures of NPM in developing nations. Especially on the economic side, structural adjustment measures such as downsizing and privatization, which are part of the NPM approach, have proven to be rather negative on the economies in the region. Moreover the prevailing political instability in many states creates great obstacles for the implementation of new public management models. In: Latin American Centre for Development Administration (CLAD.) A New Public Management for Latin America. (October 1998.) Available online at < http://www.clad.org.ve/> (13.11.2003.)

525 All these points in Minogue. "Public Management and Regulatory Governance", p. 9.

526 Larbi. "The New Public Management Approach and Crisis States", pp. 33 ff.

527 Ibid.

accountability after many agencies are privatized or even closed as a result of NPM policies.[528]

Summarizing the disparity between old administrative models and recent approaches such as NPM, it can be said that the discussion is still far from being settled. It is true on the one side that obsolete bureaucracies need to reshape their structures, especially when it comes down to combating corrupt practices therein. In this regard, NPM initiatives seem to provide an adequate platform for diminishing the risks and the proneness to corruption. However, the implementation of such model also creates new situations, in which pure management and marketing oriented schemes could turn into mechanisms to "cover up" for corruption. Therefore, further elements need to be considered for a comprehensive and effective public sector reform.

Capacity Building

Reform processes not only deal with structural managerial changes. Having skilled and trained personnel to implement and carry on with reforms is of great importance as well. Furthermore, any state undergoing a reform process should also be able to provide the adequate infrastructure in order to apply adjustment policies. Therefore, state capacity, primarily understood as the ability of the government to recruit, train and remunerate its employees, as well as to guarantee the physical means to sustain reform policies, needs to be considered in any attempt to modernize the public service.

Creating and guaranteeing a proper level of state capacity is not an easy enterprise. First of all, most problems arise as soon as there is a comprehensive change within traditional and monolithic bureaucracies. Bangura explains that the success or failure of reform attempts depends on the ability of public officers to adapt to new conditions.[529] This condition can be only achieved if there is a good education and training system to keep public officers and technocrats up to date with the latest innovations, be them technical or political-economic.

Therefore, hiring personnel with solid skills becomes a pivotal, yet difficult task for public agencies. As it was observed earlier, the "misallocation of talent" is a great impediment towards building agencies and offices with properly qualified employees. Due to the rather low wages that

528 Ibid.

529 Bangura explains, that "those who stand to benefit may be weakly organized or not strategically located to defend the reforms; doubts may exist about the commitment of reforming governments; losers may fight back or withdraw support [...]" In: Bangura. "Public Sector Restructuring", pp. 33-34

are offered in most public agencies and because of the "fear" of getting involved in corrupt activities, high potentials tend to go to the private sector instead of working for the government.[530]

In order to avoid this misallocation, many public institutions rely on training facilities, universities and public administration institutes making sure that positions are held by good candidates and that they are trained regularly[531]. However, in this context, capacity building is linked to education and thus becomes a critical issue for reform approaches, especially in developing countries.[532] The main reason is that developing countries face severe problems in areas such as education and training, thus lacking the means to have the technical know-how to implement adjustment programs on their own.[533]

Therefore, when it comes to capacity building, one suggestion could be that funds be directed towards education and training, if reforms should be undertaken by a qualified working force, which can guarantee a certain degree of state capacity. However, the costs of capacity building may become an obstacle, especially in cases in which public agencies may have to re-shape their budgets in order to afford training. These costs may rise especially when training is provided by external parties. Nevertheless, it is important to observe, that in the context of creating effective mechanisms against the incidence of corruption in the public sector, adequate education could be of utmost significance and should be included in any reform initiative. Creating awareness of the problems surrounding corruption within an educational and training approach could become a positive factor for capacity building.

Further aspects of capacity building cover the ability of the government to manage so called "recurrent costs" which deal mostly with maintenance of the basic infrastructure of the country, as well as the provision of adequate remuneration to public servants.[534] These two elements are important as they provide the "physical platform" on which reform policies should be undertaken. Moreover, as we observed in Chapter Two, although high wages do not seem to be the solution against corrupt public officers, an adequate

---

530 Murphy, Schleifer and Vishny. "The Allocation of Talent: Implications for Growth."

531 Bangura. "Public Sector Restructuring", p. 35.

532 Bangura provides a good example from how reforms in Sub-Saharan Africa were uneasy to implement due to capacity problems within public institutions. According to the author, many reform policies in the region did not pay enough attention to education in the higher level thus causing disparities in the shape and pace of reform initiatives, which needed qualified personnel in order to promote and implement them. See *Ibid.*

533 Ibid.

534 *Ibid.*, pp. 35-38.

remuneration system is still a needed element for avoiding the danger of exposing public workers to external pressures.[535]

Public Accountability

The last element that is needed for a comprehensive and solid approach of reform is to guarantee its implementation via mechanisms of public accountability. This means, that reform packages should be "socially accountably and sensitive to political realities."[536] This argument covers four main areas.

First, there needs to be a certain level of political cohesion among all reform participants, in this particular case, between the bureaucracies, the reform entrepreneurs, and the citizens. As adjustment policies have proven to go beyond technocratic changes on to major political turns, it is necessary to build a consensus on the course of action and the main objectives of public sector reforms. With strong political support, reforms will not only be undertaken properly, but moreover, they will have a greater chance to be institutionalized on a long term basis.[537] Beyond the macroeconomic outputs any reforms project might bring to the national economy, it is more important to first guarantee a certain level of governability in order to successfully implement such programs.

Second, public servants must share a common reform-oriented ideology and reach a high level professionalism at the delivery of public services. This will project a positive image to the population in terms of the results of reform projects. A sound and accountable civil service will make reforms easier to adapt on all levels of the administration, and will create a better trust relationship to the "customers", namely the citizens.[538] This point has a special important for the incidence of corruption within public rows. According to Bangura, introducing market-managerial reforms in countries without a well-developed civil service will probably encourage the growth of

535 *Ibid.*, p. 39. On this point, Bangura argues, that "the move from opaque to consolidated systems of remuneration involves calculation of real market values for such benefits as housing, transport, health and education grants and adding them to the nominal wage to arrive at a consolidated package for employees."

536 *Ibid.*, p. 41.

537 *Ibid.* The author explains that elements such as the political legitimization through democratic elections, the protection of civil rights and political liberties, a sound political culture of opposition, as well as the creation of effective public channels in order to monitor and evaluate the action of public servants and the delivery of public services are key elements for creating public accountability.

538 Ibid.

corruption and the appearance of self-interest groups seeking to unequally benefit from such policies.[539] Therefore, similar to capacity building, an accountable and professional civil working class is necessary to both implement reform and reduce the risk of corruption.

Third, when creating favourable conditions for reform, states should bear in mind the goals they want to achieve through structural changes. Especially in the second half of the 20th century, many states started to re-formulate their aspirations, as the conditions of interconnection and communication between states led to the globalization of politics and economics.[540] Moreover, as new states emerged after the last wave of decolonization, developmental goals such as democratization and market economic models started to dominate the agendas of public administrations as a viable doctrine for adapting to the pace of global economic integration. However, when implementing reform projects, some states tend to loose the main idea behind such policies. Therefore, it becomes important for generating public accountability, that states reaffirm their commitment to these objectives. In fact, Bangura rightly notes, that the definition and pursuit of social and developmental goals should enhance the provisions of reform packages. He further warns, that "[t]he failure to pay sufficient attention to these goals [...] may largely explain the high incidence of failed states, civil wars, political violence and stagnant development in large parts of the world today."[541]

Lastly, if reform policies are to last and become institutionalized, the state should generate a series of so called "robust systems of accountability." These are a series of mechanism through which the public can monitor civil servants at the performance of their duties. They include legal means such as "Citizens' Charters" that ensure that the population is properly informed and consulted on the quality and quantity of public services, allowing them to make decisions on these issues.[542] Furthermore, the introduction of Ombudsmen as well as periodical service delivery surveys within public agencies should guarantee a continuous evaluation of the public officers. This feature is particularly interesting for anti-corruption initiatives, since it would monitor processes within the governmental sector and perhaps diminish the incidence of corrupt practices.

Reforms from the outside: The Role of International Institutions

539 Ibid.

540 Held, et. al., Global Transformations. Politics, Economics and Culture.

541 Bangura. "Public Sector Restructuring", p. 45.

542 *Ibid.*, p. 46.

After having reviewed the most important aspects of public sector reform approaches, one last area still deserves our attention, namely the role of international organizations. Beyond the many reform initiatives that are generated within a state, there are many processes and policies that come from the outside. This could be related to the fact that prominent approaches such as NPM were basically elaborated in institutions such as the World Bank and the IMF. This reciprocal relationship leads to the fact that these organizations try to promote public sector reforms as main elements of their overall strategies, especially to developing and recipient nations.[543]

Therefore the following section will approach two main areas through which international organizations have an influence of external nature on the processes of government reforms, namely the promotion of "good governance" with the introduction of conditionality on development assistance on the one side, and the processes of "policy transfer" through which governments adopt public reform initiatives on the other.

Good Governance and Conditionality and Structural Adjustment

International financial institutions have a broad approach and promote public sector reform not only as a means to combat corruption, but also as one basic aspect of "good governance", a term that has shaped the entire discourse on international regimes in the past. The main idea behind this promoting good governance is summarized by World Bank's President James Wolfensohn as follows:

> "[T]he causes of financial crises and poverty are one and the same [...] [if countries] do not have good governance, of they do not confront the issue of corruption, if they do not have a complete legal system which protects human rights, property rights and contracts [...] their development is fundamentally flawed and will not last."[544]

According to public management expert Richard Common, the use of "good governance" by the international donor community denotes a shift in emphasis from economic to political doctrines which influence policy

543 See for instance: The World Bank. Reforming Public Institutions and Strengthening Governance. A World Bank Survey. (Washington, D.C.: Public Sector Group. Poverty Reduction and Economic Management Network, November 2000.)

544 *Ibid.*, p. 1

outcomes.[545] The author notes that for example, since the beginning of the 1980s, the World Bank started to reassess its goals to improve public sector management, institutional capacity and service delivery through introduction of adjustment lending.[546] These policies foresaw the compliance of recipient countries to structural adjustment programs which included neoliberal policies such as decentralization, deregulation, and the introduction of market managerial mechanisms for governance. However the difference was that loans were attached to the compliance of these policies.

This approach, mostly referred to as "conditionality of development assistance", can be interpreted as a means of introducing public sector reforms through external pressures, primarily from international financial lending institutions.[547]

The main goal of conditionality is to create the necessary budget discipline in disadvantaged economies so that they can successfully implement structural adjustment programs. Thus it is quite similar to the reform approaches presented earlier. The only difference is that these programs emerge from outside the state. The question is then: will public sector reform be more successful, if started by international organizations? Will the incidence of corruption in this context be diminished by such forces? As observed in Chapter Four, the issue of development assistance is a very important aspect of most "good governance" policies. And when we touch upon the issue of structural reform programs, lending requirements turn into a crucial factor for the implementation of such policies, especially in developing countries.

In this context, conditionality is related to international agency-state relations.[548] This leads to a definition of aid conditionality as the situation in which extra-state actors such as donor states and international financial

---

545 Common, Richard. "The new public management and policy transfer: the role of international organizations." In: Minogue, Polidano and Hulme (eds.) Beyond the New Public Management, pp. 67 ff.

546 Ibid.

547 Conditionality is not a new phenomenon. One aspect that can be considered as new since the late 1970s is that the conditions prescribing reforms by aid recipients are made open and transparent. Events such as the debt crisis in Latin America and the Caribbean in the 1980s and the intensified globalization processes of the economy after the end of the Cold War, have made the circumstances and the approaches of ODA different and therefore historically split into two major periods. The first generation is related to the original programs of the IMF in the late 1970s until the late 1980s. The second generation started in the early 1990s with the disappearance of the Soviet bloc. In: Stokke, Olav (ed.) Aid and Political Conditionality. (London: Frank Cass Publishers, 1995.)

548 *Ibid.*, p. 11. This does not deny, however, that donor states cannot imply similar requirement when offering bilateral development aid. However, this part of the analysis focuses primarily on the influence that international lending institutions can have on public sector reform.

institutions establish particular conditions which are to be met by the recipient as a requirement for entering into an aid agreement or for keeping up aid.[549] Focusing on the pressures from international financial actors such as the World Bank and the IMF, the key element of this relationship is the leverage these institutions have over recipient states because they can threaten to terminate or reduce aid.[550]

There are different levels at which conditionality can appear. The highest of them is the political intervention in the system of government and its institutions.[551] Other levels include attempts to change national policies and priorities, including specific areas such as taxation and price controls, institutional reforms and official regulations. Moreover, financial and administrative conditions within the country can be altered through conditionality packages.[552]

Different objectives of aid conditionality can be recognized. In the early stages of the ODA regime, the main concerns were to promote economic and social development and the method to achieve this goal was the implementation of comprehensive economic reform. However, the agenda of aid conditionality has widened the range of its objectives in the last decade. The current main discourse is that "good governance" and democracy are not simply desirable but essential conditions for the development in all societies.[553] Therefore, the objectives of aid conditionality have moved from a narrowly economic focused approach to the promotion of political reforms which include democracy, human rights and again, "good governance."

In the context of public sector reforms, political scientist Adrian Leftwich understands achieving "good governance" for any state as having efficient public services, independent judicial systems, accountable administration of public funds, independent public auditory, respect for law human rights at all

---

549 *Ibid.* The author agrees, however, that ODA can be affected through other channels such as non-governmental organizations (NGOs) or the private sector. These actors may set conditions for getting involved in development assistance programs in recipient countries.

550 *Ibid*, p. 12. The author notes, that "[f]oreign aid is used as a lever to promote objectives set by the donor which the recipient government would not otherwise have agreed to. The donor may set the pursuit of such objectives, by the recipient, as a condition for entering into an aid relationship (ex ante conditionality); or expectations of the recipient's progress towards meeting these objectives may be expressed beforehand and followed up afterwards (ex post conditionality)."

551 This includes pressure towards democratic reform, the introduction of a multi-party system with free elections and improved human rights standards.

552 Stokke. Aid and Political Conditionality, p. 14.

553 Leftwich, Adrian. "Governance, Democracy and Development in the Third World." Third World Quarterly (1993), Vol. 14, No. 3, pp. 605-624.

government levels, pluralistic institutional structure and free press.[554] Thus, it is quite similar to the arguments of most NPM approaches. In fact, it can be said that most NPM related policies have been "exported" worldwide within adjustment lending programs from international institutions.[555]

Nevertheless, it is still quite remarkable that the Bretton Woods institutions face several problems when targeting at states with pressures towards reform. Although this phenomenon occurs in industrialized countries as well (e.g. the adjustment policies of the European Union), there is a visible leak on this approach in development countries.[556] Moreover, the nature of the reaction is somehow different to the responses to NPM, as these are responses to the outside actors and not to internal forces.

Traditional structural adjustment reforms have reduced government expenditures by eliminating subsidies, promoting privatization and liberalizing markets. The reforms have been implemented by reducing the role of the state to a minimum and by giving more competence to transnational actors. This phenomenon currently represents a major political challenge for the internal power of states. Reducing the government's role in the national economy by placing the public sector in a secondary role have posed a direct threat to the state's legitimacy and has even threatened sovereignty as the main constitutive element of statehood.[557] This is considered one of the greatest costs of adopting structural adjustment programs and accepting the conditions of foreign aid packages.

In this context, there is considerably great external impact of international organizations towards implementing national reform projects. This is especially the case if we follow the conditionality argumentation. However, it becomes interesting to note, that the responses states offer to these pressures have been quite different. There are cases such as Croatia and other countries in Eastern Europe in which all reforms have been implemented with greater success and major acceptance from the population.[558] On the other hand, there are other instances in which these

---

[554] *Ibid*, p. 610.

[555] Common. "The new public management and policy transfer", pp. 67 ff.

[556] A great review on the problems facing structural adjustment in developing and transition economies is offered by Hewitt de Alcántara, Cynthia. "Structural Adjustment in a Changing World." Briefing Paper No. 4, World Summit for Social Development. (Geneva: United Nations Research Institute for Social Development, 1994)

[557] On this point see Wolf, "Will the Nation State Survive Globalization?"

[558] In the case of Croatia, loans from the World Bank and IMF have proved to be effective at implanting comprehensive public sector reforms. For further details see: World Bank. "Regaining Fiscal Sustainability and Enhancing Effectiveness in Croatia: A Public Expenditure and Institutional Review." (Washington, D.C.: 2002.)

approaches have failed, mostly because of a lack of comprehensive adaptation from the recipient countries to the proposed reform paths, and also due to a lack of civil confidence in the actions of the government.[559]

In the latter case, corruption once again acts as the corrosive factor in the international agency-state relations. Therefore, lending institutions have developed strategies through which the incidence of corruption can be tackled down within the framework of development aid and its conditionality. A significant example can be found in the anti-corruption strategy of the World Bank. The main pillars thereof are to minimize fraud and corruption in bank-financed projects and assisting countries at the "diagnosis" of their corruption status through capacity building and transfer of know-how.[560] Moreover, multilateral cooperation with other donor agencies such as regional banks is deemed as an adequate means to diminish the risk of corruption in development assistance transactions.[561]

International Organizations and Policy Transfer

Another area in which international organizations are of considerable importance for the implementation of public sector reforms is the role of "policy transferors" they assume at projecting approaches such as NPM onto the global level.[562] In this regard, indications of the influence of international institutions on the administration can be found at all levels. A great amount of know-how is transferred from these organizations on to national governments thus establishing a process described as "policy training."[563] This may happen on a voluntary basis as a sign of full compliance with

[559] For example, Bolivia has recently experienced the setbacks of structural adjustment approached as the government's policies did not enjoy the support of the population. Socio economic tensions increased and ended in an uprising against President Gonzalo Sánchez de Lozada at the end of 2003. See: Kruse, Tom. "The IMF and the Bolivian Crisis." Economic Justice News Online (November 2003) Vol. 6, No. 3. < http://www.50years.org>

[560] World Bank. Helping Countries Combat Corruption. Progress at the World Bank Since 1997. (Washington, D.C.: Operational Core Services. Poverty Reduction and Economic Management Network, June 2000.)

[561] *Ibid.*, p. 6. The five largest multilateral development banks joined into a working group in order to coordinate their policies in this regard. Moreover, the World Bank has established partnerships with other institutions such as UNDP, the OECD and the International Organization of Supreme Audit Institutions.

[562] Common. "The new public management and policy transfer", pp. 59 ff.

[563] *Ibid.*, p. 61.The author makes the example of the Public Management Committee at the OECD, from which member states can share valuable information on good practices and possible failures of public management initiatives.

reform approaches, or states may be forced to engage in this process, as some international organizations may have clear interests in ensuring and not only suggesting best practices.[564]

Policy transfer also deals with the ability of the political elite to cope with the provisions given be international organizations. In this context and similar to the implementation of structural adjustment programs, a successful policy transfer depends on the ability of the recipient country in matching the aspirations of the donor country.[565] Furthermore, the transfer can be undertaken by "diffusion", meaning that the elites transfer their knowledge and experiences by creating and supporting external doctrines and thus creating an "international culture of administrative reforms." According to social anthropologist Jonathan Friedman, "an international elite conformed by top diplomats, government ministers and representatives of international organizations such as the UN [have formed] a kind of cultural cohort."[566]

Most authors in this field coincide however in noting, that although the term "policy diffusion" is important for the analysis of the interaction processes between an international organization and national institutions, lacks empirical testability.[567] Therefore, Common concludes that these processes should not be described as "transfer" or "diffusion" but rather as "convergence", meaning that national governments and societies become more alike due to the influence of similar external pressures. This assumption is valid if we take into consideration that, as noted by public affairs expert John Kamensky, "the reinventing of government movement originated simultaneously in the early 1980s in foreign countries, as part of their attempts to reposition their economies to cope with increasing global competition."[568]

International organizations thus have created and disseminated policies that are accepted – yet not fully applied – in many countries regardless of their political, social and economic constituency. The insertion and convergence of externally originated policies is yet a mechanism that needs to be evaluated in terms of the effectiveness of public sector reform. Moreover, a question emerges on how effective these processes are at implementing policies

564 *Ibid.*, p. 62.

565 *Ibid.*, p. 63.

566 *Ibid.* Quoted from: Friedman. Jonathan. "Global system, globalization and the parameters of modernity" Cultural Identity and Global Process. (London: Sage Publications, 1994.) Pp. 195 ff.

567 Ibid.

568 *Ibid.* Original quote and further points in: Kamensky, John .M. "The Role of the 'Reinventing Government' Movement in Federal Management Reform." Public Administration Review (May/June 1996) Vol. 56, No. 3, pp. 247-255.

against the spread of corruption in the government. This effectiveness will be addressed in depth in Chapter Eight, in the context of international mechanisms that have been created against corruption.

Risks and Needs of Anti-corruption Public Reforms

This chapter presented the first area in which anti-corruption initiatives have focused in the last years. Parting from the earlier yet contested premise that corruption is to be found primarily in government agencies, scholars and policy makers have reacted promptly to this problem by suggesting, that the *a priori* solution to the problem should be a comprehensive reform of the public sector.

Moreover, we have observed that the processes of political, economic, social and technological globalization have put tremendous pressures on states towards modernizing their organizational and business structures, adapting them to a more market-oriented model. The decay of bureaucracy demanded new solutions and approaches in public management. Also, it was the hope of many observers that, within the anti-corruption context, reforms would bring about positive results. By doing so, the public sector would have benefited on a twofold basis by first modernizing its structures and second, at the same time, by eradicating one of its biggest long-time adversities, namely the incidence of corruption. In this regard, most of the literature on this topic still further believes that the efficiency of the state could be enhanced through the implementation of anti-corruption measures.

Nevertheless, the initiatives and thus the entire discourse of reform have faced several challenges that were observed in previous segments. One of the main findings was, that not only internal pressures from different levels of the administration and the political apparatus, but also external influences mostly from international donor institutions, have created many disparities between the overall objectives of public sector reform and its actual results. Moreover, if we follow the assumption presented earlier that an efficient state would be able to diminish the amount of corruption within its administration, then reforms seem like the best path to follow. Therefore, the conclusion of this chapter evaluates if anti-corruption initiatives within the context of public sector reforms have made a contribution to the efficiency of the government and thus to the reduction of corrupt activities therein.

The debate emerges out the arguments of Anechiarico and Jacobs presented in earlier stages of this chapter. The authors argued that the main problems of the bureaucratic model of administration and thus of the incidence of corruption were found in eight on the so called "pathologies of bureaucracy", namely decision-making delay, overcentralization, inadequate authority, defensive management, goal displacement, poor working morale, lack of interorganizational cooperation, and adaptive strategies.[569]

At first sight, one could expect from the authors to follow traditional arguments and agree on an "anti-corruption project" (understood as government action against corruption) as being a proper solution. Interesting enough and quite contrary to what most scholars would say, Anechiarico and Jacobs make an interpretative turn and argue, that it is precisely the "anti-corruption project" what is making government yet more ineffective and thus perhaps even more corrupt. As they note,

> "[just as the advocates of bureaucracy have always believed that bureaucracy is the most efficient form of administration, the advocates of the anti-corruption project have always believed that anti-corruption mechanisms and strategies contribute to bureaucratic efficiency. We have challenged those assumptions by illuminating the incompatibility and tension between the anti-corruption project and governmental efficiency."[570]

Taking on their "pathologies", the authors note that through the implementation of control mechanisms for reducing corruption, decisions may be even more delayed, as they need to be approved by more instances.[571] Moreover, the ideas of many reformers to closer monitor the work of agencies through ombudsmen and controlling agencies, have led to an even greater degree of centralization in government thus diminishing the ability of the government to respond quickly to corruption threats.[572] This leads to even greater problems of inadequate authority, as centralized agencies undermine the authority of special agencies, which operate under their supervision. A chain reaction starts creating a defensive environment of decisions, making administrative goals less flexible and reducing the working morale of public servants and policies due to the fear of absolute supervision and audit.[573] In such an environment, public offices carefully monitor the activities of their

---

569 Anechiarico, and Jacobs. The Pursuit of Absolute Integrity, pp. 174 ff.

570 Ibid.

571 *Ibid.*, p. 175.

572 *Ibid.*, p. 177. The authors add, that "[t]o the corruption controllers, decentralization means loss of control, and inevitably, corruption scandals."

573 Ibid.

counterparts and diminish the cooperation among them and try to rely more on other extra-bureaucratic channels in order to do their work.[574]

Therefore, it seems – at least from this perspective – that the main efforts of anti-corruption strategies have led to an opposite result from their original purpose. This argument can be used to stress the necessity of a new discourse of anti-corruption, as Anechiarico and Jacobs propose at the end of their book.[575] This foresees a new awareness of corruption and the fact that public servants and the public opinion in general should be examining this problem more closely.

However more importantly, if we combine this critique to some of the main ideas behind reform approaches such as New Public Management, we might observe that precisely because governmental anti-corruption initiatives seemed to have failed making the state yet more inefficient, the need for measures such as reactivating fiscal stability, implementing managerial efficiency, and promoting capacity building as well as public accountability becomes greater than ever. Anerchiarico and Jacobs warn about the dangers of increased monitoring, something that was proposed by many NPM supporters. However, it can be noted that if strategies of modernizing the state through market-oriented reforms are successful and the government is able to decentralize authority, deregulate the economy and assume a solid responsibility at the delivery of public services, state efficiency should rise and thus the propensity of corruption should become lower.

Therefore, as a concluding argument, we can observe that despite the negative experiences with public sector reform in some cases, when it comes to corruption, this strategy still maintains its validity as a main mechanism for curbing this phenomenon. If corruption is to be addressed through public sector reforms, comprehensive approaches such as NPM, should be expanded and enhanced, so that the applicability of this model can be improved and its positive elements be implemented in as many countries as possible.

---

574 *Ibid.*, p. 184 ff.

575 *Ibid.*, p. 194 ff.

Chapter Six

Non-Governmental Organizations

> "Although some autocrats operate with impunity, indifferent to domestic opinion and criticism from the outside world, others are not so self-confident or powerful. In these cases, reform may be possible with NGOs pushing the state to change and working with it to make reform happen."[576]

The influence of non-state actors in world affairs has become nowadays more visible than ever before. The notion of the classic international system with states as the main actors has been contested by the appearance of actors of non-governmental nature such as civil society networks. Some have even concluded that globalization has brought about the increasing importance these actors due to an implied "retreat" of the nation state.[577] Although this topic should have its own separate debate, three main elements therein can serve as the starting point for the observations of this chapter.

First, if it is true that the globalization of world politics has projected major political phenomena onto the transnational level, then we can easily assume, as this book has early postulated, that in the case of corruption, the emergence of a so called *pax corrupta*, an international corruption regime, has moved this particular problem onto a more transnational/global level. Second, the globalization debates on the role of the state have frequently challenged the very nature of governments as the primary entities to face and solve both national and international problems. In the field of corruption, we observed in the last chapter, that governments do confront serious obstacles while trying to promote and implement effective mechanisms against the spread of corruption. It became clear as well, that a mere public sector reform should not be the final solution for the scourge of corruption on the local, regional and international levels. Therefore, the quest at the end of the chapter was to look for alternative initiatives that deal with the same goal, but are started from a different perspective.

Last but not least, if we take the above mentioned increasing importance of non-state actors in world politics into the equation of having an

---

576 Rose-Ackermann. Corruption and Government, p. 171.

577 Scholte, Jan Aart. Globalization. A Critical Introduction. (Basingstoke/New York: Palgrave, 2000.) Pp. 21 ff.

international corruption regime, the resulting conclusion would be that NGOs and other civil society networks also perform an increasingly important role in the fight against the *pax corrupta*. Therefore, this chapter focuses on the evaluation of these organizations and networks.

In this chapter, we shall take the Berlin based non-governmental network/organization Transparency International (TI) as the leading example. It must be noted, however, that the efforts of non-state actors against corruption should not be attributed exclusively to TI. Several other NGOs have become more involved in the fight against worldwide corruption as well.[578] Moreover, as we shall see further on, TI's network is based on cooperation with other non-public organizations at regional and local levels.

The choice for TI is based on the fact that it has become the largest international anti-corruption network with over 85 independent national chapters on five continents.[579] The extent of the spheres of influence on which TI can operate as the source for mechanisms against corruption around the world has become greater than ever before. This chapter portraits the beginnings and development of the organization, presents its most recent initiatives and strategies, and reassesses the entire approach of the organization.

TRANSPARENCY INTERNATIONAL: HISTORICAL SKETCH AND CONSTITUTIVE ELEMENTS

At the beginning of the 1990s, former World Bank regional director for East Africa Peter Eigen led the initiatives for the creation of today's biggest international non-governmental network that exclusively deals with curbing corruption. According to the organization, TI was established due to the demand of several private groupings to bring the topic of corruption on top of the international agenda.[580] Moreover, due to the fact that the perception of

[578] For example, the International Chamber of Commerce revised the provisions of its statutes in 1996 in order to remind international businesses about the dangers of offering bribes to foreign public officers. Moreover, the Interparliamentary Union approved a document on 1995 to reinforce initiatives against corruption and money laundering. In: Pieth, Mark. "International Cooperation to Combat Corruption." In: Elliott (ed.) Corruption and the Global Economy, pp. 128 ff.

[579] Transparency International . "About TI." Transparency International <http://www.transparency.org> (05.02.2004.)

[580] *Ibid.* Moreover, Eigen's own experiences with dealing with corruption in the international development regime during his time at the World Bank, led him to seek for the creation of an independent organization, which would be able to canalize all previous initiatives against this problem though a single-target entity. In: Galtung and Pope. "The Global Coalition Against Corruption: Evaluating Transparency International." In: Schleder, et. al. The Self-Restraining State, pp. 257 ff.

corruption as being a global problem grew inexorably after the end of the Cold War, joint initiatives were started from the side of civil society to undertake actions against the imminent spread of corrupt practices in the world.[581] Under these premises, ten individuals from five different countries signed the founding document of TI, the charter, which contains the main directives of the institution.[582] Consequently, a Board of Directors as well as an Advisory Council – composed mostly by friends and supporters of Eigen's initiative – were established and the organization was officially launched in May 1993.[583]

The main directives of the organization of TI are reflected in the following five guiding principles:

- TI recognizes the shared responsibility of actors in all regions for corruption, and its emphasis is on prevention and on reforming systems, not on exposing individual cases;
- TI considers that the movement against corruption is global and transcends social, political, economic and cultural systems;
- Internally, TI observes the principles of participation, decentralization, diversity, accountability and transparency;
- TI is politically non-partisan; and
- TI recognizes that there are strong practical as well as ethical reasons for containing corruption.[584]

At the very beginning, TI targeted towards curbing corruption in developing countries as well as in transition economies, deriving from the

581 According to TI "Transparency International has its roots in the concern felt by a number of people throughout the developed and the developing worlds that the "grand corruption" practiced by companies in exporting countries, as they "bought" politicians and officials in the developing world, was a threat to human rights, the environment and sustainable development, and that this could be ignored no longer." In: Transparency International. "TI." Transparency International <http://www.transparency.org>

582 Ibid.

583 Galtung and Pope. "The Global Coalition Against Corruption: Evaluating Transparency International." In: Schleder, et. al. The Self-Restraining State, pp. 258 ff.

584 All guiding principles found in: Transparency International. "Mission Statement." Transparency International <http://www.transparency.org>

assumption that these countries were not able to afford the "luxury" of corruption as much as many industrialized nations did.[585] Simultaneously, TI concentrated efforts towards working with international business community as well, in order to stop the "contribution" transnational companies made to the spread of corruption by offering bribes to public foreign officials.[586] As political scientist Mark Pieth notes, TI "fulfils an essential liaison between international organizations, governments, and the business communities."[587] In this context, the founders of TI decided not to pursue their purposes by merely exposing corruption to the public, but more importantly by promoting the creation of national and international coalitions capable to reform corrupt systems.[588]

In this regard, the nature of TI's work can be classified as structural, thus meaning that it differs from other NGOs who operate as exclusive reporting agencies.[589] Therefore, the range of the organization's activities has become very wide, especially through the many *facettes* international corruption has gained over the past years. After reviewing several strategies, TI decided to concentrate on structural measures which would cover four main areas which are reflected in the following constitutive elements, as explained in TI's mission statement. Thus the organization shall focus on,

> "1) building coalitions on national, regional and global level – embracing the state civil society and the private sector – in order to fight domestic and international corruption; 2) coordinating and supporting national chapters at the implementation of this mission; 3) assisting (in conjunction with the national chapters) in the design and implementation of effective integrity systems; and 4) collecting, analyzing and disseminating information to raise

585 Galtung and Pope. "The Global Coalition Against Corruption: Evaluating Transparency International." In: Schleder, et. al. The Self-Restraining State, p. 258.

586 *Ibid.*, p. 259.

587 Pieth. "International Cooperation to Combat Corruption", p. 129.

588 Galtung and Pope. "The Global Coalition Against Corruption: Evaluating Transparency International." In: Schleder, et. al. The Self-Restraining State, p. 258.

589 An example provided by Galtung and Pope is the work of Amnesty International, which focuses primarily on reporting human rights abuses.

> public awareness on the damaging impact of corruption on human and economic development."[590]

Using both the principle guidelines as well as the main constitutive elements, TI has been able to gain considerable importance within the international community of states in the field of anti-corruption initiatives. In some aspects, TI has even become a pioneer by developing tools to analyze corruption and promote effective mechanisms for its eradication.

The Role of National Chapters

As noted earlier, the main goal of TI is to create coalitions on national and international levels in order to effectively address the issue of corruption. The physical form of civil coalitions can have many variations, as it could be independent groupings, media associations, human rights supporters and even perhaps epistemic communities.

In this regard, a particular organizational feature of TI must be highlighted, namely the ability to transfer its main directives and goals to a broad international audience through its more than 85 National Chapters spread across all regions of the world. Although National Chapters operate independent from each other, these units act as a valuable liaison between the central secretariat in Berlin and the local institutions in the respective countries. [591]

Despite their almost complete autonomy, there are two important directives in which all Chapters need to comply with the Board of Directors of TI. First, National Chapters need to be "non-partisan" thus denoting political impartiality and assuming the responsibility of carrying on with this position. This means that no prominent politician, active or inactive should assume leading positions in within the National Chapter.[592] And second, Chapters should not undertake any investigations on individual allegations of corruption.[593] This once again stresses the "structural" nature of the work of TI.

[590] Transparency International Mission Statement. Cited in: Galtung and Pope. "The Global Coalition Against Corruption: Evaluating Transparency International", p. 260

[591] *Ibid.* The authors explain, that chapters "are wholly sui generis and develop their own national programs in the light of their own perceptions of needs and possibilities."

[592] *Ibid.* The authors base this argument on the paradoxical story of Alberto Dahik, former Vice-President of Ecuador and one of the founding members of TI. Shortly after the organization was launched, the Ecuadorian congress indicted Dahik for several cases of corruption. He sought political asylum in Costa Rica, where he is still hiding from the authorities.

[593] Ibid.

As we shall see in the proceeding sections, the National Chapters not only become a mechanism of know-how transmission, but also are the sources of many best practices and good examples on how to deal with this problem from a local perspective. Additionally, countries in which there has been neither enough initiative nor enough infrastructures to build a National Chapter, points of contact have been established in order to network with TI.

FIGURE 5: TRANSPARENCY INTERNATIONAL NATIONAL CHAPTERS

Country	Status	Country	Status	Country	Status
Algeria	○	Ghana	●	Niger	⊙
Argentina	●	Greece	●	Nigeria	●
Armenia	●	Guatemala	⊙	Norway	●
Australia	●	Guinea	●	Palestine	○
Austria	●	Haiti	⊙	Pakistan	⊙
Azerbaijan	●	Honduras	●	Panama	●
Bahrain	○	Hungary	●	Papua New Guinea	●
Bangladesh	●	India	●	Paraguay	●
Belgium	●	Indonesia	●	Peru	●
Benin	●	Iran	●	Philippines	●
Bolivia	●	Iraq	●	Poland	●
Bosnia and Herzegovina	●	Ireland	●	Romania	●
Botswana	●	Israel	●	Russia	●
Brazil	●	Italy	●	Samoa	○
Bulgaria	●	Jamaica	●	Senegal	●
Burkina Faso	○	Japan	⊙	Serbia	⊙
Burundi	○	Jordan	⊙	Sierra Leone	○
Cambodia	⊙	Kazakhstan	●	Singapore	●
Cameroon	⊙	Kenya	●	Slovakia	●
Canada	●	South Korea	●	Slovenia	●
Chad	○	Kuwait	●	Solomon Islands	○
Chile	●	Kyrgyz Republic	○	South Africa	●
China	○	Latvia	●	Spain	⊙
Colombia	●	Lebanon	●	Sri Lanka	●

Costa Rica	◉	Republic of Macedonia	◉	Sweden	●
Côte d'Ivoire	●	Madagascar	●	Switzerland	●
Croatia	◉	Malawi	●	Taiwan	◉
Czech Republic	●	Malaysia	●	Tanzania	●
Denmark	●	Mali	○	Thailand	●
Dominican Republic	●	Mauritania	●	Togo	●
Ecuador	●	Mauritius	●	Trinidad and Tobago	●
Egypt	○	Mexico	●	Turkey	●
El Salvador	●	Moldova	●	Uganda	●
Estonia	●	Mongolia	○	Ukraine	●
Ethiopia	○	Montenegro	●	United Kingdom	●
Fiji	●	Morocco	●	Uruguay	●
Finland	◉	Mozambique	○	United States	●
France	●	Namibia	○	Vanuatu	◉
Gabon	○	Nepal	●	Venezuela	●
Gambia	●	Netherlands	◉	Yemen	◉
Georgia	●	New Zealand	●	Zambia	●
Germany	●	Nicaragua	○	Zimbabwe	●

● = Operational Chapter ◉ = Chapter in Formation ○ = National Contact

Source: Transparency International.

TI'S MECHANISMS FOR FIGHTING CORRUPTION

One preliminary observation should be made before we analyze the different mechanisms TI has created for addressing the issue of corruption. Picking up on the findings of Chapter One, the debate around how to cope with corruption was highly related to the very definition of this problem. Therefore, it shall be noted that the definition and thus the image of corruption TI shares is that of the "abuse of public office for private gain." This observation is important at this point, because most of the tools that TI has created are derived from the notion that corruption is not only a morality issue, but moreover has proven to bring along political, economic and social problems.[594] In this context, reforming corrupt structures within governments and creating public awareness of corruption on all possible levels become initiatives that are linked to this analytical framework and are thus influenced by this premise.

National Integrity Systems

The first approach to be analyzed is the so called "National Integrity Systems." Even since its creation, TI started to "mold" possible solution for coping with corruption both nationally and internationally. The challenge became very complex, as there were many directions in which to start, especially, as we observed earlier, due to the multiple forms corruption can take. Based on its definition of corruption, TI consequently decided to start strategies to address the problem in public institutions. Bearing in mind the imminent dangers that corruption brought to the economy, politics and society, the first main rationale was to implement anti-corruption strategies within the frameworks of a "sustainable reform" of the public sector.[595] Similar to the reform approaches observed in Chapter Five, the initial idea behind a National Integrity System is to turn the classic form of "vertical" government, in which authority is hierarchically ordered and monopolies can easily emerge, into a model of "horizontal accountability", in which the concentration of power is more disperse and every element in the chain of command can more autonomy.[596] In this context, a system of agencies is created similar to the notion of "check and balances", including all sectors of national life such as, the government and all of its branches, the media, civil society and the private sector.[597]

National Integrity Systems shall have the function of a tool for achieving reform in the public sector and thus increase accountability. On this instance, we can clearly observe that the approach of TI on corruption is merely structural, as it was noted earlier. Only a comprehensive change in the structure of government through National Integrity systems can bring about

[594] *Ibid.*, 259.

[595] Pope and Transparency International. "The National Integrity System". In: TI Source Book 2000, p. 31.

[596] *Ibid.*, p. 33. According to the author, the system of horizontal accountability creates a "vicious circle [...] on in which each actor is both a watcher and is watched, is both a monitor and is monitored. A circle avoids, and at the same time answers the age-old question: 'Who shall guard the guards?'"

[597] Ibid.

the ultimate goal of such an model, namely to "make corruption a 'high risk' and 'low return' undertaking."[598]

There are several different elements which build up National Integrity Systems in each country. This differentiation is made due to the internal composition of each country, which does vary from case to case, especially when comparing developing and industrialized countries. TI has established so called "institutional pillars", which are the necessary ingredients for the anti-corruption formula. They can be summarized in five main areas: 1) the government, including the executive as well as the judiciary and the parliament; the civil service; 2) "watchdog agencies" (e.g. Public Accounts Committee, Auditor-General, Ombudsman, Police, Anti-Corruption Agencies, etc.); 3) civil society groups including all professional sectors and the private business community; 4) the media; and 5) international agencies.[599]

After these elements are included in the approach, there are needed rules that apply for each of them. This shall enforce and compliment the institutional pillars. In an attempt to correlate both the pillars and the rules attached therein, Pope suggested the following classification, which shall not be entirely exclusive:

These categories can be mixed according to the needs and composition of each country. The approach seeks to monitor, review and examine each of the pillars and establish the enforcement of the pertinent rules. The *modus operandi* is to not isolate one institution or set of rules, but moreover to create an internal system of interdependence in which all agencies will be constantly monitoring the other.[600]

Focusing on how to export these ideas to as many countries as possible, TI quickly developed the so called "National Integrity Workshops" in order to bring together all sectors of society, the economy and politics and call upon the implementation of these measures. Integrity workshops concentrate on putting public institutions in contact with coalition partners outside the government scope in order to analyze the existing frameworks and locate areas in which reforms are needed, looking towards diminishing corruption therein.[601] In a second step, working groups are formed in order to develop a

[598] *Ibid.*, p. 35

[599] Adapted from *Ibid.*, p. 36.

[600] *Ibid.*, p. 37. For example, the author asks "what is the benefit of a sound and 'clean' Judiciary ready to uphold the Rule of Law, if there is corruption in the police, investigators, prosecutors, or the legal profession? The Judges would simply not receive the cases they should hear; they would then sit in splendid isolation – honest capable, yet able to achieve little."

[601] Galtung and Pope. "The Global Coalition Against Corruption: Evaluating Transparency International", p. 274.

set of goals, assign responsibilities for implementation of these goals, establish follow-up mechanisms and continuously report back to other working groups.[602]

The first National Integrity Workshops took place in Uganda and Tanzania, proving up to a certain point, that the doctrines and measures of TI are not entirely a product of industrialized western nations.[603] Moreover, one of the key features of the workshops is that, as Pope observes, they start at the local level as a private initiative. In this context, bringing together as many "pillars" as possible within a country, should lead to the development of comprehensive structural frameworks for reform.[604]

Furthermore, during the workshops, participants also subscribe to "integrity pledges" in which the publicly commit to the measures proposed out of the discussions of the working groups.[605] As Pope concludes, "pledges have served both to place the issue of integrity squarely on the political map and to provide critics with a weapon against those perceived as having breached the pledges."[606]

The last tool within the scope of National Integrity System is the introduction of Integrity Pacts. It is an effort to fight corruption in the field of public contracting. Integrity Pacts were first referred to as "islands of integrity", and included the initiative to enhance public trust in government contracting and increase the credibility of administrative procedures in general.[607] It includes an agreement between government agencies and

---

[602] Ibid.

[603] Pope and Transparency International. "The National Integrity System". In: TI Source Book 2000, p. 38.

[604] One example can be found in the case of the Netherlands. According to a recent country report, most elements of the National Integrity System can be found such as the provision of civil and human rights by the constitution, free elections of the legislature and their power to hold public officials to account, an independent judiciary, a free media and a diverse and active civil society. Such positive aspects notwithstanding, there are several other areas in which the country continues to denote fallacies, as in the case of the financial disclosure of high-level officials, the rules of conflicts of interest, the lack of an anti-corruption agency, limited whistle blower protection, among others. In: Huberts, Leo. "National Integrity Systems. Country Study Report. The Netherlands 2001." Presented for the Global Forum on Fighting Corruption and Safeguarding Integrity. (Prague, 2001.) Available online at <http://www.globalforum3.org/gf2/docs/Netherlands.pdf>

[605] Pope and Transparency International. "The National Integrity System". In: TI Source Book 2000, p. 39. The author makes the example of Benjamin Mkapa, President of Tanzania, who subscribed to one of the "integrity pledges" while campaigning in 1995 and publicly disclosed his assets after winning the election and assuming his post.

[606] Ibid.

[607] Transparency International. The Integrity Pact. The Concept, the Model and Present Applications. A Status Report. (Berlin, December 2002.)

private entities interested in obtaining a public sector contract. The main provisions of the agreement is that neither side will offer, demand or accept bribes, or hinder competitors to obtain the contract, before and during the bidding process.[608] Moreover, the agreement demands complete disclosure by all parties in terms of commissions or similar expenses given to any person dealing the contract.[609]

FIGURE 6 : RULES AND PRACTICES PILLARS FOR NATIONAL INTEGRITY SYSTEMS

Institutional Pillar	Corresponding core rules/practices
Executive	Conflict of interest rules
Legislative/Parliament	Fair elections
Public Accounts Committee	Power to question senior officials
Auditor General	Public Reporting
Public Service	Public service ethics
Judiciary	Independence
Media	Access to information
Civil society	Freedom of speech
Ombudsman	Records management
Anti-Corruption/watchdog agencies	Enforceable and enforced laws
Private sector	Competition policy, including public procurement rules
International community	Effective mutual legal/judicial assistance

Source: Pope and Transparency International. "The National Integrity System". In: TI Source Book 2000, p. 37.

[608] Lévy, Phillipe. "Integrity Pact." Transparency Switzerland. <http://www.transparency.ch>
[609] Ibid.

According to TI, Integrity Pacts have two primary objectives: 1) to enable companies to refrain from bribing by making sure that competitors are engaged in a clean and transparent bidding process; and 2) to enable government to reduce the high costs and damaging impact of corruption in public procurement, privatization and licensing.[610] The main operational elements include the *pact or agreement*, an undertaking by the government (or Principal), a *statement* by each bidder that it has not been involved in any illicit payment during the process in order to obtain the contract, an *undertaking* by each bidder to disclose all payments made in reference to the contract, the use and implementation of *Codes of Conduct*, the use of *arbitration* as the conflict resolution mechanism, and a set of *sanctions* for any violation of the agreement.[611] Lastly, the agreement foresees an active role of *civil society* groupings as well as of the *media* and *private organizations* as monitoring agents in the entire process.[612] It is of pivotal importance that both the government as the contractor and the private entities fully comply with the provisions explained above. Therefore, monitoring, supervision and auditing measures are included in Integrity Pacts from the very beginning, mostly reflected by inserting additional oversight mechanisms such as public hearings, publications, as well as the free access to information on the contracting process at any time.[613]

Although this might seem as a conventional agreement to pursue transparency in public constructing, the most relevant difference from other measures is that the sanctions contained in Integrity Pacts may directly affect the position of the bidders.[614] Therefore, the promotion of such tools should create the necessary reluctance of companies to use illicit mechanisms for obtaining government contracts. The effectiveness of Integrity Pacts has proven to be positive in some cases, in which governments have used such

[610] As stated in: Transparency International. The Integrity Pact, p. 4.

[611] *Ibid.*, p. 5

[612] *Ibid.*, p. 12.

[613] *Ibid.*, p. 7 ff.

[614] Galtung and Pope explain, that „[b]idders who violate their commitment not to bribe are subject to significant sanctions, such as loss of contract, liability for damages (to the government and the competing bidders), and forfeiture of the bid security. The government could also blacklist the offender from all government business for an appropriate period of time." In: Galtung and Pope. "The Global Coalition Against Corruption: Evaluating Transparency International", p. 273.

agreements to ensure transparent and correct public procurement.[615] However, the applicability of this tool is still subject to many factors such as the adherence of all bidders to the Integrity Pact, the political willingness of governments to use Integrity Pacts, and the fact that these agreements might "duplicate" the laws on contracting should a pertinent law exist already.[616]

The National Integrity Systems approach presents the first main approach of TI in fighting corruption in the public sector, and it has proven to be quite successful thus far.[617] However, tt must be observed, that this strategy does have its fallacies and critiques. For instance, it can be easily deduced that the pillars of the approach are not necessarily given in each country. Therefore the effectiveness of bringing the theoretical model of a National Integrity System into reality should be dealt with caution. Implementations may vary depending on the distinctive given elements of each nation, for instance its social structure, its political landscape as well as its economic composition.[618]

The Corruptions Perception Index (CPI)

Undoubtedly, TI's most prominent tool is the Corruption Perceptions Index (CPI) which was first launched in 1995 and is published on a yearly basis. This "poll of polls" has gained a lot of attention from international public opinion when it comes to measuring corruption by classifying states on a scale from "least corrupt" to "most corrupt".

The initiative was taken by TI's Board of Directors and German economist Johan Graf Lambsdorff, who, at that time, was professor at the University of Göttingen.[619] The index began as a yearly assessment of the incidence of corruption in the reviewed countries. However, it was noted from the very beginning, that this assessment refers to the perception of corruption given by the respondents, who have been ever since the creation

---

615 See for instance: Holsen, John. "Improving Public Sector Procurement in Latin America. A Synthesis Report on Eight Case Studies of Three Methods in Three Countries." Transparency International. (May, 2002.)

616 Lévy, "Integrity Pact."

617 Ibid.

618 For instance, in the case of Colombia, freedom of the press is guaranteed by the constitution. However, the work of journalists has been severely influenced by the ongoing violence in the country, thus creating extreme cautiousness when dealing with the issue of corruption. For a detailed description of the Colombian case, see: Ospina, Rosa Inés and Corporación Transparecia por Colombia. "National Integrity Systems. Country Study Report. Colombia 2001." Presented for the Global Forum on Fighting Corruption and Safeguarding Integrity. (Prague, 2001.) Available online at <http://www.globalforum3.org/gf2/docs/Colombia.pdf>

619 Lambsdorff and his established "Internet Center for Corruption Research" are now at the University of Passau.

of the index mostly international businessmen, risk analysts and financial journalists.[620]

The first version of the CPI included the results of seven surveys in a total of 41 countries.[621] Over the years, the significance and the impact of this index have grown considerably. The most recent version of the CPI for 2003 includes 17 sources originated by 13 independent institutions for the evaluation of 133 countries.[622]

The theoretical debate presented in this book concluded that measuring corruption is not an easy undertaking. Therefore all collected data and its evaluation should be treated with caution when making statements and observations of corruption. This is no exception for the CPI. In fact, Lambsdorff himself repeatedly adverts that the index does not determine the level of corruption of a country, but the perception thereof since,

> "[...] the data collected relates to perceptions rather than to real phenomena, it has to be considered whether such perceptions improve our understanding of what real levels of corruption may be. Since actual levels of corruption cannot be determined directly, perceptions may be all we have to guide us."[623]

An important aspect in any preliminary observation of the CPI is that all sources apply a similar definition of corruption, namely the abuse of public office for private gain.[624] This means, that all institutions from which data was obtained aimed to ask about the same phenomenon.[625] Under this

---

620 Transparency International. "1995 TI Corruption Index. Explanatory Note." (Berlin: Transparency International and the University of Göttingen, 1995.)

621 *Ibid.* The surveys came from the Institute for Management Development in Lausanne, Business International in New York, and Political & Economic Consultancy Ltd in Hong Kong.

622 The sources fort he 2003 CPI were obtained from Freedom House Nations in Transit; the Economist Intelligence Unit; PricewaterhouseCoopers (the 2001 Opacity Index); the Institute for Management Development Lausanne; the Political and Economic Risk consultancy Hong Kong; the World Bank; the World Economic Forum; the State Capacity Survey by Columbia University; Gallup International (on behalf of TI); Information International; the Multilateral Development Bank; the Business Environment and Enterprise Performance Survey; and the World Markets Research Centre. In: Lambsdorff, Johann Graf. "Framework Document 2003. Background Paper to the 2003 Corruption Perceptions Index." (Berlin: Transparency International and University of Passau, September 2003.)

623 Ibid.

624 Ibid.

625 *Ibid.* The author explains that earlier versions of the CPI were criticized by not taking into consideration the many different manifestations corruption might have,

definitional premise, a certain degree of objectivity within which the entire surveys are undertaken can be confirmed.

FIGURE 7: COUNTRIES EVALUATED BY THE CPI 1995-2003

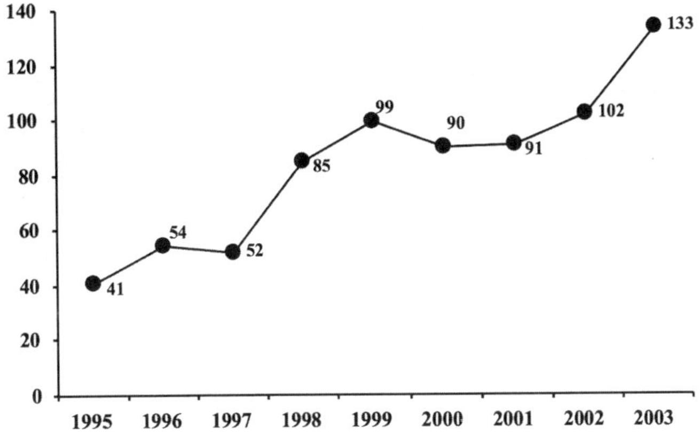

Source: Transparency International.

Nevertheless, there are two key areas that shall not be left out of the discussion. First, one shall be aware of the fact that the CPI only addresses members of the international business community as well as experts and/or journalists. Therefore, the image portrayed for any country is not necessarily complete. This feature however, could be of great advantage, given the fact that governments would not evaluate themselves in a negative matter. In this regard, it can be said that the CPI enjoys a high degree of explanatory independence, as it is not a government-influenced survey. Still, there can be serious biases due to cultural related *characteristica* of the respondents. For example, business people who are asked to evaluate their country in terms of the levels of corruption could have a different opinion that their expatriated colleagues, who share the same nationality, but who have a distinctive view of the same country and the incidence of corruption therein.[626]

626 *Ibid.* As noted by the author, this "type of bias might arise, originating from the potential dominance of a particular cultural heritage in the sample questioned or because expatriates lack a proper understanding of the country's culture."

Second, the ethical standards among the respondents might vary and this is something that can be neither measured nor monitored. The variation between locals and expatriates on this point is an issue as well. This leads back to the original effectiveness of such indexes as discussed in the earlier chapters of this book. Corruption is understood as a phenomenon that can be easily relativated due to normative and moral arguments. Thus the CPI faces a major challenge, as ethics cannot be measured and do not portray the same images that respondents have on what corruption is and what it is not.

Therefore, it can be said that the perception of a country as being "corrupt" merely based on the CPI ranking shall not determine exactly where and how corruption occurs. Moreover, the scale is subject to many methodological variations, as data may not be available for some countries, and the methodology may vary from source to source.[627] However, it is precisely the variety of sources which gives the CPI its explanatory power, since this improves its reliability and reduces the chance of misinterpretations.[628]

Despite the mentioned fallacies, the CPI is currently one of the few tools powerful enough to make a cross-country statement about the incidence of corruption in the government. There is hardly any publication on the topic that does not include the index as one element for explanation. No matter what type of publication, if journalist or academic, the CPI seems to appear anywhere where corruption is a topic.

This development should not lead to the opinion that the CPI is the only scale available for the analysis of corruption.[629] However, since TI has made increased efforts to make good publicity thereof, the CPI is known everywhere and has acquired a solid place, even in the scholarship of corruption. As Johnston observes,

> "The CPI, and many of the measures upon which is based represents a clear advance over the anecdotal evidence and hypothetical cases that dominated earlier phases of the

[627] Ibid.

[628] Andvig, Fjeldstadt, et. al. Research on Corruption. A Policy Oriented Survey, p. 42.

[629] The CPI is usually viewed as part of the „first-generation" measures of corruption. These include the surveys and state from which the CPI is elaborated (See note ###). However, new surveys are concentrating in taking private businesses, households and individuals into the analysis of corruption. As noted by: Johnston, Michael. "Measuring the New Corruption Rankings: Implications for Analysis and Reform." In: Heidenheimer and Johnston (eds.) Political Corruption, pp. 865-884.

research, and over the diffuse and emotional claims often marking public discussions."[630]

FIGURE 8 : 2003 CORRUPTION PERCEPTIONS INDEX (CPI) – SELECTION

Rank	Country	Score	SU	SD	Rank	Country	Score	SU	SD
1	Finland	9.7	8	0.3		Yemen	2.6	4	0.7
2	Iceland	9.6	7	0.3	46	Albania	2.5	5	0.6
3	Denmark	9.5	9	0.4	48	Argentina	2.5	12	0.5
	New Zealand	9.5	8	0.2		Ethiopia	2.5	5	0.8
5	Singapore	9.4	12	0.1	50	Gambia	2.5	4	0.9
6	Sweden	9.3	11	0.2		Pakistan	2.5	7	0.9
7	Netherlands	8.9	9	0.3		Philippines	2.5	12	0.5
8	Australia	8.8	12	0.9	53	Tanzania	2.5	6	0.6
	Norway	8.8	8	0.5	54	Zambia	2.5	5	0.6
	Switzerland	8.8	9	0.8		Guatemala	2.4	8	0.6
11	Canada	8.7	12	0.9		Kazakhstan	2.4	7	0.9
	Luxembourg	8.7	6	0.4	57	Moldova	2.4	5	0.8
	United Kingdom	8.7	13	0.5		Uzbekistan	2.4	6	0.5
14	Austria	8.0	9	0.7	59	Venezuela	2.4	12	0.5
	Hong Kong	8.0	11	1.1		Vietnam	2.4	8	0.8
16	Germany	7.7	11	1.2		Bolivia	2.3	6	0.4
17	Belgium	7.6	9	0.9		Honduras	2.3	7	0.6
18	Ireland	7.5	9	0.7		Macedonia	2.3	5	0.3
	USA	7.5	13	1.2	64	Serbia & Montenegro	2.3	5	0.5
20	Chile	7.4	12	0.9		Sudan	2.3	4	0.3
21	Israel	7.0	10	1.2	66	Ukraine	2.3	10	0.6
	Japan	7.0	13	1.1		Zimbabwe	2.3	7	0.3
23	France	6.9	12	1.1		Republic of Congo	2.2	3	0.5
	Spain	6.9	11	0.8		Ecuador	2.2	8	0.3
25	Portugal	6.6	9	1.2	70	Iraq	2.2	3	1.1
26	Oman	6.3	4	0.9		Sierra Leone	2.2	3	0.5
27	Bahrain	6.1	3	1.1		Uganda	2.2	6	0.7
	Cyprus	6.1	3	1.6		Cote d'Ivoire	2.1	5	0.5
29	Slovenia	5.9	12	1.2		Kyrgyzstan	2.1	5	0.4
30	Botswana	5.7	6	0.9		Libya	2.1	3	0.5
	Taiwan	5.7	13	1.0	76	Papua New Guinea	2.1	3	0.6

630 Ibid.

32	Qatar	5.6	3	0.1	77	Indonesia	1.9	13	0.5
33	Estonia	5.5	12	0.6	78	Kenya	1.9	7	0.3
	Uruguay	5.5	7	1.1		Angola	1.8	3	0.3
35	Italy	5.3	11	1.1		Azerbaijan	1.8	7	0.3
	Kuwait	5.3	4	1.7		Cameroon	1.8	5	0.2
37	Malaysia	5.2	13	1.1		Georgia	1.8	6	0.7
	United Arab Emirates	5.2	3	0.5	83	Tajikistan	1.8	3	0.3
39	Tunisia	4.9	6	0.7		Myanmar	1.6	3	0.3
40	Hungary	4.8	13	0.6		Paraguay	1.6	6	0.3
41	Lithuania	4.7	10	1.6	86	Haiti	1.5	5	0.6
	Namibia	4.7	6	1.3		Nigeria	1.4	9	0.4
43	Cuba	4.6	3	1.0	88	Bangladesh	1.3	8	0.7
	Jordan	4.6	7	1.1					
45	Trinidad and Tobago	4.6	6	1.3					

Source: Transparency International.

According to the source, the score denotes the perceptions of the degree of corruption as seen by respondents between 10 (highly clean) and 0 (highly corrupt). The Surveys Used (SU), show the number of surveys that evaluated a country's performance. At least three surveys were required for a country to be included in the index. Lastly, the Standard Deviation (SD) indicates differences in the values of the sources: the greater the standard deviation, the greater the differences of perceptions of a country among the sources.

Another contribution of the CPI, beyond the methodological contribution towards measuring corruption, is that it has become the most effective mechanism to raise international awareness on corruption. As this is one of the main goals of the entire approach of TI, the organization has achieved much since the first launching of the CPI. The index has allowed TI to make general statements about the status of corruption in the world. For instance, on the last version of the CPI, TI's chairman Peter Eigen was able to conclude that "nine out of ten developing countries urgently need practical support to fight corruption."[631] Moreover, the impact of the CPI on the public opinions of many nations has started extended debates on what to do against

[631] Transparency International. Corruption Perceptions Index. Press Release. (07.10.2003.)

this problem. TI benefits from these debates as they serve the *causa finalis* of the entire organization.[632]

The Bribe Payers Index (BPI)

A further profound critique to the CPI was that it only concentrated on one side of the corruption scope, namely those taking bribes. There was no mention of those who offered them. Therefore, Lambsdorff and TI reacted promptly by developing the Bribe Payers Index (BPI) which ranks leading exporting countries whose companies are believed to pay bribes to senior public officials in emerging economies.[633]

The BPI is not as extensive as the CPI since it only lists 21 countries and is more focused on the problem of international bribery. Accordingly, the BPI also measures the level of awareness in the evaluated countries on the implementation of the Anti-Bribery Convention from the OECD.[634] The most recent version of the BPI (2002) was polled by the Gallup International Association in 15 emerging economies.[635]Although the initiative was first taken in 1999, the impact of the BPI worldwide has been of similar scale compared to the CPI. Due to the fact that this was a more specialized survey with less participant countries, additional questions where included in order to portrait the reasons for the incidence of bribes in a more precise manner.

---

632 The most prominent negative reactions to the CPI by governments could be observed in Pakistan, Malaysia and Argentina. In Pakistan, the publication of the CPI in 1996 caused a political turmoil that ended with the dismissal of Prime Minister Benazir Butto after she angrily defied the results of the index. In the same year, Argentina's President Carlos Ménem allegedly called TI a "criminal organization" due to the bad rankings of the country therein. And lastly, Malaysian Prime Minister Mahatir Mohammed classified the CPI as a product of "western cultural imperialism." Wondered by the poor position of his country, his government quickly started to implement reforms that would diminish the incidence of corruption in the administration and thus put Malaysia on a better place on the scale. In: Galtung and Pope. "The Global Coalition Against Corruption: Evaluating Transparency International", p. 276.

633 In the exact formulation, respondents are asked "in the business sectors with which you are most familiar, please indicate how likely companies from the following countries are to pay or offer bribes to win or retain business in this country?" In: Transparency International Bribe Payers Index 2002 – Tables and FAQs. <http://www.transparency.org/ cpi/2002/bpi_faq.en.html>

634 Ibid.

635 Participant countries include: Argentina, Brazil, Colombia, Hungary, India, Indonesia, Mexico, Morocco, Nigeria, the Philippines, Poland, Russia, South Africa, South Korea, and Thailand.

FIGURE 9: TI'S BRIBE PAYERS INDEX (1999-2002)

Ran	Total sample	2002 835	1999 779
1	Australia	8.5	8.1
2	Sweden	8.4	8.3
	Switzerland	8.4	7.7
4	Austria	8.2	7.8
5	Canada	8.1	8.1
6	Netherlands	7.8	7.4
	Belgium	7.8	6.8
8	United Kingdom	6.9	7.2
9	Singapore	6.3	5.7
	Germany	6.3	6.2
11	Spain	5.8	5.3
12	France	5.5	5.2
13	USA	5.3	6.2
	Japan	5.3	5.1
15	Malaysia	4.3	3.9
	Hong Kong	4.3	n.a.
17	Italy	4.1	3.7
18	South Korea	3.9	3.4
19	Taiwan	3.8	3.5
20	China (PR)	3.5	3.1
21	Russia	3.2	n.a.
	DOMESTIC COMPANIES	1.9	n.a.

In the ranking, the perfect score denoting minimal perceived incidence of bribery is 10.0. TI indicates also that in the 15 emerging economies which were surveyed, the propensity of bribes was higher in the local companies than in the foreign firms.

Source: Transparency International Bribe Payers Index 2002.

FIGURE 10: BRIBE RY IN BUSINESS SECTORS 2002

By sector

Total Sample	2002 835
Public Works/construction	1.3
Arms and defense	1.9
Oil and gas	2.7
Real estate/property	3.5
Telecoms	3.7
Power generation/transmission	3.7
Mining	4.0
Transportation/storage	4.3
Pharmaceuticals/medical care	4.3
Heavy manufacturing	4.5
Banking and finance	4.7
Civilian aerospace	4.9
Forestry	5.1
IT	5.1
Fishery	5.9
Light manufacturing	5.9
Agriculture	5.9

0 = very high perceived levels of corruption
10 = very low perceived levels of corruption

By size of bribe

Total Sample	2002 835
Public Works/construction	46%
Arms and defense	38%
Oil and gas	21%
Banking and finance	15%
Real estate/property	11%
Pharmaceuticals/medical care	10%
Power generation/transmission	10%
Telecoms	9%
IT	6%
Forestry	5%
Mining	5%
Transportation/storage	5%
Heavy manufacturing	4%
Agriculture	3%
Fishery	3%
Civilian aerospace	2%
Light manufacturing	1%

Source: Transparency International Bribe Payers Index 2002.

The BPI has enhanced the initiatives of TI towards creating a clearer image of corrupt practices worldwide. Moreover, it helped to canalize the critiques that were made out of the CPI in terms of corruption being a problem mostly of developing countries and their administrations.[636] During the last survey in 2002, an additional index was obtained through this survey, namely the Bribery in Business Sectors, which was made in solely in 1999 and indicates in which sector bribes are more likely to occur. Another point that was implemented at the 2002 BPI was an additional question on the status of the OECD Anti Bribery Convention, which was signed off in 1997. The respondents were asked if they knew about such a convention, and to the

[636] Andvig, Fjeldstadt, et. al. Research on Corruption. A Policy Oriented Survey, p. 43.

surprise of the surveyors, the vast majority of participants had very low knowledge about the content and existence of this document.[637]

Raising Awareness (I): The Corruption Fighter's Tool Kit

Most of the work of TI is based around the notion of creation public awareness about corruption on national and international scales. Moreover, the organization's belief in the power of civil society groupings as the necessary element within a country in the fight against corruption has led to the development of other mechanisms to achieve more awareness on the incidence and dangers of corrupt activities.

Despite the imminent given prominence of the CPI and the BPI, TI has been able to create other mechanisms through, based on the organization's non-governmental character. One of them is the so called "Corruption Fighter's Tool Kit", an extensive handbook that contains over 400 pages of best practices and experiences with anti-corruption initiatives worldwide.[638] While the first version of the handbook entailed 27 tools, the newest edition collects nearly 50 different examples from civil society actions against corruption from TI's National Chapters. According to TI, the tool kit

> "[...] highlights the potential of civil society to create mechanisms for scrutiny and control of public institutions, and to demand and promote accountable and responsive public administration."[639]

The book covers a series of topics within the scope the TI's main activities starting with awareness raising through the media and culture, evaluating procurement systems, monitoring election campaigns, advocating for the access to information, surveying public institutions, implementing ethic codes for businesses and making prospect and diagnostics for the implementation of future measures.[640] Every tool presents a case from a different country in which civil society initiative have proven to be

637 Transparency International. Bribe Payers Index 2002.

638 Transparency International. The Corruption Fighter's Tool Kit. Civil society experiences and emerging strategies. (Berlin: Transparency International, 2002.)

639 *Ibid.*, p. 7.

640 Ibid.

successful.[641] After having thoroughly presented each case, an evaluation is made and prospects on its future applicability in other countries are given. Due to the multiple levels of analysis and the very changing nature of corrupt activities, the tool kit is by no means a definitive handbook and is updated on a regular basis.

The Corruption Fighter's Tool Kit has proved to be an essential part of TI's approach. It is the one tool that shows – in a more accessible language and methodologies than the indexes – what civil society groups have been able to achieve in their effort to curb corruption. It provides a more practical view of these initiatives and strategies and displays a comprehensive list of recommendations to follow.[642]

Raising Awareness (II): The Global Corruption Report

Another publication which has become quite popular among scholars and policy makes who focus on understanding international corruption is TI's Global Corruption Report, a compendium of the major topics and the latest developments in the area of corruption and the major efforts (of TI mostly) in order to eradicate the problem. It contains contributions from journalists and experts from all over the world who report on different issues and cases around the corruption pandemic.[643]

The "global" character of the publication is given by the structure of the report. On the first part, there are regional reports that concentrate on specific characteristical problems around corruption in each continent or regional domain. Thereafter, a second section is dedicated to approach global corruption issues. A third and final part evaluates the latest data on corruption as well as the status of the research on the topic.

There have been two versions of this report, in 2001 and most recently in 2003. A particular feature of the last version is a thematic focus

---

641 An example is the election monitoring in Chile, where the aim was to evaluate the role of the media and their influence on the political decision-making process as well as on the image of candidates. Surveys were carried out by PARTICIPA, a citizen participation in elections group. The results showed a quantitative measurement of candidate's appearance on the media (press, television and radio." See *Ibid.*, p. III-1 ff.

642 It must be observed, that TI's Corruption Fighter's Tool Kit is neither the first not the only of its kind. The handbook makes a resemblance to the United Nations Office on Drugs and Crime (UNODC) Anti-Corruption Tool Kit, a document which contains an extensive set of tools on how to successfully monitor and survey public institutions. See: United Nations Office on Drugs and Crime. The Global Programme Against Corruption. Anti-Corruption Toolkit. (New York. United Nations, 2000.)

643 Transparency International. Global Corruption Report 2001; and *Ibid.*, Global Corruption Report 2003.

given to the access to information. Due to the fact that some of TI's Chapters have made the topic of information their *raison d'être*, the report highlights this area as one of the keys to effectively combat corruption.[644] As we shall see in the next chapter, the role of the media as the "gatekeeper" of information – especially on corruption scandals – has gained analytical importance as well as momentum as a yet further mechanism to curb corruption.[645]

This last development might reveal a certain change in the traditional operational accentuated areas of the organization. Although the role of the media has been stressed out since the very beginnings of the National Integrity Systems, the main approach was to make recommendations for structural changes in which reform (in this case anti-corruption measures) could be better implemented. The 2003 report insists however that reforms are not enough and that the focus should be extended to further institutions such as the media in order to effectively curb corruption.

TI is not reluctant to note this approach might have its own fallacies as well since "[…] there is an abundance of cases in which the media neglect their role of watchdog and instead nurture unsuitably close ties with political leaders."[646] Therefore, after the publication of the latest report there seems to be a stronger reciprocal relationship between what the media can do against and in favour of corruption. Therefore, the Global Report 2003 focuses closely on the importance of information and its free accessibility as an alternative approach. Eigen notes at the conclusion of the report's introduction,

> "Civil society and international institutions fight corruption on many fronts […] Laws and regulations against the misuse of power must be used in this struggle. Restoring trust in public and private institutions must involve access to information to promote transparency, perhaps the most

644 TI Germany provides a good example. Great part of this national chapter's work is devoted to the promotion of a national "freedom of information act" through which more transparency in the public sector should be promoted. Germany is traditional a country in which public officers and administrations reserve themselves the right to provide full information about certain governmental procedures. Further references can be found in: <www.transparency.de>

645 Peter Eigen notes in the introduction of the 2003, that "[e]mpowered by technology – essential to the prompt and accurate flow of information – the media and the public are increasingly calling businesses and politicians to account." In: Transparency International. Global Corruption Report 2001, p. 1.

646 *Ibid.*, p. 5

> important weapon against corruption. Only by insisting on both access to information and greater transparency in every sphere of society, from the local to the intergovernmental, can civil society, business and government hope to forestall and expose corruption [...]"[647]

Civil Courage: The Protection of Whistleblowers

One last area in which TI has been showing considerable successes is promoting effective laws for the protection of those who report "wrongdoing" in public and private institutions, mostly referred to as *whistleblowers*.[648] Whenever a member of government or an employee decides to report irregularities in his/her working place, be that to the pertinent authority (superior), to external parties or to the media, he/she can face tangible risks.[649]

The conflicts that are created by this activity are readily visible. One the one hand, employees have the duty of preserving loyalty towards their institution. At the same time, on the other hand, they carry a personal responsibility to refrain from illicit activities and report them immediately, when they see it. This scenario creates a collision between these two positions, leading to both an ethical and juridical vacuum.[650] Due to this state of uncertainty, many corruption crimes are left out of prosecution, as workers do not want to face the risks of losing their jobs or – even worse – having to fear victimization to them and their families.

As explained before, the statute of TI does not allow the organization and its chapters to undertake individual investigations on corruption cases. In the same manner, the protection of whistleblowers does not take place on an individual case-to-case basis. The efforts go towards promoting more

[647] Ibid.

[648] A whistleblower is mostly defined as the person or group of persons, who "expose misconduct or malpractice in the public interest." In. Drew, Kristine. "Whistle Blowing and Corruption – An Initial and Comparative Review." UNICORN: A Global Trade Unions Anti-Corruption Project. (London: Public Services International Research Unit, January 2003.)

[649] Consequences include: discrimination/victimization by employer, discrimination by future employers (blacklisting), loss of business, loss of financial support, lawsuits for breach of confidentiality and lawsuits for libel or slander. In: Hall, David and Steve Davies. "Corruption and Whistle-Blowing – A Background Note." Paper prepared for the OECD Trade Union Advisory Committee. (London: Public Services International Research Unit, December 1999.)

[650] A scientific treatment on the topic of whistleblowing can be found in: Johnson, Roberta Ann and Michael E. Kraft. "Bureaucratic Whistleblowing and Policy Change." The Western Political Quarterly. Vol. 43, No. 4 (December 1990), pp. 849-874. Also see: Johnson, Roberta Ann. Whistleblowing: When it works – and why. (Boulder: Lynne Rienner Publishers, 2002.)

adequate judicial conditions for assessing whistleblowers and avoid the dangers involved in corruption reporting. A goal in this context is to make workers in both the public administration and the private sector show a greater amount of intolerance and "civil courage" towards corruption by ensuring the existence of "self-defence mechanisms". As consultant Harriet Fletcher comments on TI's most recent Global Corruption Report,

> "[w]histleblowers [...] need a legislative environment that protects them and a corporate culture of openness, if they are to feel secure about reporting incidents of bribery and corruption. But they also need to know where to go for advice on the complex ethical dilemmas that sometimes arise."[651]

In this regard, TI focuses on the protection and assessment of whistleblowers by cooperating with local authorities and civil society groupings in order to advocate in favour of those who show civil courage against corruption.[652]

THE "TRANSPARENCY" OF TRANSPARENCY – A REASSESSMENT

This chapter has provided a sketch of the main elements, strategies and mechanisms of the most prominent non-governmental institution engaged in the global fight against corruption and its ramifications, Transparency International. At the end of the chapter, a reassessment is needed for an adequate scientific and empirical classification of Transparency International in the entire scholarly debate about corruption.

---

651 Fletcher, Harriet. "Corporate transparency in the fight against corruption". In: Transparency International. Global Corruption Report 2003, p. 39.

652 A good example of best practices in this case can be found in South Africa, where the Open Democracy Advice Centre – an independent civil society organization – works closely with many sectors of society and government to promote the implementation and enforcement of the Protected Disclosures Act (Whistleblowing Act), passed by the South African Parliament in 2000. The program includes advocacy and training around this Act and offers services to public and private employees who are involved whistleblowing dilemmas. The Act per se foresees the protection against negative consequences towards employees who report irregularities in their workplace. In: Transparency International. The Corruption Fighter's Tool Kit, p. IV-40 ff. A more detailed analysis of this document can be found in: Camerer, Lala. "Protecting Whistle Blowers in South Africa: The Protected Disclosures Act, no. 26 of 2000." Occasional Paper N0. 47. (South Africa: Institute for Security Studies, 2001.)

This concluding reassessment has three main argumentative points: 1) TI's definition of corruption as the basis for every step taken by the organization against this phenomenon; 2) the impact and reliability of TI's most prominent product, the Corruption Perceptions Index (CPI) and the Briber Payers Index (BPI); and 3) the question of legitimacy and "transparency" of TI, as being the "world's conscience" concerning the problem of global corruption.

On the first point, we take a step back to Chapter One of this book, and use one of the main results thereof, namely, that there is more to corruption than the sole "abuse of public office or private gain." The great disadvantage of such a definition is that it completely neglects the existence of corruption in the private sector thus directing all the attention to the government and its related agencies.

Moreover, as Phillip noted, such a narrow definition needs to be specific about what and who is meant by "public office" and about how "misuse" is placed and interpreted within the context of politics.[653] These two pivotal elements of the definition proposed by the World Bank and adopted by TI do face such analytical challenges. The interesting aspect of this posture is that there does not seem to be any debate on this, when looking at the agenda of the organization. In this regard, it can be said that it has become a matter of definitional conformism for TI neither to consider not to approach the fallacies of their working definition.

Without going too deep into the definitional debate, a further clear consequence might be that TI mostly concentrates on solving just one side of the problem, namely the corrupt public administration. Although this allegation can be easily denied by looking at many instances in which TI goes beyond the government scope and focuses on the private side of corruption, it can be noted that the entire framework of the organization suffers from a limitation, as a consequence of their working definition. This means, that an organization such as TI should strongly consider the fact that corruption is not only a problem primarily generated by governments, but also by private companies and international corporations.

In this regard, many measures and strategies have successfully drifted from their government-centered notion and have evaluated the private sector as an equal source of the problem.[654] However, if the working definition of TI could be specifically extended within the context of the "private side" of

[653] Phillip. "Conceptualizing Political Corruption."

[654] For instance, the Bribe Payers Index concentrates on the evaluating which companies seem to offer the most bribes. Also, strategies on developing adequate business ethics and codes of conduct are among the initiatives from TI to focus on the private sector.

corruption, many of its directives could be followed in a more enhanced way, without the analytical restrictions discussed above.

Second, there is no doubt that both the CPI and the BPI are currently the most prominent indexes on corruption. Both the success of this approach and its contribution to the academic and public debate on corruption, are of considerable magnitude. It is said that the reliability of the CPI is its strongest point.[655] Nevertheless, several factors still remain open for the validity and precision of these indexes, especially when it comes to comparing and ranking countries. The CPI uses corruption as a one-dimensional phenomenon, meaning it does not analyze any of the ramifications thereof (embezzlement, fraud, nepotism, etc.)[656] Moreover, it has been said that both indexes could be biased in terms of depicting that the most corruption-plagued countries are developing and least developing nations.[657] Further, corruption can take place in different level and ways even within the same country. This is something that the CPI is still unable to measure.[658]

Therefore, despite their prominence, the use of such indexes should be undertaken with extreme analytical caution, as their explanatory power might be subject to severe methodological fallacies. The negation of this problem has easily led to claims and allegations made – especially by the media – on the particular ranking of a country, without considering the very fact that such classifications strictly refer to data that is not entirely representative.[659]

Finally, there is the question on the moral validity on TI as the "voice" of civil society in the area of anti-corruption initiatives. The problem that TI faces is not entirely new, but it must be noted notwithstanding, if we want to have an objective evaluation of the NGO approach against corruption. As noted at the beginning of this chapter, NGOs have gained an important place in the area of world politics, influencing the public opinion, and – at times – even forcing states to take certain courses of action. TI and its efforts on curbing corruption have not been the exception. Nevertheless, there remains the question of legitimacy and monitoring. As Louis Pauly postulated in his famous book on who elected the international *bankiers* who dictate and run

---

655 Johnston, "Measuring the New Corruption Rankings", p. 871.

656 *Ibid.*, p. 42

657 Ibid.

658 Johnston, "Measuring the New Corruption Rankings", p. 873.

659 A common mistake made in this context is to believe, that the lowest-ranked countries on the CPI are the most corrupt in the world. Considering the major fallacies in the methodology of the CPI, such a critical judgement is not entirely plausible.

the world economy, the same question can be posed in the field of corruption: who elected Transparency?

It is doubtless that the goals and directives of the organization are absolutely valuable. However, it remains unclear who (meaning societal, economic and political groupings) is really behind such organizations and under which interests and influence they operate. One example about this problem is concerned with the CPI. Although there is not any empirical evidence to it, it might occur that TI faces external pressures from states who want to "look good" on the corruption scale and thus try to influence TI negatively. Countries that have a negative image portrayed by the CPI, might undertake efforts to change the ranking through unconventional means (e.g. by making false statements or portraying a picture contrary to the TI and the CPI) in order to change the message delivered by the CPI. The lack of any clear evidence leaves these two points to speculation, however, these are scenarios that need to be considered in any objective assessment of the organization.

Lastly, and yet more important, there is no institution monitoring TI. Again, this fact does not undermine in any means the achievement of the organization. It merely points out that there is little knowledge on whose interests does TI actually serve and what kind of goals the National Chapters might have in certain countries. Recalling Rose-Ackermann's observation on the incidence of corruption in NGOs, the author did acknowledge that the existence of corruption-related activities in these institutions is not utopian anymore.[660] Only because such institutions have "noble" and "altruistic" goals, does not free them from any voluntary or involuntary illicit activities.[661] Recent initiatives such as the worldwide civil society network CIVICUS have developed strategies to closely monitor the work of civil society groupings and NGOs.[662] The results show that there is wide acceptance for the overall transparency of civil society networks and independent organizations such as TI. However, we should remain aware of the fact, that

---

660 Rose-Ackermann. "Corruption and the Private Sector", pp. 202 ff.

661 On these two points, I want to sincerely thank the participants of the seminar at LMU Munich "The International Fight Against Corruption: Tilling in the Sea?" for their valuable input and eager discussions on this matter.

662 Heinrich, Volkhart Finn. "Transparency and corruption within civil society organizations." In: Transparency International. Global Corruption Report 2003, p. 271. The author explains that in order to enhance the transparency of civil society groups and NGOs, CIVICUS undertakes periodical surveys and indexes in many countries assessing the state of civil groupings and organizations. For further reference see: <www.civicus.org>

even in the case of Transparency International, "the saints may sin inside the church."[663]

[663] See the case of Alberto Dahik in note 592.

CHAPTER SEVEN

THE MEDIA

> "Freedom of speech and a free press are generally considered human rights and powerful control instruments against government malfeasance. An independent press is the most likely mean for uncovering political trespassing. The reason is that any independent journalist has a strong incentive to investigate and uncover stories on wrongdoings. Countries with a free press should, therefore, ceteris paribus, have less corruption than countries where the press is controlled and censored."[664]

Mass communication has been recognized as a key feature of the recent processes of globalization. Nowadays, news spread all over the world faster than ever before. This has changed the traditional ways through which the media influenced public policy and its outcomes. The reasons are easily apparent. Economist David Strömberg explains that "if more informed voters receive favourable policies, then mass media should matter because they provide most of the information use in voting."[665] In the age of high speed internet connections and mobile communications, this influence has grown strong transcending from local/national level on to the international arena.

World politics has received the impact of a steady increasing presence of the media in international affairs as a result of both modern globalisation processes and technological advances. As a consequence of this "information revolution", the impact of the media on politics can be observed in four main areas.[666] First, the amount of information available to governments is so extensive, that there seems to be a news overflow.[667] Second, due to the influence of global networks, decision-making can be easily centralized or decentralized. This means, that there are so many more channels through which states communicate with each other, that they nowadays have the choice to either "micro-manage" crises or bring them out to the international

---

664 Weder and Brunetti. "A Free Press is Bad News for Corruption", p. 2.

665 Strömberg, David. "Mass media and public policy." European Economic Review (2001) Vol. 45, pp. 652-663.

666 As observed by Aronson, Jonathan. "The communications and Internet revolution." In. Baylis and Smith. The Globalization of World Politics, p. 549.

667 Ibid.

public attention.[668] Third, the globalization of mass media networks has diminished the information monopoly that states used to have on world affairs. Today, transnational media enterprises like CNN or BBC have even more information than most states, making them rely more on the media than on their own officers.[669] Lastly, and in the context of corruption certainly not less important, the media provides a certain amount of transparency in international politics, making it difficult for states to ignore the existence and importance of worldwide communication acting as *watchdogs* over the international public opinion.[670]

This last observation is the starting point for the arguments of the following chapter. Taking into consideration that the influence of the media has indeed grown stronger on states and that corruption has been globalized as a problem, then the resulting question is how much of a role does the media actually play in both the exposure of corruption scandals and as a featured element of different anti-corruption initiatives.

As the last Global Corruption Report proposed, the access of information and the presence of the media as independent and free observers has become a basic element of the current anti-corruption discourse.[671] However, the media has been exposed to criticisms in this regard as well, as observed in Chapter Six.

Therefore, this chapter provides an overview of the different aspects of the relationship between the media, journalists, and corruption considering five main elements: 1) the different roles journalists assume in society within the anti-corruption context; 2) the effects of the media when covering corruption news; 3) the critical relationship between press freedom and corruption; 4) the "ethics" of journalists; and 5) the latest recommendations to strengthen the position of the media both in the academic and practical discussion of corruption and its eradication.

---

[668] Ibid.

[669] *Ibid.* Some authors refer to this phenomenon as the "CNN effect", meaning that the latest technological innovations in the field of communication and mass media can generate greater reactions from citizens and politicians thus leading states to adapt their foreign behaviour according to "what's in the news." In: Robinson. "The CNN Effect: can the news drive foreign policy?", p. 301.

[670] Ibid.

[671] Transparency International. Global Corruption Report 2003.

THE ROLE OF THE MEDIA IN THE ANTI-CORRUPTION CONTEXT

The relationship between media and politics serves as the starting point for the analysis of the role of journalists within the area of corruption. The influence of mass communication in the agendas of politicians and in the policy outcomes of government agencies has a long tradition in the field of communication studies.[672] The main message of the scholarship is that there is a solid reciprocity between journalism and politics with attributed roles for each of the parties involved.[673]

As much as politics might actually have an influence on the media, journalists place an equal amount of pressure on politicians. This causal relationship becomes interesting for this chapter, if applied to the topic of corruption and other illicit activities. Based on this premise, the media can perform three basic roles when it comes to corruption. First, the media serves as the main *discoverer* of corruption, be that in the public administration or in private companies. Most secret corrupt deals turn into public scandals only after they have been disclosed by the media. In this context, journalists differ from criminal investigators, as they not only discover, but also disclose corruption cases.

Second, journalists are constantly viewed as *watchdogs*, who root about in national political affairs and have the choice of "exposing what they deem right for exposure."[674] Based on this premise, politicians and businessmen alike are aware of the fact that corruption is a highly dangerous enterprise since the media is constantly watching and reporting on their activities. The risks involved in the exposure of corruption scandals on the news might even diminish the rate of temptation to get involved in such activities.[675]

The third and last function attributed to the media is that of an *educator*. When reporting about corruption, journalists have the unique possibility of "teaching" the public about corruption, about its effects, and about how to fight it. They differ from criminal investigators and judges who solely present

---

672 The most prominent studies in this area include: McCombs, Maxwell and Donald Shaw. "The Agenda-Setting Function of Mass Media." Public Opinion Quarterly (1972) Vol. 36, pp. 176-187; McQuail, Denis. Mass Communication Theory. (London: Sage Publications, 1994); McCombs, Maxwell. "Building Consensus: The News Media' Agenda-Setting Role." Political Communication (1997) Vol. 14, pp. 433-444; and most recently McCombs, Maxwell. Setting the Agenda. The News Media and Public Opinion. (Cambridge, UK: Polity Press, 2004.)

673 Patterson, Thomas E. "Political Roles of the Journalist." In: Graber, Doris, Denis McQuail and Pippa Norris (eds.) The Politics of News - The News of Politics. (Washington, D.C.: Congressional Quarterly Press, 1998) p. 25 ff.

674 Herman, Edward S. "The Media's Role on U.S. Foreign Politics." Journal of International Affairs. (1993) Vol. 47, No. 1, pp. 23-43.

675 Pope. "An Independent and Free Media." In: TI Source Book, p.120.

the results of any given corruption scandal, since the media can use several more illustrative means to bring out the characteristics of corruption out to the public in a more understandable way.

As we shall see in the following sub-sections of this chapter, these roles are subject to many critics from academia and anti-corruption practitioners. Also, it must be noted that the latest technological advances in the field of information technologies have also influenced the scope and very nature of these asserted roles.

THE EFFECTS OF JOURNALISTIC CORRUPTION COVERAGE

"Corruption! Scandal! Few other words catch the reader's eye or the listener's ears as do those words [...]"[676] This observation by political scientist Harvey Kebschull denotes the imminent magnitude of the single term "corruption" when brought about in the news. This also means that the range of effects media coverage can have on politics, economics and society expands due to the allegedly wide audiences this term is able to reach.

World Bank analyst Rick Stapenhurst indicates that there are two major kinds of effects through which the media can influence the incidence of corruption.[677] *Tangible* effects refer to the immediate events that can be seen and followed after a corruption scandal has been brought up to the public by the media, while *intangible* effects are more long-term debates that arise from this disclosure of irregularities.[678] On the former, Stapenhurst notes that following most corruption scandals, the exposure of corrupt officials, the re-enforcement of the work and legitimacy of anti-corruption laws and institutions (be that governmental or non-governmental), the immediate beginning of investigations by public officials and agencies, and the shaping of public opinion about corruption become the *a priori* consequences of the work of journalists when covering corruption stories.[679] On the latter, the author notes that the media can act as a "balancing" institution, creating public awareness and strengthening partnerships with NGOs and other civil society groups in order to support them and bring them on to the public spotlight.[680]

[676] Kebschull. "Political Corruption: Making it the 'Significant Other' in Political Studies", p. 705.

[677] Stapenhurst. "The Media's Role in Curbing Corruption", p. 2.

[678] Ibid.

[679] Ibid.

[680] Ibid.

There are several examples for both tangible and intangible effects, in developing as well as in industrialized countries.[681] For the most part, the former category is the result of what is seen, read, and heard in the news every day. Whenever a corruption scandal makes it to the headlines, "the heads start rolling" almost immediately. As we shall see in the case studies, the impact of the media on politics through the disclosure of corrupt activities has been so great, that in the case of Ecuador and Argentina, entire governments have been dismantled. Therefore the exposure of officials can be considered the media's most widely used weapon against the spread of corruption.

Further on, it is important to stress the output corruption media coverage can have in terms of promoting the enforcement and empowerment of anti-corruption laws and anti-corruption agencies. As it was observed in Chapter Six, most of the prominence of Transparency International has been attributed to the extensive coverage this organization has received throughout the world. On the local level, the creation of anti-corruption agencies has been fuelled by the insistence thereof in the press.[682] Also, media coverage allows for stressing out the legitimacy of such agencies, something that has been criticized and debates in past occasions by political and social groupings.

On the more "criminalistic" side, media coverage on corruption can mark the initial moment for investigations from the government on specific cases of irregularities. Back in the 1970s, most of the official investigations on the Watergate scandal were initiated after the news were brought up by the Washington Post. In a similar way, corruption news creates enough awareness so that the government – at times – is forced to take immediate actions on the matter.[683] Moreover, news coverage can also discover the

---

681 In the case of developed countries, the French government's involvement in the scandal on Elf Aquitaine shocked the public opinion all over Europe, convicting high level officials and numerous other members of previous French governments. In these cases, the media had been the mechanism through which not only the scandals were spread, but also created the necessary momentum to push for immediate measures against corruption.

682 In the aftermath of the uprising against President Eduard Shevardnadze, members of the media have welcomed the efforts of the newly elected President Mikhail Saakashvili to curb down corruption in the country. Furthermore, the Georgian Chapter of TI has issued several key urgent recommendations for the President to follow in order to successfully tackle down the problem. Among them is the re-structuring of the anti-corruption commission as well as the establishment of the office of an Auditor General. See also. Transparency International. "TI outlines anti-corruption priorities for Georgian President Mikhail Saakashvili." Press Release.<www.transparency.ge/extra/1075816001.php> (29.01.2004.)

683 The fall, impeachment and indictment of Venezuelan President Carlos Andrés Pérez were started by an investigative article on one of the country's major newspapers. According to the source, Pérez had been involved in the misappropriation of $ 17 million missing discretionary funds. The explosion

flaws of regulatory bodies and official institutions while acting against corruption.[684]

Lastly, the impact of journalists on the public opinion should be highlighted. The general role of the media on the processes of creating and establishing public opinion is widely known. Communication scientists have preached since the 1920s that mass communication could become the main source for how people view the world, and that the media can be a tool for manipulation and social control.[685] Within the context of corruption these points sully apply. The mass media does play an imminent part in shaping the image and opinion on the phenomenon of corruption to the public. The main reason for this causal relationship can be asserted to the multi-levelled scope of corrupt practices. As criminal law professor Terttu Utriainen observes,

> "[t]he economic consequences of corruption are severe; it tends to strike at the heart of the community; it involves a conflict which has been deemed a crime; and the suspects and guilty parties are often prominent figures in society."[686]

In this context, the author explains that the media is the perfect mechanism to spread "anti-corruption values" to the public opinion. By reporting on corruption cases, the media fulfils the need of the public for being properly informed about this phenomenon and influences the image thereof.[687] Despite its importance, this point has become the "Achilles heel" of the media's involvement in anti-corruption initiatives. The main criticism is that only an independent media can assume the great responsibility behind shaping public opinion about corruption. In many instances, however, the media has been said to serve the interests of politicians and businessmen alike, and has covered up corruption, instead of the opposite, thus portraying the false image to the outside.[688]

---

of the scandal in the press led to thorough investigations that at the end forced him to resign. In: Stapenhurst. "The Media's Role in Curbing Corruption", p. 3.

684 *Ibid.*, p. 8.

685 Perse, Elizabeth. Media Effects and Society. (Mahwah, NJ and London: Lawrence Erlbaum Associates, 2001), p. 3. The author makes reference to classic communication science authors such as Walter Lippmann and Harold Lasswell.

686 Utriainen, Terttu. "The Role of the Media in Preventing Corruption." Working Paper for the 8th International Anti-Corruption Conference. (Lima: Transparency International, 1998.)

687 Ibid.

688 This is specially the case when both the media and politics are represented by the same person, for example the Italian broadcasting company RAI and its owner Italian Prime Minister Silvio Berlusconi.

Following the second category of effects of the media on corruption, Stapenhurst noted that there are certain instances, in which corruption scandals not only generate immediate consequences but also activate long-term initiatives and strategies. The first of such intangible effects deals with the fact, that the media can be used as the adequate instrument to create public awareness on corruption, perhaps even more effectively than NGOs. Due to the fact that newspapers, radio and television reach broader audiences than NGOs, they can pass on information on the incidence and effect of corruption more extendedly and with more prospects for success.

The intangible effect is that precisely NGOs and other civil society groups work hand in hand with reporters on the same goal, namely curbing corruption.[689] Therefore the partnership between the media and NGOs seems pivotal within the framework of anti-corruption measures. But again within this relationship, the independence of journalists (from the influence of the above mentioned groups) remains highly important for the objective value of what they produce, write and broadcast. As former TI Vice Chairman Frank Vogl once warned,

> "[...] the press must constantly challenge and it must challenge everyone. The press should challenge TI. It should see our balance sheets and challenge us to be open about our operations. It should challenge the relationships we have with our sponsors if it sees potential fault here. It should question our own expertise and our accountability. The press should be sure to review our methodologies before it publishes our CPI rankings. The press dare not get too close to governments, to business, to special interests and to non-governmental organisations. The battle against corruption demands an entirely independent press."[690]

PRESS FREEDOM AND THE INCIDENCE OF CORRUPTION

Following the argument of the last quote, freedom and independence (both political and economic) of the media has become the most important

Under the latter's command, independent coverage on irregularities in the government are highly limited and thus not properly presented to the viewers. In: Peters, Bettina. "The media's role: covering or covering up corruption?" In: Transparency International. Global Corruption Report 2003, p. 51.

689 Stapenhurst. "The Media's Role in Curbing Corruption", p. 9.

690 Vogl, Frank. "The Media and Corruption." Working Paper for the 9th International Anti-Corruption Conference. (Durban: Transparency International, 1998.)

element for its position towards the topic of corruption. As observed in the beginning of the chapter, politics and journalism have a strong reciprocal relationship. This relationship becomes highly volatile when the coverage of corruption is undertaken under the influence of political and economic sectors both on national as well as on international levels.

In this regard, the relationship between press freedom and the incidence of corruption becomes a necessary target of analysis. A recent study by Brunetti and Weder shows that there is enough significant evidence to defend the hypothesis that there is more press freedom in countries with less corruption.[691]

The authors note that there are three central determinants for measuring the incidence of corruption: 1) internal controls meaning official incentives to control corruption within the administration; 2) external controls, mainly performed by the judiciary power and civil society organizations; and 3) indirect factors, for example culture and levels of distortion in the economy.[692] Based on this preliminary evaluation, the Brunetti and Weder place press freedom within the second category, namely as an external control mechanism for corruption. This choice is made under the assumption, that external mechanisms such as judiciary bodies and *watchdog* agencies provide little empirical evidence on the actual power of such measures against corruption. Therefore, by using press freedom, the authors intend to gain an empirically solid factor for the determining the incidence of corruption across countries.[693]

They focus the analysis on the critical relationship between citizens and government officials in two contexts: 1) when the latter has a monopoly over a certain good or service and starts extorting the former (extortive corruption); and 2) when a government official makes informal agreements on the application of rules (collusive corruption.) In both cases the importance of the press is highlighted then any victim of corruption

> "[…] has the option of either paying the bribe or complaining to a higher official or the judiciary, i.e., use channels of internal or external control. […] However, if the costs of appealing are very high which means that the

[691] Brunetti and Weder. "A Free Press is Bad News for Corruption", p. 1802 ff.

[692] Ibid.

[693] *Ibid.*, 1806 p. The authors analyzed data from more than 125 countries based on information from both International Country Risk Guide, Transparency International and Freedom House, an independent think tank that surveys political rights, civil liberties and, since 1996, press freedom.

> formal mechanisms of internal and external control are not working well, the [citizen] might be better off by surrendering to the extortion. A free and active press constitutes an additional channel of external control which can reduce the costs of fighting extortive corruption. A firm can reveal (or credibly threaten to reveal) the bureaucrat's behaviour to a journalist and the (potential) media reports will raise the costs for the bureaucrat as the probability of being detected and punished is increased [...] Independent journalists have incentives to actively investigate *any* wrong doing."[694]

Therefore, the degree of press and media independence becomes of notable factor for the actual effectiveness of corruption coverage as mechanism to eradicate the problem. Using correlations from survey such as the CPI, Freedom House and the World Bank, Brunetti and Weder considered four categories for their investigation, namely legal, political, economic influences over media content, and last but not least, repressive actions against journalists.[695] The results were striking.

Using the level of corruption as the dependent variable and exposing it to the quality of bureaucracy, external controls, distortions and restrictions of economic competition, and cultural backgrounds in each country, Brunetti and Weder come to conclusion that for the most part, the level of press freedom correlates positively with the incidence of corruption. Moreover, in countries with sound functioning bureaucracies, an effective rule of law, the respect for political rights and liberties and a stable economy, press freedom is more likely to reduce the levels of corruption than in countries that have negative scores on these four elements.[696]

The authors do recognize that there are alternative measurements to both the incidence of corruption and the incidence of press freedom. However, the evidence they presented is solid enough to make a valid empirically tested observation on the importance of press freedom for curbing corruption. This point shall become very useful when we analyze the case studies in Section III, as both indicators (press freedom and corruption) are very different for each case.

694 *Ibid.*, p. 1804.

695 For a closer look at the data see *Ibid.*, p. 1821 and note 557.

696 Brunetti and Weder. "A Free Press is Bad News for Corruption", p. 1813. The authors note, that an improvement of 46 points on the freedom indicator could reduce corruption by at least one point on the scale.

FIGURE 11: CORRELATION BETWEEN CORRUPTION AND PRESS FREEDOM

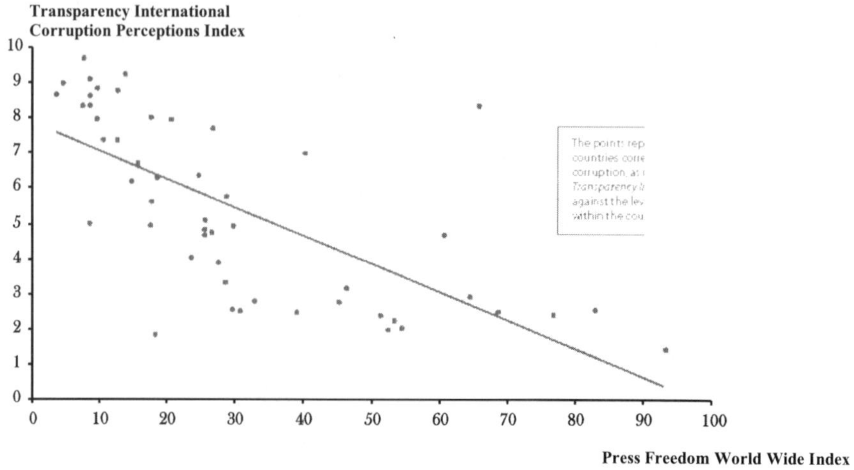

Source: Stapenhurst. "The Media's Role in Curbing Corruption", p. 2. See also: Brunetti and Weder. "A Free Press is Bad News for Corruption", p. 1811.

The points on the graph represent countries which have been correlated using the incidence of corruption measured by Transparency International's Corruption Perceptions Index (CPI) and Press Freedom World Wide Index. According to the source, the correlation rate is -0.69.[697]

JOURNALIST ETHICS

Although press freedom is a highly significant element for the position of the media in the corruption debate, there is a further aspect that deserves equal attention, namely the ethics of journalists at work. Corruption has effects on the ethics of journalists, as it has on the ethics of politicians. Although the stakes are different, journalists are exposed to corruption in a similar ways as politicians are. They can, for instance, receive perks from an organization or public agencies that want to assure positive coverage on a

697 Stapenhurst. "The Media's Role in Curbing Corruption", p. 2.

specific topic.[698] Moreover, pressures can be made on the media not to publish or broadcast a story, because an offer has been made to the editors or directly to the journalists involved.[699] There have been even instances in which journalists themselves start the corrupt transaction by "blackmailing" politicians for financial rewards in exchange for non-exposure or for good reviews, a practice referred to as "Cash for Editorial".[700]

This difficult scenario demands strong ethics from journalists in order to avoid conflicts of interest, external pressures, and the temptation of demanding bribes for news coverage. According to Utriainen, although organizations such as the UN and the OSCE have developed international journalistic codes of ethics, the implementation thereof for each country is still difficult, as each nation has its own values and opinions when it comes to ethics.[701] However, she summarizes seven important elements that should be included in any version of such codes. According to the author, any journalists should have the duty to:

1) tell the truth without malice or prejudice
2) use honest methods,
3) show respect for professional integrity and responsibility,
4) exercise discretion,
5) work for the solution of economic, social and humanitarian problems,
6) help to strengthen respect for human rights, and
7) assist in the maintenance of international peace and security.[702]

---

[698] In India and Mexico, for example, journalist earn "stipends" from the institutions they cover. In: Pope. "An Independent and Free Media." In: *Ibid.* and TI. TI Source Book 2000, p. 120 ff. In developed countries, the offers of "freebies" (meaning free travek and hospitality at hotels) for journalists are a common practice that is – at times – expected from journalistst when they take over a story. In: Peters, "The media's role: covering or covering up corruption?" p. 52 ff.

[699] Ibid.

[700] A recent survey by the International Public Relations Association (IPRA) shows that the incidence of unethical media practices is very high, especially when economic benefits for journalists are at stake. In some countries, more than half of the population believes that the content of editorials and articles is constantly influences by politicians or economic groups that accept the unethical conditions posed by journalists. See also: International Public Relations Association. "Unethical Media Practices Revealed by IPRA Report." <www.ipra.org/campaing/icmt/docs/press2.htm> (14.06.2002.)

[701] Utriainen, "The Role of the Media in Preventing Corruption."

[702] Ibid.

If applied to the topic of corruption, journalist can use these guidelines in order to have clear standards on how to proceed when interacting with politicians and businessmen. The practices of using codes of ethics are widely spread nowadays. According to the International Journalist Network (IJN) there are nearly 200 different documents in more than 50 countries which contain codes of ethics and provisions for journalists and the media.[703] Considering that there are 193 countries in the international community (per membership at the United Nations), the numbers are rather low.

Therefore, the problem remains in making journalists worldwide aware of the existence and the importance of these documents. There are many instances in which the media becomes involved in illicit activities and journalists do not know exactly how to proceed because such codes are neither available not existent. Due to the fact that corruption, as any other form of crime, is a highly ethical issue, the role of the media remains subject to the normative assessment of journalists when they cover corruption news.

FIGURE 12: SELECTED CODES OF ETHICS WORLDWIDE

Country	Document/Institution	Country	Document/Institution
Albania	Albanian Code of the Journalist's Ethics	Luxembourg	Press Council
Algeria	National Union of Journalists	Macedonia	Code of the Journalists of Macedonia
Armenia	Association of Investigative Journalists	Malawi	Media Council Of Malawi
Asia	Asian Federation of Environmental Journalists	Malaysia	Canons of Journalism
Australia	Australian Associated Press (AAP)	Mali	Code of Ethics of the Malian Journalist
Azerbaijan	Code of Professional Ethics for Journalists	Malta	Press Club (Malta) and Institute of Broadcasters
Bangladesh	Bangladesh Press	Mexico	Ethics Protocol for

703 As see in: International Journalists' Network. "Codes of Ethics" <www.ijnet.org> International Center of Journalists.

	Council		Communication and Mutual Aid
Belarus	Belarus Union of Journalists Code of Professional Ethics of Journalists	Middle East /North Africa	Arab Information Charter of Honour
Belgium	Association Générale des Journalistes Professionnels de Belgique (AGJPB)	Moldova	Journalists' Union of Moldova (JUM)
Benin	General Assembly of Journalists [1991]	Mongolia	Code of Conduct of Daily News
Bosnia and Herzegovina	General Press Code for Bosnian Journalists	Morocco	National Union of the Moroccan Press
Brazil	Código de Ética de los Periodistas Brasileños	Nepal	Press Council
Bulgaria	Union of Bulgarian Journalists Rules of Journalistic Ethics	New Zealand	New Zealand Press Council
Burundi	Code of Ethics of the Burundi Press	Niger	Etats généraux de la presse
Canada	Canadian Association of Broadcasters (CAB)	Nigeria	Nigerian Press Organization
Caribbean Countries	Association of Caribbean Media Workers	Norway	Norwegian Press Association
Chile	Code of Ethics of the Association of Journalists	Pakistan	Ethical Code of Practice
Colombia	Code of the Journalists' Circle of Bogota	Papua New Guinea	Papua New Guinea Journalists' Association (PNGJA)
Costa Rica	Association of Costa Rican Journalists	Paraguay	Ethics Code of TELEFUTURO
Croatia	Croatian Journalists' Association	Peru	National Association of Journalists of Peru
Cyprus	Union of Cyprus Journalists	Philippines	Philippine Press Institute

Czech Republic	Declaration of Principles on the Conduct of Journalists	Poland	Polish Journalists Association
DR of Congo	General Council of the Press Union of Zaire [1990]	Portugal	Syndicate of Journalists
Denmark	National Code of Conduct	Romania	Romanian Press Club
Egypt	Charter of Work and Code of Ethics in the Press	Russia	Congress of Russian Journalists
Estonia	Code of Press Ethics	Rwanda	Charter of Duties and Rights of the Journalists
Ethiopia	Ethiopian Free Press Journalists' Association	Saudi Arabia	Media Charter
Europe	European Code on the Ethics of Journalism	Senegal	Sud Quotidien
Fiji	Fiji Islands Media Association	Serbia and Montenegro	Ethical Code for Broadcasters
Finland	Union of Journalists in Finland	Sierra Leone	Sierra Leone Association of Journalists
France	National Syndicate of French Journalists	Singapore	Journalists' Code of Professional Conduct
Georgia	Independent Association of Georgian Journalists	Slovakia	Slovak Syndicate of Journalists
Germany	German Press Council	Slovenia	Code of Journalists
Ghana	Ghana Journalists Association	South Africa	South African Union of Journalists
Greece	National Council on Broadcasting	South Korea	Press Ethics Code
Guatemala	Association of Journalists of Guatemala	Spain	Federation of the Spanish Press
Hong Kong	Code of Ethics of	Sri Lanka	Sri Lanka Press

	HKJA		Council
Hungary	National Association of Hungarian Journalists	Sub-Saharan Africa	Code of Ethics of East Africa
Iceland	Union of Icelandic Journalists	Sweden	Code of Ethics for Press, Media and Television
India	Press Council of India	Switzerland	Swiss Federation of Journalists
Indonesia	Alliance of Independent Journalists	Taiwan	Association of Taiwanese Journalists
Iraq	Rules of Professional Ethics	Tanzania	Code of Ethical Practice for Public Information and Media Advertisers
Ireland	National Union of Journalists	Thailand	Press Council of Thailand
Israel	Israel Press Council [1973]	Togo	National Associations of Journalists
Italy	National Federation of the Italian Press	Tunisia	Association of Tunisian Journalists
Ivory Coast	Rights and Duties of the Ivoirian Journalist	Turkey	Association of Turkish Journalists
Japan	Nihon Shinbun Kyokai Canon of Journalism	Uganda	National Institute of Journalists of Uganda (NIJU)
Jordan	Code of Ethics of the Jordanian Journalists	United Kingdom	British National Union of Journalists
Kazakhstan	Kazakhstanskaya Pravda	United States	American Society of Newspaper Editors
Kenya	Kenyan Union of Journalists	Worldwide	Code of Conduct for Journalism and Media in Brussels [International Federation of Journalists]
Kyrgyzstan	Association of Journalists of Kyrgyzstan	Worldwide	Federation of International Editors of Journals

Latin America	Latin American Federation of Journalists	Worldwide	Forum of Journalists for Freedom of Expression and Information
Latvia	Latvian Union of Journalists	Worldwide	International Federation of Journalists - Tirana Declaration
Lebanon	Lebanon Charter of Professional Honour	Worldwide	International Principles of Professional Ethics in Journalism (UNESCO)
Liberia	Press Union of Liberia	Worldwide	Islamic Mass Media Charter
Lithuania	Lithuanian Union of Journalists	Zambia	Media Council

Source: International Journalists' Network. "Codes of Ethics."

Moreover, journalists are subject to both internal and external pressures on how to cover corruption news and this might also persuade them in their ethical commitments.

Earlier observations in Chapter One and Two showed that corruption can be a matter of personal beliefs and individual values. This also applies to the coverage of corruption news, since journalists may follow up on stories that they believe to be important or feasible according to their own perception of corruption. Therefore, any initiative against corruption through the media should include the elaboration, distribution and implementation of appropriate ethical codes so that journalists are able to know, justify and evaluate their actions accordingly. Without the existence of such guidelines, the media would much probably loose its credibility and its fundamental position in the fight against corruption.

STRENGTHENING THE ROLE OF THE MEDIA IN THE FIGHT AGAINST CORRUPTION

This chapter has portrayed the importance of journalists and the media in the fight against corruption. Moreover, it was showed that there are immense pressures that generate from the government as well as from the private sector in order to manipulate news and, especially, to diminish the risks of disclosure of corruption scandals. Lastly, it was determined that journalists need to rely on adequate levels of press freedom and independence in order to perform their job. It seems to be that there is still a great need for empowering the press and the media, in order to successfully curb corruption.

Therefore, several recommendations have been made, especially from the side of non-state actors on how to enforce initiatives which would strengthen the work of the media and ensure an adequate level of independence and press freedom so that journalists can perform their assigned roles within politics, economic and society. The following points review the most important considerations in this context.

Press and Media Ownership

As the Italian case showed earlier, the media is constantly under internal pressure due to the fact that media owners or moguls are either involved directly in politics or indirectly serve the interests of certain political groupings. According to the Global Corruption Report 2003, it has been demonstrated that, for example, state-owned media tends to be less effective than private media companies in objectively handling governmental affairs.[704]

Therefore, independence of the media in terms of ownership is a crucial factor for reassuring its position towards citizens and the government as well. A suggested solution is to privatize all state-owned or controlled media in order to assure this independence.[705] However, it must be noted that privatization should not be the only *a priori* solution, as it might happen that privatized media operate under the guidelines of the economic groups who

[704] Peters. "The media's role: covering or covering up corruption?", p. 49. The author notes that in the case of Mexico, privatization efforts in the media sector allowed the main broadcasting company to increase the coverage on corruption scandals within the Mexican administration.

[705] Pope. "An Independent and Free Media." In: TI Source Book, p. 121.

are behind them.[706] Therefore, if the concentration of media ownership could be equally dispersed between the public and the private sector, favourable conditions could be created for journalists assuring fair inter-media competition, the free exchange of opinions and thus constant and constructive dialogue within the different sectors of society. When it comes to eradicating corruption, this dialogue is keen to become one of the biggest contributions of the media to alleviate this problem.[707]

Important aspects for assuring the independence of the media are legal guarantees that codify the independence of journalists from media owners. However, not many countries have established such regulations in their jurisdiction.[708] Moreover, even when there are established rules for the press in any constitution, politicians might block the work of the media by imposing contrary regulations, especially when it comes to the access of information. Therefore, adequate provisions within the legal framework of any country are highly recommended for the freedom and independence of journalists. As Pope suggests,

> "[l]aws declaring 'freedom of expression' require support and enforcement from the courts. An independent judiciary is the handmaiden of a free media. Without an independent judiciary, media freedom is likely to be illusory. A prerequisite for building free media, therfore, is a legal system that is independent of political influence and has a firm constitutional jurisprudence supporting the concept of a free media."[709]

---

706 Stapenhurst. "The Media's Role in Curbing Corruption", p. 10. The author makes reference to the case of Russia, where the fall of the Soviet Union and the privatization of many sectors of society, including the media, have brought about new corrupt networks in which press freedom depends directly on the financial groups who support media assets.

707 A useful overview of the current debate on media ownership in the context of globalization can be found in: McChesney, Robert W. and Dan Schiller. "The Political Economy of International Communications. Foundations for the Emerging Global Debate about Media Ownership and Regulation." Technology, Business and Society Programme Paper 11. (Geneva: United Nations Research Institute for Social Development, October 2003.)

708 Pope. "An Independent and Free Media." In: TI Source Book, p. 121.

709 *Ibid.*, p. 122.

The Protection of Journalists

Similar to the case of whistleblowers in government and private agencies, journalists and media owners are severely exposed to violent repression for their actions. This sad development is a reality in many countries, especially in fragile democracies and countries facing long-term economic and social conflicts.[710] As Stapenhurst rightly points out, it is very easy to find evidence on this point and the cases of intimidation and murder of journalists and media staff grow constantly every year.[711]

Violence against journalists is a common weapon used by those involved in corruption with the aim of avoiding disclosure of scandals and also intimidating the branch for future undertakings against them. In some instances, repression can be generated from several sectors, as explained by the latest report on media casualties compiled by the International Journalist Federation:

> "In many cases, the hand of the drugs mafia and crime gangs are at work. And in far too many instances the problem of impunity, and the failure of officials to properly investigate killings of media staff, remains a persistent obstacle to justice for journalists and media staff who are killed."[712]

Under these circumstances, journalists and media workers are faced with a further dilemma apart from the ethical value of their work. As threats certainly cannot be diminished, it becomes the duty of both government institutions and society to provide adequate protection for those who work on such highly sensitive issues as corruption. This notion is, unfortunately, still regarded in most countries as *terra incognita*, as there are not enough provisions within constitutional and criminal law to effectively protect journalists who specifically deal with corruption cases.

However, since the protection of whistleblowers has been a focus of the non-governmental approach against corruption, as observed in Chapter Six,

[710] In the last year, the worst cases of violence against journalists covering corruption were found in Colombia and the Philippines, where a total of ten killings have been confirmed and further five are under investigation. In: International Federation of Journalists. Journalists and Media Staff Killed in 2003. An IFJ Report on Media Casualties in the Field of Journalism and Newsgathering. <www.ifj.org> (January 2004.) See for details also: Peters. "The media's role: covering or covering up corruption?", p. 48.

[711] Stapenhurst. "The Media's Role in Curbing Corruption", p. 11.

[712] International Federation of Journalists. Journalists and Media Staff Killed in 2003.

the ideal strategy would be to integrate journalists in the protection framework of whistle blowers, since they are – up to a certain point – whistle blowers themselves.[713] Only through a comprehensive set of laws and provisions that fully guarantee the safety of media staff and journalists in the coverage of corruption cases could be able to diminish the "fear" against repression for exposing corruption scandals and similar irregularities.[714]

The Right to Information

One of the provisions of the International Code of Practice for the Safe Conduct of Journalism reads that the government should remove obstacles to journalism.[715] The text further notes that the freedom of movement of journalists should not be restricted and that the right of gathering news, producing and disseminating information in a safety environment should not be restricted.[716] This example portrays the importance of having complete access and enjoying – most important – a right to information.

Implementing the necessary measures to guarantee the observance of this right is a fundamental element for strengthening the role of the media in the fight against corruption. Legally denying access to information has been practiced by governments all over the world, who have a problem with exposing details of their activities to the public. Moreover, political parties have also denied access to their files, fearing the discovery of irregularities that might compromise internal and external elections.[717] The private sector is not free of critique either. Banks, accountancy firms, businesses analysts and even research institutions in the field of academia also known for "hiding" behind privacy laws in order to keep corruption scandals away from

---

713 Stapenhurst makes reference to the case of South Africa, where the proposals have been made to include adequate protection for whistle blowers in documents such as the Open Democracy Bill. In: Stapenhurst. "The Media's Role in Curbing Corruption", p. 12.

714 An example of this approach is contained in the International Code of Practice for the Safe Conduct of Journalism, provided by the International Federation of Journalists. This document contains several recommendation on how to increase the safety of journalists and how to proceed to avoid risks of violent repression against them. In: International Federation of Journalists. Journalists and Media Staff Killed in 2003.

715 Ibid.

716 Ibid.

717 For example, the discovery of the scandals around the party financing of former German Chancellor Helmut Kohl not only provoked major turmoil within the Christian Democratic Union Party (CDU) in Germany. Moreover, the results of the next federal election showed that the credibility of the CDU had been utterly compromised as a result of the disclosure.

the headlines. [718] However, most sectors of civil society and the media are demanding that this position be revised, if not completely eradicated.

On a preliminary basic observation, access to information means no more than the fact that all sectors of public life should be opened to the citizens at all times. Therefore, it is a duty of governments to provide as much transparency as possible in order to create a trustworthy image towards the citizens. It is also important that the private sector plays by the same rules of accountability and transparency in order to strengthen the bonds with its clients and business partners. Nevertheless, there have been instances in which certain information is secluded in order to prevent political or economic interests to be infringed upon. Therefore, both the public as well as the private sector deny the access to information, especially to members of the media, as they are aware of the consequences of bringing irregularities out to the public eye. [719]

If this access is not freely granted, the role of the media in curbing corruption can be highly compromised, because corruption scandals can be easily covered by secrecy laws. The major reluctance from governments and businesses towards full access to information might be the fact that even journalists can belong to corrupt networks and nurture their interests instead of objectively reporting on a specific case.[720] Therefore, it should be important to combine journalist ethics and the free access to information in order to ensure the capabilities of the media as a *watchdog* of governments and societies on all forms of corrupt activities therein.

A possible solution would be legal stipulations guaranteeing the free access to information on the one hand, and, on the other hand, reassuring the correct use thereof.[721] If such a combination could be solidified, it would allow journalists to have access to all possible sources at any time and use this information rightly for exposing the problems around corruption. This scenario is however highly disputed and sadly most unlikely as governments and businesses alike still protect themselves and their employees under

[718] A recent OECD study observes that "[w]hile corporate vehicles play an essential role in the global economic system, these entities may, under certain conditions, be misused for illicit purposes, including money laundering, bribery/corruption, hiding and shielding assets from creditors, illicit tax practices, self dealing defrauding assets/diversion of assets, market fraud and circumvention of disclosure requirements, and other forms of illicit behaviour." In: Organization for Economic and Cooperation and Development (OECD.) Behind the Corporate Veil. Using Corporate Entities for Illicit Purposes. (Paris: OECD Publications, 2001.)

[719] Pope, Jeremy. "Access to information: whose right and whose information?" In: Transparency International. Global Corruption Report 2001, p. 9 ff.

[720] Peters. "The media's role: covering or covering up corruption?", p. 52 ff.

[721] Stapenhurst. "The Media's Role in Curbing Corruption", p. 13.

privacy and secrecy laws.[722] This becomes the main weakness of this approach as the ethics of journalists are not controlled by any other instance than themselves, otherwise any form of control would be easily considered as censorship.

Self-Regulation: the Role of Press Councils

The last observation brings us to the problem of absolute reliability and accountability as the biggest challenges that the media faces when it comes to corruption and its exposure in the news. Accountability from the media is elemental for its position towards politics and society.[723] The main question is: who is monitoring the media? And moreover, how can we be sure that the media is reporting independently and objectively? The answer is not entirely free of doubt and critique.

There are, however, several constraints toward maintaining a high level of accountability in media spheres. First, the race for good ratings and placements within the very competitive news market could make journalists and publishers do anything for a headline.[724] Second, the inclination of the media to favour certain groups of both government and the private sector make it hard for the public to objectively evaluate the contents of the news.[725] Lastly, denied or limited access to information and facing legal consequences of a repressive judiciary system make it even harder for the media to be accountable.[726]

Therefore, there are two key elements in improving the work of journalists in this context. First, accountability should be guaranteed as the result of press freedom. Only when the press freedom stipulations explained above are given, the media can perform its duties at its full capacity and become thus more reliable and more accountable. Under favourable conditions of press freedom, journalists have enough space to manoeuvre, improve the quality of their investigation, and increase the fairness and objectivity of their reports.

---

722 Ibid.

723 For a closer perspective on this topic, see also: Buttny, Richard. Social Accountability in Communication. (London: Sage Publications, 1993); and Bertrand, Claude-Jean. "Media Accountability: The Case for Press Councils." Intermedia. Institute of International Communications. (1990) Vol. 18, No. 6, pp.

724 Stapenhurst. "The Media's Role in Curbing Corruption", p. 15.

725 Ibid.

726 Ibid.

Second, and most necessary for the accountability factor, mechanisms of self-control must become an integral part of the entire media-anti-corruption approach. If the government watched extensively over the media, then it is mostly alleged to impose censorship. If the public monitors the media, then the issue turns somehow blurry, as there is no legal framework that includes such regulations. Therefore, in a last instance, the media should "monitor itself" in terms of developing means to evaluate the activities of journalists in order to be able to make the entire media branch more accountable to both the government and private sectors as well as to society.

The codes of ethics explained earlier are an important mechanism for self-control. However, the practices of journalists should not only be observed by documents and charters, but also through institutionalized organs of surveillance that include both internal and external input. In this regard, press councils can play a determinant role in making the press more organized, monitored and evaluated.[727] These organs are responsible for the self-regulation of the media "in any given area, free from government interference or judicial supervision."[728] The main purpose is to internally oversee the works and methods of journalists and to evaluate them, mostly using the directives of the pertaining codes of ethics.[729] Moreover, press councils serve as open fora for citizens who are wishing to express their opinions and complaints about the media and also to issue reprimands to journalists and media workers whenever irregularities have taken place.[730]

The composition of such councils is not exclusive to journalists and members and representatives of the media, but is also open to the public and members of the legislative branch. An important pre-condition for press councils is that they are independent and led by non-partisan widely respected individuals.[731] This should enhance the credibility of such an organ to the outside. Moreover, these monitoring bodies should not have real sanction power as for instance the judiciary or the police, since this will create another struggle for power between journalists, citizens and politicians.[732] Therefore, one of the main solutions that has been considered by practitioners and scholars alike is that more press councils should be

727 Stapenhurst. "The Media's Role in Curbing Corruption", p. 17 ff. A classic overview of the nature of press councils can be found in: Robertson, Geoffrey. People Against the Press: An Enquiry into the Press Council. (London: Quartet Books, 1983.)

728 Independent Press Councils. "What is a Press Council?" <www.presscouncils.org>.

729 Ibid.

730 Stapenhurst. "The Media's Role in Curbing Corruption", p. 17

731 Ibid.

732 Ibid.

established as the main bodies of moral integrity to which journalists must look up to.

FIGURE 13: SELECTED INDEPENDENT PRESS COUNCILS AROUND THE WORLD

Country	Estanlished	Ethics Code	Complaints	Country	Established	Ethics Code	Complaints
Australia	1976	Yes	400 (30)	Italy	1963	Yes	n.a.
Austria	1961	Yes	41 (0)	Lithuania	1996	Yes	200 (180)
Belgium (Flemish)	2002	Yes	3 (1)	Luxembourg	1979	Yes	3 (2)
Bosnia and Herzegowina	2001	Yes	30 (3)	Macedonia	2001	Yes	21 (15)
Burkina Faso	2000	Yes	10 (3)	Malta	1999	Yes	12 (8)
Canada (Alberta)	1972	Yes	17 (2)	Netherlands	1948	No	60 (¤)
Canada (British Columbia)	1983	Yes	40 (2)	New Zealand	1973	No	87 (10)
Canada (Manitoba)	1984	No	2 (0)	Norway	1928	Yes	207 (51)
Canada (Maritimes Atlantic)	1980	Yes	60 (0)	Papua-New Guinea	1988	Yes	20 (0)
Canada (Ontario)	1972	No	100 (7)	Peru	1997	No	n.a.
Canada (Québec)	1971	Yes	80 (26)	Russia	1998	Yes	11 (8)
Chile	1991	No	10 (10)	Slovakia	2002	Yes	14 (10)
China (Hong Kong)	2000	Yes	25 (11)	Slovenia	1995	Yes	25 (17)
Cyprus	1990	Yes	12 (3)	South Korea	1961	Yes	600 (162)
Denmark	1964	Yes	134 (47)	Spain (Catalunya)	1997	Yes	30 (25)
Eastern Caribbean	2003	Yes	n.a.	Sweden	1916	Yes	383 (57)
Estonia	2002	Yes	14 (11)	Switzerland	1972	Yes	91 (23)
Fiji	1996	Yes	7 (0)	Taiwan	1963	Yes	20 (16)
Finland	1927	Yes	128 (14)	Tanzania	1997	Yes	22 (16)
Germany	1956	Yes	701 (145)	Thailand	1997	Yes	24 (0)

Great Britain	1953	Yes	2630 (19)	Turkey	1988	Yes	133 (62)
Iceland	1963	Yes	10 (10)	United States (Honolulu)	1970	Yes	10 (0)3
India	1965	No	1213 (197)	United States (Minnesota)	1971	No	126 (n.a.)
Israel	1963	Yes	83 (2)	United States (Washington)	1998	No	5 (1)

Source: Independent Press Councils. <www.presscouncils.org>

The source indicates that there are several other bodies in other countries that could qualify as press councils as well. However, the composition and fields of action are so broad that they can be identified as general journalist associations. Moreover, this table presents a selection of national and local councils (as in the cases of the US and Canada.) The numbers in the "complaints" columns indicate the total numbers of received complaints and, in brackets, the number of upheld complaints.

Currently, there are about 50 press councils at national and local levels, with different constitutive elements in over 40 countries worldwide.[733] The further creation of these bodies is highly recommendable for solidifying the media as a powerful actor in the fight against corruption. The moral authority press councils create should reaffirm the objectives and monitor the methods of journalists in order to establish a culture of "responsibility" from the media to its audience and to the government.[734]

Journalist Training

A final area in which the role of journalists and thus of the entire media can be strengthened in their efforts to combat corruption is continuous training and on-the-job training. The issue of corruption can become at times so complex, that many journalists cannot cover this topic without facing the

733 Independent Press Councils. World Press Councils 2003. <www.presscouncils.org>.

734 For further reference see also: Pritchard, David (ed.) Holding the Media Accountable: Citizens, Ethics and the Law. (Bloomington: Indiana University Press, 2000.)

risk of displaying wrong facts.[735] This affects the reliability of the press and can lead to serious consequences for all actors involved be they the media, the public and/or the government.[736]

Therefore journalists need, above all, to have a solid knowledge about what is actually meant by the term corruption, its different forms and ramifications. This would allow them to objectively localize the problem and isolate it from other forms of crime, so that the content of the news can be objective and based on asserted knowledge of the facts and not on mere speculations. In this regard, organization such as TI and the World Bank offer journalists and media staff training seminars on the topic of corruption.[737] Such courses are directed to all branches of the media and provide participants with basic information about the current debates on corruption both in academia and practice. Moreover, training seminars are a good opportunity for journalists and media workers to exchange their experiences on working on and covering corruption cases. Through this dialogue, the image of corruption as well as the role of the media therein can be portrayed from different perspectives thus providing a broad a reliable picture of this problem and its numerous implications.

Also, the very basics of investigative journalism should be constantly trained and mastered.[738] The effectiveness and, more important, the reliability of treating corruption cases in the media depends highly on the skills that a journalist is capable of using for the research, writing and publishing of a story. Therefore, journalists must also have a sound knowledge of politics, economics and society in order to make their judgements solid enough to become credible to the public.[739] Although practice shows that this is not a

[735] Common mistakes refer to the collection of facts and data, the interpretation and evaluation thereof and, in the last instance, the resulting statement delivered by media and journalists. In: Stapenhurst. "The Media's Role in Curbing Corruption", p. 19.

[736] For instance, false incriminations and the dissemination of stories without proper research can create legal problems for journalists and media owners.

[737] A good example can be found in TI Germany. In January 2002, the German national chapter organized a media symposium in collaboration with independent journalist and civil society associations. The main topic of the event was the fight against corruption and the role of the media. This forum allowed practitioners as well as academics to exchange views and experiences on the topic. At the end, a publication with all presentations was made to the public. See: Netzwerk Recherche, Transparency International and Bund der Steuerzahler (eds.) Korruption: Schatten der demokratischen Gesellschaft. Fakten, Trends, Gegenstrategien. (Kronberg im Taunus, March 2002.)

[738] Stapenhurst. "The Media's Role in Curbing Corruption", p. 19.

[739] *Ibid.* Thor author explains that "if journalists are expected to cover and present news fairly and accurately, they have to possess the tools and appropriate knowledge for it. This becomes especially important when they are required to provide an easy, although truthful, explanation of the news to the public."

condition sine qua non, as many journalists do not have share the same skills and knowledge about the topic of corruption, this element should not be left out of the discussion. Only with a good overview and proper vision of political, economic and social affairs within a country, and nowadays, on the international arena, journalists and media workers can cover corruption cases with a high rate of credibility.[740]

Lastly, journalists and media staff need to be up to date with all advancements in the field of research and communication technologies. As the methods of corruption are getting more sophisticated every day (e.g. money laundering through electronic banking), the media should also improve its techniques to research, cover, and communicate corruption news not only to local or national outlets, but also worldwide. The globalization of information technologies can be easily used as an effective weapon against the spread of corruption. However, if the main actors involved in globalized mass communication are not properly trained and do not have the skills to use these new information technologies, the role of the media in this regard can decrease rapidly. Therefore, technical training is a pivotal element of this approach. Because the very nature of journalism has changed through the implementation of the Internet and the latest advancements in the telecommunication industry, journalist must be aware of these developments and adapt quickly to these conditions.[741] Technically versed personnel will increase the probability of coverage on corruption to become quickly and broadly available to the public.

Corruption News Beyond Scandal

Nowadays, there is no doubt that corruption makes the news. As it has been analyzed previously, the consequences of the illegitimate use of private or corporate authority for personal benefits can go far beyond the scope of a scandal. Journalists have become important actors in this topic, as they can perform different roles that influence the entire scope of corrupt activities, regardless of the sector in which they take place. This chapter provided an overview of the most important aspects of the role of the media in the fight against corruption and observed the main recommendations that are needed for strengthening its position in the anti-corruption debate. Summarizing the

[740] An overview on journalist training can be found in: Gaunt, Philip. Making the Newsmakers. International Handbook of Journalism Training. (Westport: Greenwood Publishing Group, 1992.)

[741] On this topic see for further reference: Berkman, Robert I. and Christopher A. Shumway. Digital Dilemmas: Ethical Issues for Online Media Professionals. (Ames: Blackwell Publishing Press, August 2003); and Stoval, James Glen. Web Journalism. Practice and Promise of a New Medium. (Boston: Pearson Allyn and Bacon, 2003.)

findings, there are three important concluding observations that need to be made.

First, the role of the press freedom in the context of politics and corruption has become of particular importance for the analysis of the entire media approach to the topic at hand. Weder and Brunetti took upon the highly difficult task of analyzing the relationship between the incidence of corruption and the level of press freedom in several countries. According to their results, the higher scores in the corruption scale coincided with low levels of press freedom. This means that the latter can be seen a pre-condition of the former thus leading to the question: can press freedom be a solution against the endemic corruption? Through the analysis of the case studies in Section III, we shall be able to gain a more proper answer to these questions.

Second, this chapter analyzed some of the working elements of journalists and media workers when it comes to covering corruption news, as well as the serious difficulties, challenges and risks involved in their profession. The roles of *discoverer*, *watchdog*, and *educator* adhered to journalists, made it clear that they not only can have a great range of influence on public opinion. More important, journalists have a yet greater amount of responsibility towards their audience as they are the prime channel through which information about corruption both filtered and disseminated. As a result of the analysis, it has become clear that the role of the media has been somehow underestimated in the last few years in the context of anti-corruption strategies. This deals with the many adverse aspects of the profession such as a lack of credibility and reliability as well as the constant danger of becoming the target of repression and violence from those who were exposed in corruption scandals. However, it has become clear why these reverse scenarios should not diminish the presence of the press, radio, television, the internet in the anti-corruption context. Only with a strong presence of the media can enough deterrence be created both at national and international levels to prevent possible corruption from taking place.

Third, as the media can face serious problems of reliability and credibility when it comes to corruption, the importance of training and solidifying the skills of media staff is not to be left out of the analysis. Only good trained journalists, versed in the latest technological communication advancements and with an equal amount of political, economic and social vision can be effective, credible and reliable "corruption fighters." Therefore, initiatives that strive through educating and mastering journalists in substantive as well as technical and logistical matters should be supported in any anti-corruption strategy involving the media.

Lastly, although the corruption scenario has not entirely changed in its pathology and the cases of corruption have, if anything, increased, we must remain cautious of the amount of news that is generated from corruption scandals. This assumption can be misleading, because its initial simpleness would certainly lead to the following dilemma: is there currently more corruption around the world or is it just more news about it in the media? Statistics would tell us that the rate of publications about corruption has indeed increased in the last years. [742] Nevertheless, the problem has remained somehow intact. However it is not necessarily the number what has grown, but moreover the implications, effects and results of corruption, especially in the political arena. And precisely in this regard, the media plays a preponderant role. As the case studies will show, the work of journalists has been the key factor for the shape of the anti-corruption debate and for the dismantling of entire corruption regimes and networks, both nationally and internationally.

[742] Poelchau, Normativer Wandel im Internationalen System, p. 117 ff. See note 43.

CHAPTER EIGHT

INTERNATIONAL MECHANISMS

> "Corruption's effects on economic development and political legitimacy spill over a given country's borders, affecting global peace and prosperity. Thus, it is natural that corruption concerns the international community as a whole, just as distortions in international trade and investment flows are also concerns. The most important role of the international community is [...] of providing financial and technical support to countries undertaking difficult anticorruption reforms."[743]

The problem of corruption has been treated in this book from many different perspectives thus far. However, the internationality of this phenomenon has been constantly in the background, since one of the main reasons for this analysis is the fact, that corruption has turned into a global problem, gaining much importance on the agendas of several international fora.

It is precisely because of its transnational nature that the last chapter of this section concentrates on reviewing major international initiatives against corruption. The focus will directed toward the different patterns of reaction by the community of states against corruption. As it has been argued earlier, if the nature of corruption has transformed from being a single-case national phenomenon into a major international threat, then the solutions for its eradication should be found in international initiatives. Therefore, this chapter analyzes these initiatives on two main levels.

First, a brief sketch of the development of the international agreements in form of codified conventions and treaties will be presented. Ever since the Foreign Corrupt Practices Act (FCPA) was passed in the United States in 1977, the importance given to corruption in binding international law has increased and, most recently it has reached new hypes. In December 2003, the first comprehensive United Nations Convention against Corruption was signed in Mérida, Mexico by 95 member states.[744]

---

743 Elliott, Kimberly. "Corruption as an International Policy Problem: Overview and Recommendations." In: Elliott (ed.) Corruption and the Global Economy, p. 216.

744 Transparency International Quarterly Newsletter. (December 2003.)

Thus, it shall be of particular interest to take a closer look at how these anti-corruption mechanisms evolved and what kind of provisions they include. More importantly, it will be necessary to discuss how effective these initiatives have been for the purposes of curbing corruption.

Second, the work of international organizations will be highlighted, as they have been major actors in implementing comprehensive strategies against corruption.[745] The major efforts in this regard can be found in the work of the United Nations, the World Bank and the OECD. These organizations have become the major sources of information and recommendations about how to cope with national and international corruption. However, due to the nature of the chosen case studies, a further organization will be taken under consideration, namely the Inter-American Development Bank (IDB) and the Organization of American States (OAS), which build the so called Inter-American System. The major contribution these organizations have made for the region of Latin America in the context of anti-corruption efforts is the adoption of the Inter-American Convention against Corruption, which will be discussed in the following subsections of the chapter.

MAJOR TREATIES AND CONVENTIONS AGAINST CORRUPTION 1977-2003

An initial differentiation must be made at this point between the work of international organizations on corruption and the international treaties that have emerged within the same context. The former can have multiple approaches and initiatives for fighting corruption while the latter contain specific provisions, especially on penalizing and criminalizing corrupt activities. Therefore, we shall have a look at the treaties first, in order to understand the legal nature of the international strategies against corruption. Nowadays all major regional and international organizations have an Act, a Treaty or Convention that contains provisions on how to prevent and penalize corruption and its different typologies.[746] The selection presented here

---

[745] In his analysis of corruption, Poelchau comes to the conclusion that there are two major factors for a normative transformation in the views of the international community on this phenomenon thus leading towards a stronger involvement towards the eradication of this problem. The first one is the involvement of the United States and the second one the work of international organizations such as the World Bank, the United Nations, and the OECD. In: Poelchau. Normativer Wandel im Internationalen System.

[746] An overview of selected cases can be found in: Ofosu-Amaah W. Paatii, Raj Soopramanien and Kishor Uprety. "International Efforts Against Corruption." In: Combating Corruption. A Comparative Review of Selected Legal Aspects of State Practice and Major International Initiatives. (Washington, D.C.: The World Bank, 1999), pp. 68-81.

contains the main instruments that have had an impact on the development of an international anti-corruption legislation.

The Foreign Corrupt Practices Act

Although the existence of corruption was acknowledged by the international community of the post war era, no concrete measures were undertaken against several illicit activities among, and, within states. Back in the 1970s, the Watergate scandal in the United States became the ignition moment for the development of international law mechanisms against corrupt practices.[747] The repercussions of this incident had dramatic consequences for the position of the Nixon Administration at that time. The notable aspect of this case is that it started a public debate in the United States about corruption and its detrimental effects. Moreover, the hearings related to the Watergate case led to further investigations about the different types of irregularities which took place in day-to-day international business transactions between many US American companies and several countries.[748] To the eyes of public opinion, it soon became clear that there was an urgent need for bringing the adverse effects of such practices out to public debate and create awareness on the fact that this phenomenon was actually not an integral part of a healthy body politic. Such discussions were intensively undertaken and led to pressuring top level politicians, legislators and members of the judiciary to start concrete steps to diminish the occurrence of corrupt deals.

Until that time, it was very common (and fully compliant with legal regulations) that big companies would offer different kinds of payments to foreign government while doing business. However, after the US American legislative and judiciary branches followed up on several instances in which the government and private companies had equally been involved in bribery activities abroad, a decision was adopted on prohibiting any kind of economic exchanges that were not contained in official statutes.[749] As a

[747] Posadas, Alejandro. "Combating Corruption under International Law." Duke Journal of Comparative and International Law. (Spring 2000), Vol. 10, No. 2, pp. 345-414.

[748] For example, one of the most prominent cases was the exposure of Lockheed Corporation's illicit payments of $ 25 million to Japanese officials to secure the sale of an aircraft to Japan. As a consequence, Japanese Premier Kakuei Tanaka resigned and was soon convicted by Japanese laws. In: Pieth. "International Cooperation to Combat Corruption", p. 17.

[749] Investigations led by the Securities and Exchange Commission of Congress led to a disclosure of irregularities in many cases. As much as 400 US companies recognized that they had been involved in illicit payments to foreign government officials amounting over $300 million therein. In: United States Department of Justice Fraud Section, Criminal Division (DOJ.) "Foreign Corrupt Practices Act. Antibribery Provisions." (Washington D.C., 2002.)

result, in 1977, the Foreign Corrupt Practices Act (FCPA) was signed into law by US President Jimmy Carter in order to "bring a halt to the bribery of foreign officials and to restore public confidence in the integrity of the American business system."[750]

This act primarily makes bribing a foreign official a felony. It also contains provisions regarding accounting practices.[751] As a consequence, all actors involved in international business transactions in and out of the United States can be prosecuted under the FCPA, if a breach of it provisions is determined.[752] Moreover, the penalties included in the document for those who are found guilty of bribing foreign officials can be both of criminal and civil kind amounting up to $ 2,000,000 for companies and $ 100,000 for individuals, as well as up to five years of sentenced prison.[753] On the accounting provisions, the FCPA turned requirements of compliance by previous documents into mandatory standards for the future. These include recommendations for companies to keep books, records and accounts in an accurate manner as well as implementing systems of internal oversight in order to better monitor all organizational processes.[754]

The importance of the FCPA for the international law approach in anti-corruption efforts is that this document became the first comprehensive treaty that strictly codified the penalization of bribery and made specific provisions on how "not to proceed" when doing business on an international levels.[755] Also, it was the first time that an international anti-corruption document was created as a result of domestic pressures towards a clean image of governmental business activity.

Nevertheless, the criticisms of the FCPA came almost immediately after its adoption. Most US corporations urged to a revision of the provisions of the Act as they easily started to argue about the competitive disadvantage in which this document left US American companies compared to firms based

750 *Ibid.*

751 Pieth. "International Cooperation to Combat Corruption", p. 18.

752 Posadas. "Combating Corruption under International Law", p. 360. The author explains, that "the FCPA's liability rests on two alternative jurisdictional grounds. Firstly, jurisdiction may lie when there is use of the mails or other means of interstate commerce corruptly in the United States in furtherance of a foreign corrupt practice. Secondly, jurisdiction lies when there have been foreign corrupt practices outside the United States. Foreign corporations and foreign natural persons, their officers, directors, employees, agents, and stockholders acting on their behalf can also be liable under the FCPA for acts of furtherance of foreign corrupt practices while within the territory of the United States."

753 DOJ. "Foreign Corrupt Practices Act. Antibribery Provisions", p. 5.

754 Posadas. "Combating Corruption under International Law", p. 363.

755 There had been other multilateral proposals introduced to the UN General Assembly prior to the signing and adoption of the FCPA, however they lacked the binding character of a strong international law mechanism and were soon withdrawn. In: *Ibid.*, p. 365.

in other countries.[756] In 1988, concerned with the fact that in some countries bribes in international business transactions were legal and even – in some jurisdictions – tax deductible, US Congress started recommendations to amend the FCPA in order to put pressure on other countries to create similar anti-bribery statutes.[757] The opinions on the validity of these complaints are difficult to underline, as most of the information still remains classified.[758]

The vast majority of studies that have taken a closer look at the performance of US companies after 1977 indicate that there is in deed a certain loss that can be attributed to the new anti-bribery provisions.[759] However, scholars observe that the amount is relatively low, compared to the usual costs involved for a bribe. As economist Kimberly Ann Elliott points out,

> "[w]ith globalization and democratization making corruption less and less acceptable around the world, however, US firms that have been forced by the FCPA to become more innovative and aggressive should be well placed to reap the benefits. The FCPA could also be a competitive advantage in some newly democratizing countries where politicians or public officials concerned about negative publicity might prefer a US firm because they can more credibly claim that no corruption was involved."[760]

The notable aspect of the FCPA, however, is that it became the cornerstone for the development of further internationally binding mechanisms against the spread of corruption. The impact of the FCPA could be observed in the way the community of states reacted to the long-known issue of corruption. During the 1980s, both industrialized and developing countries joined further efforts to create similar initiatives that would finally combat bribery and other forms of corruption through multilateral treaties and international legal obligations.

---

756 Goldbarg, Andrea. "The Foreign Corrupt Practices Act and Structural Corruption." In: Boston University International Law Journal (Fall 2000) Vol. 18 No. 273, pp. 273-289.

757 Pieth. "International Cooperation to Combat Corruption", p. 18.

758 DOJ. "Foreign Corrupt Practices Act. Antibribery Provisions", p. 2. See also: Goldbarg. "The Foreign Corrupt Practices Act and Structural Corruption."

759 For a detailed overview, see: Pieth. "International Cooperation to Combat Corruption", p. 18 ff.

760 Elliott. "Corruption as an International Policy Problem: Overview and Recommendations", p. 207.

FIGURE 14: THE PARTIES OF THE 1997 OECD CONVENTION

Country	Date of deposit of acceptance, approval or ratification	Country	Date of deposit of acceptance, approval or ratification
Iceland	17. August 1998	Spain	14. January 2000
Japan	13. October 1998	Czech Republic	21. January 2000
Germany	10. November 1998	Switzerland	31. May 2000
Hungary	4. December 1998	Turkey	26. July 2000
United States	8. December 1998	France	31. July 2000
Finland	10. December 1998	Brazil	24. August 2000
United Kingdom	14. December 1998	Denmark	5. September 2000
Canada	17. December 1998	Poland	8. September 2000
Norway	18. December 1998	Portugal	23. November 2000
Bulgaria	22. December 1998	Italy	15. December 2000
Korea	4. January 1999	Netherlands	12. January 2001
Greece	5. February 1999	Argentina	8. February 2001
Austria	20. May 1999	Luxemburg	21. March 2001
Mexico	27. May 1999	Chile	18. April 2001
Sweden	8. June 1999	New Zealand	25. June 2001
Belgium	27. July 1999	Slovenia *	6. September 2001
Slovak Republic	24. September 1999	Ireland	22. September 2003
Australia	18. October 1999	*= Slovenia has not yet enacted full implementing legislation	

Source: Organization for Economic Cooperation and Development. <www.oecd.org>

The OECD Anti-Bribery Convention

The actions against international bribery and thus against global corruption considerably gained momentum by the end of the 1980s, as the end of the Cold War and the demise of the Soviet empire led to a incredible turn in all aspects of international life. At that time, the traditional security threats imposed by bloc politics changed in nature, leaving world leaders to pay attention to other problems in international life. As Tanzi pointed out, the topic of corruption became a high priority for governments all over the world, because of the immense transnational danger it had carried on over the years.[761]

Bearing this development in mind, and after the FCPA had entered the international arena as the first comprehensive international law mechanism against bribery, the world soon witnessed the impact of this change of attitude in the states community. As noted above, the FCPA was amended in 1988 with several recommendations to make it more effective and also to diminish the burden of complaints by companies who claimed to have been put in disadvantage thereby.[762] One of the amendments also requested consecutive actions, led by the US President, for negotiating an international agreement among member countries of the OECD in order to curb the bribery of foreign officials through a multilateral treaty.[763] During the President William J. Clinton's first term, negotiations were started with other OECD countries. After several rounds, Council of the OECD adopted the 1994 Recommendations on Bribery in International Transactions, which built the fundament for the 1997 adopted Convention on Combating Bribery of Foreign Public Officials in International Business Transactions (referred to as OECD Convention.)[764]

This document became the first multilateral binding mechanism under which countries committed themselves to penalize the bribing of foreign officials. The Convention thus obliges states to make almost every transaction or payment outside the legal scope and the provisions of a contract be penalized.[765] Two major positive aspects of this document can be observed. First, it relies on the political agreement among states for changing domestic laws in order to ban illicit payments to foreign officials instead of agreeing upon the creation of an international regulatory agency, which

---

761 Tanzi, "Corruption Around the World. Causes, Consequences, Scope and Cures", p. 560 ff.

762 Goldbarg. "The Foreign Corrupt Practices Act and Structural Corruption", p. 275 ff.

763 The FCPA applies strictly to US companies and is subject to US law.

764 George, Barbara C., Kathleen A. Lacey and Jutta Birmele. "On the Threshold of the Adoption of Global Antibribery Legislation: A Critical Analysis of Current Domestic and International Efforts Toward the Reduction of Corruption." Vanderbilt Journal of Transnational Law (January, 1999) Vol. 32, No. 1, p. 35.

765 It must be noted, that there exists a difference between bribery and so called "facilitating" or "grease" payments. Both the FCPA and the OECD Convention made "facilitating payments" an exception in their provisions. According to US Congress, such payments covered "nominal payments used to expedite a business transaction that were made to persons whose duties did not include policy-making functions." Therefore, the Act and the Convention do not apply to foreign officials whose duties are "essentially ministerial or clerical." Moreover, such payments are considered "routine governmental action" and other cases in which governmental decisions are not based on the discretion of higher ranking officials, who may want to seek illicit benefits for their approval. In: *Ibid.*

might not necessarily make control, monitoring, and sanctioning any easier.[766] And second, the Convention approached for the first time the "demand" side of corruption by focusing on those actors who initiate a great percentage of corruption transactions, namely transnational corporations.[767]

From the political perspective, however, the Convention has two major shortcomings. First, it does not specifically deal with illicit payments in political parties. The document solely bans bribery-related payments to foreign officials made *through* political parties, as well as bribes directed to political parties from public officials.[768] And second, the Convention does not make any specific application as to family members of foreign officials being bribed thus making it easy for signatories to circumscribe the provisions included therein.[769]

Since the Convention was modelled after the FCPA, it also included some accountability measures to be undertaken by its parties. For example, it is demanded from the signatories, that they implement necessary measures in order to refrain from using "off-the-books" accounts for hiding the bribes of/for foreign officials.[770] Moreover, issues such as the non-deductibility of dubious foreign payments and the establishment of proper codes of conduct for international business transactions were approached.[771]

On the matter of penalties, it must be noted that due to the multinational nature of the Convention, sanctions are determined individually within the context of each national penal system. Moreover, the Convention includes requirements for the seizure and confiscation of the goods involved in bribes, as well as other illegal transactions.[772]

In a general evaluation, it must be stressed out, that the OECD Convention is a major contribution to the international fight against corruption via international law. Although its full implementation relies heavily on the individual actions of governments, practices within the

[766] Glynn, Kobrin and Naim. "The Globalization of Corruption", p. 22.

[767] Ibid., The authors defend this position by observing that "[i]n the long run, to prevent companies in well-ordered industrial countries from proffering bribes is clearly a far more manageable task than achieving the necessary legal and political reforms in the scores of developing countries where such bribes are routinely accepted [...]"

[768] George, Lacey and Birmele. "On the Threshold of the Adoption of Global Antibribery Legislation", p. 37.

[769] Posadas. "Combating Corruption under International Law", p. 381.

[770] George, Lacey and Birmele. "On the Threshold of the Adoption of Global Antibribery Legislation", p. 37.

[771] Posadas. "Combating Corruption under International Law", p. 382

[772] Quiñonez, Enery. "Implementing the Anti-Bribery Convention: an update from the OECD." In: Transparency International. Global Corruption Report 2001, p. 199.

international business regime have been positively affected by the Convention in terms of reducing the political dangers and economic losses caused by bribery and, at the same time, promoting more transparency and accountability between states and transnational corporations. This is of particular importance for the perception of corruption worldwide, as it becomes clear that this phenomenon can also be best fought against through a binding international treaty.

The commitment of OECD countries to the provisions and further recommendations of the Convention did not stop in 1997. Ever since the treaty entered into force, constant follow-up mechanisms and reports have been gathered by the organization and made available to the public, so that every citizen can see, how much (or how little) it has been accomplished thus far in the fight against international bribery.[773]

The Inter-American Convention against Corruption

Both the FCPA and the OECD Convention addressed a specific form of corruption, namely the offering and acceptance of bribes. However, it becomes hard to believe that until 1996, no multilateral treaty addressed the issue of corruption in concrete. The anti-corruption law status quo changed in 1996 when 21 Latin American countries, the United States and Canada signed the Inter-American Convention Against Corruption. This document is the first of its kind and its provisions go beyond the penalizing of bribes on to addressing corruption as a whole with all its different forms and ramifications.[774]

Latin America was always known for being a region endemically affected by corruption. Therefore, the political need to undertake efforts against this problem grew as a consequence of the latest negative turns in several countries which suffered from the consequences of corruption. In 1994, during the Summit of the Americas in Miami, 34 heads of government agreed in at the signing of the Declaration of Principles and Plan of Action that an "effective democracy requires a comprehensive attack on corruption

[773] A comprehensive review of the latest developments in each of the signatory countries can be found in: Organization for Economic Cooperation and Development. "Steps taken and planned future actions by participating countries to ratify and implement the Convention on Combating Bribery of Foreign Public Officials in International Business Transactions." OECD. <http://www.oecd.org/dataoecd/50/33/1827022.pdf> (17.12.2003.)

[774] The original text of the Convention is available online at: Organization of American States (OAS.) Secretariat for Legal Affairs: Technical Secretariat for Legal Cooperation Mechanisms. "Inter-American Convention Against Corruption." <http://www.oas.org/juridico/english/Treaties/b-58.html>

as a factor of social disintegration and distortion of the economic system that undermines the legitimacy of political institutions."[775] This initial commitment foresaw regional multilateral negotiations for the creation of a comprehensive document which would include a holistic approach to corruption by isolating the issue from other related problems such as drugs and organized crime.

In 1995 and under the auspices of the Organization of American States, the drafted text was negotiated and by March 1996, 23 countries signed the Convention in a Special Conference which took place in Caracas.[776] As stated before, the particularity of the Convention was its focus on corruption exclusively. For example, under Article III, states agreed to:

- enact standards of conduct for public employees and create mechanisms for the enforcement of such standards;
- develop asset disclosure systems for selected officials;
- reform national procurement and hiring systems;
- exclude individuals and/or corporations which have violated local anti-corruption laws from favourable tax conditions;
- increase the protection for whistleblowers;
- strengthen the creation and functioning of independent internal oversight agencies;
- consider the relationship between equal wages for public servants and the incidence of corruption in the public sector.[777]

Although the Inter-American Convention does rely heavily on both the FCPA and the OECD Convention, its main difference is that it concentrates on fighting corruption from within governments thus approaching also the passive side of corruption (penalizing bribed government officials.) The scope of the Inter-American Convention seems broader as it not only covers illicit activities in the international business regime (mostly involving a private company), but also any kind of economic or commercial transaction (involving both internal and external government actors.)[778]

---

[775] Original text quoted in Posadas. "Combating Corruption under International Law", p. 382.

[776] *Ibid.* Currently, the Inter-American Convention has been signed by 28 OAS Member States. In: OAS. "Inter-American Convention Against Corruption." <http://www.oas.org/juridico/english/Sigs/b-58.html>

[777] Brandolino, John. "Fighting Corruption. The Role of Diplomacy and International Agreements." The Journal of Public Inquiry (Fall/Winter 2001), pp. 9-12.

[778] For a detailed comparison of the two documents see also Posadas. "Combating Corruption under International Law", p. 386 ff.

In addition, the Convention requires all parties to establish a new offence of "illicit enrichment" in cases where a government official has significantly increased his/her personal assets without being able to explain to the superiors or central authorities about the sources of the new earnings.[779] The important aspect of this provision is that it calls upon states where no legal provisions exist for this kind of crime to cooperate with other states in creating and implementing national laws that criminalize such incidents.[780]

The European Union's Convention and other regional laws

The mechanisms for anti-corruption legislation did not evolve solely in the Americas. In Europe, several institutions of the European Union have addressed this topic as well. The European Council and the European Commission have led the initiatives. In November 1998, the Criminal Law Convention on Corruption was adopted by the Committee of Ministers of the Council of Europe intending coordinated action against a wide range of corruption activities.[781] Another important document passed by the Council is the Civil Law Convention on Corruption which aims to implement compensation mechanisms in national legal systems to help individuals who have been harmed by corrupt practices. This Convention however, has not yet had a wide impact with only three countries having ratified.[782] Several other documents have been elaborated such as the Twenty Guiding Principles Against Corruption, the Model Code of Conduct for Public Officials and the Convention of the European Union on the Protection of its Financial Interests, thus making the fight against this phenomenon a highly relevant topic in the EU agenda.[783]

---

779 Ofosu-Amaah, Soopramanien and Uprety. "International Efforts Against Corruption", p. 71.

780 *Ibid.*

781 In: United Nations Office for Drug Control and Crime Prevention (UNODCCP.) United Nations Manual on Anti-Corruption Policy (Draft Version.) (Vienna: June 2001), p. 64 ff.

782 *Ibid.* The countries are Albania, Bulgaria and Estonia.

783 Ibid., p. 65 ff.

FIGURE 15: PARTIES TO THE 1997 INTER-AMERICAN CONVENTION AGAINST CORRUPTION

Country	Deposit of acceptance, accession or ratification	Country	Deposit of acceptance, accession or ratification
Haiti	29.03.1996 (S)	Nicaragua	6 May 1999
Paraguay	28 January 1997	Dominican Rep.	8 June 1999
Bolivia	4 February 1997	Bahamas (CW)	14 March 2000
Ecuador	2 June 1997	Canada	6 June 2000
Venezuela	2 June 1997	United States	29 September 2000
Mexico	2 June 1997	St. Lucia	08.02.2001 (AD)
Costa Rica	3 June 1997	Guyana	15 February 2001
Peru	4 June 1997	Jamaica	30 March 2001
Argentina	9 October 1997	Barbados	06.04.2001 (S)
Trinidad and Tobago	15 April 1998	St. Vincent & Grenadines	05.06.2001 (AD)
Honduras	2 June 1998	Guatemala	3 July 2001
Panama	8 October 1998	Grenada	16 January 2002
Chile	27 October 1998	Suriname	04.06.2002 (AD)
Uruguay	7 December 1998	Brazil	24 July 2002
Colombia	10 January 1999	Belize	6 September 2002
El Salvador	18 March 1999	Antigua & Barbuda	23 February 2004

(S)= Signatory, yet not ratified
(AD)= Accession, yet not ratified

Source: Organization of American States.
<www.oas.org>

Noteworthy is also the European Union's Convention on the Fight Against Corruption Involving Officials of the European Communities or Officials of Member States of the European Union, referred to as the

European Convention, which has become an integral part of the anti-corruption strategies for the governments of EU member states.[784] The Convention concentrates on the penalization bribes of both EU officials and government agents of member states. However, it does not criminalize transnational crimes outside of the borders of the EU. The current debate in Europe in this regard is to implement anti-corruption legislation that guarantees free market competition and the harmonization of trade flows. Moreover, the penalization of bribes and fraud in private companies has also been the topic of the recent EU recommendations.[785]

Lastly, there are other regional multilateral treaties that also address the problem of corruption within their geographical sphere. The prominence of these instruments might not necessarily be as great as that of the OECD Convention or the Inter-American Convention. However, their existence within the specific regions is a step forward in the strategies against corruption. In some cases, a regional convention is the initial point for further measures in this context. Also, it is important to note, that such "smaller" conventions might even have less problems of applicability, since they are developed under specific regional/cultural backgrounds.[786] Among the many law initiatives are worth mentioning: the Dakar Declaration on the Prevention and Control of Organized Transnational Crime and Corruption, adopted by the African Regional Ministerial Workshop on Organized Transnational Crime and Corruption; and, in the same fashion, the Manila Declaration on the Prevention and Control of Transnational Crime, adopted by the Asian Regional Ministerial Workshop on Organized Transnational Crime and Corruption.[787]

The United Nations Convention

Most recently, the endeavours of the biggest international forum in creating a universal document against corruption and its related forms

[784] George, Lacey and Birmele. "On the Threshold of the Adoption of Global Antibribery Legislation", p. 40.

[785] *Ibid.* For the most recent developments on regional anti-corruption initiatives, see also: European Council's Group of States against Corruption. <www.greco.coe.int/>

[786] See for instance the case of Africa, where regional conventions are developed out of recommendations of regional for a such as the African Union. In: Ofosu-Amaah, Soopramanien and Uprety. "International Efforts Against Corruption", p. 76 ff.

[787] United Nations Office for Drug Control and Crime Prevention (UNODCCP.) Global Dynamics of Corruption. The Role of the United Nations Helping Member States Build Integrity to Curb Corruption. (Vienna: October 2002), p. 15.

became a reality when 95 states gathered in Mérida, Mexico to sign the United Nations Convention Against Corruption. This document marks a new era in the efforts of the international community to curb corruption on a global level since it becomes attempts to become the first universal tool containing legally binding obligations for the parties involved.[788]

The history of international anti-corruption law making in the UN has a long tradition. Although there were plenty recommendations from several bodies during the 1970s, the efforts never went any further than resolutions with no binding character.[789] However, in the second half of the 1990s the impetus grew inexorably from two major events. First, the end of the Cold War created a new *raison d'être* for the different organisms of the United Nations System. Not only new topics such as development, health and social issues received higher priorities in the different agendas. Moreover, the end of the bipolar animosities between member states, gave the entire organization a new political vitality. Second, the implementation of other international law mechanisms such as the FCPA, the OECD Convention and all other regional treaties demanded from the UN the development of an own legal tool for the eradication of corruption.

The direct mandate for the UN Convention was originally given by the General Assembly (GA) in resolution A/RES/55/61, which recommended the establishment of an Ad Hoc Committee for the negotiation of the document.[790] The issues related to corruption such as transnational organized crime and the international transfer of illicit funds built the basis for the consensus found for the urgent need of a broad legally binding convention which would address corruption and all its related forms. In this regard, GA resolution A/RES/56/260 decided that the Ad Hoc Committee should take a multidisciplinary approach to the topic and draft the specifics of the

---

788 The universal character derives from the fact, that all other Conventions are either for members of industrialized and developed countries (i.e. OECD) or required regional membership (i.e. OAS, EU.) Therefore, the UN Convention is open to all member states for signature and ratification.

789 The First resolutions to the topic date back to 1976 when a group of states presented recommendations to both the General Assembly and the Economic and Social Council. In: Posadas. "Combating Corruption under International Law", p. 367 ff.

790 United Nations. An effective international legal instrument against corruption. Resolution A/RES/55/61, (22 January 2001.) This resolution reflects the content of prior UN documents that deal with the issue including: Transnational organized crime. Resolution A/RES/53/111, (20 January 1999); Action against corruption and bribery in international commercial transactions. Resolution A/RES/53/176, (25 January 1999); Draft United Nations Convention against Transnational Organized Crime and the draft protocol thereto. Resolution A/RES/54/126, (20 January 2000); Prevention of corrupt practices and illegal transfer of funds. Resolution A/RES/54/205, (27 January 2000); Action against corruption. Resolution A/RES/54/128, (28 January 2000), High-level Political Signing Conference for the United Nations Convention against Transnational Crime. Resolution A/RES/54/129, (28 January 2000.)

Convention, taking into consideration the recommendations from specialized agencies such as the Commission on Crime Prevention and Criminal Justice.[791] Since 2001, the Ad Hoc Committee held three sessions per year and concluded its work by the end of 2003. Accordingly, México offered to host a High Level Signing Conference for the Convention after the work of the Ad Hoc Committee was finished.[792]

FIGURE 16: SIGNATORIES TO THE 2003 UN CONVENTION AGAINST CORRUPTION

Country	Signature	Country	Signature	Country	Signature
Australia	09.12.2003	Thailand	09.12.2003	Lithuania	10.12.2003
Bolivia	09.12.2003	Uganda	09.12.2003	Luxemburg	10.12.2003
Brazil	09.12.2003	United Kingdom	09.12.2003	Madagascar	10.12.2003
Cape Verde	09.12.2003	Tanzania	09.12.2003	Nepal	10.12.2003
Cyprus	09.12.2003	United States	09.12.2003	Netherlands	10.12.2003
Egypt	09.12.2003	Uruguay	09.12.2003	New Zealand	10.12.2003
France	09.12.2003	Algeria	09.12.2003	Nicaragua	10.12.2003
Germany	09.12.2003	Angola	10.12.2003	Panama	10.12.2003
Guatemala	09.12.2003	Argentina	10.12.2003	Peru	10.12.2003
Iran	09.12.2003	Austria	10.12.2003	Poland	10.12.2003
Ireland	09.12.2003	Barbados	10.12.2003	Republic of Korea	10.12.2003
Italy	09.12.2003	Belgium	10.12.2003	Switzerland	10.12.2003
Japan	09.12.2003	Benin	10.12.2003	Timor-Leste	10.12.2003
Jordan	09.12.2003	Bulgaria	10.12.2003	Togo	10.12.2003
Kenya *	09.12.2003	Burkina Faso	10.12.2003	Turkey	10.12.2003
Kuwait	09.12.2003	Cameroon	10.12.2003	Venezuela	10.12.2003
Malaysia	09.12.2003	China	10.12.2003	Vietnam	10.12.2003
Mali	09.12.2003	Colombia	10.12.2003	Brunei	11.12.2003

[791] UNODCCP. Global Dynamics of Corruption, p. 15 ff.
[792] *Ibid.*

				Darussalam	
Mauritius	09.12.2003	Comoros	10.12.2003	Chile	11.12.2003
Mexico	09.12.2003	Costa Rica	10.12.2003	Portugal	11.12.2003
Morocco	09.12.2003	Côte D' Ivoire	10.12.2003	Serbia and Montenegro	11.12.2003
Namibia	09.12.2003	Croatia	10.12.2003	Trinidad and Tobago	11.12.2003
Nigeria	09.12.2003	Denmark	10.12.2003	Ukraine	11.12.2003
Norway	09.12.2003	Dominican Republic	10.12.2003	Yemen	11.12.2003
Pakistan	09.12.2003	Ecuador	10.12.2003	Zambia	11.12.2003
Paraguay	09.12.2003	El Salvador	10.12.2003	Albania	18.12.2003
Philippines	09.12.2003	Ethiopia	10.12.2003	Indonesia	18.12.2003
Romania	09.12.2003	Finland	10.12.2003	Libyan Arab Jamahiriya	23.12.2003
Russian Federation	09. 12.2003	Gabon	10.12.2003	Saudi Arabia	09.01.2004
Senegal	09.12.2003	Greece	10.12.2003	Central African Republic	11.02.2004
Sierra Leone	09.12.2003	Haiti	10.12.2003	Afghanistan	20.02.2004
Slovakia	09.12.2003	Hungary	10.12.2003	Zimbabwe	20 .02.2004
South Africa	09.122003	Kyrgyzstan	10.12.2003	Azerbaijan	27.02.2004
Sweden	09.12.2003	Lao's PDR	10.12.2003	Seychelles	27.02.2004
Syrian Arab Republic	09.12.2003	Liechtenstein	10.12.2003	Sri Lanka	15.032004

*Kenya ratified the Convention upon signature

Source: United Nations Office on Drugs and Crime
< http://www.unodc.org/unodc/crime_signatures_corruption.html>

A total of 26 different countries made recommendations to the text of the convention, all based on the original provisions of previous GA resolutions on actions against corruption. The submitted recommendations covered several key areas including: a proper definition and scope of corruption; guarantees for the protection of state sovereignty; the creation of applicable preventive measures; deliberations on proper criminalization and sanctions; establishing mechanisms for confiscation and seizure; jurisdiction issues; determining the liability of legal persons; the need for adequate protection of both witnesses and victims; implementing provisions for solid international anti-corruption cooperation; the development of measures to prevent the transfer of illicit funds; providing technical assistance; knowledge sharing and analysis of collected data; and long-term follow-up mechanisms.[793]

At the Mérida Conference, signatories agreed to enter into legal binding obligations to criminalize corrupt practices, develop national institutions for the prevention and prosecution of corruption offences, cooperate in order to recover stolen assets from corrupt deals and help each other through technical assistance and information sharing for reducing the incidence of corruption worldwide.[794]

It must be noted, that the text of the Convention is very broad, because the purposes are to have as many countries as possible ratify the document. Nevertheless, there are "UN-Convention typical" shortcomings. For instance, there are declarations and reservations to the agreement, so that states do not have to adhere to or comply with specific articles contained in the Convention.[795] Moreover, no concrete follow-up mechanisms have been decided upon, since it was only decided that the monitoring phase should start one year after the Convention enters into force.[796]

At this time, it is too early to make any evaluation or even a forecast on the success of the UN Convention, as it has just been signed. From a general perspective however, it can be said that the success of the document will rely

793 *Ibid.*

794 United Nations. "Countries gather to sign on to tough new treaty against corruption, beginning 9 December in Mérida, Mexico." Press Release (8.12. 2003.)

795 For example, Iran has already submitted reservations to Article 66 of the Convention in which the settlement of disputes is specified. The country reserves the right to settle disputes according to the provisions of its national law system and constitution. In: United Nations Office on Drugs and Crime. "United Nations Convention Against Corruption." <http://www.unodc.org/unodc/crime_signatures_corruption.html>

796 In this regard, Transparency International is helping countries coordinate efforts for establishing the framework for a comprehensive follow-up process by signatories as soon as 2005. Transparency International Quarterly Newsletter. (December 2003.)

on willingness and momentum. The UN has scored a success by actually drafting the Convention text so quickly and, more importantly, by bringing enough states to sign it. Nevertheless, the effectiveness of this document is yet to be tested since its entering into force is still far away in the future. Until today, only one country, Kenya, has ratified the UN Convention Against Corruption.[797]

THE ROLE OF INTERNATIONAL ORGANIZATIONS

Besides providing logistical and substantive support for the creation of multilateral anti-corruption laws, intergovernmental institutions have more to offer as actors in the fight against corruption. For example, Chapter Five observed the role of international financial institutions at the different levels of public sector reform that aim to curb corruption in several countries. Moreover, Chapter Six analyzed the contribution of a new, yet equally important actor in the international eradication of corruption, namely Transparency International. This non-governmental forum has gained the interest and respect from the international community as one of the biggest anti-corruption networks worldwide.

These two examples lead to a particular interest in briefly observing the activities of intergovernmental organizations in the context of anti-corruption approaches. After the major international law initiatives have been discussed above, the following section will portrait the role, features and challenges of international organizations as active elements in the anti-corruption debate. Basically, international organizations concentrate their efforts against corruption on five key areas, as observed by Rose-Ackermann, namely: 1) the effective use of the resources provided to recipient countries; 2) support of anti-corruption efforts for the implementation of public sector reforms; 3) reducing the incidence of international bribery, especially in the international business and trade regimes; 4) control the flow and transfer of illicit flows; and 5) the establishment of new international institutions which may deal specifically with corruption.[798] Although at the moment, this last point has not yet become a reality, the following observations will portrait these features as we proceed with the analysis of the biggest international actors in the anti-corruption regime.

---

797 The text of the convention can be found in: United Nations Office on Drugs and Crime. United Nations Convention Against Corruption <www.unodc.org/pdf/crime/convention_corruption/signing/Convention-e.pdf>

798 Rose-Ackermann. Corruption and Government, p. 178.

The World Bank

The increased importance given to the topic of corruption reached a turning point in 1996, after World Bank's President James Wolfensohn publicly committed the work of the World Bank to "fight the cancer of corruption."[799] In this regard, a traditionally ignored issue became the center of the organization's approach towards good governance. During the following year, the Bank developed a comprehensive framework of integrity around its operations considering four key elements:

- making efforts to prevent the incidence of illicit deals and corruption in projects funded by the bank;
- assisting countries that need help in fighting corruption;
- "mainstreaming" corruption as a factor in the analysis of lending decisions;
- and cooperating with other international institutions in the fight against corruption.[800]

The first area of this strategic framework foresaw the creation of internal mechanisms that would effectively monitor the activities of the Bank both to the inside and to the outside. In 1998, an Oversight Committee on Fraud and Corruption took over the responsibility of receiving and processing allegations on illicit activities and corruption by any member of the World Bank Group[801] Additionally, the area of procurement has been reformed so that the goods and services that are circulated and transferred to/from the Bank are properly used and to make sure that the funds granted by the Bank are reaching the right addresses.[802] Another important point is the revision of the conducts of ethics for employees at all levels. Lastly, an internal Sanctions Committee has taken the lead on investigating and prosecuting those staff members who are involved in corruption.[803]

---

799 World Bank. Helping Countries Combat Corruption, p. 1.

800 *Ibid.*, p. 2 ff.

801 Shortly after corruption was declared a high priority, the body was created after recommendations from the Bank's Internal Audit Department. World Bank. "Preventing Corruption in World Bank Projects." <http://www1.worldbank.org/publicsector/anticorrupt/preventing.htm>

802 See also: World Bank. Guidelines: Procurement under IBRD Loans and IDA Credits. (Washington, D.C. : 1999.)

803 World Bank. "Preventing Corruption in World Bank Projects." Much progress has been made within the Bank after the implementation of these measures. The oversight mechanisms were able to

As to the second aspect of the World Bank's approach, it can be observed that providing assistance to those countries which cannot combat corruption on their own is based on a "multipronged strategy" including economic policy reform, administrative and civil service reform, improving the legal and judicial systems, enhancing public expenditure and financial management, and strengthening public and external oversight mechanisms for internal control (see Figure 17).[804] The Bank believes that this broad strategy should help countries strengthen their institutions and make them less prone to corruption. Moreover, the improvement of the judiciary becomes important for proper criminalization and penalization of corrupt agents.

FIGURE 17: THE WORLD BANK'S STRATEGY TOWARDS COUNTRY ASSISTANCE AGAINST CORRUPTION

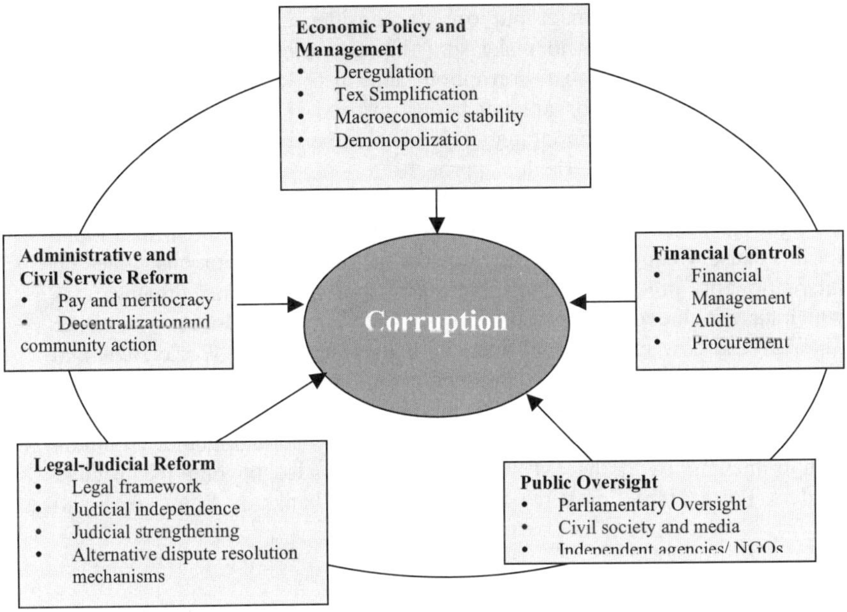

locate staff-belonging perpetrators involved in cases of misuse of funds, breach of contract for personal benefit and conspiracy.

804 World Bank. Helping Countries Combat Corruption, p. 21 ff.

Source: World Bank. Helping Countries Combat Corruption, p. 22

In order to make this strategy work, the contribution of the World Bank has been the development and application of several "diagnostic tools", which are instruments for locating cases of corruption and explore their causes, effects and scope.[805] These mechanisms allow both the Bank and member countries (especially the recipient ones) to better determine the incidence of corruption in their national institutions thus making the relationship between donors and recipients more transparent.[806]

The third key element of the overall strategy deals with taking corruption into account in the Bank's lending program. This relates heavily to the first two elements explained above. It requires Bank personnel to consider the incidence of corruption as a factor for the analysis of countries, as well as for the decisions concerning lending and the delivery of technical assistance. This change in the traditional procedures of the Bank is new, and, for the first time, mandatory. The main purpose of considering corruption in every decision or agreement is to make sure that countries are really taking all necessary steps to combat corruption and also to reassure the donor community that the funds are not being misused. Therefore, the constant revision of anti-corruption strategies in all member countries is an integral part of this element of the Bank's approach.[807]

The last area in which the World Bank has vested most of its interest in the fight against corruption is cooperating with other international institutions for this cause. Chapter Four highlighted the fact that corruption has gained on internationality precisely because there are more international organizations which have included the topic at the top of their agendas. Moreover, Chapter Six analyzed how international financial bodies such as the World Bank and the IMF can help countries better implement public sector reforms.[808]

Therefore, the importance of combining efforts with other institutions cannot be mistaken. In this regard, the World Bank works together within its own framework with the IMF and the UN, but also beyond its juridical borders. For example, most regional development banks in Asia, Africa and

[805] *Ibid.*, p. 23 ff.

[806] "Diagnostic Tools" include: Institutional and Governance Reviews (IGRs), Anticorruption Surveys, Public Expenditure Reviews (PERs) and the County Procurement Assessment Review (CPAR). In: *Ibid.*, p. 24 ff.

[807] *Ibid.*

[808] Rose-Ackermann. Corruption and Government, p. 182 ff.

Latin America rely heavily on the approaches of the World Bank for curbing corruption in their respective countries.[809] Additionally, the Bank also establishes its links with non-governmental groups in order to reach all sectors of society. Therefore, the international cooperation element reaches out to NGOs as well. Transparency International, once again, becomes the major partner in this relationship.

Summarizing, it can be said that the World Bank has a holistic approach to fighting corruption, as the four main pillars of its anti-corruption strategy cover all areas of action, both governmental and non-governmental. The concrete steps that this organization is able to take may depend on the willingness of states to adhere to its recommendations. However, the newest measures against corruption in Bank related projects and, more importantly, the "anti-corruption conditionality" in the lending policy can be quite effective to deter those countries among the recipients to take the eradication of all forms of corruption as a *conditio sine qua non* for accessing to development aid and assistance.

The United Nations

The strategy of the United Nations does not entirely differ from the one of the World Bank. In fact, both approaches are very similar. The only difference lies in the nature of both organizations. While the World Bank is a lending institution that provides financial aid for development, the United Nations is the universal forum of all states and covers more than exclusive development issues. Therefore, the approach of the United Nations is also much broader than the one of the World Bank.

The original efforts of the United Nations against corruption, as observed earlier, are related to the international fight against the illicit transfer of funds and the incidence of transnational organized crime. However, during the last ten years, the approach of the organization has been focused more intensively on corruption *per se*, rather than on its related forms. The UN Convention Against Corruption confirms this new posture.

Besides providing the legal and political framework for the adoption of the Convention, there have been other UN-led initiatives against corruption. The advantage of the United Nations as an organization is that anti-corruption efforts can be started by different subsidiary bodies and specialized agencies, each of them approaching the problem from its own expertise's perspective.

[809] World Bank. Helping Countries Combat Corruption, p. 44 ff.

For example, the United Nations Development Programme focuses on prioritizing on improving integrity as a means to curb corruption. The approach includes capacity development at local and national levels, assessing the implementation of effective measures for a better working public sector, creating adequate channel for active citizen participation in the government decision making and building partnerships between different sectors of society.[810] Moreover, UNDP's Programme for Accountability and Transparency (PACT) includes recommendations and initiatives for strengthening financial management and accountability, as well as mechanisms for fostering national capacity in order to reduce the incidence of corruption.[811] Through cooperation with national and local authorities across many regions of the world, such coordinated strategies can become a beneficial, especially for those states that lack a comprehensive initiative against corruption.

Currently, the UN Department of Economic and Social Affairs (DESA) concentrates on improving the role of the public administration underlining the importance of transparent and accountable governance institutions in the context of anti-corruption efforts.[812] The contribution of DESA is providing assistance in intergovernmental deliberations and providing states with the adequate means (capacity building) to strengthen public institutions and make them more resistant to corruption.

Another important initiative is the Global Program Against Corruption, promoted by the Center for International Crime Prevention (CICP). This program approaches the role of the judiciary and strengthens judicial capacities in both industrialized and developing countries by promoting the integrity, effectiveness and efficiency of judges.[813] The mechanisms for this initiative are based on technical cooperation, research, information sharing of best practices, reinforcing judiciary integrity, and inter-agency coordination regarding corruption activities.[814] This last point is an important feature of the UN's approach against corruption. Due to the fact that the UN system is so extensive and that anti-corruption strategies can be started from different perspectives and at different levels, the coordination among agencies has become a central part of the overall strategy.

---

810 UNODCCP. Global Dynamics of Corruption, pp. 18 ff.

811 *Ibid.*

812 *Ibid.*, p. 19

813 *Ibid.*, p 20.

814 *Ibid.*

This multiplicity can be however one of the short-comings of the entire UN involvement in the anti-corruption regime. Precisely because of the scope of the UN system, many programs and initiatives might overlap similar ones and, more important, a lot of resources might be used for the inter-agency coordination on the first place, instead of focusing on implementing concrete mechanisms to fight corruption. Another problem could be the incidence of corruption inside the organization, as the UN bureaucracy is one of the biggest of its kind. However, similar to the World Bank, the latest reforms brought up by Secretary-General Kofi Annan have included the creation of an Internal Oversight Office in order to better monitor the processes within the organization and keep UN staff well-trained and with a clear vision of the negative aspects of corruption. As Annan himself noted at the time of the adoption of the convention,

> "Corruption hurts the poor disproportionately—by diverting funds intended for development, undermining a government's ability to provide basic services, feeding inequality and injustice, and discouraging foreign investment and aid"[815]

The Organization for Economic Cooperation and Development

The approach of the OECD is more concentrated than the one of the United Nations. Since its main contribution to the international anti-corruption regime has been the OECD Convention against bribery, the organization focuses mostly on helping member countries at the implementation of the Convention as well as to coordinate and disseminate periodical information on the status of the document.[816]

Additionally, the OECD focuses on the private business sector, trying to implement measures that would make international business less prone to corruption. In this context, the organization makes specific recommendations on money laundering and establishes concrete mechanisms for its eradication.[817] The Financial Action Task Force (FATF), which was created by the G-7 in 1989 and has been housed at the OECD ever since, strives

[815] UNODC. United Nations Convention Against Corruption.

[816] Monitoring has been delegated to the OECD Working Group on Bribery in International Business Transactions. Signatories were asked to report on two phases about the status of the Convention in their respective countries. Individual documents on Phase 1 and Phase 2 can be downloaded at <www.oecd.org>

[817] OECD. "Basic facts about money laundering."

towards a better management of money laundering measures. In the early 1990s, the group drafted a document with 40 recommendations focusing on three main areas: the criminal justice system and law enforcement; the financial system and its regulation; and international cooperation.[818]

Another important area of action of the OECD is the adequate treatment of conflicts of interest for public sector. On this topic, the OECD Public Management Service works closely with governments in order to make them aware of the risks and consequences such conflicts might carry. The organization hosts workshops as well as high-level fora for issuing recommendations for concrete mechanisms to better prepare public servants when a conflict of interest might take place.[819] The OECD also approaches the issue of ethics in business transactions as an integral part of its anti-corruption strategy. Using the provisions included in the OECD Convention, the organization focuses on capacity building for both the public and private sectors in order to create a culture of anti-corruption ethics, or, to put it in the organization's own terms to apply "core values" within government agencies and transnational corporations.[820] The strategy is based on identifying risk areas of public life in regards to corruption and making policy recommendations on how to cope with them *via* proper ethic codes. Management measures such as creating a transparent working environment and merit-based promotion system are the basis elements of this approach.[821] More importantly, building public trust to the outside is fundamental for achieving the objectives of this strategy. In this regard, the OECD also targets at strengthening the public image of governments and corporate entities in order to diminish the public distrust, a major factor that has been previously been considered as another source for the incidence of corruption within any given country.

Lastly, the cooperation with civil society is another worth mentioning area within the framework of the OECD. The implementation and follow-up of the multiple OECD mechanisms and recommendations on bribery, money laundering and other types of corrupt related activities relies heavily on the

---

818 *Ibid.*

819 See for further reference: Organization for Economic and Cooperation and Development (OECD.) Managing Conflict of Interest in the Public Service: OECD Guidelines and Country Experiences. (Paris: OECD Publications, 2004); and Organization for Economic and Cooperation and Development (OECD.) Trust in Government: Ethics Measures in OECD Countries. (Paris: OECD Publications, 2000.)

820 Organization for Economic and Cooperation and Development (OECD.) "Building Public Trust: Ethics and Measures in OECD Countries." OECD Public Management Policy Brief. (September 2000.)

821 *Ibid.*

input provided by countries. In this regard, civil society organizations have played a key role as facilitators, initiators and policy-recommendation contributors.[822] Organizations such as Transparency International, the International Chamber of Commerce (ICC), the Business and Industry Advisory Committee to the OECD (BIAC) and the Trade Union Advisory Committee to the OECD (TUAC) have been the main partners of the organization thus far.[823] Their contribution can be seen on an *ante*, as well as on a *post* level. First, these independent entities supported the adoption of the 1997 Convention by generating political will within the member countries and the international business community to criminalize the bribery of foreign officials. This has been considered one of the main catalysts for the adoption of the Convention.[824] Second, these four organizations took an active role on the implementation of the two evaluation phases for the Convention in the last years. Collecting data, evaluating best practices and providing country-based input to the OECD has allowed the organization to periodically monitor the successes (and losses) of the OECD Convention thus far. Another important aspect of these organizations is that they cooperate with the OECD at solidifying initiatives at the regional level in order to broaden the reaching spectrum of the Convention's anti-corruption endeavors.[825]

It can be said, therefore, that when it comes to a comprehensive anti-corruption approach, the support between civil society and the OECD becomes mutual. These organizations guarantee the continuity of the initiatives and the development for OECD-sponsored effective mechanisms against bribery, money laundering and similar crimes.

The Inter-American Development Bank and the Organization of American States

Due to the specific thematic approach of this book, it becomes necessary to have a look at the major regional organizations in Latin America, especially in regards to their efforts towards the eradication of corruption on the continent. The two pillars of the so called Inter-American system are the

822 Organization for Economic and Cooperation and Development (OECD.) Fighting Corruption. What Role for Civil Society? The Experience of the OECD. (Paris: OECD Publications, 2003.)

823 *Ibid.*

824 *Ibid.*

825 Examples of these regional initiatives are the Stability Pact Anti-Corruption Initiative for South Eastern Europe (SPAI), the Asia-Pacific Anti-Corruption Initiative, and the Governance and Anti-Corruption Forum for Latin America. In: *Ibid.*, p. 19.

Organization of American States, as the principal political forum, and the Inter-American Development Bank, as the principal development bank.[826] These two institutions work together to promote integration and development in the region. The focus on corruption is also an important aspect of the work of both the OAS and the IDB, since the main legal mechanisms for the fight against corruption have developed out of these fora.

The first measures taken within the Inter-American System for combating corruption date back to 1992 when different institutions within the two main institutions started to include the topic of corruption in their agendas.[827] The efforts gave the desired results after the adoption of the Inter-American Convention in 1997, as observed earlier.

Similar to the case of the OECD, it can be observed that the Convention provides the main framework around which the system undertakes most of its anti-corruption actions. For example, the Convention has served as the basis for the establishment of the Inter-American Program for Cooperation in the Fight Against Corruption, an anti-corruption framework adopted in Lima in 1997 at the General Assembly of the OAS.[828] The document is one of the most significant ongoing efforts to promote greater cooperation in the region in order to effectively combat corruption.

As noted in the case of the World Bank, regional development banks incline towards learning from its established anti-corruption approaches and then apply them on a respective region. The IDB and the OAS are no exception. The Bank's approach towards diminishing corruption is closely linked with the strategies undertaken by the World Bank. Five key areas are included: 1) prevention of fraud and corruption within the institutions of the Bank; 2) prevention of fraud and corruption within Bank-approved and financed projects; 3) acting as a forum for and supporting international efforts to reduce corruption; 4) taking corruption explicitly into account in country assistance and lending considerations; and 5) helping countries that require help from the Bank in their strategies to reduce corruption.[829]

---

[826] Vargas Carreño, Edmundo. "The Inter-American Convention Against Corruption." Working Paper for the Conference on Transparency and Development in Latin America and the Caribbean. (Washington, D.C., 2000.)

[827] *Ibid.* The Inter-American Judicial Committee adopted the topic "First Approach to Focus the Law on Corruption in the Americas." Also, the Inter-American Legal Committee adopted resolution 1559 (XXII-92) stated the concern of the body that corrupt practices in international business as a constraint for development.

[828] *Ibid.*

[829] Bannon. "The Fight Against Corruption, A World Bank Perspective."

Furthermore, the IDB works together with other international and regional institutions such as the OECD and UNDO in order to address common concerns, share experiences and best practices, and design futures strategies for intervention and assistance in the field. It can be observed once again, how important the inter-agency dialogue is for an international anti-corruption approach. In addition to the inter-organizational exchange, the IDB and the OAS constantly serve as coordination fora, hosting conferences, symposia, workshops and other related activities in order to maintain the anti-corruption momentum within member states.[830] This provides a great opportunity for government officials, experts of international finance institutions, scholars, as well as NGOs to strategically approach the impact of corruption in the region and work out possible strategies to follow.

Besides improving the internal system of the IDB and the OAS by updating their ethical guidelines and make its structures transparent and accurate, special attention has been given to public sector reform, especially fiscal control, revenue collection accounting, and auditing of tax systems, as Latin American nations seem to be very sensitive to corruption in these areas.[831] Within this area, the IDB and the OAS seek to improve the role of the judiciary, as it is their belief that corruption could be best approached in countries in the region, if the judicial sector maintains adequate levels of independency and transparency for punishing corruption perpetrators.[832]

A noteworthy aspect of the work of the OAS is the follow-up and monitoring of the Inter-American Convention. This is mainly managed by the OAS Secretariat for Legal Affairs and the Technical Secretariat for Legal Cooperation Mechanisms therein. It comprises periodical national progress reports on the implementation of the Convention, based on a questionnaire that the signatories have to periodically provide answers to.[833] An expert committee of the Secretariat evaluates the reports, makes recommendations and distributes the information to the other member countries and to the public in general. Moreover, the Secretariat is in charge of acting as a liaison between civil society groups, NGOs and other organizations with the OAE in matters related to the Convention.

---

830 One example is the Conference on Transparency and Development in Latin America and the Caribbean hosted by the IDB and the OAS in Washington, D.C. in May 2000.

831 Quick, Steven. "Inter-American Bank Initiatives against Corrupion." In: Tulchin and Espach. Combating Corruption in Latin America, p. 217.

832 *Ibid.*

833 Organization of American States (OAS.) Secretariat for Legal Affairs: Technical Secretariat for Legal Cooperation Mechanisms. <http://www.oas.org/juridico/english/fightcur.html>

Although the approach is very similar to the other organizations presented in this section, the Inter-American system has its own dynamics and characteristics, due to the regional limitation of both the OAS and the IDB. There is a certain emphasis on some of the aspects of anti-corruption strategies (i.e. public sector reforms) based on the experiences of countries in the region with specific challenges in the field of corruption.

This chapter has presented the main approaches of the international community to confront the problem of corruption. It has become clear that, at the moment, there is no lack of strategies and legal instruments that have been developed for the eradication of this phenomenon, especially during the last ten years. The approaches are multiple and can be found in all regions.

However, two main aspects should be mentioned at the end of this section, as we approach the case studies. First, every international treaty, covenant, convention or similar document relies heavily on both the ability and the political willingness of states for its implementation. This has been a shortcoming in each of the cases explained above. When it comes to the topic of corruption, the normative element comes again to the foreground, giving a lot of space for individual interpretation of what is understood under "corruption" or "bribery". This gives states the opportunity to issue binding reservations to several provisions included in the documents analyzed in this chapter thus relativizing the original purposes thereof. As a consequence, one should remain cautious of the fact, that simply because there is a legal mechanism out there, this does not mean that a solution to corruption is near. Although there has been enormous progress in this area (especially in Latin America), the problem of ratification, implementation and follow-up is still a potential factor for the failure of international mechanisms against corruption.

The second observation can be obtained from the analysis of the work of the organizations presented in this chapter. In each one of the cases, it became clear that holistic approaches must rely heavily on a constant inter-agency dialogue. Finding solutions to a problem that is so broad is a difficult enterprise, especially if these solutions are to be of international nature. As we have seen in this chapter, most international organizations do provide a series of solutions and strategies that are very similar, if not equal, to the ones of other partner organizations. In order to avoid this overlapping of strategies, international institutions have to steadily communicate with their counterparts and regional branches. This again relies on the skills and mechanisms that these fora implement to cooperate with other anti-corruption institutions. Only a comprehensive dialogue, based on a common goal, namely the eradication of corruption via international mechanisms, can enhance this approach.

Regime theory has taught us that regimes facilitate the communication between actors in order to solve problems more effectively. After the findings of this chapter, it has become notable that the international corruption regime referred to in Chapter Four as the *pax corrupta* has found a very strong contestant, namely an international regime of inter-governmental, non-governmental and civil society institutions which have a series of remedies for the current scourge of worldwide corruption. The proceeding chapters should exemplify both successes and failures in order to prove the hypotheses and solve the main puzzle of the book.

CHAPTER NINE

ARGENTINA

If the research proposed in this book was undertaken for each of the 27 Latin American (and Caribbean) nations, not only the size of the book but – much worse – the main analytical tasks would become less concise and utterly unpredictable. Therefore, in order to make the comparative exercise effective and successful, this book will focus on three Latin American countries, namely Argentina, Chile, and Ecuador. Although the arguments for this particular choice are not entirely exclusive, thus meaning the analyzed countries may vary in other studies, an outlook of history, political composition, economic development, and societal elements should clarify why these three countries serve the analytical purposes of this book.

The main puzzle and thus the main goal is to give a comprehensive yet solid explanation to why corruption is so imminent in Latin American countries by making a comparison of three of them. Therefore, it will be helpful to have a look some of the similar and differential aspects of the highlighted nations in order to underline the importance of the choice and the comparative method used for the analysis. This shall be done by making three introductory observations on the elements mentioned above, namely recent history, the political landscape and tradition, economic performance and the role of society in national affairs.

First, in terms of historical political development, it can be observed that all three countries are post-colonial democracies that emerged under almost identical backgrounds and followed the European tradition of governmental and economic models for state constituency. This point makes all countries similar and thus increases the interest for approaching the question of corruption as being a product of patrimonial heritage and not of regional particularity. This means that the mainstream argument for Latin American countries simply being inevitably corrupt *per natura* opposed to Europeans/Western nations lacks an absolute historical and empirical underpinning.[834]

Economically, Argentina, Chile and Ecuador developed at a quite different pace. Right after World War II, Argentina was one of the most economically advanced countries in the world, with very high levels of

[834] Tulchin and Espach. Combating Corruption in Latin America, p. 10. See also note 84.

industrialization and trade and a solid public sector. Chile developed in a similar way in the 1950s and 1960s, expanding the role of the state to a maximum and becoming one of the strongest (yet most protectionist) economies as well. Ecuador however, did not yet advance to the same extent as the other two countries within the first decades of the post-war era. This was mostly due to the difficulties of the Ecuadorian economy to cope with trade drawbacks around its main export goods, bananas and cacao in the 1960s which made the country successively more dependent on foreign loans than on national production. Nowadays, Chile is the leading emerging economy in Latin America, while Argentina and Ecuador are suffering from the worst economic austerity since the return of democracy. Can this difference be attributed to the incidence of corruption? An answer to this question demands a comparison of the three countries using economic performance as an evaluation *criterium*.

In terms of political systems, all the three countries have installed democratically elected governments by now. However, all of them have had experiences with social turmoil and the constant change from military to democratic rule in the past 50 years. Ecuador was the first of the three to install an independently elected government in 1979. Contrary, Argentina and Chile entered the 1980s under military dictatorships from which they suffered major human rights atrocities. In the case of the latter, military rule lasted until the early 1990s. Having a look at the political landscape of each country will enable us to find out if political culture – also understood in terms of political legacy and heritage – plays a role in the incidence of corruption in each of the cases.

From a societal perspective, Chile and Argentina share a common characteristic as opposed to Ecuador. These two countries have a greater European influence since only a small percentage of the population can be considered as being "indigenous people." In Ecuador, nearly one third of the population belongs to indigenous groups. This contrast makes society-state relations quite unique in the country, especially due to the fact, that the indigenous movement in Ecuador has gone far beyond being a mere grouping of tribes and cultures, on to becoming one of the nation's most powerful political forces of the new millennium. If it is said that the incidence of corruption can be related to societal/anthropological factors, then the comparison of these three countries should exemplify up to what level this progressive approach to corruption can prove its explanatory power.

Section II presented the main approaches against the expansion of corrupt practices worldwide. Therefore, it must be explained that precisely these four areas will be considered individually in the analysis of all cases.

This means that the efforts and initiatives towards public sector reform, the role and participation of NGOs, the media landscape and press freedom, and the national implementation and follow-up of international anti-corruption mechanisms such as the OAS Convention will be evaluated in each country as well. Such an analytical step will allow us to better understand how these nations are coping with the problem of corruption and what challenges remain ahead.

ARGENTINA: RECENT DEVELOPMENTS

Back in the early stages of the 20th century, Argentina was considered a developed economy. According to the World Bank however, the country's economic growth did not improve noticeably from the 1940s until the early 1990s, when one of the worse crises in the nation's republican history hit all sectors of Argentine affairs.[835] Since the establishment of the *Plan de Convertibilidad* in 1991, which locked the peso to the US dollar in a 1:1 relationship, the trade imbalance grew rapidly and made it impossible for the country to earn enough money to keep current on its foreign debt obligations.[836] Consequently, Argentina accumulated a total foreign debt amounting to over 140 billion US dollars in 2001, which represented nearly 50 percent of the country's GDP.[837] The final stage of the crisis was again an inevitable devaluation of the *peso*, as the government of Fernando de la Rúa could not fulfill its financial duties. The current state of affairs in Argentina is far from reaching neither an end nor a comprehensive solution. Although the tone of the crisis might have seemed economic at first, social and political breakdowns have been present during this tumultuous period in Argentina's history as well. It becomes striking to observe how one of the richest countries in Latin America is now among the poorest and heavily indebted ones.

An unprecedented economic crisis creates a perfect scenario for the spread of crime and social unrest throughout the country. Recent reports on crime in Argentina show that the rate of criminal activity has experienced a significant rise, especially since 1994.[838] Experts recognize income inequality, poor economic performance, and a lack of public security services

[835] World Bank. Country Brief – Argentina. <http://www.worldbank.org> Washington, D.C. 2000.

[836] Feldstein, Martin. "Argentina's Fall. Lessons from the Latest Financial Crisis." Foreign Affairs (March/April 2002), Vol. 81, Nr. 2, pp. 8-14.

[837] *Ibid.* See also Country Brief – Argentina.

[838] Lederman, Daniel. Crime in Argentina: A Preliminary Assessment. World Bank, 1999.

as the main reasons for this development.[839] Poverty and underemployment levels have increased reciprocally to the economic outsets in the last decade.[840]

The major breakdowns in the economy and social affairs of Argentina did not escape the political elites. Quite to the contrary, Argentine politics entered the new millennium in probably the most unstable period since the return to democracy in 1983. Back then, the debt crisis was still in its infancy after the last military dictatorship destabilized the economy and created a public distrust by oppressing the population through the horror of a "dirty war".[841] However, the re-installment of democratic rule created high expectations among the Argentine political community, as former presidents Raul Alfonsín and Carlos Ménem undertook the difficult task of bringing the country back to the right economic, social and political tracks after years of military rule.

At the end of Ménem's second administration, the country's economic indicators were not very promising for the new government of radical Fernando de la Rúa. Highly impacted by the havoc of the Argentine economy and after only two years in office, de la Rúa's was unable to stay in power. Besides the general social discontent in most cities and provinces across the country, de la Rúa also faced a serious political backslash, as he split the Senate and went into direct confrontation with all opposition parties and even with his coalition partners. In August of 2000, the president's "inner circle" was involved in accusations allegedly concerning bribes in the Argentine Senate for positive votes for the executive's labor reform plans.[842] As a consequence, de la Rúa was forced to reshuffle his cabinet and witnessed the resignation of the popular vice-president Carlos Alvarez.[843] Within months, Congress accepted a letter from de la Rua stating his resignation as well.

In the following few days, the world witnessed a political roller-coaster ride *à la Argentina*, as the seat of the president turned into the bonfire of the vanities for the Argentine political elite. The situation was managed miserably and after only seven days after being appointed president by

839 *Ibid.*

840 According to the World Bank Country Brief, the poverty status in Argentina is at 18 percent and the unemployment rate has risen to almost 16 percent.

841 Zuleta Puceiro, Enrique. "State Reform and Deregulatory Strategies in Argentina." In: Naim, Moises and Joseph Tulchin (eds.) Competition Policy, Deregulation and Modernization in Latin America. (Boulder: Lynne Rienner Publishers, 1999.)

842 Transparency International. Global Corruption Report 2001. p. 169.

843 Faiola, Anthony. "Bribery Scandal Singes Argentine Anti-Graft Crusader." The Washington Post. (11th October 2000.)

Congress, de la Rúa's successor Adolfo Rodríguez Saá quit, leaving the president's seat to Eduardo Duhalde until general elections are to be held in 2003. The general discontent with this situation was brought out to the streets of Buenos Aires, Rosario and other major cities as the people claimed with one voice: *"que se vayan todos!"* (engl.: "let them *all* go away!") This motto has had great repercussion in Argentina symbolizing the distrust of the population towards the political institutions and its representatives.

Duhalde performed poorly as well and thus was forced to call elections ahead of schedule. This last electoral race did not lack a theatrical tone, after a resented Carlos Ménem, afraid of low electoral results, stepped out of the second decisive round, leaving the win to Néstor Kirchner, a left oriented neo-peronist who has already claimed the failure of the neoliberal economic model in Argentina and other Latin American economies.

During the dramatic events in Argentina, especially during in the 1990s, corruption played a determinant role for the fate of the last two governments. Not only de la Rúa was accused of bribery thus leading to his resignation. Moreover, former president Carlos Ménem has been recently taken to court on charges of fraud and illegal arms sale to Croatia and Ecuador during his administration, through which he and his family benefited from the deal's outcome. Although he was able to finish his two terms in power, many observers blame Ménem and his administration for the misery in Argentine politics and economics.

Political Landscape

Argentine politics in the last two decades have been the result of the amalgamation of three major events in the history of the country, namely the rise and fall of Peronism during the 1940s, the struggle for power by the military armed forces starting the 1950s and the return to democracy in the early 1980s.[844] These elements build the political structure of modern Argentina. Therein included are decisive factors which shaped national politics such as the antagonism between a socialist left and a conservative right, the role of trade unions and the working class as political actors, populism as a feasible mechanism for political action, the active presence of the military in all areas of politics and thus a cycle between democracy and authoritarian rule, the former having been intensified in the 1970s.[845]

844 Tedesco, Laura. Democracy in Argentina. Hope and Disillusion. (London: Frank Cass, 1999.)

845 Since 1930, Argentina has witnessed the overthrown of six democratically elected governments. Along came six countercoups, and between 1952 and 1994, no democratically elected president was

Since the end of the last military Junta, Argentine politics have diversified towards pluralism and an open dialogue between the different affiliations. Although system is very much bipartisan, there are currently 32 different political parties covering all major traditions from conservatives, on to moderates and left wing communism.[846] The most influencing political streams are the former party of national leader Juan Perón, namely the Justicialist Party *(Partido Justicialista – PJ)*, and Argentina's oldest political party, the Redical Civic Union *(Unión Cívica Radical – UCR)*, founded in 1890.[847] In the last ten years, a "third way" has been highly recognized by the electorate namely the Solidarity National Front *(Frente del País Solidario – FREPASO)*, which offers an moderate alternative to both the PJ and the UCR. The major force has been, however, the peronist PJ from which three out of the last four presidents have emerged.[848] Moreover, the major economic breakdowns in the 1990s severely damaged the political image and strength of the UCR, leaving the last elections to be decided among PJ candidates.

The political apparatus of Argentina presents a modern federalist structure with Western democratic features. The executive is carried out by the President, who is at the same time the commander in chief of the armed forces. Presidential elections are held after a maximum of two terms of four years each.[849]

The legislative branch is bicameral, composed by a Congress (Chamber of Deputies, 257 members) and a Senate (72 members), both of which are directly elected for a period of four and six years respectively. One half of Congress stands for re-election every two years, while one third of the Senators follow the same pattern.[850] By obtaining majorities in both chambers, the President can be ousted from power.

The federalist element in the Argentine political structure is reflected in 23 states (or provinces) and one federal district. Both have independence

able to finish his term. In: Teichman, Judith A. The Politics of Freeing Markets in Latin America. Chile, Argentina and Mexico. (Chapel Hill and London: The University of North Carolina Press, 2001), p. 30.

846 As found in: Georgetown University. "Argentina Political Parties." Political Database of the Americas. <http://www.georgetown.edu/pdba/Parties/Resumen/Argentina/desc.html> (December 2003.)

847 *Ibid.*

848 Fernando de la Rúa (1999-2002) has been the only UCR-affiliated President since 1989.

849 Economist Intelligence Unit. "Political Forces." In: Country ViewsWire Argentina. (October 2003.) Also available online at <http://www.economist.com/countries/Argentina/index.cfm>

850 Senators are elected from each state considering the following distributional key: two from the leading party, one from the major contestant. In: *Ibid.*

from the central government in matters that are not vested therein and elect their own representatives.[851]

On the legislative side, Argentine federal judges are appointed by the National Council of Magistrates. The Supreme Court is composed by members of all provinces and need a two-third majority from the Senate to be appointed.[852]

The Economy

As observed earlier, Argentina began the second half of the 20th Century with a positive image and was able to be placed among the most prosperous nations of the Western Hemisphere.[853] Although the political and human rights abuses from the military rule severely damaged the country at many levels, the economic downfall of Argentina paradoxically coincided with its return to democracy. Until the late 1970s, the economic policy of the country was based on the traditional protectionist import substitution model with a considerable degree of internationalization via trade within the Americas and with Europe.[854]

Until the last military dictatorship (1976-1983), the private sector was a vital part of the economic life of Argentina. Nevertheless, the instalment of the new Junta started a more state-oriented economic approach thus giving preference to state owned industries and enterprises for managing the Argentine economic front.[855] This caused both stagnation and a weakening of private entrepreneurial actors and, at the same time, an overload of the public administration. The economic doctrine imposed by the ministry of economy at that time, José Martínez de Hoz hit the middle class and established a solid network between the military and the high spheres of the Argentine economy, who were mostly industrial and financial groups close to the state leadership.[856] The results were not too surprising, as political scientist Judith Teichman explains,

[851] *Ibid.*

[852] *Ibid.*

[853] World Bank. Country Brief – Argentina.

[854] Tedesco. Democracy in Argentina, pp. 15 ff.

[855] Teichman, Judith. "Private sector power and market reform: exploring the domestic origins of Argentina's meltdown and Mexico's policy failures." Third World Quarterly (2002) Vol. 23, No. 3, pp. 491-512.

[856] *Ibid.*

> "[t]he positions of minister of foreign trade and director of the national planning office were filled by individuals with ties to the highest financial circles. At the same time, economic policy hit small and medium enterprises hard especially industry, and concentrated economic power in the hands of favoured big business interests. Trade liberalization in consumer goods industries produced a sharp increase in bankruptcies, especially among small and medium firms producing got the domestic consumer market."[857]

These bonds were solidified through the 1970s creating a separate economic class that benefited from special treatments such as access to markets, tax privileges (exemption) and easy credits from the state owned Bank.[858] The biggest economic legacy left by the military governments was a very extensive accumulated foreign debt. The war over the Falkland Islands (Malvinas) increased public spending and left the economy in the ruin.[859]

The elections of 1983 brought in the hope for a rapid economic reorientation and recovery. However, by the time Raúl Alfonsín was appointed President on a democratic ticket, he continued to base his economic policies on the provisions given by the country's same most powerful business actors. These economic elites kept their ties to the dictatorship era, and Alfonsín let them decide on which economic pattern to follow at the dawn of Argentina's new democratic phase. Thus it is interesting to observe how the Argentine model of economy relied heavily on the public sector as the main actor in all areas of the national economy both during and after the last military government.

This position changed with the return of the Peronist Party PJ to power through Carlos Ménem after the elections of 1989. Quickly after he assumed power, Ménem announced that he would – for the first time ever – renounce to some of the traditional postures of the Peronist economic doctrine by adopting a new liberal market oriented course for the Argentine economy.[860] He did not let critical voices and sceptics wait too long. By 1994, privatizations of most public companies in all sectors including telecommunications, energy and transportation were either fully completed

---

857 *Ibid.*

858 *Ibid.*

859 Tedesco. Democracy in Argentina, pp. 45 ff.

860 Economist Intelligence Unit. "Political Forces."

on the way thereto, and the pace would not slow down.[861] This showed a complete rejection from the original credo of Peronism, as it always strived for a greater role of the state in national affairs.

One particular aspect of this liberalization and deregulation course taken by the first Ménem administration was the fact that he took these efforts as a personal initiative, delegating very few tasks to actors outside his closest perimeter (see Figure 18.) Moreover, the president relied on a new generation of technocrats who had been abroad in the United States and Europe and brought economic plans of neoliberal tone. These new technocrats took it upon themselves to implement the new doctrines of economic reform in Argentina.[862]

FIGURE 18: ARGENTINE POLICY NETWORKS (STATE AND SOCIETY PARTICIPATION BY POLICY AREA)

State	Society
Major policy reforms: privatization, trade liberalization (policy initiation)	
▪ President ▪ Minister of Economy ▪ Key Cabinet Members and their teams	▪ Private sector excluded
Trade policy	
▪ Minister of the Economy ▪ Minister of Foreign Affairs	▪ Private sector excluded ▪ Export conglomerates consulted ▪ (only on Mercosur matters)
Labour and social security reforms	
▪ Minister of the Economy ▪ Minister of Labour	▪ Conglomerated consulted (periphery) ▪ Trade union leaders

861 In the 1990s, 154 privatization contracts were completed in Argentina amounting ca. $ 19.5 billion in revenues for the federal government. While in the initial years, the revenues represented only 1% of the country's GDP and 10% of the entire revenue, by the end of the decade, the latter figure rose up to 60% of the entire amount given to the public treasury. In: Ennis, Huberto M. and Santiago M. Pinto. "Privatization and Income Distribution in Argentina." Inter-American Development Bank Project: The Effects of Privatization in Income Distribution in Latin America. (Washington, D.C./Mexico, D.F.: Inter-American Development Bank Sustainable Development Department, 2001.)

862 Teichman. The Politics of Freeing Markets in Latin America, p. 114.

	(collaborationist on periphery)
Public enterprise restructuring and privatization	
▪ Minister of the Economy ▪ Minister of Public Works (until 1991) ▪ Public enterprise managers ▪ Military commanders (from companies under military control)	▪ Private contractors linked to conglomerates ▪ Trade union leaders (collaborationist on periphery)

Source: Teichman. The Politics of Freeing Markets in Latin America, p. 109.

The project of modernizing the economy was a widely debatable undertaking with several positive and negative consequences. In economic terms, the Washington institutions highly welcomed the new economic doctrine and entered into an era of mutual cooperation and assistance with the country.[863] The role of the *persona* Ménem continued to grow inexorably with the pace and the scope of reform. This led to a parallel development of a new political class that emerged from the anti-Peronist posture of the PJ. The observations on Argentina's social components and the impact of *Menemismo* shall be undertaken below.

Important is to note however, that the hopes of the government to earn the fruits of the neoliberal harvest were let down by a severe economic breakdown that has taken the Argentine economy hit rock bottom almost every year. It all started in 1991 when Ménem's minister of economy, Domingo Cavallo announced the Convertibility Plan, which tied the Argentine Peso to the US Dollar on a 1:1 relationship. This measure was highly criticized by most sectors of the Argentine political, economic and social classes. Additionally, the Mexican crisis of 1994 had its so called "tequila effect" on almost every country in Latin America. Such external shocks caught the Argentine economic front liners almost by surprise and led to a rapid deterioration the situation in the country. Although the *Convertibilidad* had ended the currency chaos of the era of Alfonsín, it had a deep impact on other sides of the economy. The most important problem, as observed at the beginning of the chapter was an uncontrollable foreign debt

[863] The relationships with the IMF were not always harmonious. In 1988, the Fund denied Argentina a standby loan. However, the World Bank intervened and initiated thereby further agreements with the government. In: *Ibid.*, p. 107.

accumulation and an overspent public treasury. Privatization was very costly for the government and the revenues thereof did not reach the intended levels.[864]

By the end of the 1990s, the wave of privatization had come to an end thus diminishing the inflow of private capital flow. The economy entered into a fear recession with an overvalued peso which led to a stagnation of exports and left a considerable deficit in the trade balance. Additionally, the devaluation of the Real in Brazil brought terrible consequences for Argentina's regional and international trade position. Nevertheless, by the next elections, the Argentine voters put their trust in Ménem once more, as the nation was in need of a continuous political and economic line. He was re-elected in order to saver Argentina from the collapsing course it had taken in the past year.

The electorate's hopes where once more taken for granted. The already very adverse background of Ménem's first term made the government incapable of supporting the currency board anymore and thus had to continuously borrow from international institutions and private banks. Additionally, inflation rates were shockingly high, as well as unemployment. Citizens began to entirely loose faith in the collapsing financial system and thus soon begun to secure their reserves by withdrawing them directly from banks or by transferring them into a third country. And the debt continued to grow.

This accumulation of debt increased drastically until the end of Ménem's second term and the beginning of the presidency of de la Rúa. When he entered office, he found literally the ruins of a country with high rates of unemployment, an uncontrollable inflation rate, low levels of international trade and, again, an empty public treasury. Paradoxically enough, de la Rúa did not reverse the economic roller-coaster implanted by his predecessor. Despite the fact that he and the UCR defeated Ménem and thus the steadily less Peronist PJ, he rehired the already highly unpopular former Minister of the Economy Cavallo (who had quit Ménem's cabinet earlier due to differences with the President) and put him once again on the lead of the economic front. Although the old new Minister took a decisive neoliberal course of action, this remedy did not bring the cure to the country's critical condition. In addition, the political weakness of de la Rúa as president took the country into a yet mote desperate state, namely a complete political breakdown.

[864] Ennis and Pinto. "Privatization and Income Distribution in Argentina."

FIGURE 19. ARGENTINA – ECONOMIC INDICATORS (1999-2002)

	1999	2000	2001	2002
GDP per head ($ at PPP)	12,330	12,402	12,000	10,640
GDP (% real change pa)	-3.39	-0.79	-4.41	-11.30
Government consumption (% of GDP)	13.72	13.78	14.16	12.22
Budget balance (% of GDP)	-1.68	-2.39	-3.25	-1.45
Consumer prices (% change pa; av)	-1.17	-0.94	-1.07	25.87
Public debt (% of GDP)	42.99	45.04	53.76	111.50
Labour costs per hour (USD)	4.16	4.23	4.06	1.35
Recorded unemployment (%)	13.03	14.55	16.40	18.80
Current-account balance/GDP	-4.20	-3.12	-1.69	8.60
Foreign-exchange reserves (m$)	26,252	25,147	14,553	10,489

Source: Economist Intelligence Unit. Country Data Argentina.

The debacle about Cavallo's and de la Rúa cessation by political and civil forces in 2003 left the country with a poor international image for investors. Moreover, the failure to undertake comprehensive public reforms made the country take severe damage from the privatization waves and the conditionality of international loans. As the crisis has not yet reached an ending point, institutional deficiencies and inadequate currency appreciations remain the main obstacles towards investment and sustained growth.[865] Moreover, the foreign debt still casts a shadow over all the positive developments of the Argentine economy. The economy thus will not really recover, despite forecasts, if these three problems, namely institutional weakness, currency depreciation and external debt service are not properly faced.

Social Factors in the 1990s: From *Peronismo* to *Menemismo*

During the heights of his political career, Juan Perón mobilized the masses striving for more equality and fairness towards those who had less. This altruistic undertaken brought him great popularity. However, the gap

[865] Cañonero, Gustavo. "Latin America: Economic Analysis – Argentina." Deutsche Bank. Emerging Markets Monthly. (November 2003.)

between the rich and the poor in Argentina was something not even he was able to close.

Instead, Argentine society became polarized between the traditional rich elites and the new forces driven by Perón, especially the working class. After his first term, Perón was capable of changing average Argentine workers on to politically active and motivated elements. In this regard, political parties were confronted by the unions, who had come stronger than ever before. During the years after Perón, internal social struggles were never ceased, especially after the military took over the affairs of the country until 1983.

The horrendous experience of the dictatorial rule in Argentina shaped the way its society developed in the course of the 1980s. Although the military decided to "back off", they still played a decisive part in all sectors of the Argentine system. Only Ménem's election did bring along a comprehensive transformation in the state-society relations.

As observed in the analysis of the Argentine economy, the new Peronist *impetus* that started in the country after Ménem assumed power became a major turning point in history. This turn could also be observed in some aspects of Argentine society. Teichman notes that

> "[t]he predominant feature of [Ménem's] leadership style and the authority it established was patrimonial. As such, Ménem's appointments to state and party positions were based on personal loyalty to himself. These appointments produced a downgrading of the importance of Peronist militancy and the appointment of many outsiders to government and party positions."[866]

Thus the beginning of Menemist patrimonialism became the emerging societal struggle in Argentina, as a new elite has formed and intended to climb to the highest spheres of the social ladder. The common features of such an enterprise soon appeared in the country in form of networking clans, clientelism and up to a certain point, a modern form of caudillismo.[867] Under these conditions, societal relations in Argentina became highly explosive, especially if the economic situation is added thereto. The traditional

[866] Teichman. The Politics of Freeing Markets in Latin America, p. 114.

[867] *Ibid.* The author observed that "[t]he predominantly patrimonial authority established by Ménem has been linked to his political origins as governor of one of the country's poorest provinces, La Rioja [...] in such context, politics is much more personalistic, even more heavily based on clans, caudillismo, and clientelism than is Argentine national politics generally."

industrial elites of the country did not loose their influence on the country. However, due to the pressing nature of the crisis, new pseudo-elites soon became increasingly powerful, mostly because of the dynamics of an energic closed group around the highest spheres of power within economically devastated scenario.

Ménem started as a low key governor and suddenly became a global player with a Peronist twist. This was something that was soon found to become a problem for many people in the country, especially deeming the fact that Ménem, as a President, tried establish the same political and society patterns as when he was governor. As Teichman concludes,

> "[i]t is for this reason that Ménem and his closest collaborators have been termed an 'antielite' – a group that, because it lacked the acceptance by the established elite groups, recognition, and prestige, was able to act much more autonomously and flexibly than would otherwise be the case."

The post-Ménem society in Argentina still suffers from this disruptive development. The economic crisis had its impact on all levels of society, hitting the middle and lower classes the most. Living standards heavily decreased due to the recession and the stagnation of all forms of economic activity, forcing many people to involuntarily give up their jobs. As a consequence, high levels of unemployment led to a continuously growing lack of social cohesion. Also it is important to observe, that the population soon made the government directly responsible for the adverse situation. In this scenario, civic mistrust towards politics grew inexorably leading the administration towards a complete loss of political grip to manage the affairs of country and provide basic public services.

This kind of disjunctions was obviously nothing new in a country that was traditionally critical and demanding towards its political leadership. Nevertheless, Argentine society during the Ménem years developed such mistrust towards the government that, as observed in the beginning of the chapter, the main approach for the solution of the country's problems was to get rid of the political elites and start "from scratch" all over again (*"que se vayan todos!"* - (engl.: "let them *all* go away!")

This sentiment was present during the latest elections in which Ménem once again proved his intentions of regaining power by running for President. Although he made it to the second round, he decided to withdraw, fearing an unprecedented defeat. Nestor Kirchner won the election and intended to re-establish electoral confidence and economic stability.

Explaining Corruption in Argentina

This brief sketch of Argentina's politics, primary economic indicators and selected social factors have provided valuable input for the explanation of corruption in this country. In order to explain how corruption has been a damaging force of the Argentine system, the following aspects must be considered.

According to the CPI, Argentina is ranked 92 between Albania and Ethiopia. Although this classification does only provide with perceptions of corruption, we can still observe that the incidence thereof can be related to the dramatic incidents of the last few years. The Argentine economy has suffered severe damages and the political trust is lost. Moreover, the social gap between those who have access to adequate living standards and those who do not has widened leaving an unbalanced social climate.

Bringing the factor of corruption into the discussion, we can observe that the existence of corrupt activities in Argentina, especially during the years of President Ménem's administration is a crucial factor for the development of the country on many levels. Menemismo transformed the political arena through a revival of popular Peronist-like paroles that led to a new wave of populism and thus clientelist politics. Moreover, the economy was transformed through Menemist technocrats, who adopted radical measures of neo-liberal tenure. Lastly, the Argentine society suffered a great amount of transformation, since the economic crisis raised the unemployment rate leading to higher inequality and a greater incidence of crime.

This is not to say that Ménem and his government are the sole cause for the higher levels of corruption in Argentina. In all previous administrations, this phenomenon was not entirely absent.[868] However, the decade of the 1990s did bring a unique turn over in the country, whose consequences are visible until today. The consequences explained above, political dismantlement, complete loss of civic trust and economic desolation have never been so visible in the country.

According to the National Anti-Corruption Office, the main causes for corruption in the Argentine public administration are referred to a lack of effective controls, excessive discretion, and a diminished amount of

[868] See also Tedesco. Democracy in Argentina.

transparency and accountability.[869] As it was observed in Section I, all these factors can be attributed to a lack of political leadership and a demoralization of public servants. This is precisely what happened during the administration of Carlos Ménem. Therefore, it is possible to establish a relationship between the poor performance of the administration during those days and the increase of corrupt activities in the public sector as a consequence of mismanagement for the sake of reform.

Argentina's Anti-Corruption Efforts

In terms of what the country has done against its high levels of corruption, it can be noted that the role of international finance institutions, international anti-corruption mechanisms, the media, NGOs and national programs of public sector reform are of considerable importance. These approaches have been considered thoroughly in Section II, however, it seems necessary to have a quick overview of the country's performance in this regard.

First, the World Bank and the IMF are the principal lenders of Argentina. As it was observed in Chapter Eight, these institutions have made recommendations against corruption, especially in the context of development aid, an integral part of their lending policy. Argentina is not an exception and over the last years, international finance institutions have demanded from the country to be as cooperative and transparent as possible in order to guarantee that the funds provided are directed to the right hands.[870] Similar approaches are followed by the IMF and the Inter-American Development Bank (IDB), the country's regional lending institution. The overall goal is to cooperate with the country at achieving economic and financial development on the one hand, and curbing corruption on the other hand.

Argentina is a signatory of the OAS Convention, as well as the OECD Anti-Bribery Convention. The latest reports on the progress of the implementation of such mechanisms in the country denote a considerable amount of progress in terms of promoting transparency and accountability,

---

869 De Michele, Roberto. "The Role of the Anti-Corruption Office in Argentina. Lessons in Corruption and Anti-Corruption: Policies and Results." The Journal of Public Inquiry. (Fall/Winter 2001) pp. 17-20.

870 For example, the World Bank has established Country Assistance Strategies (CAS), in order to help countries assess national priorities and include proper analysis on the level and composition of the Bank's assistance. These deliberations are also based on the overall strategy of the Bank according to the country's portfolio performance. In: World Bank. "The World Bank and Civil Society in the Latin American and Caribbean Region." <www.worldbank.org>

especially in public institutions. The country has recognized the provisions of both documents and has been adapting them according to the contents of its national jurisdiction. This is not an easy undertaking. However, it is a necessary step towards the eradication of illicit activities in the country's public administration.[871]

The media landscape in Argentina is very rich, in terms of a wide variety of media outlets in press, radio and television. The treatment of the corruption *problematique* is much extended, since freedom of the press is one of the key features of the country after the last military dictatorship. The performance of the media in this regard has improved. The economic crisis has demanded some greater changes, especially in the composition and range of some publications, however, the overall role as a watchdog, as remained constantly strong.[872]

The presence of Poder Ciudadano, the Argentine National Chapter of Transparency International, cannot remain unmentioned. This is a non-governmental civil organization seeking to promote a wider citizen participation in the public political debate in Argentina, as well as making specific recommendations and follow-ups, especially in matters such as corruption and the implementation of the provisions of the Inter-American Convention on both national and local levels in the country.[873]

Lastly, it is worth mentioning, that the projects of public sector reform seem to be extensive in numbers, however minor in efficiency.[874] There are mainly three reasons for this pessimistic evaluation, according to economist Andrew Nickson. After making a general assessment for the region of Latin America and its recent experience with approaches such as NPM, he comes to the conclusion, that the absence of a solid civil service career, the rigid presidential system of government, which allows less flexibility for reform due to strong centralist component, and the interpretation of the processes of administrative law in terms of means and

---

871 Reports on Argentina's performance with both the OECD Convention and the Inter-American Convention can b found in: OECD. Argentina. Review of Implementation of the Convention and 1997 Recommendation. <www.oecd.org/dataoecd/31/50/2078382.pdf> Also, the follow-up to the Inter-American Convention contains detailed information on the progress achieved thus far. In: OAS. Secretariat for Legal Affairs: Technical Secretariat for Legal Cooperation Mechanisms. Follow-Up Mechanism for the Implementation of the Inter-American Convention Against Corruption. Argentina. (This report, is also available online at <www. www.oas.org/juridico/spanish/mec_avance_argV.pdf>)

872 For a comprehensive review, see also: Waisbord, Sylvio. Watchdog Journalism in South America. News, Accountability, and Democracy. (New York: Columbia University Press, 2000.)

873 Poder Ciudadano. <http://www.poderciudadano.org.ar>

874 Nickson, Andrew. "Transferencia de políticas y reforma en la gestión del sector público en América Latina: el caso del New Public Management." Reforma y Democracia (October 2002) No. 24, pp. 1-15.

not of goals constitute the main impediments for adequate public sector reforms.[875] Since the end of the military rule, Argentina's public administration has been characterized by these three elements and thus has no success stories to report from this perspective. This is not to say that Argentina has not been improving in other aspect of reform, such as market sector and finance, however, in terms of the public administration, there is still much to do for the next years.

[875] *Ibid.*

CHAPTER TEN

CHILE

The 2002 report of Transparency International identified Chile as the country with the lowest corruption levels in Latin America.[876] Furthermore, economic analysts conclude that within all nations in the region, Chile leads in development standards.[877] Since Chile is often categorized as the most economically progressive country of the Southern Cone, one might ask if this perception could be related to the country's low corruption levels.

Looking back in recent history, the first thing that is commonly associated with Chile is the military dictatorship that ruled the country between 1973 and 1990. For nearly 20 years, since General Augusto Pinochet successfully led a coup against socialist president Salvador Allende, Chile was politically "subdued".[878] After the introduction of censorship and the disablement of all democratic institutions, the military Junta reversed the nationalization plans of the former government and re-directed the country into a different course, aiming at the establishment of an unprecedented free-market economic model.[879] This particular formula was accepted by the middle and upper classes of the Chilean population, which benefited from the sale of public enterprises and from a massive inflow of foreign capital.[880] In this scenario, the Armed Forces became the principal actor for the implementation of this rigid form of capitalism, using extremely repressive methods to guarantee its intended success.[881]

---

[876] Transparency International. Global Corruption Report 2002, p. 264.

[877] According to the World Bank, the incidence of poverty in Chile dropped from 40 percent in 1987 to 17 percent in 1998. Moreover, primary education is said to cover more than 95 percent of the age specific population; nearly 90 percent of births take place in appropriate health conditions; public services such as electricity and water reach over 70 percent of the citizens. Facts taken from: The World Bank. Country Brief – Chile. <http://www.worldbank.org> Washington, D.C. 2000; and Raczynski, Dagmar. "Overcoming Proverty in Chile." In: Tulchin, Joseph and Allison Garland (eds.) Social Development in Latin America. The Politics of Reform. (Boulder: Lynne Rienner Publishers, 2000), p.119.

[878] Calvert and Calvert. Latin America in the Twentieth Century, p. 138.

[879] *Ibid.*

[880] *Ibid.*

[881] See also Garreton, Manuel Antonio. "Military Regimes, Democracy, and Political Transition in the Southern Cone: The Chilean Case." In: Lopez and Stohl. Liberalization and Redemocratization in Latin America, p. 192.

Although the extraordinary economic development has been attributed to the "tight hand" of the military regime, it cannot justify the atrocities committed by the government between 1973 and 1990 against its own people. The human rights abuses that took place during this period combined with the expansion of the economy gave birth to a remarkable breach within Chile's society between those who benefited from the *dictadura* and those who were oppressed thereby. However, when General Pinochet called for a referendum on the prolongation of his administration in 1988, the people of Chile took their opportunity and showed a joint commitment to democracy by turning their back on dictatorial rule and demanding a constitutional, political transition.[882]

In 1990, Patricio Aylwin, the center-left leader of the Concertation of Parties for Democracy *(Concertación de Partidos por la Democracia - CPPD)* was inaugurated as the first democratically elected president after 17 years of harsh military rule. Aylwin confronted the uneasy task of creating adequate political, social and economic frameworks for properly guiding the country through the transition from dictatorial rule to democracy. But most important, Aylwin had to choose between following the economic pattern established by Pinochet or returning to the populist practices of the past.[883] His administration chose to base its main directives on the premise that the neoliberal model should continue in order to foster economic growth and stability, however, complementary social policies aimed at promoting greater equality needed be introduced as well.[884] This posture achieved great results during the 1990s as Chile recorded its highest average growth rates and least economic volatility since the late nineteenth century.[885] The following presidents Eduardo Frei (1994-1999) and Ricardo Lagos (2000-present) continued with the neoliberal course intensifying privatization efforts, deregulating the economy, implementing effective social policies, decreasing poverty levels and maintaining constant economic growth.[886] Despite the side

[882] Tulchin, Joseph and Augusto Varas (eds.) From Dictatroship to Democracy. Rebuilding Political Consensus in Chile. (Boulder & London: Lynne Rienner Publishers, 1991.)

[883] Vergara, Pilar. "In Pursuit of 'Growth with Equity': The Limits of Chile's Free-Market Social Reforms." The North American Congress on Latin America (NACLA) Report on the Americas (May/June 1996).

[884] *Ibid.*

[885] Aninat, Eduardo. "Chile in the 1990s. Embracing Development Opportunities." Finance & Development (March 2000), pp. 19-21.

[886] *Ibid.*

effects brought about by the Asian crisis in the late 1990s, the numbers of the Chilean economy are still the most favorable in Latin America.[887]

On the political side, the transition to democracy brought the revival of the traditional left stream in Chilean politics. Aylwin and Frei belonged to the center-left dogma of *Concertación*, and Lagos – once a member of Allende's administration – became the first socialist president since 1973. Although Lagos's party and his coalition partners are situated within the same political platform as his predecessors, the current government marked a renewed rejection towards the pro-Pinochet right wing conservatives. In this regard, the political landscape of Chile denotes certain continuity in terms of political orientation and economic doctrine.

Since the end of its military rule, Chile has not experienced economic, political and social shakedowns to the degree of magnitude experienced by its neighbours. Although the Asian crisis left clear marks on the Chilean economy raising the unemployment rate and slowing down the constant growth pace, the government has been able to maintain the country's stability for the most part. Even the considerable political and social repercussions of the conviction and trial against Pinochet in London and in Santiago did not bring the country to a social standstill or to a political breakdown.

This stability does not imply a total absence of corruption in Chilean politics. Although Chileans tend to differentiate themselves from the rest of Latin American nations by perceiving their society and political system as relatively "corruption-free", the existence of corruption cases cannot be neglected.[888] During the past ten years, cases of malfeasance and bribery within the government have been confirmed marring Chile's near impeccable corruption record.[889] Most recently, two major corruption scandals caught the Chilean public opinion by surprise. In the beginning of 2002, former Minister of Public Works, Transport and Communication, Carlos Cruz resigned and was later arrested for illegally transferring money to employees of his ministry in order to finance political campaigns.[890] Cruz, a former close collaborator of Lagos and long-time member of *Concertación*, was recently

[887] Raczynski, "Overcoming Proverty in Chile."

[888] Little and Posada-Carbó. Political Corruption in Europe and Latin America, p. 11.

[889] *Ibid.* The authors note that during the government of Patricio Aylwin, allegations were made against several public servants of the Concon Oil Refinery for fraud and bribery.

[890] Aguillon Espinoza, Paola. "Cuando las institutciones funcionan." Tiempos del Mundo Chile. (16.-22.01.2003)

denied bail by a local court.[891] In November of the same year, five congressmen faced allegations of being directly involved in a bribery scandal under the name *"Caso Coimas"*.[892] The congressmen had their legal immunity removed by the prosecutor Carlos Aránguiz in order to be convicted in a case of using their influence to grant third parties the rights to operate car inspections and grant circulation permits in the town of Rancagua.[893]

Although these cases constitute a first-time, major political crisis within the *Concertación* and the Lagos administration, analysts conclude that these scandals could have negative effects only on the electoral future of the parties involved.[894] Unlike the situation faced in other Latin American countries, Chile's economic policy and economic growth will remain unscathed seeing as the amounts of money involved in both cases were not significant enough to effect the national economy. Moreover, the impact of these cases on the Chilean population has not caused massive discontent leading to a political maelstrom, as had been the case in Argentina, Perú and Ecuador, and endangering the position of President Lagos.

To the surprise of analysts and policy makers, these scandals have brought along positive effects despite the negative repercussion of these cases on Chilean politics. To some extent, Chile's judicial institutions have been able to show the public how fast and accurate they operate in order to prosecute those involved in illicit activities, thus, standing up for the good international anti-corruption rankings the country has received.[895] Within 30 days from the publication of the *"Caso Coimas"*, the prosecutor issued the arrest warrant for all those involved. And the recent removal of legal immunity of the five congressmen for proper prosecution has affirmed President Lagos' motto or slogan, *"caiga quien caiga"*, meaning that whoever falls into the hands of justice, should fall with no exceptions.[896]

Chile's case proves that no country is immune to corruption regardless of outward appearances. Having said this, a government's ability

---

891 BBC News. "Deniegan libertad bajo fianza en Chile." BBC Mundo. <www.bbcmundo.com> (11.01.2003)

892 BBC News. "Chile: Desafueros por corrupción." BBC Mundo. <www.bbcmundo.com> (27.11.2002)

893 *Ibid.*

894 Aguillon, "Cuando las institutciones funcionan."

895 *Ibid.*

896 Berguido, Fernando. "Dos Caras de la Corrupción". Ministry of Government <www.gobiernodechile.cl>

to effectively counter corruption will differentiate it from those governments who promote it. Many observe that the effectiveness of Chile's institutions is a reflection of the constant denial of society towards such practices.[897] Consequently, immediate questions beg discourse: what are the factors that make Chile "less corrupt" than its neighboring countries? Is it the political heritage of Pinochet's hardline regime, or has the political system in Chile always been less prone to corruption? Is the Chilean society so different than other Latin American societies, that it can be attributed for the general rejection of illicit activities?

Political Landscape

Chile's political spectrum is divided into three main streams, namely right wing conservatives, centered social democrats and left wing socialists along with the remains of the communist legacies. There have been three events in recent Chilean history that have changed they way politics operate in the country. First, the agrarian reform which too place in the late 1960s and was led by the Christian Democratic Party. Second, the rise of the socialist intellectuals around Salvador Allende between 1970-1973. And lastly, the installment of the military regime by General Augusto Pinochet, which lasted for nearly 17 years.[898]

Although immediately after the end of the Second World War, Chile was one of the most stable democracies in the world, the political partitions, reflected throughout each of the mentioned events above, that the disparity among parties was bigger than it seemed. All major political streams had representatives within the Chilean party landscape. Socialists and communists dominated the left, liberals and conservatives were preponderant on the right wing, and the center was represented by the anticlerical Radical Party. Political pluralism allowed the country to become one of the most stable nations in the world. However, discrepancies grew inexorably on to a point in which open multi-party political dialogue turned into dubious political maneuver to attempt to gain power and remain therein.[899]

The political conflict was based on ideological differences and the ongoing debate would soon be silenced by a brutal military regime that

---

[897] *Ibid.*

[898] Economist Intelligence Unit. "Political Forces." In: Country ViewsWire Chile. (December 2003.) Also available online at <http://www.economist.com/countries/Chile/index.cfm>

[899] Barrett, Patrick S. "Chile's Transformed Party System and the Future of Democratic Stability." Journal of Interamerican Studies and World Affairs (Fall 2000) Vol. 42, No. 3, pp. 2 ff.

practically downsized or completely shut down any form of political pluralism.[900] The main impact of the military rule on the political landscape was that politics suddenly became centralized. The authorities did not destroy the political party system in its entirety. However, they constantly kept silencing alternative political voices, as soon the turned too loud.[901] During the first weeks of Pinochet's rule, the antipathy towards all parties soon became the trademark of major authorities within the military government for years to come.[902]

After having split and outset the political landscape, Pinochet begun to transform the regime from a joint military Junta, on to a more personal type of rule. Therefore, he purposely institutionalized his persona around the key areas of Chilean politics, as well as economics and society. Although there was a separation of powers and many Generals of the Junta welcomed this fact, Pinochet became the main person of the regime. As political scientist Robert Barros explains,

> "Typically, Pinochet's position as commander in chief of the army and president emerges as the cornerstone for characterizing the dictatorship as 'personalist': as commander in chief, Pinochet molds and manipulates the army, checking any internal challenges to his dominance; as president, he attains policy control and subordinates the commanders of the other forces to mere legislative activities, which purportedly he dominated as well. From this perspective [this kind of leadership] allowed Pinochet to avoid the corrosive factionalism, inter-military divisions, and subsequent institutional pressures for military withdrawal which scholars have identified as factors that explain the lesser longevity of military as against personalist or single-party regimes."[903]

900 See also: Barros, Robert. Constitutionalism and Dictatorship. Pinochet, the Junta and the 1980 Constitution. (Cambridge: Cambridge University Press, 2002.)

901 *Ibid.*, p. 123 ff.

902 Barret, "Chile's Transformed Party System and the Future of Democratic Stability" p. 4. The authorobserves that Pinochet "regarded [political parties] as major culprits behind the socio-political and economic instability of the 1960s and 1970s."

903 Barros. Constitutionalism and Dictatorship. Pinochet, the Junta and the 1980 Constitution, p. 69.

Even after the adoption of the Law of Political Parties in 1987, the operational conditions for political parties remained highly difficult. Nevertheless, the opening of the leadership towards democracy, ending with the elections of 1989, showed that the political forces in Chile were only kept silent, but never refrained from being representative of the free electorate. The rise of the CPPD or *Concertación* after the election of Patricio Aylwin as the first center-left president since the 1940s, represented a new era of pluralism and democracy for all Chileans, who were still coping with the early stages of transition from a year-long military rule. The main challenge was to make the party strong enough to govern over the affairs of the country, keep the multiparty dialogue going, and increasingly diminish the influence of the military in national affairs.

Today, Chile presents a presidential system, with a bicameral legislative and an independent judiciary. As for the president, he can be elected for a one-time term of six years. He is also the head of state and appoints the cabinet. The Chilean legislative is composed by the Senate (38 elected members, 10 appointed members) and the Chamber of Deputies (120 members elected for four year terms.) The judicial branch is formed by the Chilean Supreme Court, with 21 appointed judges. They must have the approval of both the president and obtain a two-third majority vote in the Senate. On the regional level, there are 16 courts of appeal whose members are appointed by the Supreme Court.[904]

Economic Reforms

Unlike the beginning of the 1950s, the Chilean economy hit the ground shortly before the takeover by the military in the early 1970s. The division between left and right and the absence of sound economic policies left the country in a desolate status. In this context, the establishment of the military regime could be seen as an opportunity to achieve some sort of economic stability.[905]

The major initiatives for Chile's efforts of economic and market reforms were undertaken by a group of right-wing technocrats under the name of "Chicago Boys", a group of young economists who were trained at the University of Chicago's Department of Economics.[906] The impact of this

---

[904] Economist Intelligence Unit. "Political Structure." In: Country ViewsWire Chile. (January 2004.) Also available online at <http://www.economist.com/countries/Chile/index.cfm>

[905] Teichman. The Politics of Freeing Markets in Latin America, p. 65.

[906] *Ibid.*, p. 66.

group on the economic development of Chile since the 1970s is of great importance. The reason is, that Pinochet was able to use these "experts" in order to start an rigid economic doctrine, focusing on solidifying the national economy, both to the inside, through privatization, deregulation, and cuts in the public expenditure, and to the outside, by opening Chile's market to its neighbors and international partners in North America and Europe.[907] These kind of measures were undertaken in Argentina and Ecuador with almost 10-15 years of difference.

Therefore, the main feature of the Chilean economy during the military rule was the premature adoption of neo-liberal measures of liberal tone. Although there were great discrepancies about this economic course, especially with representatives of the working class and union leaders, the government was capable of maintaining these policies ongoing for more than a decade.

When power returned to the hands of a democratically elected government, president Aylwin had to choose between a new start and a continuity of this economic plan. The country demanded change after the horrific experiences of a repressive government. Nevertheless, on the economic front, the new government deliberately chose to continue the neo-liberal legacy of the Chicago Boys. In fact, the failures of short-term, chance-based populism in Latin America provided a great amount of influence for Aylwin to not jeopardize the gains achieved by the adopted economic policy.[908]

The social debt left by Pinochet included grave deficiencies in the public health and education sectors. However, the new government decided to face these challenges with responsible, non-inflationary measures, keeping an overall condition of stability.[909] Economic cautiousness became the main guideline of *Concertación*, as political scientist Kurt Weyland observes:

> "The Aylwin and Frei administrations did have some room to choose how much pressure to put on their socioeconomic and political opponents. In principle, they could have made

[907] *Ibid.*, p. 74 ff. In fact, one of the most influential figures of the Chicago Boys, former Finance Minister Sergio de Castro, undertook a comprehensive economic solidification program including measures such as the removal of all restrictions on foreign borrowing by banks, a reform of the labour code, a social security reform, a law prohibiting fiscal deficit, inclusion of market reforms in the 1980 constitution and the reduction of public companies.

[908] Weyland, Kurt. "Economic Policy in Chile's New Democracy." Journal of Interamerican Studies and World Affairs (Fall 1999) Vol. 41, No. 3, pp. 67 ff.

[909] *Ibid.*, p. 69.

> greater efforts to mobilize their supporters against the Right; instead, they privileged accommodation over confrontation [...] Chile's economic stability and sustained growth in the late 1980s put the center-left coalition that took power in 1990 into the domain of gains and included it to adopt a clearly risk-adverse posture. Therefore, rather than rock the boat, the Concertación decided to seek further improvements, especially social reforms, with 'prudence'."[910]

Therefore, Aylwin and Frei, and more recently the current president Ricardo Lagos have followed an establish path, that seems to be proving the right one to follow. Despite criticisms from the opposition and the external shocks from economic breakdowns in neighboring countries, most recent forecasts for the country show, that the Chilean economy remains strong, with positive balances, low inflation, a strong currency and adequate levels of development.[911]

Social Aspects and Political Disenchantment

Chile's military legacy was also a societal division, between those who benefited from the dictatorship and those who were opposed to it. This gap became even wider when former president Augusto Pinochet was put under arrest in the United Kingdom in 1998 and then released in 2000. The magnitude of these events on Chilean society showed, that there are great differences on the country's past, thus leading towards differentiating positions towards the political parties and the government.
Although Chile is one of the most prosperous countries in Latin America, most recently, the amount of trust from the electorate on politicians has decreased considerably.[912] The main reason is that political elites built a pact of many parties in order to avoid any new intervention by the military in government affairs. Therefore, *Concertación* works around making policies

---

910 *Ibid.*, p. 70.

911 De Faria, José Carlos. "Latin America: Economic Analysis – Chile." Deutsche Bank. Emerging Markets Monthly. (November 2003.)

912 Posner, Paul W. Popular Representation and Political Dissatisfaction in Chile's New Democracy. Journal of Interamerican Studies and World Affairs (Spring 1999) Vol. 41, No. 1, pp. 60 ff.

through exclusive political elites thus causing a certain distance between many parties and their base constituents at the grass root level.[913]

FIGURE 20: CHILE – ECONOMIC INDICATORS (1999-2002)

	1999	2000	2001	2002
GDP per head ($ at PPP)	9,080	9,730	10,150	10,373
GDP (% real change pa)	-0.76	4.17	3.07	2.15
Government consumption (% of GDP)	12.40	12.43	12.53	12.64
Budget balance (% of GDP)	-1,36	0.12	-0.27	-0.79
Consumer prices (% change pa; av)	3.34	3.84	3.57	2.49
Public debt (% of GDP)	13.39	12.98	14.71	13.30
Labour costs per hour (USD)	2.37	2.33	2.07	1.99
Recorded unemployment (%)	9.69	9.22	9.18	8.95
Current-account balance/GDP	0.14	-1.02	-1.75	-0.80
Foreign-exchange reserves (m$)	14,616	15,034	14,379	15,341

Source: Economist Intelligence Unit. Country Data Chile.

In this regard, popular sectors of the Chilean society are impeded from directly participating in the political process and thus articulate their interests to the outside. These impediments appear at both national and local levels. When Chile's military agreed to turn the country over to a democratically elected government, the transition was successfully made by a political pact among the country's most influential forces. However, these groups belonged only to established political elites. Therefore, leaders of other non-political groups did not get the same opportunity to participate in Chile's turn to democracy.

Thereafter, Chile's electoral system, has enabled congressmen, senators, and judges to benefit from the system and have political power secured and guaranteed by the constitution. Political leaders and party elites have *de facto* more opportunities than grass root leaders and other non-politically affiliated figures to enter and influence the national political process. In this scenario, unrepresented groups have recently presented their rejection to the lack of

913 *Ibid.*, p. 64.

accessibility to the system by not taking part in elections or by casting invalid votes.[914] Political scientist Paul Posner observes that

> "[t]he effects [of the Chilean electoral/political system] on popular sector political apathy results from limiting the Concertación parties' ability to enact beneficial legislation (for example, labor code reform) or democratic reforms (for example, terminating the appointment of designated senators) and by increasing the parties' reluctance to respond to popular sector demands. Institutional arrangements at the local level of government, by comparison, exacerbate the split between the political parties and their popular sector constituents."[915]

Therefore, we can conclude that one of the key features of the current Chilean society is an entrenched division on two levels. First, those who benefited from the military rule and welcome the policies of the new governments. And second, those who are not given access to the political building process and therefore portray certain disenchantment with the "Chilean miracle" and the many positive things it has brought to the nation, especially on the economic side.

Assessment of Corruption in Chile

Chile is the best ranked Latin American country in the most recent version of the CPI, having reached place 18, behind the United States (!) and ahead of Israel. This score seems somehow impressive. However, we should re-assess some of the points presented in this chapter, in order to explain possible reasons for this state of affairs.

The picture Chile presents is somehow different than the two other selected case studies. On the one hand, Chile comes from the same historical tradition of the post-war Latin American economies with strong political participation and an active economy. However, Chile suffered the repression of the last military Junta of the 20th century. As we have seen above, the military had two main directives: first, to eradicate the multiplicity of the political landscape and shut down all major political streams; and second, to

[914] *Ibid.*, p. 74.
[915] *Ibid.*, p. 78.

bring the economy back on track by imposing a very rigid neo-liberal model. If we take the latter aspect into consideration, it might help us understand why the incidence of corruption can be perceived as lower in Chile than in the other cases.

Neo-liberal type reforms include a reduction of the role of the state and promote a more flexible model of bureaucratic government. Moreover, measures such as deregulation, tax reform and privatization should increase public revenues and thus reduce the risk of inflation and thus an overload of the public sector capacities. In the discussion of the so called "decay of bureaucracy" in Chapter Five, it became clear that the neo-liberal reform approach could be – from case to case – be useful for curbing corruption, especially in emerging economies. The case of Chile presents a country, which had already been taking this pattern, even before the return to democracy.

Therefore, we can prove a valid point by observing that the rigid economic course taken by the Pinochet government led to a strengthening of national institutions and thus to a lesser danger of corruption. This by no means retracts from the belief, that corruption was in deed a problem for Chile, even during the military Junta. However, compared to the other cases, the country benefited from the adopted economic doctrine, which affected political and economic aspects of the nation likewise.

Moreover, the fact, that *Concertación* did not deviate from this posture, gave the Chilean institutions the consistency and strength to overcome a much needed transition without the dangers of loosing grip of the political apparatus. Even when corruption scandals appear, as it was explained at the beginning of the chapter, Chileans institutions seem to be strong enough to quickly repeal such instances and lower the damage of corruption scandals.

On the other hand, the observations made on the marginalized sectors of Chilean society, could serve as an element for explaining at least one aspect on the incidence of corruption in the country. Samuel Huntington postulated in Chapter One, that corruption can emerge as the struggle for power between groups in society. Moreover, the incidence and danger of corruption can be elevated when certain groups do not gain access to power (regardless of local or national) and start operating outside the jurisdictional frame. Just as Chile's political parties are strong, so has the opposition grown, especially from grass roots leader, who feel unrepresented. Such a "leak" could lead to both the illegitimate use of authority (in this case from the political elites to remain in power) and to an increase of interest (by unrepresented groups) of getting things done via unofficial channels.

This prediction is subject to interpretation by the reader and does not intend to be a definitive and exclusive postulate. However, after having analyzed the case of Chile, the juxtaposition of the lesser incidence, and, at the same time, high risk of corruption deserves to be mentioned in this part of the analysis.

Chile's Anti-Corruption Policy

The main features of Chile's anti-corruption efforts are based around the idea of maintaining strong institutions for the impediment of wide-ranged corruption cases in the country. The return to democracy demanded a comprehensive approach for the revitalization of public institutions in the new area of Chile's history. Within this approach, several observations were made to the fact, that many institutions under the old military legacy denoted the presence of illicit networks and dubious procedures within their structures.[916] Therefore, it became highly relevant to create adequate mechanisms to re-enforce the positions and the work of national institutions. In 1994, the government created a National Commission on Public Ethics, which should monitor the implementation of the latest anti-corruption approaches in the public sector.[917]

Chile signed and adopted the OAS convention by 1998, as well as the OECD Convention by 2001. These two mechanisms have been successfully implemented in order to eradicate the incidence of corruption within the Chilean government and to prevent the bribing of foreign officials by Chilean officers. The latest reports from both organizations make clear that Chile's efforts are constant and that there is still much to achieve.

Moreover, TI's National Chapter in Chile is one of the most active and includes a wide range of activities such as monitoring the implementation of the OAS Convention and creating awareness about the problems around corruption. Numerous seminars have been coordinated by TI Chile for audiences of all kinds, ranging from merely public officers, to private entrepreneurs to civil society organizations.[918] One particular highlight was a direct proposal to president Lagos under the name *Por un Chile Transparente*

---

916 In: Chile Transparente. Capítulo Chileno de Transparencia Internacional. Seguimiento de la Convención Interamericana Contra la Corrupción (CICC-OEA) Informe desde la Sociedad Civil. <http://www.chiletransparente.cl/informe_oea.htm>

917 *Ibid.*

918 Chile Transparente. Capítulo Chileno de Transparencia Internacional. <http://www.chiletransparente.cl/>

- Towards a Transparent Chile, including direct recommendations from civil society to a better approach on public sector reform, more transparency on the mechanisms of public procurement, more accessibility to the political building process, and better representation of all sector of society within the government, among many others.[919]

The media in Chile is very active in the fight against corruption. Having faced nearly 17 years of censorship, Chilean journalists have learned to value pluralism as the true mechanism for an adequate role of the media in society.[920] Nevertheless, most of the media outlets are still the property of two corporations, who are known to serve specific political groupings.[921] Although there is no censorship anymore, some outlets might prefer to portray different images to the public, especially when it comes to politics. Nevertheless, the approach of the Chilean media is to promote diversity in the country's journalist landscape in order to achieve greater competition and thus better quality of journalism.

Lastly, the work of international organizations such as the IMF, the World Bank, and the IDB in Chile has proven to be quite successful in their endeavors against corruption. Promoting transparency in government institutions is one of the most important aspects of lending conditions. Chile has been one of the role models of the international recipient community, proving again that through solid institutions, development assistance can reach its ends more properly than in a high-risk corrupt environment. Additionally, Chile's impressive economic performance has improved its image towards bilateral and multilateral donors, so that the levels of ODA have not decreased in the last few years.[922]

---

919 Ibid.

920 Baltra, Lidia. Chile: towards true pluralism and cultural diversity. In: United Nations Educational and Scientific Organization (UNESCO) (eds.) Media and democracy in Latin America and the Caribbean. (Paris: UNESCO Publications, 1996), p. 166.

921 *Ibid.*

922 See also: Aninat. "Chile in the 1990s. Embracing Development Opportunities."

Chapter Eleven

Ecuador

Although it is one of the smallest countries on the continent, Ecuador has always commanded a particular place in Latin American affairs. Ecuador was among the first countries to declare full independence from Spain and began its republican life in 1832.

From thereon, the country's political landscape was marked by the struggle between conservatives and liberals, which became the main characteristic of Ecuadorian politics.[923] A further conflict widened this breach, namely the regionalist disputes among the elites from Ecuador's most influential geographical regions, the Pacific coast and the Andes' *sierra.*[924] Under these two factors, Ecuador's politics and society have not only been the products of an unresolved ideological and regional disjuncture. Moreover, the country is deeply marked by a social separation between the white upper class, the mostly Creole-Spanish middle class and the indigenous people, who – as in most Latin American countries – occupy the lowest rank of the nation's social structure.

Despite the fact, that Ecuador was not able to escape the wave of military regimes that took hold across Latin America, its political, social and economic structures remained relatively unmarked by the many Juntas that ruled the country from time to time.[925] The latest transition to democracy took place in 1979, when the military triumvirate called for general elections and Jaime Roldós became – at 38 years of age – Latin America's youngest president.

The new period of constitutional governance soon became a turning point in Ecuador's political life. It was expected that democracy would bring prosperity in the economic sector, more equality in the social sector and, most important, a durable stability on the political arena. However, the governments that followed Roldós were not able to fulfill any of these

---

[923] Calvert and Calvert. Latin America in the Twentieth Century, p. 139.

[924] *Ibid.*

[925] *Ibid.* After 1945, there were at least 5 major military coups in Ecuador, all of them installing either one President or a Junta. Moreover, all there regimes have been qualified as "soft dictatorships", as they did not achieve greater repercussion on the country's destiny. This point is further explained in: Martz, John D. "The Fate of a Small State: Ecuador in Foreign Affairs." In: Muñoz and Tulchin. Latin American Nations in World Politics, p. 129-147.

expectations. On the economic side, the country entered a major crisis in the mid-1980s. Suffering the effects of the market crashes in Argentina and Mexico, Ecuador accumulated a great amount of foreign debt overloading on public spending. On the political side, the division between left and right became more visible, as all administrations following former President Osvaldo Hurtado alternated between these two camps. But more important, the return to democracy in the late 1970s led Ecuador to the greatest period of political instability since the civil war in 1895.

Although all governments between 1981 and 1997 were installed after democratic elections, the appointment of populist candidate Abdala Bucarám started a chain reaction with unprecedented consequences. Bucarám, a lawyer from Guayaquil and member of Ecuador's most influential political clan, had been involved in politics since 1979 and ever since, he became known by the Ecuadorian public due to his aggressive and unconventional campaigning style.[926]

Soon after his inauguration in August 1996, his government became the platform for Ecuador's biggest political scandals, most of them related to corruption, fraud and nepotism.[927] Only six months after his appointment, Bucarám embarrassed not only himself, but the entire country with public appearances on national television singing and inviting the poor to the government's palace, in order to give away his salary.[928] Many of his ministers were already accused of malfeasance of public funds, clientelism and bribery, forcing the great majority to either resign or be removed. On 6th February, in an extraordinary session, Congress declared Bucarám "mentally

[926] In the 1980s, when Bucaram was elected mayor of Guayaquil, he was accused of fraud and fled the country to political exile in Panamá. Ever since then, he and his party proclaimed to represent the lower classes of Ecuador. When he returned to pursue his presidential campaign, he publicly insulted his opponents and distributed self-recorded jingles against them. A further analysis can be found in: De la Torre, Carlos. "Populism and Democracy: Political Discourses and Cultures in Contemporary Ecuador." Latin American Perspectives (May, 1997) Vol. 24, No. 3, pp. 12-24.

[927] Bucaram took advantage of his position as constitutional president and placed many members of his family and his closest circle of friends on the country's key positions. His brother Adolfo became Minister of Social Affairs, his sister Elsa was appointed personal adviser to the President, and his two cousins Jose Salem and Averroes Bucaram respectively turned into Head of the Central Bank and Deputy Minister of Government. Moreover, two Bucaram brothers, Santiago and Jacobo were elected to Congress. In: "Biografías de Líderes Políticos: Abdalá Bucaram Ortiz." Fundación CIDOB. Center of International Relations and International Cooperation. (Barcelona: 2002.)

[928] HOY, Quito's second biggest daily, published the entire scope of the scandals during his administration in: Cornejo, Diego (ed.) '¡Que se vaya!' Crónica del Bucaramato. (Quito: Edimpres S.A., 1997)

ill" and forced him to resign in accordance to the Ecuadorian constitution.[929] The following days were tainted by a political dispute over the Presidency between Vice-President Rosalia Arteaga and the President of Congress Fabian Alarcón, both claiming the Presidency with just a few hours of difference. After the military demanded a quick solution to the sudden power vacuum, Alarcón was appointed interim President until new elections were held in 1998. While the Congress was solving the crisis, Bucarám was "evacuated" and left the country for a new political exile period in Panama.[930]

This entire episode often referred to as the *'Bucarámato'* took place in the middle of Ecuador's worst economic crisis. The country's currency was devaluated on a constant basis and the neoliberal programs implemented by the former administrations did not bring along any positive results. Moreover, the scandals around Bucarám created wide public mistrust towards the political elite in Ecuador. The interim government was expected to bring the country back to stability and somehow re-build the damage made by the last administration. However, Alarcón did not accomplish any of these tasks. Quite on the contrary, at the end of his term, he was accused and later on jailed because of his involvement in a bribery scandal within Congress.

The elections of 1998 gave the country a further opportunity to start a new political era and eradicate the poor "heritage" left by Bucarám. Jamil Mahuad, the former mayor of Quito, was elected with a very tight difference of votes over Alvaro Noboa, Ecuador's most important banana tycoon and richest entrepreneur. Mahuad had won the trust of the people as he proved to be one of Quito's best mayors and a historically "clean" politician. Although the economic crisis had worsened, the new government was confident of bringing political stability, social equality and economic prosperity to the all sectors of the country.

Nevertheless, the new administration turned once more into a great disappointment. After the introduction of the first austerity measures in March 1999, Mahuad had to face serious social discontent, as his "recovery plan" foresaw the striking of subsidies for gas and electricity, the devaluation of Ecuador's national currency, and an extensive wave of privatizations. During the first general strike, Mahuad's image of the serious and competent leader decreased dramatically. Nonetheless, he took one of the most controversial decisions in the modern economic history of Ecuador in 1999 when he decided to prevent the collapse of the Ecuadorian financial system

---

[929] CNN World News. "Invoking 'mental incapacity' rule, Ecuador fires President." <www.cnn.com> (06.02.1997)

[930] Cornejo. '¡Que se vaya!' Cronica del Bucaramato, p. 94.

by freezing all private accounts. After this decisive step, the government took control over more than half of the country's banking system and temporarily closed all banks. The president's goal was to stop the capital leak, which became the major factor for the deterioration of the Ecuadorian economy. Opposition movements grew strong and the crisis reached its highest peak in early 2000, when Mahuad presented a convertibility plan sponsored by Argentina's former Minister of the Economy, Domingo Cavallo. This plan foresaw the introduction of the US dollar as official currency, locking it to the Ecuadorian Sucre. It was well known by the Ecuadorian public that the plan had failed in Argentina. Nevertheless, Mahuad insisted on adopting this measure, in order to end the constant currency devaluation.

The reaction from all sectors of Ecuador's society was as immediate as it was extensive. Mass protests took hundreds of thousands out to the streets to reject Mahuad's economic plans. Due to the intensity of the social unrest, the entire government apparatus soon became fragile, and on 21st January thousands of marching civilians, the vast majority from the indigenous part of the population, joined forces with dissident ranks of the military and occupied the facilities of the Congress and the Supreme Court of Justice. The result was the immediate installment of a National Salvation Junta *(Junta de Salvacion Nacional)* led by representatives of the indigenous people, the military, and civil society. A provisional government was proclaimed and Mahuad fled the country within the same day. After several disputes, the Junta decided to advocate power to Congress, which rapidly designated Vice-President Gustavo Noboa as the new constitutional President for the rest of Mahuad's term. Noboa was able to finish his term, despite the fact that his administration continued with the old government's economic plans.

Most recently, Lucio Gutierrez, a former member of the National Salvation Junta and former military advisor to former Presidents Bucarám and Alarcón became the newly elected President of Ecuador. In his inaugural speech, he proclaimed the fight against corruption as an essential backbone of his government. However, his government soon became a completely different version from what he announced at the beginning of his term. Among many broken promises and poorly sustained alliances, Gutierrez' government faces serious problems of nepotism and clientelism, since he put several family members and close friends on strategic positions of the administration. Most recently, he has been accused of being involved in an electoral campaign scandal, which included bribes from many illegal donors possibly including the Colombian and Ecuadorian drug mafias.

The particular characteristic of the agitated episodes of Ecuador's recent political life is that the country's political instability and economic deterioration have a direct relationship with the alarming indexes of corruption in the Ecuadorian system. While being evacuated, Bucarám and his collaborators are said to have stolen more than half of the national reserves.[931] Alarcón was taken into prison, because of bribery within Congress.[932] Mahuad is currently facing charges on economic mismanagement and fraud. In the mean time, Ecuador's economy has not yet revealed any significant steps towards recovery. The question is then: why is such relatively small country so prone to corruption? Ecuador's economy and political system differ in size compared to other Latin American countries. Furthermore, Ecuador's social structure has transformed radically, as the indigenous population has risen from the "social basement" into the highest spheres of influence on Ecuadorian politics.[933]

Lastly, Ecuador's political past does not denote a clear devotion to military or authoritarian ruling, as the country's dictators have been considered as rather *soft* compared to the Juntas in Argentina and Chile. These factors make Ecuador a suitable case study for the intended investigation of corruption in Latin America. Taking a closer look into the politics of this small, culturally diverse, economically damaged and politically agitated country shall enhance the comparison to the other two country cases, as it clearly differs from them in its size, cultural heritage and political past. This differentiation will enable an adequate test of the working hypotheses and will provide valuable insights on the economic damage that corruption has caused, not only in this country, but on the whole region.

Political Landscape

Ecuador presents a very agitated political landscape, mainly influenced by the eternal opposition between right-conservative and left-

---

931 Cornejo. '¡Que se vaya!' Cronica del Bucaramato.

932 The scandal included the hiring of staff for Congress, most of which never took office. In: BBC News: "Ecuadorian President Accused of Corruption." BBC World Service. <www.bbc.co.uk> (17.12.1997)

933 The fall of Mahuad was, in great part, attributed to the strength of indigenous movements. They have gained much influence on national politics ever since. As a matter of fact, during the elections of 2002, the indio-supported parties gave President Gutierrez the necessary support for winning the run-off against Alvaro Noboa. In exchange for this support and as a symbol of the new power of indigenous peoples in politics, one of its highest representatives, Nina Pacari, was appointed the first-ever indigenous woman in charge of the Minister of Foreign Affairs. A further prominent member of the indigenous community, Luis Macas, became Minister of Agriculture.

socialist. Traditionally, the Catholic Church in Ecuador would have much influence on the proceedings in politics. Nevertheless, in the course of the early 20th century, this influence was diminished, partly because of the new "anticlerical" political voices which would soon be heard across the nation.

During the 1930s and 1940s, the political landscape was dominated by populist figures such as José María Velasco Ibarra, who became president for a total of five times.[934] His contenders were built around other populist leader such as Asaad Bucarám and his party Concentration of Popular Forces (Concentración de Fuerzas Populares – CFP.)

However, one of the most influencing post-war new political streams emerged in Ecuador during the 1950s, out of the Catholic-Roman tradition. The Christian Social Party *(Partido Social Cristiano – PSC)* was formed by upper-middle class settled in the capital.[935] This group would experience many ups and downs in Ecuadorian politics, having several of its top figures running for the presidency and obtaining victory in many instances. The latest of them was in 1984 when León Febres-Cordero assumed the presidency after defeating center-left candidate Rodrigo Borja. A particular feature of his term is that, ever since he was in power, his influence on the political and economic course of the country has not diminished at all.[936]

The military Juntas of the 1960s and 1970s did not impede the development of other political groupings in the country. Parallel forces to the PSC are the center-left Democratic Left *(Izquierda Democrática-ID)* with a more radical tone and leaning towards a more social democrat posture, pledging for more equal shares of national wealth to all levels of society. The ID reached the peak of its political power when candidate Rodrigo Borja assumed the presidency after having lost the run twice already.[937]

The CFP had not lost its influence in its entirety, even after the PSC and the ID started to dominate the Ecuadorian political scene. In fact, the first president after the last military triumvirate, Jaime Roldós Aguilera belonged to the CFP. Unfortunately, after a plane crash in 1981, the hopes of many Ecuadorians towards a smooth transition to democracy vanished. His brother

---

934 For a detailed overview, see: De La Torre, Carlos. "Velasco Ibarra and 'La Revolucion Gloriosa': The Social Production of a Populist Leader in Ecuador in the 1940s." Journal of Latin American Studies (October 1994) Vol. 26, No. 3, pp. 683-711.

935 Economist Intelligence Unit. "Political Forces." In: Country ViewsWire Ecuador. (July 2003.) Also available online at <http://www.economist.com/countries/Ecuador/index.cfm>

936 Popular voices claim Febrés-Cordero to be the "owner of the country", as most presidents rely on his opinion and support in order to govern the country.

937 Fundación CIDOB. "Biografías de Líderes Políticos: Rodrigo Borja Cevallos." Fundación CIDOB. Center of International Relations and International Cooperation. (Barcelona: 2002.)

in law, Abdalá Bucarám, started a new independent force, which soon became one of the main pillars of politics in the nation. The Roldosist Ecuadorian Party (Partido Roldosista Ecuatoriano – PRE), was found after the deceased president and was able to climb on to the top of the political ladder, having Abdalá serving as president of the country between 1996 and 1997.[938]

Other forces emerged out of the constant dialogue and struggle between left and right such as the intellectual integrated party around former president Osvaldo Hurtado the Popular Democracy *(Democracia Popular – DP)* or the more left oriented wings such as the communist Popular Democratic Movement (Movimiento Popular Democrático – MPD) and the Radical Alfaro Front, named after former president Eloy Alfaro *(Frente Radical Alfarista – FRA.)* These were the main political streams of Ecuador until the early 1990s out of a total of 22 different official parties.[939] It is interesting to note again, that during the years of military rule, the political activism in Ecuador remained high, as the Juntas were not pursuing an absolute control of the country, as it was the case on Argentina and Chile.

The most recent political force that has entered the arena and has found a solid place therein is the Plurinational Unity Movement Pachakútik *(Movimiento Unidad Plurinacional Pachakútik.)* This party constitutes the political arm of numerous indigenous organizations, social movements and trade unions, which have been capable of organizing themselves and take an active part in the political processes of the country.[940] The particular feature of Pachakútik has been its ability to become a vital partner for government coalitions. Gutierrez' victory in 2003 for instance, would have not been possible without the help of Pachakútik. In fact, the government of Ecuador witnessed the return of representatives of the indigenous population to the legislative and executive branches after several hundred years of remaining mostly local, mostly unheard leaders.[941] The political posture of Pachakútik is more radical than the other parties. For example, it rejects neoliberal structural adjustment programs in the country, as well as the most recent

---

[938] De la Torre. "Populism and Democracy: Political Discourses and Cultures in Contemporary Ecuador", pp. 15 ff.

[939] As found in: Georgetown University. "Ecuador Political Parties." Political Database of the Americas. <http://www.georgetown.edu/pdba/Parties/Resumen/Ecuador/desc.html> (January 2002.)

[940] Economist Intelligence Unit. "Political Forces." In: Country ViewsWire Ecuador.

[941] An in-depth analysis of the situation of the indigenous people in Ecuador and their relationship with the upper class can be found in: Gerlach, Allen. Indians, Oil and Politics. A Recent History of Ecuador. (Wilmington, DE: Scholarly Resources, 2003.)

currency change from the national *Sucre* to the US dollar.[942] The particular feature of this new political force is the forum it provides for all members of the Ecuadorian indigenous community to articulate and defend their interests and positions, and also for lobbying their political weight in the government.[943]

Besides this wide variety in the area of political parties, Ecuador presents a democratic structure of government. Its system is presidential, with elections taking place every four years. The legislative is composed by a single-chamber Congress of 100 members, who are elected by proportional representation from open slates and serve for a four-year term. The judicative is built around the Ecuadorian Supreme Court, whose 32 members with life tenure are selected by Congress from nomination lists approved by electoral colleges and civil groups. The Ecuadorian legal system foresees a Supreme Constitutional Court composed by nine judges appointed by Congress and portraying the party composition thereof.[944]

Economy

The Ecuadorian economy was traditionally based on agricultural products such as bananas, coffee and cacao beans. However, the discovery of oil reserves in 1967 in the north east part of the Ecuadorian rainforest entirely changed the economy. The pipeline, that was built to extract and transport the crude barrels to the coast and then to the outside, remained in private hands for nearly 25 years.[945] During the first years of the petroleum exports, Ecuador was able to re-live the economic booms it has experienced in the 1950s and 1960s with the bananas and the cacao beans.

Nevertheless the "black gold high" would soon run down, as most Latin American countries entered the 1980s to face serious economic grievances and breakdowns of unprecedented consequences. In order to sustain the demands of the oil exports, as well as of the pursued import-substitution economic model, the last military Junta around Guillermo Rodríguez Lara borrowed heavily from international investors and countries

942 Economist Intelligence Unit. "Political Forces." In: Country ViewsWire Ecuador.

943 *Ibid.*

944 All these facts from: *Ibid.* "Political Structure." In: Country ViewsWire Ecuador.

945 Gerlach. Indians, Oil and Politics. A Recent History of Ecuador, pp. 33 ff. The author explains, that "[t]he oil bonanza lasted a decade and a half as prices skyrocketed. In 1972 the cost per barrel for Ecuadorean crude stood at $2.50, and the next year it came close to doubling at $4.20. By 1974 the charge soared severalfold to $13.70. It climbed to $23.50 in 1979 and reached its summit in 1980 at $35.26 following the Iranian revolution and conflict in the Middle East."

and compromised the oil reserves, which were mostly given away as loan guarantees.[946] Ecuador's external debt grew exponentially as it began to export oil, quadrupling from $380 million in 1973 to $1.263 billion in 1977.[947] During the first years of the newly established democracy, Ecuador's economy was severely affected by the inability of the government to meet its debt obligations. Additionally, oil prices began to sink reaching $12.70 in 1986.[948]

This situation demanded prompt action from the government in order to prevent a complete default as in the Mexican case in the early 1980s. The problem of servicing the foreign debt became a directive of the Ecuadorian economic front. During the years of the oil boom, the government traditionally assumed most of the responsibility in the economic, finance and trade areas, leaving not much room for private actors and foreign investors. The promises made by the government to investors and lenders that the country would be able to pay its debts by relying on the oil revenues became soon utopian, after prices dropped again and, in 1987, an earthquake severely damaged the oil pipeline for nearly 5 months, thus leaving the Ecuadorian economy in a desolate status.

In this situation, president Hurtado was forced to reschedule all external payments to the IMF and implemented a highly unpopular austerity plan.[949] The results of such a decision became visible as the IMF approved the deal by imposing stabilization programs which included classic neoliberal measures such as privatization, downsizing, rigid fiscal policies and opening the economy to the outside. These policies were followed by Febres-Cordero as well as Borja in the mid-1980s and early 1990s.

The former approached the crisis with a more business-like attitude and focused on export-led growth welcoming broad packages of neoliberal programs and structural adjustment measures.[950] He was convinced that if the economy performed well, the rest of the county would follow. Therefore, he attracted the attention of the IMF and the United States obtaining a $105 million loan on the condition of adopting a very strict monetary policy in

---

[946] *Ibid.*, p. 39.

[947] Weiss, Wendy. "Debt and Devaluation: The Burden on Ecuador's Popular Class." Latin American Perspectives (July 1997) Vol. 24, No. 4, p. 11.

[948] *Ibid.*

[949] *Ibid.*, p. 15. Measures included cut downs on subsidies, as well as elevations in the prices of combustibles and milk.

[950] *Ibid.*, p. 16.

order to stop inflation and properly service the debt.[951] In this scenario, Febres-Cordero betrayed his initial electoral promises by undertaking severe measures such as rising fuel prices, which led to an increase of transportation costs as well. He bypassed Congress by passing emergency measures within only two weeks of open debate.[952] This posture did not change for the governments that followed Febres-Cordero. The presidential terms of Rodrigo Borja and Sixto Durán-Ballén had to face similar constraints in order to avoid the complete collapse of the Ecuadorian economy.

Surely one of the most comprehensive changes that took place in recent years has been the dollarization of the economy, which was started by Jamil Mahuad and completed by Gustavo Noboa. The second half of the 1990s brought an increased damage to the Ecuadorian economy, mainly for two reasons. First, the country was not prepared to resist the external shocks of crisis such as the ones in Mexico and Asia. And second, a considerable amount of money was destined to the last armed encounter with its southern neighbour Perú, which lasted several months in 1995. Thus the already weakened Ecuadorian economy had to take two enormous burdens which were not accounted for any of the economic predictions.

After the highly polemic presidency of Abdalá Bucarám, who only understood to properly steal the left-overs of the national reserve, the economic panorama became even worse. The crisis of the economy was accompanied by a major political turmoil, as explained at the beginning of the chapter. The results of the presidential fanfare, the many corruption scandals on all levels o government and the external debt pressures facing the economy, led the government of Jamil Mahuad to opt for the path of giving up the national currency and adopting the US Dollar as the official monetary unit.

Many economists agree that this step was necessary on long-term basis. Ecuador was devaluating its currency on a daily basis up to rates o 25 percent. Therefore, the project of dollarization was set in order to avoid further devaluations and stop inflation immediately. However, on a short-term basis, the plan has become very unpopular among the population, especially among low-income groups and the rural, mostly indigenous, population. The current Finance Minister Mauricio Pozo, a true defender of neoliberal policies, has been dealing with the IMF seeking for new loans to re-establish the confidence on the economy, despite the unpopular tenure of his policies. Nevertheless, the economic disparities in the country are still

[951] Gerlach. Indians, Oil and Politics. A Recent History of Ecuador, pp. 44 ff

[952] *Ibid.*

extended, leaving no really good forecasts for the future, unless the country is able to adapt to the conditions of the IMF and pursue comprehensive structural reforms in the upcoming months.[953]

FIGURE 21: ECUADOR – ECONOMIC INDICATORS (1999-2002)

	1999	2000	2001	2002
GDP per head ($ at PPP)	3,340	3,400	3,585	3,680
GDP (% real change pa)	-6.30	2.80	5.12	3.41
Government consumption (% of GDP)	12.52	9.81	10.15	10.83
Budget balance (% of GDP)	-3.90	1.49	0.05	0.68
Consumer prices (% change pa; av)	52.24	96.09	37.68	12.48
Public debt (% of GDP)	100.55	88.92	67.21	57.98
Labour costs per hour (USD)	0.94	1.71	2.75	3.31
Recorded unemployment (%)	15.14	14.10	10.42	8.60
Current-account balance/GDP	5.64	5.81	-3.07	-5.01
Foreign-exchange reserves (m$)	1,642	946	839	714

Source: Economist Intelligence Unit. Country Data Ecuador.

Recent Social Trends

Modern society in Ecuador is composed of five major groups: the rich entrepreneurs, who are mostly based on the coastal side; the working middle class; a working low class; the indigenous population; and the military. On a selective basis, societal relations in Ecuador will be analyzed by considering three of the most current developments in this area. First, it must be noted, that the Ecuadorian social composition differs from other Latin American countries, due to its high rate of indigenous people among the total amount of the population.[954] The amount of influence that these groups have gained in the last couple of years deserves the attention of the scholarship. Second, the immense wave of emigration, which has been taken place in the country as a

[953] Cañonero, Gustavo and Alice Fabieshenko. "Latin America: Economic Analysis – Ecuador." Deutsche Bank. Emerging Markets Monthly. (December 2003.)

[954] See also: Gerlach. Indians, Oil and Politics. A Recent History of Ecuador, pp. 51 ff.

consequence of the economic catastrophe, must be observed. And third, the vigilant role of the military, "directing from the back" in terms of supporting government for their success or withdrawing the support for their abolishment, and also as a more engaged actor on many levels of Ecuadorian society since the inauguration of the last government.

While other countries witness social disequilibria between the rich and the working classes, Ecuador's indigenous population has been able to set the tone and take the lead on the debate about equal participation and representation in society and the government. During the last ten years, the representatives of numerous tribes and other grouping were able to organize themselves in a Confederation of Indigenous Nationalities *(Confederación de Nacionalidades Indígenas del Ecuador - CONAIE)*, which has become one of the most powerful force in politics, society, and – up to some point – the economy.[955]

The power of the indigenous lobby has been able to bring down two governments within the last five years. The demands they make are simple: the government should give power to the people and establish an order of more social justice and equality for the indigenous people.[956] In this regard, CONAIE has turned into a watchdog for the government offering open debate with the authorities, however, undertaking mostly activist turns in form of general strikes throughout the nation.

The economic crisis that has hit Ecuador for so many years has caused a severe wave of migration to Europe and the United States. This phenomenon is changing Ecuadorian society in many ways, as there seems to be a constant exodus of much higher extent than in the past.[957] For many people, leaving the country seems to be the only solution for the desperate needs that have grown inexorably as a result of the ongoing economic crisis of the past few years. The societal effects can be found in a growing disparity in the Ecuadorian society between those who leave, and those who decide to stay. While the former might become bigger opportunities in other countries, the latter have to remain in the country and deal with what the government has to offer. This might cause a general discontent and thus social distrust among

---

[955] *Ibid.*

[956] In: Confederation of Indigenous Nationalities of Ecuador. <http://conaie.nativeweb.org/>

[957] It has been estimated, that between 1999 and 2000, more than 267,000 Ecuadorians have emigrated to Europe and North America. The monthly rate of emigrants rose up to 7,000 in the same year. In: Jokish, Brad and Jason Pribilsky. "The Panic to Leave: Economic Crisis and the 'New Emigration' from Ecuador." International Migration (2002) Vol. 40 No. 4, pp. 76 ff.

these two groups and, more dangerously, it might engender great antipathy towards the political leadership.

Moreover, massive migration causes a non-stoppable leak of talented people to countries such as the United States and Spain leaving the country with few possibilities for the promotion and replacement of available jobs. A proper transition or generation change, especially in the public sector, can be severely affected in many aspects, due to the loss of qualified personnel. This point brings us back – in some way – to the argument presented in Chapter Three about the misallocation of talent. A similar phenomenon can be observed by the extensive emigration rates, as people with skills will most probably use the opportunity of serving other countries, simply because the native environment has little to offer.

The last aspect of the Ecuadorian society is the role of the military therein. As observed in the beginning of the chapter, Ecuador was not free of military dictatorships in the last 50 years. However, these Juntas were referred to as "soft", because they did not show the degree of brutality as those in Argentina or Chile. Nevertheless, the presence of the military in society has been something that cannot be denied for a country like Ecuador. It is a much respected yet at the same time highly criticized institution. Since the return to democracy in the early 1980s, the military have assumed a vigilant role, especially towards politicians and their sometimes overwhelming ambitions. During the collapse of Bucarám and, thereafter, Mahuad, the military were the decisive piece needed for finishing the puzzle. These two governments fell only after the military withdrew support for them. Nowadays, the current president Gutierrez, a military man himself, has introduced the military back into politics and society by posting and appointing many members of the military to all sorts of positions. The answers of the civilian population are much discrepant, depending on the context and the rank of the position.

Therefore, it can be said, that the military in Ecuador have left the margin of society, and have become more involved therein than ever before. It is still unclear, how the role of the military will further develop, after Gutierrez finishes his term. However, as of now, they are considered a pivotal group for the social cohesion in the country.

Explaining Corruption in Ecuador

The latest version of the CPI classifies Ecuador at number 113, between the Republic of the Congo and Iraq. After having taken a brief overview at the basic components of Ecuadorian recent history, politics, economy and society, it can be seen that the country has become so prone to corruption due to one main reason, namely institutional weakness. This factor can be related to the dramatic economic crisis that the country has faced in the last 20 years. Contrary to Chile, Ecuador was not able to recover from neither from internal economic breakdowns, nor from external financial shocks.

Since very first democratic administration, the governments inherited a tremendous amount of foreign debt. This was accumulated in the hopes that the oil exports would cover the debts, someday. However, when oil prices fell and Ecuador had to face the reality of a debt, which was too big for a country of its size, policies failed and institutions started to crumble. Despite the efforts of all former presidents to somehow diminish the damage, the situation got worse every year. The last major breakdown after the decision to close all banks, freeze out the entire financial system and replace the Sucre for the US Dollar, proved once more that the country was (and still is) nowhere near recovery.

Additionally, traditional clientelism between political parties contributed to the further weakening of public institutions. Although Febres-Cordero only served for a four-year term, he has been on top of every political decision in Ecuador for almost 20 years now. In this regard, a crucial element for the devastation of civil trust towards the government was the rise of Abdalá Bucarám. After his inauguration as president, it became clear that politics in the country were based on nepotism more than ever before. This is not to say that there were not similar patterns in previous administrations. However, Bucarám, with his very extravagant way of governing over a country were something not ever seen before in the national republican life of the country.[958]

These events triggered an extreme weakness of all three branches of government. The executive was not trusted anymore, as well as the legislative. And the judiciary was not able to remain untouched from the influences of ambitious politicians either.

In this context, the defrauded electorate was not only able to express its discontent on at local and national levels. Moreover, it was able to mobilize enough people to bring down the entire government. The amount of respect

[958] The scandals around Abdalá Bucarám cover a wide range of areas such as the energy sector, education, defense and security, as well as foreign policy. The rationale behind his presidency was supposedly his "mad" obsession with being in power. See also: De la Torre, Carlos. "Populism and Democracy: Political Discourses and Cultures in Contemporary Ecuador"; and Cornejo. '¡Que se Vaya!' Crónica del Bucaramato.

paid to public institutions was brought to a minimum by the end of the 1990s. As a matter of fact, survey of that time clearly showed that 61 percent of citizens asked were even not so "unhappy" with the theoretical scenario of going back to military rule.[959]

This clearly denotes that the institutional weakness provided the best scenario for the spread of corruption in Ecuador. The very fact that the authorities did not really care about the fate of their institutions – since they were not working on the first place – left structures unprotected against those who wanted to get private or corporate advantage of this scenario. The events prior to the fall of Bucarám proved this point clearly, as they were filled with one scandal after the other.

Anti-Corruption Efforts

The anti-corruption efforts in Ecuador have been increased, however, there is still much to do. The reason again is that the institutions in the country are so weak, that there is little space to maneuver. Four main areas will be briefly analyzed, namely efforts in the public sector, the work of the media, the role of NGOs and the implementation of international anti-corruption mechanisms.

Internal reforms are not bringing the desired results, as they are not undertaken in a proper way. This means, that any initiative by the government soon becomes the target of multiple critique by the population, the media, or by the opposition in congress. In many instances, the president has either retracted from the original proposal or has appointed either a close friend or a relative to undertake reforms.[960]

Another interesting example for this weakness within the public sector was the creation of an Anti-Corruption Unit.[961] This "independent" body should have become the main tool of the president for monitoring and perhaps even curbing corruption within the administration. The body covered the areas of the presidency, vice-presidency, as well as all the ministries. However, before the first reports of the agency, it soon became clear that it was going to be an ineffective measure, as the president himself mandated to

[959] Fitch, J. Samuel. "Ecuador." In: Arnson, Cynthia (ed.) The Crisis of Democratic Governance in the Andes. (Washington, D.C.: Woodrow Wilson International Center for Scholars, 2001), p. 64.

[960] One example is the appointment of Napoleón Villa, Gutierrez' brother in law as head of the Solidarity Fund, which is supposed to administer public funds for the poor. He is also the deputy chief of Gutierrez' party and led the presidential campaign in 2002.

[961] El Comercio. "Ejecutivo: El gobierno crea su ente anti-corrupción." El Comercio <www.elcomecio.com> (26.03.2003)

be the first one to receive the reports and approve them, before any information was disseminated.

The Ecuadorian constitution does provide with enough anti-corruption laws that penalize any acts of this kind. However, the great handicap of the country is that the judiciary is extremely independent of politicians and therefore, even when perpetrators get caught, there is little for judges to do, as most of them serve the interests of the political elite.

Press freedom in Ecuador is guaranteed in the constitution and has served to create more awareness to the public about the incidence of corruption. In fact, HOY, one of the most influential daily newspapers was the principal channel for the protests against Bucarám, which led to the collapse of his government. However, clientelist constellations do appear in terms of editors and owners of media outlets being at times too close to the political spheres of power.[962] More recently, the government has done a good job in terms of using the media for the purposes of creating awareness about the dangers of corruption. Public messages to the population in the press, television and radio have been sent on how to recognize and prevent corruption.

In terms of civil society, Ecuadot has a very active TI National Chapter, namely the Latin American Corporation for Development *(Corporación Latinoamericana para el Desarrollo.)* One of the highlights of recent activities by this chapter has been the introduction to the use of electronic methods for procurement in order to create more transparency for governmental procedures. Also, this project aims at providing better information for citizens about public institutions and what they have to offer.[963] Ecuador thus became a pioneer in this field by making use of the latest technological advancements for establishing a better flow of information between citizens and public servants.

Lastly, it can be observed that Ecuador is party to the OAS Convention and signed the UN Convention as well. The last report from the OAS on the follow-up for the implementation of the Convention in Ecuador notes, that the country is actively involved in the fight against corruption on a

[962] For example, after the fall of Bucarám, the director of HOY, Benjamín Ortiz joined the cabinet of the newly elected president Jamil Mahuad.

[963] Transparency International. Global Corruption Report 2003, p. 29.

regional level by coordinating actions with anti-corruption commissions in Perú, Argentina and Colombia.[964]

[964] OAS. Secretariat for Legal Affairs: Technical Secretariat for Legal Cooperation Mechanisms. Follow-Up Mechanism for the Implementation of the Inter-American Convention Against Corruption. Ecuador. (This report, is also available online at <www. www.oas.org/juridico/spanish/mec_avance_ecuV.pdf>)

CONCLUSION

TILLING IN THE SEA?

The topic of corruption has been the main focus of this book. One of the preliminary findings has been that corruption is much too extended of a problem, to make a simple observation without risking a lack of validity and/or reliability. Moreover, the impossibility of obtaining accurate measurable data for this topic demanded the use of a comparative/empirical method for the treatment of the questions.

This last chapter summarizes and evaluates the findings of this book by giving a last glimpse on the three main areas of analysis. Such a *resumé* is much needed for making an attempt to debrief on the arguments presented earlier and for pointing out some concluding remarks on the main findings of the research project.

Before doing so, it is important to note that the observations provided in this book are not exclusive and that their scope might be limited in time and analytical space. However, the area of corruption studies clearly showed that it is very difficult to write and learn about corruption without the danger of becoming "obsessed" with one particular posture, be that in terms of theoretical understanding or empirical treatment of the topic.

Therefore, this book ends with an evaluation of the findings presented in order to better understand the numerous analytical undertakings attempted in the previous pages. Moreover, it will be portrayed in this chapter if the main puzzle had been solved and if, through the comparative analysis of the three chosen case studies, the hypotheses could be either verified or falsified.

TOWARDS AN END OF THE ACADEMIC DEBATE?

Section I of this book approached the most important aspects of the academic debate about corruption, searching for answers on how to define this phenomenon. Additionally, the causes, consequences and effects of corruption were observed. By the end of the section, the internationality of corruption was discussed within the evolvement of a possible *pax corrupta*, in order to locate corruption as a phenomenon of international relations.

The first main finding of the Section was that there is no easy way for any scholar to attempt a general definition of corruption. However, this should not discourage the academic *esprit* while looking and defending adequate definitions. This book worked with a definition of corruption that is not exclusive, yet based on the recent debates on the area. The *illegitimate or illegal use of public (and private) authority for personal or corporate benefit* entailed all relevant aspects of the scholarly as well as the practical discussions about corruption and its ramifications. The attempt of such a definition is to better portray all the levels at which corruption makes an appearance, both in private as well as in governmental spheres. It must be noted that the benefits of having such a definition are that it covers a wide range of issues, which were subject to heated debate in the past such as the division between public and private benefit and the particular *vis a vis* relationship between the use of authority and the responsibility thereof.

Another feature of Section I was to highlight how corruption can take different forms and when corruption is initiated. Corruption seems to appear in many different shapes ranging from nepotism, patronage, conflicts of interest, business corruption, fraud, theft, abuse, organized crime and racketeering.[965] How can the main manifestations be recognized? In order to give an answer to this question, the analysis was supported by three different views from economics, political science and anthropology. The answer about the causes of corruption is multiple, as it can occur in any instance and regardless of the form of government (authoritarian or democratic.) Economists would deem it is a market failure, political scientists would say it a misinterpretation of power and authority, and sociologists/anthropologists would assert to note that it is a disjuncture of norms and values that are created in every society. There is a lot of truth in each answer. Instead of focusing on just one approach, this book proposes to use these three approaches to locate the causes of corruption. Furthermore, the cases of Argentina, Chile and Ecuador proved that the explanation of corruption in these countries cannot rely just on one particular answer.

The empirical analysis of the case studies showed that the effects of corruption can be found in all three levels, economic, political and social. Argentina's effects on corruption are the complete weakening of the governmental institutions, the division of society, and a considerable economic breakdown. Chile, proved to be more permeable to – yet not free of – the problems, and Ecuador seems to be lost in a mixture between political chaos and economic despair. Again, the book does not promote to focus on one single effect of corruption. This could be undertaken by other research projects that might want to deal with one problem specifically.

[965] Gardiner. "Defining Corruption", p. 27 ff.

However, it is important to observe that different effects observed in Chapter Two offer a wide range of elements for an assessment of the effects of corruption. Taking the political approach, decisive consequences such as the lack of political participation and political development, the decrease of quality of government performance, the disappearance of public trust leading toward political instability and total decay of the governmental apparatus show how powerful the damage of corruption can be. Economists offered also a wide range of aspects to consider such as impact on growth and investment, unprecedented revenue losses and an increased public expenditure as well as the loss of governmental control over economic activity. Lastly, sociologists – with the help of economists - approached the question on the effects of corruption by focusing on the social impact of corrupt practices, questioning issues such as of poverty and unequal access to services, the levels of poverty, income inequality, social spending, and the incidence of crime.

Lastly, Chapter Four undertook an analysis on one of the main messages of this dissertations, namely that corruption has evolved to become an international regime of its own. Issues such as the close relationship between the incidence of transnational organized crime and corruption, as well as the phenomenon around money laundering (a special type of corruption *per se*), gave many reasons to believe on a conceptualized international regime of corruption, that operates on its own rules. The appearance of corruption in the context of development constraints and development aid fueled the arguments for explaining the new internationality of this phenomenon.

Too Many Problems For Too Many Approaches

Taking a more empirical approach, Section II moved on to the explanation of the main approaches on those areas that are engaged in fight against corruption. One of the big questions that arise after having discussed on the nature and effects of the problem is how to solve it. Since corruption was traditionally seen both as a problem of government and as a result of the decay of bureaucracy, state reform seemed to be the most urgent solution to implement. Therefore, practices such as New Public Management seemed to give a lot of input in terms of how to get rid of corruption by segregating bureaucracy and making the public sector a much more efficient area of national life.

The reform approach was extensively observed in Chapter Five and it became interesting to note how much attention it has gained over the past years. Nevertheless, it seems to be that there is much room for improvement, since you cannot apply the same remedy on different patients, despite the similarity of their diseases.

Another important approach against corruption included the increasing role of non-governmental actors. Until the beginning of the 1990s, corruption was a silenced issue, which was dealt with by states and their respective international fora only. Nevertheless, the issue became both so wide and so pressing that elements in civil society started to take initiative against the spread of corruption, especially after the end of the bipolar animosities of the Cold War. A new independent approach was needed for bringing the issue and its ramifications on to the international public. The creation of organizations such as Transparency International helped to create concrete mechanisms for a comprehensive framework against corruption. Not only that the organization per se was a *novum*, it also became responsible for the most widely used indicator on the status of corruption in states. The Corruption Perceptions Index (CPI) has been pivotal for the newest debates about corruption. However, this book argued on several analytical reservations to the CPI. Although it has been a great step in terms of providing a tangible mechanism for understanding corruption, the index is based on perceptions. This particular feature makes any attempt on proving the accuracy and the validity of the data a very reserved issue. Moreover, the approach of NGOs led to new questions such as the legitimacy of such actors and the internal oversight that does not seem to be clear until now.

There is no doubt that corruption makes good news. In this regard, the assessment of the role of the media within the discussion of corruption brought up interesting conclusions. Among them, is the issue of the difficult relationship of media assets and government institutions, which turns very tense when corruption is "in between." Therefore, the proper conduct of journalists ranges between professionalism on the one hand and ethical standards on the other one. It was observed that strengthening the role of the media is in deed a powerful approach against corruption. The effect of media coverage in the aftermath of corruption scandals can be decisive for the measures and sanctions taken against perpetrators. Moreover, recent studies showed that there is – up to a certain point – a relationship between press freedom and the incidence of corruption. It was determined that those countries who have better guarantees in terms of press freedom and civil rights, seem to denote lesser levels of corruption. Although these observations may be changed by altering the causalities, it proves the point that a free press is a key element in every democracy and a necessary element in any anti-corruption approach. However, in some instances, journalists may become actors in the corrupt transactions' side, assuming both initiative and recipient roles. Therefore, this book advocates for a solid training for journalists and for the spread and implementation of codes of conduct, as well as press councils as needed tools for enhancing the media approach against the spread of corruption.

Since it became clear that corruption needs to be treated as an international problem, Section II concluded with both a presentation and evaluation of the most extensive international treaties and covenants against corruption and portrayed the work of international organizations in this regard. Although there was a selection on the institutions and documents analyzed, it soon became clear that this approach still has several deficiencies that can be found mostly in the lack of political initiative of many states in actions against corruption. The relevant legal instruments are plenty and ever since "milestones" such as the OECD Convention and the Inter-American Convention, the number of international treaties has grown considerably. Also, in some cases, states have shown great interest in implementing the provisions of such documents. The clear example is the signing of what should become the major international treaty against corruption, namely the UN Convention Against Corruption. However, there remains resilience to make international standards become national laws. Therefore, its can be concluded that the approach of combating corruption via international law mechanisms will not fail on the scope or amount of existing documents, but much rather on the political compromise that must be found within states to implement the different provisions thereof. In this regard, the work of international organizations by accompanying the efforts of states against corruption can be the perfect enhancement for this approach.

LATIN AMERICAN PERSPECTIVES

Section III concluded the entire book by making a brief analysis of three Latin American countries that were used to better understand the findings of the two preceding sections. The methodological background of using three countries and compare them can be found in the lack of reliable data about corruption. The CPI is the only scale that can be used for such an analysis, and since it became clear that corruption is a non-measurable phenomenon, the comparative path is the most appropriate one. Therefore, the analysis of the three chosen cases presented many aspects which could be reflected both in theory, as well as in the approaches presented in Section II.

Argentina proved to be an adequate candidate for the analysis proposed on this book, since the incidence of corruption in the country led to most of the damages found in form of political instability, economic despair and social disparity. The case of Argentina proved how corruption evolves through the appearance of elites and networks that manipulate politics and democracy for their own purposes. Also, Argentina's economic development, if related to the position of the country in the CPI, strengthens the argumentative posture of countries with high levels of corruption lacking standard levels of development. Moreover, the current deplorable situation of the Argentine population denotes clearly how corruption can have effects on the access to public services, on the income inequality, on the levels of poverty and on the incidence of crime. At the end, the picture of the Argentine corruption landscape has too many colors that cause a general dislike both to the inside and to the outside.

Analyzing Chile with the same elements, namely politics, economic performance, and societal factors, proved to be useful in terms of obtaining a different image of a country within the same regional block as for Argentina. It must be noted that Chile is not free of corruption. However, the country's institutions have been able to cope with the problem much better than in the other two cases. Some of the cases presented in Chapter Ten proofs that the problem of corruption of Chile served as an indicator of how good national institutions can work. Therefore, the comparison to Argentina and Ecuador served to prove the point, that corruption does not necessarily have the same scope, if placed in geographical/cultural context.

Lastly, the analysis of Ecuador proved to be very useful and interesting, because of the relative small size and political weight of the country but, at the same time, because of the enormous implications of corruption for the fate of the country. Having had six presidential changes in six years and an awful amount of social unrest, led by one of the traditionally marginalized sectors of the population, namely the indigenous people, contributed to directly observe how a government is dismantled after being accused of corruption. The events of 1998 around the unfinished presidential term of Abdalá Bucarám, clearly portrayed how corruption acts as a corrosive on the political institutions of a country, thus leading toward a complete government breakdown. However, the events of the following years soon became the results of the spread of corruption in government since the re-instalment of democracy in the early 1980s. Also, compared to the other cases, especially Chile, corruption in Ecuador seems to be the product of a severe weakness of institutions, such as the judicative. The book stressed the role of strengthening institutions for a better eradication of this problem.

However, for the case of Ecuador, institutions seem to fail and leave the path free for corruption to develop.

PUZZLE: WHY IS CORRUPTION STILL SO PRESENT IN THIS REGION?

After the analysis, we can observe that the multidisciplinarity of corruption can help us answer this question properly. As Tulchin and Espach observed earlier, the postulate of Latin American countries as being corrupt per nature lacks any validity and empirical foundation. Since these nations have all been founded in the light of European political and economic frameworks, it would be also too easy to say that the *conquista* needs to be considered in the explanation of the incidence of corruption in the region.

Therefore, this book chooses three answers from three different perspectives. First, the case studies have delivered a clear picture of what seems to be a common problem for all Latin American nations, namely *political institutional weakness*. Therefore, this element shall be considered as the main political explanation for the incidence of corruption in Latin American countries. This weakness denotes many of the aspects entailed in Section I, especially in Chapter Two. It means that the lack o political cohesion within and between governmental agencies, the low moral of public workers, low wages, the power struggles among new and old elites, has led to a decrease of the strength needed in government to operate properly. Therefore, corruption in these countries, as Argentina and Ecuador have illustrated, is the product of such a weakness. In such scenario, as many authors have agrees, corruption finds fertile soil to spread and infect all areas of national life.

Second, the *severe economic breakdowns* that Latin America countries have suffered in the last 20 years has led to a greater incidence of illicit enrichment. This is not to say that typical Latin American phenomena such as the debt crisis are responsible for the increase of corruption in the region. However, if we recall the arguments of Vito Tanzi, there were to types of initial motives for getting involved in illicit activities, namely "corruption due need and corruption due to greed."[966] For the case of Latin America, we can see both types, in different contexts however with a similar relationship, namely the deplorable state of the national economy. There are those who find themselves in "petty" corruption deals because they need to access to a public service or because the waged are too low. However, there are many who are involved in corruption, because the benefits they receive

[966] Tanzi, "Corruption Around the World. Causes, Consequences, Scope and Cures", p. 572.

do not seem sufficient. Both scenarios can be related to the poor economic performance of each country, which acts as a catalyzer, especially for "corruption due to need". Economic impediments such as lower rates of foreign investments and low levels of growth fuel this argument. Lastly, economic breakdowns lead to yet more institutional weaknesses thus resulting in a more adequate scenario for the appearance and spread of corruption. After the analysis of the case studies, it became clear how, in the cases of Ecuador and Argentina, low level corruption can most likely be attributed to "corruption to need", because of the situation of a great amount of citizens, while on the top spheres of government, "corruption due to greed" takes precedence over other forms of illicit enrichment. As for the case of Chile, it seems to be that the positive economic performance has allowed vast sectors of society, if not to refrain, then to at least not immediately become a part of corrupt deals.

Third, there are two key features in Latin American societies that can be identified as main factors for persistence of corruption in these societies. The *extended culture of networking and "gift-giving"* has made the line between what is legal and what can be considered as corruption utmost blurry. Chapter One debated about the fact that corruption is a very wide phenomenon and, as such, it is subject to infinite interpretations. Moreover, anthropologists such as Tone Sissener adverted the dangers of not considering the role of cultural networks and societal values in the definition of corruption.[967] As observed in the case of Argentina, Ménem and his closest collaborators established a network that was in charge of modernizing the country, but at the same time, these networks benefited enormously of their privileged position. Bucarám and his clan in Ecuador operated similarly. Further cases in Latin America denote the same problem, namely that elites or networks, once in power, deny both the access and delivery of public goods. And this is precisely the point in which corruption starts. Not being able to draw the line between a favor and a bribe is a weakness of many parts of the population. If we apply this weakness to the government and private sectors, then we obtain as result, that Latin American societies, influenced by the European but developing own characteristics, developed a unique cultural system of networking and "gift giving" that has made it difficult to delineate the initial moment of corruption. It must be said that such networks are nothing new and are certainly present in each region of the world. However, for the explanation of the incidence of corruption, after the analysis proposed

[967] Sissener. "Anthropological perspectives on corruption."

in this book, this factor adds a solid element to the general answer of the puzzle.

Based on these deliberations and bearing in mind the main characteristic of the case studies presented in this book, the answer to the puzzle can be formulated as follows: *Corruption in Latin America can be explained by three elements and its incidence is attributed to the combination thereof. First, political institutional weaknesses, especially in the public sector provide the perfect scenario of the spread of corrupt activities. Second, the consequences of major economic breakdowns have led all sectors of the population to more likely engage in corrupt deals. Third, the role of networks and the culture of "gift giving", which are both unique due to the regional and cultural contexts, make it impossible to draw a clear line between corruption and non-corruption.*

TESTING HYPOTHESIS 1: IF ECONOMIC DEVELOPMENT IS LOW, THEN CORRUPTION LEVELS REMAIN HIGH

The argumentation presented by Paulo Mauro in Chapter Two entailed some relevant aspects related with this hypothesis. In his contribution on the effects of corruption, the author defended the position that there was indeed a relationship between high levels of corruption and growth rates. The results of his work have become the *canon* of many anti-corruption strategies, namely that corruption and growth can be correlated and that the former has a negative impact on the latter.

Taking this observation as an initial point, the cases of Argentina, Chile and Ecuador proved to be useful for understanding how the relationship between the two variables could look like. First of all, however, it should be determined that growth rates are an adequate indicator for economic development (among many others of course.) In a preliminary observation, if we part from the fact that the Argentine economy has been severely damaged, especially in the last five years, and if we relate to that the levels of perceived corruption as indicated in the CPI, then we could most probably verify the hypothesis. However, it still deserves our attention to try to make a general statement, no only for the chosen countries, but also for the entire region.

Economic development is the basis for good governance and strong public institutions. If we should follow the findings of the three case studies, we can see that there is some analytical validity which could be helpful to our purposes. If compared, the economic performance of each country has declined severely, with some recoveries, however not consistent enough to observe a constant positive trend.

Taking a look at the latest ratings of the CPI, we can observe that the chosen countries have dropped in the scale considerably. Only Chile has been able to remain among the top 20. This means that severe economic breakdowns and thus low levels of development can be interpreted in function of corruption. This means, that for most Latin American, this observation is valid and the hypothesis can be thus verified. We should be cautious about the validity of this verification. It must be noted that the analytical roots of such an assumption are based on two scales that are compared to each other. Thus the relationship can be easily changed by swapping the order of the variables. This undertaking is noteworthy. Nevertheless, it is also beyond the scope of the purposes of this book.

TESTING HYPOTHESES 2: NATIONAL HISTORY AND POLITICAL CULTURE INFLUENCE THE LEVELS OF CORRUPTION

Clientelism is a mechanism for achieving political power in almost every country in the world. Moreover, political culture can be understood the way through which citizens perceive the amalgamation of political action at all levels. Taking these two elements into consideration, we can conclude the following for the chosen cases and – up to some point – for the vast majority of Latin American countries: politics in the region are strongly based in clientelism, due to the "gift-giving" idiosyncrasy of its citizens and to the way the look at politics.

In Latin America, as in most regions as well, there has hardly been a President who did not have to return the support given to his election in form of patronage and other clientelist ways. In the case studies, it was easily observed that Ménem privatized in Argentina in the 1990s appointing members of his closest personal circles. During the same decade, Bucaram "sold" the country to the interests of his family and those around it. In Chile, the influence of the military remained high, with the *Concertación* government having to make vast personal arrangements to succeed at the transition from military rule to democracy.[968]

Therefore, an assessment of this hypothesis considers the following points, which have been provided after having had taken a closer look at the case studies. All three countries have a similar national history that dates back to the struggles against the *conquista* followed by the establishment of free and independent governments thereafter. These governments were based

[968] One example is the appointment of Augusto Pinochet as Senator for Life with all sorts of privileges and immunities.

on the premise, that an accumulation of power by one particular sector should not be the adequate way to avoid the despotism of the early 19th Century. Nevertheless, the political struggle in all three countries, mostly between conservatives and liberals, has led to an intense change of policies and political frameworks, depending on who is in power.

Moreover, all three countries have experienced several military regimes, which have shaped the general understanding of politics and thus influenced the ways of citizens of viewing the government as a political entity. Due to the common history of most Latin American countries, this assimilation of government and development of a political culture seems to be similar. Nevertheless, the duration of military dictatorships and the degree of their brutality have also influenced the political culture. The best example for this point is Chile, where people know have an imminent sense of respect, due to the impact of the last military regime.

The phenomenon of corruption appears here not much so on the history side, but more on the political cultural side. First, the fact that all countries shared to the most part common historical patterns does not imply that corruption is present as a consequence of this element. Chile proves once again to be the exception to the rule, because corruption levels seem low despite similar historical patterns since the early 19th Century. Argentina and Ecuador have shared this historical trajectory as well. However, corruption in these countries seems to be out of control, compared to the Chilean political scene. *Therefore, at the end of the analysis, this book discards national history as the explanatory mechanism for corruption in the chosen countries.*

Turning on to the political culture, and in this case, clientelism and "gift-giving", we can observe that the way politicians and citizens alike view national politics is one of the main elements which can account for a valid explanation. The arguments explained earlier for Argentina and *Menemismo* and the like, showed that the incidence of corruption in these countries is directly related to the ways of politics, meaning that clientelism sets up the stage for corruption to evolve. Moreover, the "gift-giving" attitude of most politicians fuels the postulate of corruption being a product of such political practices. *Therefore, we can conclude that having observed how politics work in Argentina, Chile and Ecuador, the appearance, incidence and spread of corruption can be directly attributed to the clientelist factor in each of the countries.*

TESTING HYPOTHESES 3: IF THE MODERN LIBERAL DEMOCRATIC MODEL OF GOVERNANCE IS FOLLOWED, CORRUPTION LEVELS WILL BE LOW

Of all the four hypotheses presented in this book, this is the one with the most probability of falsification. In order to provide a solid test of this hypothesis, we must focus on both the political and the economic level.
From the political perspective, previous Chapters focused on the importance of having solid, democratic and transparent institutions for an adequate combat of corrupt practices. On a more general note, in Latin America, the return to democracy in the 1970s and 1980s, promised to bring comprehensive change at all levels, political, economic and social. The atrocities against human rights would be brought to an absolute minimum, political diversity will be guaranteed, the economy would benefit from liberalizations of the trade and services market, and society would be able to develop and act freely in a non-repressive and open environment. In terms of corruption, the hopes were also to at least try to comprehensively approach this problem and not to hide it under military secrecy.

Nevertheless, the return to democracy, especially for Argentina and Ecuador, meant the beginning of the most politically unstable and economically disastrous period in the history of these countries. And in terms of corruption, it meant the spread of the phenomenon in ways that have never been experienced before. This is not to say that Chile has not had its problems since the re-instalment of an elected government. However, Argentina and Ecuador serve as adequate examples for the denial of the neoliberal democratic model as an adequate approach against corruption.

The lack of political stability was recognized in this book as one major effect of corruption. The immediate consequence of such a scenario is the mistrust of the citizens towards the political leadership, ending at times in a complete dismantlement of the entire government apparatus. Argentina and Ecuador seem to best portray this development, due to the events of the fall of President de la Rúa in the former, and the falls of Presidents Bucarám and Mahuad in the latter. In these countries, there seems to be a low amount of belief for the fate of democracy as an adequate framework for the eradication of corruption. In fact, since 1996, corruption levels have increased according to the CPI.[969] *Therefore, we must conclude, that from the government/political perspective, the democratic model has not brought about little – if any – real improvement to the status of corruption in the chosen cases.* In Ecuador, President Gutierrez announced on his inaugural speech, that the fight against corruption would be the cornerstone of his

[969] If a counterfactual experimental thought would be possible at this point, it would be interesting to observe what kind of a placement these countries would have received under military rule. However the CPI is a relatively new tool and such surveys were limited – if not existent at all – at that time.

administration's work. Today, his image has been damaged due to the intense nepotist character of his government with many relatives and friend in the key positions. In Chile, *Concertación* was surely no easy undertaking after so many years of dictatorship. Nevertheless, corruption within the governmental institutions has flourished as well, with the only difference, that in Chile, public institutions seem to function well enough to diminish the damage and quickly bring those responsible to justice, as the *"Caso Coimas"* showed.

Taking the economic perspective into account, we find a more positive scenario. The democratic/liberal model proposed many reforms, especially in the public sector. In Chapter Five of this book, the numerous attempts towards public reform in the context of anti-corruption initiatives were analyzed. By the end of the Chapter, it became clear that approaches such as NPM, which are of strong neo-liberal tone, could strengthen public institutions and thus make them more permeable to corruption. Moreover, reforms can bring transparency in the public sector and this should reduce the incidence of corruption therein.

The chosen case studies have shown that they take public sector reform as a strong element in their agendas. Reform packages should be shaped individually to every country, according to its characteristics and to its needs. Of the three cases, Chile denotes the most successes with this approach, having been able to already successfully privatize and deregulate its economy in a constant and comprehensive way during the Pinochet regime.

Therefore, if taken from the economic view, this book concludes in regard to hypotheses 3, that the economic aspects of the liberal/democratic of governance, if applied correctly, can offer a feasible solution to corruption.

TESTING HYPOTHESES 4: IF INTERNATIONAL NORMS AGAINST CORRUPTION ARE ESTABLISHED AND EFFECTIVELY IMPLEMENTED, LEVELS OF CORRUPTION WILL DIMINISH

There are three levels in which we can give a proper answer to this question. First, there is the role of international mechanisms such as treaties and conventions. Second, there are certain international norms such as freedom of the press that have been promoted throughout the world as a remedy against corruption. Lastly, the international development assistance regime has proven to be equally valid for explaining how external standards influence the willingness of governments to engage in corrupt practices.

Taking the first level, international mechanisms, it seems to premature to say with certainty, if anti corruption documents such as the conventions of the OAS, OECD, and most recently, the UN, could offer an adequate solution to the problem. The main weakness of such an approach is that it is still subject to the will of sovereign states. They have to sign and ratify the treaties in order to make them effective. More important however, as observed in Chapter Eight, they can have as many reservations they want on issues they deem necessary. Although the three cases have been integral parties to the numerous anti-corruption treaties, it would not be surprising if they would not behave accordingly, simply because states will always pursue what is on their own interest first, and only afterwards, they would consider what the will of the community might be. Also another weakness point is the lack of comprehensive sanctions due to a breach of contract. All international treaties have provisions on what to do if a state discovers that it is being affected by corruption. However, the provision on how to behave if the state itself has taken the initiative to engage in corruption actions, are somehow blurry, if not existent at all.

Therefore, this book concludes that international treaties are a good first step towards the eradication of corruption. However, they fail as soon as they are subject to the states' approval for implementation.

However, if we consider press freedom as a norm that has become international in the last couples of years, we might be able to confirm the hypotheses, at least up to some point. Brunetti and Weder showed us in Chapter Seven, that there is enough evidence to postulate that countries with high rates of press freedom and civil rights are most likely to denote lower levels of corruption. In this regard, if we understand press freedom as an international norm that should be kept in all countries of the world, then we can confirm the hypotheses. *Therefore, this book concludes, that when considering press freedom as an international norm, levels of corruption have been found to be lower in those countries, which can guarantee for this norm in a comprehensive way.*

Lastly, Chapter Four and Chapter Eight portrayed the importance, and at the same time, the *problematique*, around the concept of official development assistance. The first problem was that ODA was not being granted to the right countries in terms of lower incidence of corruption.[970] Second, the main criticism was that the more funds are granted, the more money there is available to corrupt agents. And third, the conditionality attached to ODA was in many cases so difficult for some countries, that they had to take austerity measures in order to receive the much needed funds.

[970] Goldfarb. "Who gets CIDA Grants? Recipient Corruption and the Effectiveness of Development Aid."

It is precisely this point that leads us towards relating the international aid regime to the test of the hypotheses. It was observed earlier, that the entire approach of ODA contains several norms that have become international such as the implementation of adequate public sector reforms, deregulation of the economy, privatization, and downsizing, among others. Chapter Five showed clearly, that such an approach can be very useful in the fight against corruption. Moreover, Rose-Ackerman was wise in observing that external pressures such as conditionality can be a great incentive for states to start broad strategies against the spread of corruption. The case studies have shown that ODA and conditionality are integral parts of the countries' approach towards development, and in this context, of national anti-corruption strategies. *Therefore, this book concludes that the international norms included in the development aid regime can be powerful external mechanisms for the fight against corruption.*

ARE WE TILLING IN THE SEA?

When analyzing the vast aspects of corruption, its definition, its causes and effects, as well as the efforts towards its eradication, it may seem as if we were constantly "tilling in the sea", an phrase often used by the great Libertador Simón Bolívar, when he described ho difficult it was to achieve unity among Latin American nations. Therefore, at the end of the book, I ask: what are the main concluding messages of this research? There are at least five concluding points that need to be made before "closing the book."

First of all, the analysis of corruption can be a very difficult enterprise, if a statistical method is chosen. There is hardly any data that can be considered reliable, simply because governments will most likely reserve this kind of information for other purposes, not for academic research. Therefore, I strongly believe that the analysis of corruption in the social sciences finds a perfect place in the comparative method. Choosing countries or regions can say much more about the reasons for the existence of corruption than any statistical database available.

Second, the analysis of corruption turns even more difficult when one considers the different definitions that have been proposed both by scholars and practitioners. Within this definitional sea, there is a further problem, namely that there will always be a normative component in which the "breach" or the "abuse" of any standard will be subject to personal interpretations. We were able to observe in Chapter One certain actions were considered bribery in some countries, while in others they belonged to day-to-day practices. Therefore, we must always remain aware of the fact, that corruption will never become a universal concept accepted everywhere by everyone.

Third, a proper academic assessment of corruption in the social sciences should no be limited to a single discipline. Politics, economics, sociology, anthropology, and history should be included in every analysis of corruption. The reason is that this phenomenon is so complex and can take so many shapes, that the more flexible the analysis is, the more understanding we will gain about it.

Fourth, solutions to corruption are as frequent as its definitions. And again, there is not only one solution that can work. The multidisciplinarity of corruption also brings along several approaches. Section II of this book presented what seem to be the most current and comprehensive approaches. However, it is also equally valid note, that there might be other approaches, not mentioned in this book that could be equally applied to the theory and to the case studies. However, it is important to consider that solutions might be interrelated to each other, and that some of the greatest strategies against corruption have evolved out of the combination of solutions and strategies.

Lastly, case studies present good input for the verification and/or falsification of the hypotheses. The case of Latin America turned out to be interesting in terms of having countries that are within the same regional block, share many common historical and cultural elements, however differ from each other in so many levels. Making comparisons between countries is helpful for acknowledging that corruption has many faces and although it may appear in similar ways, it is different for every case.

Therefore, as this book has come to an end, it must be appraised that the research on corruption still needs to continue in a comprehensive way. Simply because we face definitional or measuring problems, we shall not give up in our endeavours to understand the many facettes of this phenomenon, which has caused so many damages, not only to Latin American countries, but to nations all around the world.

***

Ades, Alberto and Rafael Di Tella. "Rents, Competition, and Corruption." The American Economic Review (September 1999), Vol. 89, No. 4, pp. 982-993.

Aguillon Espinoza, Paola. "Cuando las institutciones funcionan." Tiempos del Mundo Chile. (16.-22.01.2003.)

Alesina, Alberto, Sule Ozler, Nouriel Roubini and Phillip Swagel. "Political Instability and Economic Growth." Journal of Economic Growth (1996) Vol. 1, pp. 189-211.

Alesina, Alberto and Beatrice Weder. "Do Corrupt Governments Receive Less Foreign Aid?" Working Paper 7108. National Bureau of Economic Research. (May 1999.)

Amudsen, Inge. "Political Corruption: an introduction to the issues." Chr. Michelsen Institute Working Paper (1999.)

Andvig, Jens, Odd-Helge Fjeldstad, et. al. Research on Corruption. A Policy Oriented Survey. (Stockholm: Chr. Michelsen Institute (CMI) & Norwegian Institute for International Affairs (NUPI), December 2000.)

Anechiarico, Frank and James b. Jacobs. The Pursuit of Absolute Integrity. How Corruption Control Makes Government Ineffective. (Chicago and London: The University of Chicago Press, 1996.)

Aninat, Eduardo. "Chile in the 1990s. Embracing Development Opportunities." Finance & Development (March 2000), pp. 19-21.

Appelbaum, Elie and Eliakim Katz. "Seeking Rents by Setting Rents: The Political Economy of Rent-Seeking." The Economic Journal (September 1987) Vol. 97, No. 387, pp. 685-699.

Arnson, Cynthia (ed.) The Crisis of Democratic Governance in the Andes. (Washington, D.C.: Woodrow Wilson International Center for Scholars, 2001.)

Ashley, Richard. "The Poverty of Neorealism." International Organization (1984), Vol. 38, pp. 225-286.

Banfield, Edward C. "Corruption as a Feature of Governmental Organization." The Journal of Law and Economics (1975) Vol. 18, pp. 587-605.

Bangura, Yusuf. "Public Sector Restructuring: The Institutional and Social Effects of Fiscal, Managerial and Capacity-Building Reforms." Occasional Paper No. 3. (Geneva: United Nations Research Institute for Social Development, February 2000.)

Bannon, Ian. "The Fight Against Corruption, A World Bank Perspective." Workshop on Transparency and Governance. Consultative Group Meeting for the Reconstruction and Transformation of Central America.

<http://www.iadb.org/regions/re2/consultative_group/groups/transparency_workshop6.htm> (04.06.2000.)

Batley, Richard. "The Role of Government in Adjusting Economies 1994-1999 – An Overview of Findings." Research Programme at the International Development Department. University of Birmingham. <www.idd.bham.ac.uk/research> (04.11.2003.)

Bardhan, Pranab. "Corruption and Development: A Review of Issues." Journal of Economic Literature. (September 1997), Vol. 35, No. 3, pp. 1320-1346.

Barrett, Patrick S. "Chile's Transformed Party System and the Future of Democratic Stability." Journal of Interamerican Studies and World Affairs (2000) Vol. 42, No. 3, pp. 1-32.

Barros, Robert. Constitutionalism and Dictatorship. Pinochet, the Junta and the 1980 Constitution. (Cambridge: Cambridge University Press, 2002.)

Baylis, John and Steve Smith. The Globalization of World Politics. An Introduction to International Relations. (Oxford: Oxford University Press, 1997.)

BBC News. "Chile: Desafueros por corrupción." BBC Mundo. <www.bbcmundo.com> (27.11.2002)

BBC News. "Deniegan libertad bajo fianza en Chile." BBC Mundo. <www.bbcmundo.com> (11.01.2003)

BBC News: "Ecuadorian President Accused of Corruption." BBC World Service. <www.bbc.co.uk> (17.12.1997)

Berguido, Fernando. "Dos Caras de la Corrupción". Ministry of Government <www.gobiernodechile.cl>

Berthélemy, Jean-Claude, Celine Kauffmann, Laurence Renard and Lucia Wegner. "Political Instability, political regimes and economic performance in African countries." OECD Development Center. March 2002.

Birdsall, Nancy and Juan Luis Londoño. "Asset Inequality Matters: An Assessment if the World Bank's Approach to Poverty Reduction." American Economic Review, Papers and Proceedings. (1997) Vol. 87 No.2, pp. 32-37.

Birdsall, Nancy and John Nellis. "Winners and Losers: Assessing the Distributional Impact of Privatization." Working Paper No 6. (Washington DC: Center for Global Development, May 2002.)

Bliss, Christopher and Rafael Di Tella. "Does Competition Kill Corruption?" The Journal of Political Economy (October 1997), Vol. 105, No. 5, pp. 1001-1023.

Boix Carles. "Democracy, Development and the Public Sector." American Journal of Political Science. (January 2001) Vol. 45, No. 1, pp. 1-17.

Booth, Ken and Steve Smith (ed.), International Relations Theory Today (University Park, PA: Penn State Press, 1995.)

Brandolino, John. "Fighting Corruption. The Role of Diplomacy and International Agreements." The Journal of Public Inquiry (Fall/Winter 2001), pp. 9-12.

Brunetti, Aymo and Beatrice Weder. “A Free Press is Bad News for Corruption.” WWZ Discussion Paper Nr. 9809. (Basel: Center of Economics and Business Administration, University of Basel, 1998.) Reprinted in: Journal of Public Economics. (2003) Vol. 87, pp. 1801-1824.

Buttny, Richard. Social Accountability in Communication. (London: Sage Publications, 1993.)

Byers, Michael (ed.) The Role of Law in International Politics. (Oxford: Oxford University Press, 2000.)

Calvert, Peter and Susan Calvert. Latin America in the Twentieth Century. (London: Macmillan Press, 1990.)

Camerer, Lala. “Protecting Whistle Blowers in South Africa: The Protected Disclosures Act, no. 26 of 2000.” Occasional Paper N0. 47. (South Africa: Institute for Security Studies, 2001.)

Cañonero, Gustavo. “Latin America: Economic Analysis – Argentina.” Deutsche Bank. Emerging Markets Monthly. (November 2003.)

Cañonero, Gustavo and Alice Fabieshenko. “Latin America: Economic Analysis – Ecuador.” Deutsche Bank. Emerging Markets Monthly. (December 2003.)

Casals, Beatriz C. and Sergio Díaz-Briquets. “Policy Framework to Address Corruption in the Cuban Transition.” Cuba in Transition. (ASCE), (August 1999), Vol. 9, pp. 443-452.

Chalmers, Alan F. What Is This Thing Called Science? (Indianapolis: Hackett Pub. Co., 1999.)

Chile Transparente. Capítulo Chileno de Transparencia Internacional. Seguimiento de la Convención Interamericana Contra la Corrupción (CICC-OEA) Informe desde la Sociedad Civil. <http://www.chiletransparente.cl/informe_oea.htm>

CIVICUS. World Alliance for Citizen Participation. <www.civicus.org>

Clark, Anne Marie, et. al. "The Global Limits of Civil Society." World Politics (October 1998), Vol. 51, pp. 1-35.

Clark, Ian. Globalization and International Relations Theory. (Oxford: Oxford University Press, 1999.)

CNN World News. "Invoking 'mental incapacity' rule, Ecuador fires President." <www.cnn.com> (06.02.1997)

Confederation of Indigenous Nationalities of Ecuador. <http://conaie.nativeweb.org/>

Cornejo, Diego (ed.) '¡Que se vaya!' Cronica del Bucaramato. (Quito: Edimpres S.A., 1997)

Crozier, Michel. The Bureaucratic Phenomenon. (Chicago: University of Chicago Press, 1964.)

De Faria, José Carlos. "Latin America: Economic Analysis – Chile." Deutsche Bank. Emerging Markets Monthly. (November 2003.)

De la Torre, Carlos. "Populism and Democracy: Political Discourses and Cultures in Contemporary Ecuador." Latin American Perspectives (May 1997) Vol. 24, no. 3, pp. 12-24.

De La Torre, Carlos. "Velasco Ibarra and 'La Revolucion Gloriosa': The Social Production of a Populist Leader in Ecuador in the 1940s." Journal of Latin American Studies (October 1994) Vol. 26, No. 3, pp. 683-711.

De Michele, Roberto. "The Role of the Anti-Corruption Office in Argentina. Lessons in Corruption and Anti-Corruption: Policies and Results." The Journal of Public Inquiry. (Fall/Winter 2001) pp. 17-20.

Della Porta, Donatella and Alberto Vannucci. Corrupt Exchanges. Actors, Resources, and Mechanisms of Political Corruption. (New York: Walter de Gruyter Inc., 1999.)

Dobel, J. Patrick. "The Corruption of the State." The American Political Science Review (September 1978), Vol. 72, No. 3, pp. 958-973.

Dogan, Mattei and Dominique Pelassy. How to Compare Nations. Strategies in Comparative Politics. (Chatham, NJ: Chatham House Publishers, Inc., 1990.)

Doig, Alan and Robin Theobald (eds). Corruption and Democratization. (London: Frank Class and Co. Ltd, 2000.)

Doig, Alan and Stephanie Mclvor. "Corruption and its control in the developmental context: an analysis and selective review of the literature." Third World Quarterly (1999) Vol. 20, No. 3, pp. 657-676.

Drew, Kristine. "Whistle Blowing and Corruption – An Initial and Comparative Review." UNICORN: A Global Trade Unions Anti-Corruption Project. (London: Public Services International Research Unit, 2003.)

Dunne, Tim, Michael Cox and Ken Booth. The Eighty Year's Crisis. International Relations 1919-1999. (Cambridge: Cambridge University Press, 1998.)

Eckstein, Harry. "Case Study and Theory in Political Science." In: Greenstein, Fred and Nelson W. Polsby. Handbook of Political Science. Volume 7: Strategies of Inquiry. (Reading, MA: Addison-Wesley Publishing Company, 1975), pp. 79-137.

Economist Intelligence Unit. Country Data Argentina. (June 2003.)

Economist Intelligence Unit. Country Data Chile. (June 2003.)

Economist Intelligence Unit. Country Data Ecuador. (June 2003.)

Economist Intelligence Unit. Country ViewsWire Argentina. (October 2003.)

Economist Intelligence Unit. Country ViewsWire Chile. (December 2003.)

Economist Intelligence Unit. Country ViewsWire Chile. (July 2003.)

Ehrlich, Isaac and Francis T. Lui. "Bureaucratic Corruption and Endogenous Growth." The Journal of Political Economy (December 1999) Part 2: Symposium on the Economic Analysis of Social Behavior in Honor of Gary S. Becker. Vol. 107, No. 6, pp. 270-293.

Elliott, Kimberly Ann (ed.) Corruption and the Global Economy. (Washington D.C.: Institute for International Economics, 1997.)

Ennis, Huberto M. and Santiago M. Pinto. "Privatization and Income Distribution in Argentina." Inter-American Development Bank Project: The Effects of Privatization in Income Distribution in Latin America. (Washington, D.C./Mexico, D.F.: Inter-American Development Bank Sustainable Development Department, 2001.)

European Council's Group of States against Corruption. <www.greco.coe.int/>

Evans Lewis, Arthur Grimes, Bryce Wilkinson and David Teece. "Economic Reform in New Zealand 1984-95: The Pursuit of Efficiency." Journal of Economic Literature (December 1996) Vol. 34, No. 4, pp. 1856-1902.

Faiola, Anthony. "Bribery Scandal Singes Argentine Anti-Graft Crusader." The Washington Post. (11th October 2000.)

Feldstein, Martin. "Argentina's Fall. Lessons from the Latest Financial Crisis." Foreign Affairs (March/April 2002), Vol. 81, Nr. 2, pp. 8-14.

Ferreiro, Alejandro. "Dinero, Política y Transparencia: el imperativo democrático de combatir la corrupción." Working Paper for the 9th International Anti-Corruption Conference. (Durban: Transparency International, 1999.)

Finnemore, Martha and Kathryn Sikkink. "International Norm Dynamics and Political Change." International Organization (Fall 1998), Vol. 52, pp. 887-917.

Fisman, Raymond and Roberta Gatti. "Decentralization and corruption: evidence across countries." Journal of Public Economics (2002), Vol. 83, pp. 325-345.

Flanary, Rachel and David Watt. "The state of corruption: a case study of Uganda." Third World Quarterly (1999), Vol. 20, No. 3, pp. 525-536.

Florini, Ann. "The Evoution of International Norms." International Studies Quarterly (September 1996), Vol. 40, pp. 363-390.

Fosu, Augustin Kwasi. "Political Instability and Economic Growth: Evidence from Sub-Saharan Africa." Economic Development and Cultural Change (1999), Vol.40, No. 4, pp. 87-107

Friedrich, Carl. The Pathology of Politics: Violence, Betrayal Corruption, Secrecy and Propaganda. (New York: Harper & Row, 1972.)

Friedman. Jonathan. Cultural Identity and Global Process. (London: Sage Publications, 1994.)

Fukuyama, Francis. "The End of History?" The National Interest (Summer 1989), Vol. 16, pp. 3-18.

Fundación CIDOB. "Biografías de Líderes Políticos: Abdalá Bucaram Ortiz." Fundación CIDOB. Center of International Relations and International Cooperation. (Barcelona: 2002.)

Fundación CIDOB. "Biografías de Líderes Políticos: Rodrigo Borja Cevallos." Fundación CIDOB. Center of International Relations and International Cooperation. (Barcelona: 2002.)

Gambetta, Diego. The Sicilian Mafia. (Cambridge, MA: Cambridge University Press, 1993.)

Geddes, Barbara. "How the Cases You Choose Affect the Answers You Get: Selection Bias in Comparative Politics." In: Stimson, James A. (ed.) Political Analysis. An Annual Publication of the Methodology Section of the American Political Science Association. Vol. 2 (Ann Arbor: The University of Michigan Press, 1990), pp. 131-150.

George, Alexander L. and Timothy L. McKeown. "Case Studies and Theories of Organizational Decision Making." In: Coulam, Robert F. and Richard A. Smith. Advances in Information Processing in Organizations, Vol. 2. (Greenwich, CN.: JAI Press, 1985), pp. 21-58.

George, Barbara C., Kathleen A. Lacey and Jutta Birmele. "On the Threshold of the Adoption of Global Antibribery Legislation: A Critical Analysis of Current Domestic and International Efforts Toward the Reduction of Corruption." Vanderbilt Journal of Transnational Law (January, 1999) Vol. 32, No. 1, pp. 1-48.

Georgetown University. "Argentina Political Parties." Political Database of the Americas. <http://www.georgetown.edu/pdba/Parties/Resumen/Argentina/desc.html> (December 2003.)

Georgetown University. "Ecuador Political Parties." Political Database of the Americas. <http://www.georgetown.edu/pdba/Parties/Resumen/Ecuador/desc.html> (January 2002.)

Gerlach, Allen. Indians, Oil and Politics. A Recent History of Ecuador. (Wilmington, DE: Scholarly Resources, 2003.)

Goldbarg, Andrea. "The Foreign Corrupt Practices Act and Structural Corruption." In: Boston University International Law Journal (Fall 2000) Vol. 18 No. 273, pp. 273-289.

Goldfarb, Danielle. "Who gets CIDA Grants? Recipient Corruption and the Effectiveness of Development Aid." Backgrounder. C.D. Howe Institute. (November 2001.)

González, Andrés. "Preventing and Combating the International Flow of Illicit Funds within the International Business and Trade Regime. A Background Guide." The National Model United Nations Conference. (October, 2002.)

Graber, Doris, Denis McQuail and Pippa Norris (eds.) The Politics of News - The News of Politics. (Washington, D.C.: Congressional Quarterly Press, 1998.)

Gradstein, Mark. "Rent Seeking and the Provision of Public Goods." The Economic Journal (September 1993) Vol. 103, No. 420, pp. 1236-1243.

Gray, Cheryl and Daniel Kaufmann. "Corruption and Development." Finance & Development (1998), pp. 7-10.

Gupta, Akhil. Blurred Boundaries: The Discourse of Corruption, the Culture of Politics and the Imagined State." American Ethnologist (May 1995), Vol. 22, No. 2, pp. 375-402.

Gupta, Sanjeev, Hamid Davoodi and Rosa Alonso-Terme. "Does Corruption Affect Income Inequality and Poverty?" Working Paper of the International Monetary Fund WP/98/76 (May, 1998.)

Hall, David and Steve Davies. "Corruption and Whistle-Blowing – A Background Note." Paper prepared for the OECD Trade Union Advisory Committee. (London: Public Services International Research Unit, December 1999.)

Handelman, John. "Introduction: The Idea of Bureaucratic Organization." Social Analysis (December 1981), Vol. 9.

Hartle, D.G. "The Theory of 'Rent Seeking': Some Reflections." The Canadian Journal of Economics. (1983) Vol. 16, No. 4, pp. 539-554.

Hartnagel, Timothy F. "The Perception and Fear of Crime: Implications for Neighborhood Cohesion, Social Activity, and Community Affect." Social Forces (September 1979) Vol. 58, No. 1, pp. 176-193.

Hedge, David M., Michael J. Sticchitano and Patricia Metz. "The Principal-Agent Model and Regulatory Federalism." The Western Political Quarterly (December 1991) Vol. 44, No. 4, pp. 1055-1080.

Heidenheimer, Arnold and Michael Johnston (eds.) Political Corruption. Concepts and Contexts. Third Edition. (New Brunswick, New Jersey: 2002.)

Heidenheimer, Arnold, Michael Johnston, and Victor LeVine (eds.) Political Corruption – A Handbook. (New Brunswick and Oxford: Transaction, 1989.)

Heidenheimer, Arnold. Political Corruption: Readings in Comparative Analysis. (New York: Holt, 1970.)

Held, David, Anthony McGrew, David Goldblatt and Jonathan Perraton. Global Transformations. Politics, Economics and Culture. (Cambridge, UK: Polity Press, 1999.)

Herman, Edward S. "The Media's Role un U.S. Foreign Politics." Journal of International Affairs. (1993) Vol. 47, No. 1, pp. 23-43.

Hewitt de Alcántara, Cynthia. "Structural Adjustment in a Changing World." Briefing Paper No. 4, World Summit for Social Development. (Geneva: United Nations Research Institute for Social Development, 1994.)

Holloway, Richard. "Corruption and Civil Society Institutions in Indonesia." Working Paper for the 10th International Anti-Corruption Conference. (Berlin: Transparency International, 2000.)

Hollway, Wend and Tony Jefferson. "The Risk Society in Age of Anxiety: Situating Fear of Crime." The British Journal of Sociology (June 1997) Vol. 48, No. 2, pp. 255-266.

Holsen, John. "Improving Public Sector Procurement in Latin America. A Synthesis Report on Eight Case Studies of Three Methods in Three Countries." Transparency International. (May, 2002.)

Hood, Christopher. The Art of the State. Culture, Rhetoric and Public Management. (Oxford: Oxford University Press, 1998.)

Huberts, Leo. "National Integrity Systems. Country Study Report. The Netherlands 2001." Presented for the Global Forum on Fighting Corruption and Safeguarding Integrity. (Prague, 2001.) Available online at <http://www.globalforum3.org/gf2/docs/Netherlands.pdf>

Huntington, Samuel. Political Order in Changing Societies. (New Haven and London: Yale University Press, 1970.)

Independent Press Councils. <www.presscouncils.org>

Independent Press Councils. World Press Councils 2003. <www.presscouncils.org>

International Federation of Journalists. Journalists and Media Staff Killed in 2003. An IFJ Report on Media Casualties in the Field of Journalism and Newsgathering. <www.ifj.org> (January 2004.)

International Journalists' Network. "Codes of Ethics" <www.ijnet.org> International Center of Journalists.

International Public Relations Association. "Unethical Media Practices Revealed by IPRA Report." <www.ipra.org/campaing/icmt/docs/press2.htm> (14.06.2002.)

Johnson, Roberta Ann. Whistleblowing: When it works – and why. (Boulder: Lynne Rienner Publishers, 2002.

Johnson, Roberta Ann and Michael E. Kraft. "Bureaucratic Whistleblowing and Policy Change." The Western Political Quarterly. Vol. 43, No. 4 (December 1990), pp. 849-874.

Johnston, Michael. "Measuring the New Corruption Rankings: Implications for Analysis and Reform." In: Heidenheimer and Johnston (eds.) Political Corruption, pp. 865-884.

Johnston, Michael. "The Political Consequences of Corruption: A Reassessment." Comparative Politics (July 1986), Vol. 18, Issue 4, pp. 459-477.

Johnston, Michael. "The Political Costs of Corruption." Paper presented at the First Latin American Conference on the Fight against Bureaucratic Corruption. (Santa Fe de Bogota: November, 1993.)

Johnston, Michael. "Unpredictable Rules, Dishonest Competition, and Corruption: Costs for Development and Good Governance." Paper submitted for the Conference on Combating Corruption in Asian and Pacific Economies. (29. September, 1999.)

Jokish, Brad and Jason Pribilsky. "The Panic to Leave: Economic Crisis and the 'New Emigration' from Ecuador." International Migration (2002) Vol. 40 No. 4, pp. 75-101.

Kamensky, John .M. "The Role of the 'Reinventing Government' Movement in Federal Management Reform." Public Administration Review (May/June 1996), Vol. 56, No. 3, pp. 247-255.

Kaufmann, Daniel and Shang Jin Wie. "Does ‚Grease Money' Speed Up the Wheels of Commerce?" IMF Working Paper 00/64. (Washington DC: International Monetary Fund, 2000.)

Kaufmann, Daniel and Paul Siegelbaum. "Privatization and Corruption in Transition Economies" Journal of International Affairs (1996), Vol. 50, No. 2, pp. 419-58.

Kebschull, Harvey G. "Political Corruption: Making it the 'Significant Other' in Political Studies." PS: Political Science and Politics. (December 1992), Vol. 25, Issue 4, pp. 705-709.

Key, V.O. Southern Politics in State and Nation. (New York: Vintage Books, 1949.)

Klitgaard, Robert. "International Cooperation Against Corruption." In: Finance and Development. (March 1998), pp. 3-6.

Klitgaard, Robert. Controlling Corruption. (Berkeley: University of California Press, 1988.)

Knutsen, Torbjørn L. A History of International Relations Theory. 2nd Edition, (Manchester, University of Manchester Press, 1997.)

Krasner, Stephen. "Regimes and the Limits of Realism: Regimes as Autonomous Variables." International Organization (1982), Vol. 36, pp. 497-510.

Krasner, Stephen. "Structural Causes and Regime Consequences: Regimes as Intervening Variables." International Organization (1982), Vol. 36, pp. 185-205.

Kratochwil, Friedrich. Rules, Norms and Decisions. (Cambridge: Cambridge University Press, 1989.)

Krueger, Anne O. "The Political Economy of the Rent-Seeking Society." The American Economic Review (June, 1974) Vol. 64, No. 3, pp. 291-303.

Kruse, Tom. "The IMF and the Bolivian Crisis." Economic Justice News Online (November 2003) Vol. 6, No. 3. < http://www.50years.org> (30.01.2004.)

Lapid, Yosef. "The Third Debate: On the Prospects of International Theory in a Post-Positivist Era." International Studies Quarterly (1989), Vol. 33, pp. 235-254.

Larbi, George A. "The New Public Management Approach and Crisis States" Occasional Paper No. 112. (Geneva: United Nations Research Institute for Social Development, September 1999.)

Latin American Centre for Development Administration (CLAD.) A New Public Management for Latin America. (October 1998.) Available online at < http://www.clad.org.ve/> (13.11.2003.)

Lambsdorff, Johann Graf. "Framework Document 2003. Background Paper to the 2003 Corruption Perceptions Index." (Berlin: Transparency International and University of Passau, September 2003.)

Lasswel, Harold D. Politics: Who Gets What, When, How. (New York: Peter Smith, 1950. Reprinted version. Originally published by the McGraw-Hill Book Company, 1936.)

Lebow, Richard Ned. "The Long Peace, the End of the Cold War and the Failure of Realism." International Organization (Spring 1994), Vol. 48, pp. 249-277.

Ledeneva, Alena. Russia's Economy of Favours: Blat, Networking and Informal Exchange. (Cambridge, MA: Cambridge University Press, 1998.)

Lederman, Daniel. Crime in Argentina: A Preliminary Assessment. World Bank, 1999.

Leff, Nathaniel. "Economic Development Through Bureaucratic Corruption." American Behavioral Scientist. (November 1964), Vol. 8, No. 3, pp. 8-14.

Leftwich, Adrian. "Governance, Democracy and Development in the Third World." Third World Quarterly (1993), Vol. 14, No. 3, pp. 605-624.

Legro, Jeffrey. "Which Norms Matter?" International Organization (Winter 1997), Vol. 51, pp. 31-64.

Lévy, Phillipe. "Integrity Pact." Transpareny Switzerland. <http://www.transparency.ch>

Lijphart, Arend. "Comparative Politics and the Comparative Method." American Political Science Review. (September 1971) Vol. 65, No. 3, pp. 682-693.

Lipshutz, Ronnie. "From Place to Planet: Local Knowledge and Global Environmental Governance." Global Governance. (1997), Vol. 3, pp. 83-102.

Liska, Allen E. and Barbara D. Warner. "Functions of Crime: A Paradoxical Process." American Journal of Sociology. (May 1991) Vol. 96, No. 6, pp. 1441-1463.

Little, Walter and Eduardo Posada-Carbó. Political Corruption in Europe and Latin America. (London: Macmillan Press Ltd., 1996.)

Lopez, George A. and Michael Stohl (eds.) Liberalization and Redemocratization in Latin America. (New York: Greenwood Press, 1987.)

Lynch, John. Latin America Between Colony and Nation: Selected Essays (London: Palgrave Macmillan, 2001.)

Maingot, Anthony P. "Confronting Corruption in the Hemisphere: A Sociological Perspective." Journal of Interamerican Studies and World Affairs. Special Issue: Summit of the Americas – Issues to Consider. (Autumn, 1994), Vol. 36, No. 3, pp. 49-74.

Mauro, Paolo. "Corruption: Causes, Consequences, and Agenda for further Research." Finance & Development (1998), pp. 11-14.

Mauro, Paulo. "Corruption and Growth." The Quarterly Journal of Economics. (August 1995) Vol. 110, No. 3, pp. 681-712.

Mauro, Paulo. "Corruption and Growth." The Quarterly Journal of Economics. (August 1995) Vol. 110, No. 3, pp. 681-712.

Mauro, Paulo. "The Effects of Corruption on Growth, Investment, and Government Expenditure: A Cross-Country Analysis." In: Elliot. Corruption and the Global Economy, pp. 83-107.

Mauro, Paulo. "Why Worry About Corruption?" Economic Issues. No. 6 (Washington D.C.: International Monetary Fund, 1997.)

McChesney, Robert W. and Dan Schiller. "The Political Economy of International Communications. Foundations for the Emerging Global Debate about Media Ownership and Regulation." Technology, Business and Society Programme Paper 11. (Geneva: United Nations Research Institute for Social Development, October 2003.)

McCombs, Maxwell. "Building Consensus: The News Media' Agenda-Setting Role." Political Communication (1997) Vol. 14, pp. 433-444.

McCombs, Maxwell. Setting the Agenda. The News Media and Public Opinion. (Cambridge, UK: Polity Press, 2004.)

McCombs, Maxwell and Donald Shaw. "The Agenda-Setting Function of Mass Media." Public Opinion Quarterly (1972) Vol. 36, pp. 176-187.

McQuail, Denis. Mass Communication Theory. (London: Sage Publications, 1994.)

Mill, John Stuart. A System of Logic. (London: Spottiswoode, Ballantyne & Co. Ltd. Reprinted Version, 1967.)

Minogue, Martin. "Getting the Ideas Right: Public Management, Corruption and Development." Paper presented at the Workshop: "New Public Management: Challenges for Improved Accountability and Corruption Control. World Bank Annual European Conference on Development Economics (Oslo, June 2002.) Available online at <http://www.worldbank.org>

Minogue, Martin, Charles Polidano and David Hulme (eds.) Beyond the New Public Management. Changing Ideas and Practices in Governance. (Cheltenham: Edward Elgar Publishing, 1998.)

Mittelman, James H. and Robert Johnston. "The Globalization of Organized Crime, the Courtesan State, and the Corruption of Civil Society." Global Governance (1999), vol. 5, pp. 103-126.

Moody-Stuart, George. "Grand Corruption in Third World Development" Transparency International (1994.)

Moody-Stuart, George. Grand Corruption. How Business Bribes Damages Developing Countries. (Oxford: WorldView Publications, 1997.)

Moravscsik, Andrew "Taking Preferences Seriously: A Liberal Theory of International Politics." International Organization, (Autumn 1997), Vol. 51, pp. 513-554.

Morris-Cotterill, Nigel. "Money Laundering." Foreign Policy (May/June 2001) Issue 124, pp. 16-22.

Morris, Stephen. "Corruption and the Mexican political system: continuity and change." Third World Quarterly (1999) Vol. 20, No. 3, pp. 623-643.

Muñoz, Heraldo and Joseph Tulchin (eds.) Latin American Nations in World Politics. (Boulder: Westview Press, 1996.)

Murphy, Kevin M., Andrei Shleifer and Robert W. Vishny. "The Allocation of Talent: Implications for Growth." The Quarterly Journal of Economics. (May, 1991) Vol. 106, No. 2, pp. 503-530.

Naim, Moises and Joseph Tulchin (eds.) Competition Policy, Deregulation and Modernization in Latin America. (Boulder: Lynne Rienner Publishers, 1999.)

Nas, Tevfik F., Albert C. Price and Charles T. Weber. "A Policy-Oriented Theory of Corruption." The American Political Science Review (March 1986), Vol. 80, No. 1, pp. 107-119.

Netzwerk Recherche, Transparency International and Bund der Steuerzahler (eds.) Korruption: Schatten der demokratischen Gesellschaft. Fakten, Trends, Gegenstrategien. (Kornberg im Taunus, March 2002.)

Nickson, Andrew. "Transferencia de políticas y reforma en la gestión del sector público en América Latina: el caso del New Public Management." Reforma y Democracia (October 2002) No. 24, pp. 1-15.

Niskanen, William A. "Bureaucrats and Politicians." The Journal of Law and Economics (1975) Vol. 18, pp. 617-643.

Nye Joseph. "Corruption and Political Development: A Cost-Benefit Analysis." American Political Science Review (June 1967), Vol. LXI, No.2, pp. 417-427.

Ofosu-Amaah W. Paatii, Raj Soopramanien and Kishor Uprety. Combating Corruption. A Comparative Review of Selected Legal Aspects of State Practice and Major International Initiatives. (Washington, D.C.: The World Bank, 1999.)

Organization of American States (OAS.) Secretariat for Legal Affairs: Technical Secretariat for Legal Cooperation Mechanisms. Follow-Up Mechanism for the Implementation of the Inter-American Convention Against Corruption. Argentina. <www. www.oas.org/juridico/spanish/mec_avance_argV.pdf>)

Organization of American States (OAS.) Secretariat for Legal Affairs: Technical Secretariat for Legal Cooperation Mechanisms. Follow-Up Mechanism for the Implementation of the Inter-American Convention Against Corruption. Ecuador. <www. www.oas.org/juridico/spanish/mec_avance_ecuV.pdf>)

Organization of American States (OAS.) Secretariat for Legal Affairs: Technical Secretariat for Legal Cooperation Mechanisms. "Inter-American Convention Against Corruption." <http://www.oas.org/juridico/english/Sigs/b-58.html>

Organization of American States (OAS.) Secretariat for Legal Affairs: Technical Secretariat for Legal Cooperation Mechanisms. "Inter-American Convention Against Corruption." <http://www.oas.org/juridico/english/Treaties/b-58.html>

Organization for Economic and Cooperation and Development (OECD.) Argentina. Review of Implementation of the Convention and 1997 Recommendation. <www.oecd.org/dataoecd/31/50/2078382.pdf>

Organization for Economic and Cooperation and Development (OECD.) Behind the Corporate Veil. Using Corporate Entities for Illicit Purposes. (Paris: OECD Publications, 2001.)

Organization for Economic Cooperation and Development (OECD.) "Building Public Trust: Ethics and Measures in OECD Countries." OECD Public Management Policy Brief. (September 2000.)

Organization for Economic and Cooperation and Development (OECD.) Fighting Corruption. What Role for Civil Society? The Experience of the OECD. (Paris: OECD Publications, 2003.)

Organization for Economic Cooperation and Development (OECD.) "Government of the Future." OECD Public Management Policy Brief. (June 2001.)

Organization for Economic and Cooperation and Development (OECD.) Managing Conflict of Interest in the Public Service: OECD Guidelines and Country Experiences. (Paris: OECD Publications, 2004.)

Organization for Economic Cooperation and Development (OECD.) "Steps taken and planned future actions by participating countries to ratify and implement the Convention on Combating Bribery of Foreign Public Officials in International Business Transactions." OECD. <http://www.oecd.org/dataoecd/50/33/1827022.pdf> (17.12.2003.)

Organization for Economic and Cooperation and Development (OECD.) Trust in Government: Ethics Measures in OECD Countries. (Paris: OECD Publications, 2000.)

Ospina, Rosa Inés and Corporación Transparecia por Colombia. "National Integrity Systems. Country Study Report. Colombia 2001." Presented for the Global Forum on Fighting Corruption and Safeguarding Integrity. (Prague, 2001.) Available online at <http://www.globalforum3.org/gf2/docs/Colombia.pdf>

Palan, Ronen. "Tax Havens and the Commercialization of State Sovereignty." International Organization (Winter 2002), Vol. 56, no. 1, pp. 151-176.

Patterson, Thomas E. "Political Roles of the Journalist." In: Graber, McQuail and Norris (eds.) The Politics of News - The News of Politics, pp. 17-32.

Pauly, Louis. Who Elected the Bankers? Surveillance and Control in the World Economy. (Ithaca and London: Cornell University Press.)

Peters, John G. and Susan Welch. "Political Corruption in America: A Search for Definitions and Theory, or If Political Corruption Is in the Mainstream of American Politics Why Is it Not in he Mainstream of American Politics Research?" The American Political Science Review (September 1978), Vol. 72, Issue 3, pp. 974-984.

Perse, Elizabeth. Media Effects and Society. (Mahwah, NJ and London: Lawrence Erlbaum Associates, 2001)

Pharr, Susan J. "Public Trust and Corruption in Japan." In: Heidenheimer and Johnston (eds.) Political Corruption, pp. 835-859.

Pharr, Susan J. and Robert Putnam (eds.) Disaffected Countries: What's Troubling the Trilateral Countries? (Princeton: Princeton University Press, 2000.)

Poder Ciudadano. <http://www.poderciudadano.org.ar>

Poelchau, Daniel. Normativer Wandel im Internationalen System. Ein Erklärungsansatz für das zunehmende Engagement im Kampf gegen die Korruption. (Munich: Geschiwster-Scholl-Institut für Politische Wissenschaft, 2002.)

Pollit, Christopher and Geert Bouckaert. Public Management Reform. A Comparative Analysis. (Oxford: Oxford University Press, 2000.)

Pope, Jeremy and Transparency International. TI Source Book 2000 – Confronting Corruption: The Elements of a National Integrity System. (Berlin: Transparency International, 2000.)

Posadas, Alejandro. "Combating Corruption under International Law." Duke Journal of Comparative and International Law. (Spring 2000), Vol. 10, No. 2, pp. 345-414.

Posner, Paul W. Popular Representation and Political Dissatisfaction in Chile's New Democracy. Journal of Interamerican Studies and World Affairs (Spring 1999) Vol. 41, No. 1, pp. 67-96.

Pritchard, David (ed.) Holding the Media Accountable: Citizens, Ethics and the Law. (Bloomington: Indiana University Press, 2000.)

Pryce, William T. Congressional Testimony. Inter-American Convention Against Corruption. Council of the Americas. <www.americas-society.org> (02.05.2000)

Quirk, Peter J. "Money Laundering: Muddying the Macroeconomy." In: Finance and Development (1997) Vol. 34 No. 1, pp. 7-9.

Risse-Kappen, Thomas (ed.) Bringing Transnational Relations Back In. Non-State Actors and International Institutions. (Cambridge, UK: Cambridge University Press, 1995.)

Robertson, Geoffrey. People Against the Press: An Enquiry into the Press Council. (London: Quartet Books, 1983.)

Robinson, Piers. "The CNN effect: can the news media drive foreign policy?" Review of International Studies (1999), Vol. 25, pp. 301-309.

Rose-Ackerman, Susan. Corruption and Government. Causes, Consequences, and Reform. (Cambridge: Cambridge University Press, 1999.)

Rose-Ackerman, Susan. Corruption: A study of political economy. (New York: Academic Press, 1978.)

Rose-Ackerman, Susan. "The Political Economy of Corruption." In: Elliot. Corruption and the Global Economy, p. 45.

Rousseu, Jean-Jacques and Donald A. Cress (Translator.) Discourse on the Origin of Inequality. (Indianapolis: Hackett Pub. Co, 1992); and *Ibid.* and Maurice Cranston (Translator.) The Social Contract (New York: Penguin, June 1968.)

Russet, Bruce M. International Regions and the International System. A Study in Political Ecology. (Chicago: Rand McNally & Company, 1969)

Schedler, Andreas, Larry Diamond and Marc Plattner (eds.) The Self-Retaining State – Power and Accountability in New Democracies. (Boulder, London: Lynne Rienner Publishers, 1999.)

Schleifer, Andrei and Robert W. Vishny. "Politicians and Firms." The Quarterly Journal of Economics. (November 1994), Vol. 109, No. 4, pp. 995-1025.

Scholte, Jan Aart. Globalization. A Critical Introduction. (Basingstoke/New York: Palgrave, 2000.)

Scott, David. "Money Laundering and International Efforts to Fight It." Public Policy for the Private Sector. Note 48 (May 1995.) Available online at: <http://rru.worldbank.org/viewpoint/HTMLNotes/48/48scott.pdf>

Scott, James C. Comparative Political Corruption. (Englewood Cliffs, NJ: Prentice Hall, 1972.)

Seligson, Mitchell A. "The Impact of Corruption on Regime Legitimacy: A comparative Study of Four Latin American Countries." The Journal of Politics. (May 2002), Vol. 64, No. 2, pp. 408-433.

Shapiro, Carlo and Joseph Stiglitz. "Equilibrium unemployment as a worker-discipline device." American Economic Review (1984), Vol 74 ,pp. 433-444.

Shaw, Martin. Global Society and International Relations. Sociological Concepts and Political Perspectives. (Cambridge, UK: Polity Press, 1995.)

Shleifer, Andrei and Robert W. Vishny. "Corruption." The Quarterly Journal of Economics. (August 1993), Vol. 108, No. 3, pp. 599-617.

Sissener, Tone Kristin. "Anthropological perspectives on corruption." Chr. Michelsen Institute Working Paper (2001.)

Stapenhurst, Rick. "The Media's Role in Curbing Corruption." The World Bank Institute (2000.)

Stokke, Olav (ed.) Aid and Political Conditionality. (London: Frank Cass Publishers, 1995.)

Strömberg, David. "Mass media and public policy." European Economic Review (2001) Vol. 45, pp. 652-663.

Svensson, Jakob. "Foreign Aid and Rent-Seeking." Journal of International Economics (2000) Vol 51, pp. 437-461.

Swartz, Mimi and Sherron Watkins. Power Failure: The Inside Story of the Collapse of Enron. (New York: Double Day, 2003.)

Tanzi, Vito and Hamid Davoodi. "Corruption, Public Investment and Growth." Working Paper of the International Monetary Fund WP/97/139 (October, 1997.)

Tanzi, Vito and Hamid R. Davoodi. "Corruption, Growth and Public Finances." IMF Working Paper 00/182 (2000.)

Tanzi, Vito. "Corruption Around the World. Causes, Consequences, Scope and Cures." IMF Staff Papers. (December 1998) Vol. 45, No. 4, pp. 559-594.

Tanzi, Vito. Policies, Institutions and the Dark Side of Economics. (Cheltenham, UK: Edward Elgar Publisching, 2000), p. 145 ff.

Tavares, José. "Does Foreign Aid Corrupt?" Economic Letters (2003) No. (79), pp. 99-106.

Tedesco, Laura. Democracy in Argentina. Hope and Disillusion. (London: Frank Cass, 1999.)

Teggemann, Stefanie. "Corruption, Poverty and Inequality." The World Bank. <www.worldbank.org> (26.03.2002)

Teichman, Judith A. "Private sector power and market reform: exploring the domestic origins of Argentina's meltdown and Mexico's policy failures." Third World Quarterly (2002) Vol. 23, No. 3, pp. 491-512.

Teichman, Judith A. The Politics of Freeing Markets in Latin America. Chile, Argentina and Mexico. (Chapel Hill and London: The University of North Carolina Press, 2001.)

Theobald, Robin. "So what is really the problem about corruption?" Third World Quarterly (1999) Vol. 20, No. 3, pp. 491-502.

Thompson, Victor A. Bureaucracy and Innovation. (Alabama: University of Alabama Press, 1969.)

Thompson, Victor A. Modern Organization. A General Theory. (New York: Alfred A. Knopf, 1969.)

Trang Duc V. (ed.) Corruption and Democracy. Political Institutions, Processes and Corruption in Transition States in East-Central Europe and in the former Soviet Union. (Budapest: Institute for Constitutional & Legislative Policy, 1994.)

Transparency International. Bribe Payers Index 2002 – Tables and FAQs. <http://www.transparency.org/ cpi/2002/bpi_faq.en.html>

Transparency International. Corruption Perceptions Index. Press Release. (07.10.2003.)

Transparency International. Global Corruption Report 2001. (Berlin: Transparency International, 2001.)

Transparency International. Global Corruption Report 2003. (Berlin: Transparency International, 2003.)

Transparency International. The Corruption Fighter's Tool Kit. Civil society experiences and emerging strategies. (Berlin: Transparency International, 2002.)

Transparency International. The Integrity Pact. The Concept, the Model and Present Applications. A Status Report. (Berlin, December 2002.)

Transparency International. "TI outlines anti-corruption priorities for Georgian President Mikhail Saakashvili." Press Release. <www.transparency.ge/extra/1075816001.php> (29.01.2004.)

Transparency International. "1995 TI Corruption Index. Explanatory Note." (Berlin: Transparency International and the University of Göttingen, 1995.)#

Transparency International Quarterly Newsletter. (December, 2003.)

Tulchin, Joseph and Allison Garland (eds.) Social Development in Latin America. The Politics of Reform. (Boulder: Lynne Rienner Publishers, 2000.)

Tulchin, Joseph and Augusto Varas (eds.) From Dictatroship to Democracy. Rebuilding Political Consensus in Chile. (Boulder & London: Lynne Rienner Publishers, 1991.)

Tulchin, Joseph S. and Ralph H. Espach. Combating Corruption in Latin America. (Washington, D.C.: The Woodrow Wilson Center Press, 2002.)

United Nations. Action against corruption and bribery in international commercial transactions. Resolution A/RES/53/176, (25 January 1999.)

United Nations. Action against corruption. Resolution A/RES/54/128, (28 January 2000.)

United Nations. An effective international legal instrument against corruption. Resolution A/RES/55/61, (22 January 2001.)

United Nations. Draft United Nations Convention against Transnational Organized Crime and the draft protocol thereto. Resolution A/RES/54/126, (20 January 2000.)

United Nations. High-level Political Signing Conference for the United Nations Convention against Transnational Crime. Resolution A/RES/54/129, (28 January 2000.)

United Nations. Prevention of corrupt practices and illegal transfer of funds. Resolution A/RES/54/205, (27 January 2000.)

United Nations. Transnational organized crime. Resolution A/RES/53/111, (20 January 1999.)

United Nations. "Countries gather to sign on to tough new treaty against corruption, beginning 9 December in Mérida, Mexico." Press Release (8.12. 2003.)

United Nations Educational and Scientific Organization (UNESCO) (eds.) Media and democracy in Latin America and the Caribbean. (Paris: UNESCO Publications, 1996.)

United Nations Development Programme (UNDP). Corruption and Governance. Discussion Paper 3. New York, 1997.

United Nations Development Programme (UNDP). "Public Sector Downsizing. Early Retirement Schemes and Voluntary Severance Pay." (Beirut: 1999.)

United Nations Office on Drugs and Crime (UNODC). The Global Programme Against Corruption. Anti-Corruption Toolkit. (New York: United Nations, 2000.)

United Nations Office on Drugs and Crime. United Nations Convention Against Corruption. <www.unodc.org/pdf/crime/convention_corruption/signing/Convention-e.pdf>

United Nations Office on Drugs and Crime. "United Nations Convention Against Corruption." <http://www.unodc.org/unodc/crime_signatures_corruption.html>

United Nations Office for Drug Control and Crime Prevention (UNODCCP.) Global Dynamics of Corruption. The Role of the United Nations Helping Member States Build Integrity to Curb Corruption. (Vienna: October 2002)

United Nations Office for Drug Control and Crime Prevention (UNODCCP.) United Nations Manual on Anti-Corruption Policy (Draft Version.) (Vienna: June 2001.)

United States Department of Justice Fraud Section, Criminal Division (DOJ.) "Foreign Corrupt Practices Act. Antibribery Provisions." (Washington D.C., 2002.)

Utriainen, Terttu. "The Role of the Media in Preventing Corruption." Working Paper for the 8th International Anti-Corruption Conference. (Lima: Transparency International, 1998.)

Van Rijckeghem, Caroline and Beatrice Weder. "Corruption and the Rate of Temptation: Do Low Wages in the Civil Service Cause Corruption?" Working Paper of the International Monetary Fund WP/97/73 (1997.)

Vargas Carreño, Edmundo. "The Inter-American Convention Against Corruption." Working Paper for the Conference on Transparency and Development in Latin America and the Caribbean. (Washington, D.C., 2000.)

Vergara, Pilar. "In Pursuit of 'Growth with Equity': The Limits of Chile's Free-Market Social Reforms." The North American Congress on Latin America (NACLA) Report on the Americas (May/June 1996).

Vogl, Frank. "The Media and Corruption." Working Paper for the 9th International Anti-Corruption Conference. (Durban: Transparency International, 1998.)

Vogl, Frank. "The Supply Side of Global Bribery." In: New Perspectives on Combating Corruption. (Kuala Lumpur: Transparency International and the World Bank, 1998), pp. 55-64.

Waisbord, Sylvio. Watchdog Journalism in South America. News, Accountability, and Democracy. (New York: Columbia University Press, 2000.)

Weber, Max, Mills C.Wright (ed.) Gerth Hand (Translator.) Essays in Sociology. (Oxford: Oxford University Press, 1958.)

Weder, Beatrice. "Institutions, Corruption and Development and their Ramifications for International Cooperation."In: van Ginkel, Hans et. al. (eds.) Human Development and the Environment – UNU Millennium Series. (Tokyo: United Nations University Press, 2002.)

Wei, Shang-Jin. "Corruption in Economic Development: Beneficial Grease, Minor Annoyance, or Major Obstacle?" Discussion Paper for the Workshop on Integrity in Governance in Asia. (Bangkok, June 19-July 1, 1998.)

Weiss, Wendy. "Debt and Devaluation: The Burden on Ecuador's Popular Class." Latin American Perspectives (July 1997) Vol. 24, No. 4, pp. 9-33.

Weyland, Kurt. "Economic Policy in Chile's New Democracy." Journal of Interamerican Studies and World Affairs (Fall 1999) Vol. 41, No. 3, pp. 67-96.

Wilson, James Q. Bureaucracy: What Government Agencies Do and Why They Do It. (New York: Basic Books, 1989)

Wolf, Martin. "Will the Nation State Survive Globalization?" Foreign Affairs, (January/February 2001) Vol. 80 No. 1, pp. 178-191.

World Bank. Assessing Aid. What Works, What Doesn't and Why. (New York: Oxford University Press, 1998.)

World Bank. Country Brief – Argentina. <http://www.worldbank.org> Washington, D.C. 2000.

World Bank. Country Brief – Chile. <http://www.worldbank.org> Washington, D.C. 2000.

World Bank. Helping Countries Combat Corruption. Progress at the World Bank Since 1997. (Washington, D.C.: Operational Core Services. Poverty Reduction and Economic Management Network, June 2000.)

World Bank. Guidelines: Procurement under IBRD Loans and IDA Credits. (Washington, D.C. : 1999.)

World Bank. "Preventing Corruption in World Bank Projects." <http://www1.worldbank.org/publicsector/anticorrupt/preventing.htm>

World Bank. "Regaining Fiscal Sustainability and Enhancing Effectiveness in Croatia: A Public Expenditure and Institutional Review." (Washington, D.C.: 2002.)

World Bank. Reforming Public Institutions and Strengthening Governance. A World Bank Survey. (Washington, D.C.: Public Sector Group. Poverty Reduction and Economic Management Network, November 2000.)

World Bank. "The World Bank and Civil Society in the Latin American and Caribbean Region." <www.worldbank.org>

Young, Oran. International Cooperation: Building Regimes for Natural Resources and the Environment (Cornell Studies in Political Economy.) (Ithaca: Cornell University Press, 1989.)

bei. Darüber hinaus wird durch eine konstruktiv-spekulative Argumentation versucht, die z. Z. wenig innovative Theorie- und Methodendiskussion in der Politikwissenschaft anzuregen.
Bd. 7, 2003, 224 S., 25,90 €, br., ISBN 3-8258-6091-4

Politik: Forschung und Wissenschaft

Wolfgang Gieler
Handbuch der Ausländer- und Zuwanderungspolitik
Von Afghanistan bis Zypern
In der Literatur zur Ausländer- und Zuwanderungspolitik fehlt ein Handbuch, dass einen schnellen und kompakten Überblick dieses Politikbereichs ermöglicht. Das vorliegende Handbuch bemüht sich diese wissenschaftliche Lücke zu schließen. Thematisiert werden die Ausländer- und Zuwanderungspolitik weltweiter Staaten von Afghanistan bis Zypern. Zentrale Fragestellung ist dabei der Umgang mit Fremden, das heißt mit Nicht-Inländern im jeweiligen Staat. Hierbei werden insbesondere politische, soziale, rechtliche, wirtschaftliche und kulturelle Aspekte mitberücksichtigt. Um eine Kompatibilität der Beiträge herzustellen beinhaltet jeder Beitrag darüber hinaus eine Zusammenstellung der historischen Grunddaten und eine Tabelle zur jeweiligen Anzahl der im Staat lebenden Ausländer. Die vorgelegte Publikation versteht sich als ein grundlegendes Nachschlagewerk. Neben dem universitären Bereich richtet es sich besonders an die gesellschaftspolitisch interessierte Öffentlichkeit und den auf sozialwissenschaftlichen Kenntnissen angewiesenen Personen in Politik, Verwaltung, Medien, Bildungseinrichtungen und Migranten-Organisationen.
Bd. 6, 2003, 768 S., 98,90 €, gb., ISBN 3-8258-6444-8

Harald Barrios; Martin Beck;
Andreas Boeckh; Klaus Segbers (Eds)
Resistance to Globalization
Political Struggle and Cultural Resilience in the Middle East, Russia, and Latin America
This volume is an important contribution to the empirical research on what globalization means in different world regions. "Resistance" here has a double meaning: It can signify active, intentional resistance to tendencies which are rejected on political or moral grounds by presenting alternative discourses and concepts founded in specific cultural and national traditions. It can also mean resilience with regard to globalization pressures in the sense that traditional patterns of development and politics are resistant to change. The book shows the that the local, sub-national, national, and regional patterns of politics and development coexist with globalized structures without yielding very much ground and in ways which may turn out to be a serious barrier to further globalization. Case studies presented focus on Venezuela, Brazil, the Middle East, Iran, and Russia.
Bd. 7, 2003, 184 S., 20,90 €, br., ISBN 3-8258-6749-8

Michael Neu; Wolfgang Gieler;
Jürgen Bellers (Hg.)
Handbuch der Außenwirtschaftspolitiken: Staaten und Organisationen
Afrika, Amerika, Asien, Europa, Ozeanien
Das vorliegende Handbuch ist die erste umfassende Darstellung der Außenwirtschaftspolitiken der Staaten dieser Welt. Die klar strukturierten Beiträge sind in verständlicher Sprache verfasst. Sie geben Wissenschaftlern, Studierenden und sonstigen interessierten Personen des öffentlichen und privaten Lebens einen fundierten und soliden Überblick über die nationalen Wirtschaftsstrukturen und Außenwirtschaftsbeziehungen der einzelnen Länder. Darüber hinaus werden in diesem Zusammenhang relevante internationale Organisationen behandelt.
Bd. 8 (2 Bde.), 2004, 1136 S., 149,90 €, br.,
ISBN 3-8258-6920-2

Ellen Bos; Antje Helmerich
Neue Bedrohung Terrorismus
Der 11. September 2001 und die Folgen. Unter Mitarbeit von Barry Adams und Harald Wilkoszewski
Die terroristischen Anschläge des 11. September 2001 haben die Weltöffentlichkeit erschüttert. Ihre weitreichenden Auswirkungen auf die Lebenswirklichkeit des Einzelnen, den Handlungsspielraum der Nationalstaaten und das internationale System stehen im Mittelpunkt des Sammelbandes. Er basiert auf einer Ringvorlesung, in der sich Wissenschaftler der Ludwig-Maximilians-Universität München aus den Fächern Amerikanistik, Jura, Geschichte, Politik-, Religions-, Kommunikations- und Wirtschaftswissenschaft mit den geistigen Hintergründen und den Konsequenzen des Terrorismus auseinandersetzten.
Bd. 9, 2003, 232 S., 19,90 €, br., ISBN 3-8258-7099-5

Heinz-Gerhard Justenhoven;
James Turner (Eds.)
Rethinking the State in the Age of Globalisation
Catholic Thought and Contemporary Political Theory
Since Jean Bodin and Thomas Hobbes, political theorists have depicted the state as "sovereign" because it holds preeminent authority over all the denizens belonging to its geographically defined

territory. From the Peace of Westphalia in 1648 until the beginning of World War I in 1914, the essential responsiblities ascribcd to the sovereign state were maintaining internal and external security and promoting domestic prosperity. This idea of "the state" in political theory is clearly inadequate to the realities of national governments and international relations at the beginning of the twenty-first century. During the twentieth century, the sovereign state, as a reality and an idea, has been variously challenged from without and within its borders. Where will the state head in the age of globalisation? Can Catholic polilical thinking contribute to an adequate concept of statehood and government? A group of German and American scholars were asked to explore specific ways in which the intellectual traditions of Catholicism might help our effort lo rethink the state. The debate is guided by the conviction that these intellectual resources will prove valuable to political theorists as they work to revise our understanding of the state.
Bd. 10, 2003, 240 S., 19,90 €, br., ISBN 3-8258-7249-1

Gesine Foljanty-Jost (ed.)
Japan in the 1990s
Crisis as an impetus for change
The 1990s in Japan have been a period of far-reaching changes in Japanese society, which have not come to an end yet. These developments demand a reexamination of our accumulated knowledge of Japan. This volume looks at them from different perspectives; the contributions deal with issues from the fields of economy, education, political and social science. The volume is a collection of papers from the 2002 meeting of the German Association of Social Scientific Research of Japan (VSJF) at Halle-Wittenberg University.
Bd. 11, 2004, 224 S., 24,90 €, br., ISBN 3-8258-7346-3

Wolfgang Gieler; Dietmar Fricke (Hg.)
Handbuch Europäischer Migrationspolitiken
Die EU-Länder und die Beitrittskandidaten
Migrationspolitik ist ein zentrales Thema in der politischen Diskussion. Es ist zu erwarten, dass sowohl die Diskussion um eine restriktivere Migrationspolitik als auch die sich dort abbildenden Befürchtungen und Stereotype in der Bevölkerung mit der EU-Osterweiterung neue Nahrung erhalten. Andererseits ist das allgemeine Wissen über die jeweilige Migrationspolitik der EU insgesamt und noch mehr die der einzelnen EU-Länder als auch die der Beitrittskandidaten sehr gering. Das vorliegende Handbuch möchte hier ein Lücke schließen und zur Versachlichung der Diskussion beitragen. Die Publikation versteht sich als ein grundlegendes Nachschlagewerk, das eine schnelle und differenzierte Orientierungshilfe in dem komplexen Feld der europäischen Migrationspolitiken ermöglichen soll.
Bd. 12, 2004, 320 S., 29,90 €, gb., ISBN 3-8258-7509-1

Patrick van Schie; Gerrit Voerman (Hg.)
The dividing line between success and failure
A comparison of liberalism in the Netherlands and Germany in the 19th and 20th centuries
Since the Second World War, liberalism has been much stronger in the Netherlands than in Germany. The present volume compares the development of liberalism in both countries – which took place under quite different conditions and without much mutual interaction – from the early beginnings in the nineteenth century down to the twenty-first century. It tries to explain why Dutch liberals are nowadays doing better than their German counterparts.
Bd. 13, 2006, 168 S., 19,90 €, br., ISBN 3-8258-7668-3

Stephan Bierling; Karlfriedrich Herb; Jerzy Maćków; Martin Sebaldt
Politischen Wandel denken
Herausforderungen der Demokratie in europäischer und globaler Perspektive. Antrittsvorlesung Institut für Politikwissenschaft der Universität Regensburg 26./27. Januar 2004
Dass Wandel mit Fortschritt einhergeht, ist ein moderner Gedanke. Er hat heute seine Selbstverständlichkeit verloren. Den vielfältigen Fragen des politischen Wandels geht die gemeinsame Antrittsvorlesung nach, mit der sich die Professoren des Regensburger Instituts für Politikwissenschaft am 26. und 27. Januar 2004 präsentierten. Politischen Wandel denken. Herausforderungen der Demokratie in europäischer und globaler Perspektive – so lautete die gemeinsame Fragestellung. In ihrer Vielfalt und Eigenheit spannen die Vorträge den Bogen von der Reflexion auf das Verhältnis von Wandel und Fortschritt bis hin zu den Herausforderungen, denen die Demokratie heute begegnet.
Bd. 14, 2004, 72 S., 9,90 €, br., ISBN 3-8258-7920-8

Lutz Roemheld (Hg.)
Erinnerung an P.-J. Proudhon
Zur Aktualität seines Denkens für die Zukunft der Sozialdemokratie
P.-J. Proudhon – „nur der Kleinbürger, der beständig zwischen dem Kapital und der Arbeit, zwischen der politischen Ökonomie und dem Kommunismus hin- und hergeworfen wird"? (K. Marx: Elend der Philosophie, 1847). Diese Diskriminierung hat wohl am meisten zur Verdrängung Proudhons aus dem kollektiven Gedächtnis von Sozialisten und

Sozialdemokraten beigetragen. Nach dem Scheitern des Sozialismus Marx-Engels'scher Provenienz kann ein Erinnern an Proudhons libertären Sozialismus Hinweise auf die Möglichkeit der Entwicklung einer „sozialpflichtigen Moderne" (Gerhard Senft) im 21. Jahrhundert geben.

Bd. 15, 2005, 296 S., 24,90 €, br., ISBN 3-8258-8292-6

Jürgen H. Wolff

Entwicklungshilfe: Ein hilfreiches Gewerbe?

Versuch einer Bilanz

Die Lebensbedingungen auf der Welt, insbesondere in den Entwick-lungsländern, sollen sich, so hört man es oft, laufend verschlechtern. Insbesondere Institutionen, die von und für die Entwicklungshilfe leben, vertreten diese These. Mit reichem Datenmaterial be-legt der Verfasser, daß fast überall auf der Welt die Lebenserwartung steigt, sich Bildungsstand und Ernährungslage verbessern, kurz, der Wohlstand zunimmt. Mit einer Ausnahme: Schwarzafrika. Wolff geht weiter, er warnt vor dem Trugschluß, dies sei auf Entwicklungshilfe zurückzuführen und erfolgreiche Entwicklungsprojekte seien mit erfolgreicher Entwicklung gleichzusetzen. Reformvorschläge für die Entwicklungshilfe schließen den Band ab.

Bd. 18, 2005, 320 S., 19,90 €, br., ISBN 3-8258-8162-8

Wolfgang Gieler (Hg.)

Internationale Wirtschaftsorganisationen

Entstehung – Struktur – Perspektiven. Ein Handbuch

Das „Handbuch Internationale Wirtschaftsorganisationen" informiert über die Außenwirtschaftspolitiken internationaler Organisationen. Zur besseren Handhabbarkeit verfügen die einzelnen Beiträge über einen vergleichbaren Aufbau – Gründungsgeschichte und Gründungsmotivation, vertragliche Grundlage und Struktur, integrationstheoretische Einordnung und Perspektiven sowie eine Auswahlbibliographie. Der Band wendet sich an einen breiten Benutzerkreis in Forschung und Lehre, in Politik, Verwaltung und Medien sowie an alle politisch Interessierten.

Bd. 19, 2005, 416 S., 24,90 €, br., ISBN 3-8258-8532-1

Michael Weigl (Hg.)

Folgenlose Nachbarschaft

Spuren der DDR-Außenpolitik in den deutsch-tschechischen Beziehungen

Als „moderne Diktatur" beanspruchte die SED ein Weltanschauungsmonopol, das sie jeder Zeit in der Gesellschaft durchzusetzen trachtete. Dass diese Bemühungen Spuren hinterlassen haben im vereinten Deutschland, ist unbestritten. Während ihnen allerdings bereits in zahlreichen Politikfeldern nachgegangen wurde, stellt die Frage nach über den 3. Oktober 1990 hinaus identifizierbaren Wirkungen Ost-Berliner Außenpolitik noch ein Forschungsdesiderat dar. Der Sammelband möchte vor diesem Hintergrund Impulse geben, indem er sich am Beispiel der deutsch-tschechischen Beziehungen auf „Spurensuche" begibt.

Bd. 20, 2006, 176 S., 19,90 €, br., ISBN 3-8258-8552-6

Christiane Lemke

Amerika-Bilder: US-Politik zwischen Moralisierung und Macht

Die transatlantischen Beziehungen zeichnen sich durch widersprüchliche Deutungsmuster aus. Einerseits gilt die US-amerikanische Gesellschaft als weltoffen und innovationsfreudig, andererseits erscheint sie aber auch als konservativ und traditionell. Die Spannungen zwischen Tradition und Moderne speisen das ambivalente Bild von „zwei Amerikas", welches den Blick von Europa auf die Vereinigten Staaten prägt. Basierend auf langjährigen Forschungsarbeiten und eingehenden Kenntnissen gesellschaftlicher und politischer Entwicklungen in den Vereinigten Staaten analysiert die Verfasserin, ausgehend von den Präsidentschaftswahlen 2004, längerfristige Veränderungen in der amerikanischen Politik. Sie zeigt die Widersprüche und Ungleichzeitigkeiten auf, die die amerikanische Politik in einer Zeit kennzeichnen, welche durch einen wachsenden Einfluss von moralischen Werte- und Orientierungsmustern in der Politik charakterisiert ist.

Bd. 21, 2005, 128 S., 14,90 €, br., ISBN 3-8258-8701-4

Reidar Visser

Basra, the Failed Gulf State

Separatism and Nationalism in Southern Iraq

Is Iraq "artificial", on the verge of disintegrating? All too often, the answers to this question ignore Iraq's own history. In fact, the literature on indigenous attempts at dismembering Iraq is surprisingly patchy, especially with regard to the oil-rich south. This book presents, for the first time, an actual case of southern Iraqi separatism: a daring bid to turn Basra into a pro-British mercantile mini-state. The study uncovers the dynamics and limits of southern separatism, casts new light on the victory of Iraqi nationalism in the south and discusses the challenges of post-2003 regionalism in a federal Iraq. *"From the abundance of recent publications on modern Iraq, Reidar Visser's work on the origins and development of twentieth-century separatism in the southern region of that country stands out. For anyone seriously interested in the current conflict in Iraq over the question of federalism versus centralism, this meticulously researched study provides a highly instructive historical perspective."* –

Werner Ende, professor emeritus of Islamic Studies at Albert-Ludwigs-Universität, Freiburg, Germany
Bd. 22, 2005, 256 S., 29,90 €, br., ISBN 3-8258-8799-5

Barbara Wasner
Alterssicherung in Europa: Institutionenwandel durch Europäisierung?
Europäisierung wird in der öffentlichen Diskussion häufig mit der „Fremdbestimmung aus Brüssel" gleichgesetzt. Und auch im sozialwissenschaftlichen Diskurs bleibt der Begriff unbestimmt und wenig eindeutig. In diesem Buch werden die verschiedenen Begriffsbedeutungen geordnet, zueinander in Beziehung gesetzt und so zu einem theoretischen Konzept ausgearbeitet, das auf die Wandlungen der Alterssicherungssysteme konzeptionell angewandt werden kann. Das Buch stellt eine umfassende Analyse der verschiedenen Alterssicherungssysteme der Mitgliedstaaten der EU und ihre Reaktionen auf die europäische „Herausforderung" dar.
Bd. 23, 2005, 376 S., 24,90 €, br., ISBN 3-8258-8855-x

Mario Petri; Ulrich Schnier; Jürgen Bellers (Hg.)
Handbuch der transitorischen Systeme, Diktaturen und autoritären Regime der Gegenwart
Gefestigte und intakte sowie gesellschaftlich akzeptierte und vor allem „funktionierende", demokratische Strukturen sind heutzutage keine Selbstverständlichkeit, schon gar nicht in globaler Perspektive. Auf dem steinigen Weg zu demokratischen Strukturen liefert das Handbuch der transitorischen Systeme, Diktaturen und autoritären Regime eine Bestandsaufnahme anhand einer Vielzahl ausgesuchter nationalstaatlicher Beispiele. Die strukturell ähnlich angelegten Beiträge skizzieren neben der Historie das gegenwärtige politische System und liefern einen Ausblick zu Chancen und Perspektiven des weiteren Demokratisierungsprozesses. Ergänzt werden die aktuellen Nationalstaatsbeispiele um Betrachtungen der „klassischen" totalitären, diktatorischen und autoritären Regime des deutschen Nationalsozialismus, des italienischen Faschismus, des spanischen Franquismus sowie des Austro-Faschismus.
Bd. 24, 2006, 584 S., 39,90 €, br., ISBN 3-8258-9070-8

Hartmut Elsenhans
Globalization Between A Convoy Model and An Underconsumptionist Threat
There are different types of globalization. Today's globalization is characterized by the worldwide disempowerment of labor. This is the result not of low real wages in backward countries but of devaluation-driven exports from relatively prosperous catch-up countries. An alternative form of globalization, the convoy model, is possible if the causes of devaluation-driven exports are eliminated. This does not call for a worldwide alignment of labor costs, but worldwide full employment policies. The latter require a strong state in labor-surplus economies of the underdeveloped South in addition to social and economic reforms in favor of the poor.
Bd. 25, 2006, 312 S., 29,90 €, br., ISBN 3-8258-9219-0

Elkhan Nuriyev
The South Caucasus at the Crossroads
Conflicts, Caspian Oil and Great Power Politics
Written by a highly respected expert in the field, the book addresses some of this little known region's most vital issues: territorial conflicts, oil and natural gas resources, geopolitical complexities and pipeline politics, as well as the successes and failures of democratic processes in the post-Soviet countries of Armenia, Azerbaijan, and Georgia. The future of these newly independent states, where Iran and Turkey, as well as Russia, the U.S. and the EU are vying for political and economic influence is still being determined, and it is more clear every day that events in the Caucasus and Caspian Sea region have the potential to impact European security. The author looks at the challenges faced by these young South Caucasian countries and examines the prospects for future peace and prosperity in the region. The „South Caucasus at the Crossroads" is essential reading for students and researchers of post-Soviet history and Caucasus studies, sociology, Caspian Sea politics, political science and international relations.
Bd. 26, 2007, 384 S., 25,90 €, br.,
ISBN 978-3-8258-6216-9

Austria: Forschung und Wissenschaft – Politikwissenschaft

René Cuperus; Karl A. Duffek; Erich Fröschl; Tobias Mörschel (eds.)
The EU – A Global Player?
vol. 1, 2006, 208 pp., 24,90 €, br.,
ISBN-DE 3-8258-9581-5, ISBN-AT 3-7000-0582-2

Erich Reiter (Hg.)
Europa ohne Sicherheit?
Chancen und Risiken einer Europäischen Sicherheits- und Verteidigungspolitik
Bd. 3, 2007, 120 S., 14,90 €, br.,
ISBN-DE 978-3-8258-0314-8,
ISBN-AT 978-3-7000-0647-3

LIT Verlag Berlin – Hamburg – London – Münster – Wien – Zürich
Fresnostr. 2 48159 Münster
Tel.: 0251 / 620 32 22 – Fax: 0251 / 922 60 99
e-Mail: vertrieb@lit-verlag.de – http://www.lit-verlag.de